MW01154351

Multimodal Literacies and Emerging Genres

Pittsburgh Series in Composition, Literacy, and Culture

David Bartholomae and Jean Ferguson Carr, Editors

MULTIMODAL LITERACIES

AND EMERGING GENRES

EDITED BY

TRACEY BOWEN AND CARL WHITHAUS

Published by the University of Pittsburgh Press, Pittsburgh, Pa., 15260

Manufactured in the United States of America
Printed on acid-free paper
10 9 8 7 6 5 4 3 2

Cataloging-in-Publication data on file at the Library of Congress

In memory of Nathaniel "Nacho" Córdova

CONTENTS

PART II. Multimodal Literacies and Pedagogical Choices

PART III. The Changing Structures of Composition Programs

ACKNOWLEDGMENTS

THE IDEA FOR THIS COLLECTION had its origin at a Writing Across the Curriculum (WAC) conference at Clemson University a number of years ago. As the book has evolved, we have been privileged to have conversations with many students, teachers, and researchers who are thinking about how multimodal composition is changing what we think of as "writing." All the contributors as well as the manuscript reviewers deserve thank-yous. While the complete list of other colleagues who have contributed to the development of our thoughts would go on for pages, we want to acknowledge the special contributions of the following people: Linda Adler-Kassner, UC–Santa Barbara; Jonathan Alexander, UC–Irvine; Kris Blair, Bowling Green State University; Gail Desler, Area 3 Writing Project; Danielle DeVoss, Michigan State University; Elyse Eidman-Aadahl, the National Writing Project at UC–Berkeley; Kory Ching, San Francisco State University; Daniel Gross, UC–Irvine; Will Hochman, Southern Connecticut State University; Virginia Kuhn, University of Southern California; Karen Lunsford, UC–Santa Barbara; Lanette

Jimerson, Bay Area Writing Project; Chuck Jurich, High Desert Writing Project; Becky Rupert, Hoosier Writing Project; and Joe Wood, Area 3 Writing Project.

For Carl, the group of graduate students and faculty in the Writing, Rhetoric, and Composition Studies (WRaCS) program at UC–Davis have provided a rich series of conversations over the past five years; particular thanks go to Rebekka Andersen, Dana Ferris, Aaron Lanser, Cynthia Carter Ching, Jenae Cohn, Jeff Magnin, Sandra Murphy, Sarah Perrault, Tara Porter, Manuel Senna, Aparna Sinha, Mary Stewart, Chris Thaiss, and Juliet Wahleithner. Of course, a coedited book requires "two to tango," as they say, and Carl would like to thank Tracey for the e-mails and phone conversations that kept this project going. Thanks are also due Carl's family—Shannah, Lillian, Hannah, AJ, and Rosalee—for putting up with him and for providing much multimodal inspiration (Facebook, tweets, tumblr, and beyond).

Tracey would like to thank Cleo Boyd, of the Robert Gillespie Academic Skill Centre, for her continuous support of multimodal pedagogical adventures; Penny Kinnear for her constant collaboration and her willingness to use her writing classes as a place for visual experiments; and all the students in CCT310 Mass Communications and Popular Culture at the University of Toronto Mississauga for taking up the multimodal challenge and pushing their imaginations. Tracey would also thank Carl for his ongoing enthusiasm, his collaborative spirit, and his commitment to this project. Finally, Tracey thanks her husband, Robert, for his boundless love and support.

Multimodal Literacies and Emerging Genres

INTRODUCTION

"What Else Is Possible": Multimodal Composing and Genre in the Teaching of Writing

Tracey Bowen and Carl Whithaus

In *Releasing the Imagination*, Maxine Greene (2000) maintains that educators are responsible for asking students to reflect on what they do, what they think, and what they produce. But she also argues that faculty and students need to consider "what else is possible" in educational spaces. Greene's work is hopeful and forward looking. When combined with emerging understandings of genre in writing classrooms, Greene's "what else is possible" sketches an outline for pedagogies of hope, difference, and challenge to the status quo. Within college writing courses, the emergence of a wide array of information and communication technologies (ICTs) in the past twenty years has opened up new possibilities for the types of compositions that students can create.

The chapters in *Multimodal Literacies and Emerging Genres* demonstrate how faculty and students are already exploring "what else is possible" in these new media writing spaces. When students are given access to pedagogical spaces and learning opportunities for experimenting with different ways to make meaning, they are drawing on the stuff of everyday social interaction to rethink the shape of written academic knowledge. But this process of rethinking what is possible in academic writing is not without its challenges and failures. The developing forms of student writing, pedagogy, and writing program organization explored in *Multimodal Literacies and Emerging Genres* acknowledge that new media and new genres are not some achieved utopia for perfect learning but rather are sites where conflict and agreement, success and failure, coexist. The aim of this edited collection is to report on a range of classroom and programmatic practices where multimodal forms of writing are reshaping what is possible in college and university writing courses.

UNDERSTANDING GENRE IN THE CLASSROOM

Taken together, the chapters in *Multimodal Literacies and Emerging Genres* argue that as educators, we need to help students become more aware of these ways of working across multiple modes of communication. One way of engaging students not only in the process of making multimodal compositions but also in building their knowledge about how these compositions work within social spaces is to make explicit how readers experience multimodal compositions and how those experiences are shaped by expectations from other genres and other media. Whether one subscribes to a theory of genre that sees text forms as relatively stable social constructs or a theory of genre that defines text forms as fluid enactments influenced by a variety of social contexts, naming a text as belonging to a particular genre helps situate that text within an interpretative framework. Influenced by Michael Halliday's functional linguistics (1977), scholars Gunther Kress (2003, 2010), Kress and Theo van Leeuwen (2006), Bill Cope and Mary Kalantzis (2000), and Kalantzis, Cope, and Andrew Harvey (2003) have pushed forward the concept of genres as relatively stable social constructs. In contrast, David Russell (1999) and Thomas Kent (1999) have drawn on Mikhail Bakhtin's (1986) semiotic theory of genre to argue for a more fluid view of how genres are shaped by social activities.

In the space between Halliday's systemic functional linguistics and a Bakhtian approach to genre, Paul Prior (2005, 2009) and Anne Wysocki (2005) have carved out a space where genre and multimodality can be understood as cross-fertilizing influences that shape the development of written documents. The contributions in *Multimodal Literacies and Emerging Genres* are informed by systemic functional linguistics and Bakhtin's semiotics, but they are most closely aligned with the praxis found in Prior's and Wysocki's writing. *Multimodal Literacies and Emerging Genres* asks what students are doing when they compose multimodal works in postsecondary writing environments and how those practical compositions reinforce or challenge existing genre theories.

Understanding how readers' and users' experiences with works in other media shape their responses to multimodal student compositions helps students imagine and predict some of the dynamics that will shape the interpretative framework in which their multimodal pieces will be read and evaluated. Readers' and users' experiences with works in other media can vary widely. Readers' prior experiences could include thinking about longer, featured news articles published in print magazines or shorter journalistic news stories delivered via paper. When interacting with *Second Life*, these experiences with other genres could be a user's experiences with a first-person shooter video game or multiuser dungeon (MUD). The variety is nearly endless. But within *Multimodal Literacies and Emerging Genres*, the contributing authors take up the questions raised by Halliday (1977), Bakhtin (1986), Kress (2003, 2010), Prior (2005, 2009), and Wysocki (2005). The contributors consider how understandings of genre and media can be used in classrooms to help facilitate students' development as writers able to work across modes and across genres.

It is important to note that throughout this edited volume, genre is considered distinctive from the text-tool used to create a work and from the medium in which it is created and received. That is, the authors are careful not to conflate genre and medium or genre and text-tool. When a text form is still emerging, the act of naming a genre has often confused genre with the text-tool or the medium. For instance, at the beginning of *A Better Pencil*, Dennis Baron (2010, xvi) promises to "examine the new genres that the computer has enabled: email, the instant message, the web page, the blog, social networking pages such as MySpace and Facebook, and communally generated wikis like Wikipedia and the Urban Dictionary." Baron equates text-tools such as e-mail, instant messaging, blogs, and wikis with genres. But each of these text-tools can be used to generate a number of different genres. Take wikis, for example. They can be used to create encyclopedia-like entries, dictionary-like entries, or a variety of other communally written and edited texts. Wikis are text-tools that use the medium of the Web to distribute texts that remediate existing print genres into something new. This act of remediation puts into play text-tools, media, and genres. Keeping these terms distinctive within *Multimodal Literacies and Emerging Genres* allows authors to talk about how students are creating new hybrid genres.

The chapters in this edited volume explore the possibilities that exist as both students and teachers experiment with the malleability of these new forms of communication during the early stages of integration into academic practices. Questions arise regarding the shifts that occur when new media forms evolve as genres that further splinter through social and institutional practices. Social media sites, for instance, began as portals for connecting "friends" within particular social circles. Only a few years later, they have spawned new ways of writing (140 characters or fewer) and reconsidered social practices that extend beyond the content on a website.

BEING LITERATE IN THE WORLD TODAY

The contributors in this collection document the changing landscape of writing in college. They show that what it means to be literate in the world today is changing and that the shapes and forms of academic knowledge within undergraduate writing are undergoing transformations opened up by the revolution in ICTs. In developing an understanding of literacy practices in today's college classrooms, these chapters attend to the social aspects of the increasing use of multimodal texts in college writing programs. They also advocate for pedagogical techniques that incorporate approaches where social contexts are considered in the evaluation of a work's effectiveness (Inoue 2005; Warnock 2009; Whithaus 2005). Multimodal student writing is doing something new—it's reshaping genre boundaries and changing what counts as academic knowledge. Faculty, students, and writing program administrators are responding to these new forms of literacy by creating in them, by writing in them, by pushing concepts and practices of what is possible to accomplish and create in a college writing course.

At first glance, this process of increasing students' awareness of the relationships among text-tools (that is, pieces of software and their interfaces), readerly and "userly" expectations, and authorial composing techniques seems to promise an almost endless sense of empowerment for students as creators of entirely new forms of texts. However, the literacy practices described in the following chapters develop within classroom spaces where the promises of multimodal pedagogies are not always achieved. Composing digital videos for YouTube, creating avatars and structures within *Second Life*, or using PowerPoint slides to present an interpretation of a Marge Piercy poem do open the new modes of understanding that Maxine Greene encourages teachers to move toward. Yet, including these activities in college writing courses is difficult and not always as successful as faculty would like. There are risks in trying to incorporate multimodal composing techniques in a writing class; these risks are magnified when writing program administrators (WPAs) try to integrate multimodal composing into a university-wide program. It is this tension between what is possible with multimodal composing and what actually happens in classrooms when faculty and students try to innovate that we explore in this edited volume. Some techniques work, others do not. Many have promising moments but also instances of failure amid their successes.

Our way of understanding this tension is to think about how genre expectations—and here we mean "genre" as associated with film, video games, speeches, photographs, and visual graphics as well as with written works—can both constrain and enable students and teachers. At the time of writing this introduction, new forms of writing are emerging all around us: students are writing on the Internet, in our classrooms, on cell phones, and continuously within some form of digital environment. They are seeing what else is possible. Our job is neither to lead them into this changing world of multimodality nor to hold them back from it. Rather, we are in the midst of a shift that is affecting how we write, why we write, and where we write . . . or don't. The chapters in this collection ask us to think about how writing programs—the students who take the courses, the faculty and graduate students who teach writing courses, and the faculty administrators who run the programs—are responding to shifts and how our various purposes for writing converge with our writing curricula.

The impact of multimodal composing upon writing practices has been documented in Moje 2004; Cope and Kalantzis 2000; Kalantzis, Cope, and Harvey 2003; Kress 2003, 2010; Kress and Leeuwen 2006; Herrington, Hodgson, and Moran 2009; Reiss, Young, and Selfe 1998; Selfe and Hawisher 2004; Wysocki 2005; Wysocki et al. 2004; and Yancey 2004. Alphabetic literacy has privileged words, their sequencing, and rules of usage as the primary organizing system for articulating experiences as texts. Alphabetic literacy has historically been at the core of what Western cultures have perceived as the act of writing and composing. However, as Kress (2003, 7) has suggested, the structure of using words on a page to be read as text is now affected by a "reorganization" of what we perceive the page to be. Kress describes this shift in relation to the screen that affords a diverse range of graphic representations beyond words in which case, conventions, and rules of usage applied to words are no longer plausible. This shift also affects genre. Traditionally, genres have organized the ways in which we explain experiences through sets of recognizable rules and conventions that frame the production of the texts we are creating and reading. Genres are ways for students to organize their experiences and, through identified conventions, relate those experiences to others within a particular social context. Thinking through genres can both constrain and open up student compositions.

A reciprocal relationship between multimodal composing and the creation of hybrid genres exists as new media forms afford continuous experimentation. Anne Herrington and Charles Moran's (2005) work on genre theory recognized that the conventions which guide student writing practices often need to be challenged, shifted, or morphed to accommodate emerging practices. During the first decade of the twenty-first century, it became clear that learning the rules, learning how to break the rules, and then developing new rules was part of the experimentation process inherent in multimodal composing as well as the development of individual students' writing skills (Kahn and Kellner 2005; Kress 2010; Lankshear and Knobel 2003; Shipka 2011; Sirc 2002; Wardle 2009; Watkins 2008). In a similar way, as the contributors in this collection asked students to redefine their composing practices, the students were rewriting the rules, redefining the constraints, and testing the boundaries. Encouraging multimodal compositions in writing courses was itself creating spaces within which new genres were emerging and helping to define "what else is possible" through student learning.

THE CHAPTERS IN THIS COLLECTION

Some of the chapters in this edited volume speak to breaking with conventions in both pedagogy and production by using multimodalities as liberating vehicles. However, other chapters caution that many of these new modes of composing create their own set of conventions that shape or even limit students' composing processes. The point is to grapple with how the emerging genres of early twenty-first-century cyberspace are influencing, and being influenced by, writing practices found in postsecondary classrooms. The collection is divided into three parts:

- Part I, "Multimodal Pedagogies That Inspire Hybrid Genres," examines how students are themselves shaping and reshaping the genres of writing when they compose multimodal texts as part of college courses.

- PART II, "Multimodal Literacies and Pedagogical Choices," considers the challenges teachers are facing as they include multimodal composing in their writing courses. The chapters in part II move back and forth from practice to theory and discuss multimodal literacy and genre on a classroom level.
- PART III, "The Changing Structures of Composition Programs," explores how writing program administrators are reshaping their programs to accommodate new media literacy practices.

Underlying all of these chapters is the problem of defining multimodal composing. The term "multimodality" has been appropriated by composition studies as well as new media and communications. It is now becoming more common within many curricula as technological innovations are incorporated into writing classes. Educators are striving to complement in-class learning with out-of class communications and networking practices. Our definition of "multimodal composing" within the context of these chapters, however, is that it involves the conscious manipulation of the interaction among various sensory experiences—visual, textual, verbal, tactile, and aural—used in the processes of producing and reading texts. (Jody Shipka's contribution in part I, "Including, but Not Limited to, the Digital," and the opening chapter of part II, Nathaniel Córdova's "Invention, Ethos, and New Media in the Rhetoric Classroom," both have extended discussions about how we define multimodal composing based on practice and theory.) Although our definition may seem broad to many academics and practitioners, it is our belief that we cannot restrict how individuals might interpret and employ multimodality as a way of thinking about designing and composing beyond written words. It is a dynamic way of thinking about expressing ideas; on its best days "multimodal composing" can become an embodiment of Paulo Freire's (1970 and 1991) notion of praxis. Understanding the interactions and relationships between different expressive modes is integral to understanding the composing processes and enabling students to develop their own writing techniques fully.

Through the chapters in this collection, we see that students who are composing within hybrid genres and developing new spatializing practices have always known multiple spaces of living, playing, and learning. Many of today's students do not know a world without the Internet. They move naturally between physical and virtual worlds—they push and publish as much content as they retrieve and collect. However, they must learn to see their communication acts through writing, visual representations, image and sound production as ethical acts that are affected by the spaces in which they are produced and further affect the spaces in which they are received (Cooper 2005). We cannot talk about multimodal composing and production without understanding the ethical considerations of this production as creating particular spaces for meaning making. The tools and technologies we use to communicate cannot be separated from their social and historical practices across time and space (Wysocki 2005). As we see multimodal practices becoming natural curriculum considerations for some undergraduate programs, we must also be aware of the contracted history of multimodal communications practices (at least those that are digitally based) and new ethical questions that arise from issues of access.

Anne Frances Wysocki (2005) has maintained that we use communicative tools in particular ways because of past practices that hold particular conventions and constraints. We learn and adopt these practices and spatial understandings (i.e., the spacing of words on a page or screen or the use of black Times Roman text on white paper without questioning the origins or diversities of those practices). These conventions are tied to other dominant social practices within our lived world (ibid., 57). Building on Cooper's and Wysocki's critiques, the chapters in this collection show us that the ways in which we privilege text create dichotomies between words and images rather than fostering approaches to multimodal composing, which include analysis, critique, and production. In fact, the contributions in this edited volume not only extend Cooper's and Wysocki's concepts but also outline pedagogical practices that show concrete alternatives to writing instruction as merely alphabetic composing. We believe the authors address multimodal pedagogy as an essential lens for thinking about program development, curriculum design, teaching, learning, and preparing students for the new global economy. Throughout the collection, the authors wrestle with Greene's (2000) immensely important pedagogical question for students and teachers: What else is possible?

CLOSING AND NOT CLOSED

The chapters in this collection show that in the first decade of the twenty-first century, students were not just being asked to write in genres that they knew or that were well established. Because of the speed with which information and communication technologies were emerging, the genres of the multimodal assignments were themselves unstable. Bakhtin's (1986), Kent's (1999), and Russell's (1999) notions of genres as always undergoing transformations because they are located within social activity systems seemed to be multiplying by a power of ten. Genres were not just transforming, they were fundamentally unstable—being made and remade within months rather than within years. With Twitter, Facebook, and other social networking sites, students represent themselves textually in a myriad of contexts simultaneously like never before.

These contexts, however, do not require a conscious awareness of older text-based literacies. Rather, they require an understanding of the social conventions at that moment and what is acceptable to the receiving community. So how do we teach students to identify, investigate, and interrogate genre within this "new normal" of instability? We begin to answer this question by examining how the environments into which our students will send their texts are elastic, expanding and contracting in relation to context with mutable genres that respond to the moment. Exploring these new compositional spaces, we examine how students, faculty, and writing programs are responding to, and incorporating, new multimodal forms of discourse into college writing courses. In the end we can see the fissures in the compositional landscape—writing is not what it was in 1990, nor is it now what it will be in 2020—but this collection reminds us that we still return to our classrooms and the daily realities of teaching, learning, and grading. Each of these actions is about writing, and about how a piece of writing—no matter what its new forms are—works.

Multiliteracies and multimodal composing present a set of questions that reach from the structure of departments within postsecondary education toward global economic systems, but multimodal composing is also an intimate experience—it is the student writer working on a composing task. It is the student having to make choices about what visual elements to add to her work or about how to prepare a speech in tandem with a PowerPoint or Prezi presentation. Multimodal composing is the teacher trying to decide how to organize a new assignment sequence that will include forms of composing not previously seen as serious, academic modes of inquiry. For writing program administrators, multimodal literacies bring new challenges—faculty and students need to explore the potentials of multimodal composing without losing the programmatic structures that facilitate the development of discrete writing skills. This collection employs multimodal pedagogy as a way of carving out spaces where different modes of composing and creating are used to explore the lived world and make meaning from experience.

Changes to composition programs, however, only happen as individuals begin to avail themselves of the opportunities to present and create knowledge in new formats. The chapters in this collection take us inside the programs and classrooms where writing curricula are being transformed. Students and faculty discuss their work and begin to describe how particular assignments requiring multimodal compositions are using information and communication technologies to create the spaces where new genres can emerge. Students are using rich and varied ICTs and while they do so, they draw on equally rich and varied concepts of genre to help them organize their new forms of writing. Ultimately, students will continue to make and remake what writing looks like within emerging multimodal discourse environments; however, faculty and administrators can help shape student experiences, so that the learning that occurs in college writing courses prepares writers for the challenges they will face later in life.

REFERENCES

Bakhtin, Mikhail. 1986. *Speech Genres and Other Late Essays*. Austin: University of Texas Press.

Baron, Dennis. 2010. *A Better Pencil: Readers, Writers, and the Digital Revolution*. Oxford: Oxford University Press.

Cope, Bill, and Mary Kalantzis. 2000. "Multiliteracies: The Beginning of an Idea." In *Multiliteracies: Literacy Learning and the Design of Social Futures*, edited by Bill Cope and Mary Kalantzis, 3–37. London: Routledge.

Cooper, Marilyn. 2005. "Bringing Forth Worlds." *Computers and Composition* 22 (1): 31–38.

Freire, Paulo. 1970. *Pedagogy of the Oppressed*. New York: Seabury.

———. 1991. *Pedagogy of the City*. New York: Continuum.

Greene, Maxine. 2000. *Releasing the Imagination*. San Francisco: Jossey-Bass.

Halliday, Michael. 1977. *Explorations in the Functions of Language*. New York: Elsevier.

Herrington, Anne, Kevin Hodgson, and Charles Moran. 2009. *Teaching the New Writing: Technology, Change, and Assessment in the Twenty-First-Century Classroom*. New York: Teachers College Press.

Herrington, Anne, and Charles Moran. 2005. *Genre across the Curriculum*. Logan: Utah State University Press.

Inoue, Asao B. 2005. "Community-based Assessment Pedagogy." *Assessing Writing* 9 (3): 208–38.

Kahn, Richard, and Douglas Kellner. 2005. "Reconstructing Technoliteracy: A Multiple Literacies Approach." *E-Learning and Digital Media* 2 (3): 238–51.

Kalantzis, Mary, Bill Cope, and Andrew Harvey. 2003. "Assessing Multiliteracies and the New Basics." *Assessment in Education* 10 (1): 15–26.

Kent, Thomas. 1999. *Post-Process Theory: Beyond the Writing-Process Paradigm*. Carbondale: Southern Illinois University Press.

Kress, Gunther. 2003. *Literacy in the New Media Age*. New York: Routledge.

———. 2010. *Multimodality: A Social Semiotic Approach to Contemporary Communication*. New York: Routledge.

Kress, Gunther, and Theo van Leeuwen. 2006. *Reading Images: The Grammar of Visual Design*. Oxon, UK: Routledge.

Lankshear, Colin, and Michele Knobel. 2003. *New Literacies*. Buckingham, UK: Open University Press.

Moje E. B. 2004. "Powerful Spaces: Tracing the Out-of-School Literacy Spaces of Latino/a Youth." In *Spatializing Literacy Research and Practice*, edited by Kevin Leander and Margaret Sheehy, 15–38. New York: Peter Lang.

Prior, Paul. 2005. "Moving Multimodality beyond the Binaries: A Response to Gunther Kress's 'Gains and Losses.'" *Computers and Composition* 22 (1): 23–30.

———. 2009. "From Speech Genres to Mediated Multimodal Genre Systems: Bakhtin, Voloshinov, and the Question of Writing." In *Genre in a Changing World*, edited by Charles Bazerman, Adair Bonini, and Debora Figueiredo, 17–34. Fort Collins, CO: WAC Clearinghouse; West Lafayette, IN: Parlor Press.

Reiss, Donna, Art Young, and Richard Selfe. 1998. *Electronic Communication Across the Curriculum*. Urbana, IL: NCTE.

Russell, David. 1999. "Activity Theory and Process Approaches: Writing (Power) in School and Society." In *Post-Process Theory: Beyond the Writing-Process Paradigm*, edited by Thomas Kent. Carbondale: Southern Illinois University Press.

Selfe, Cynthia, and Gail Hawisher. 2004. *Literate Lives in the Information Age: Narratives of Literacy from the United States*. Mahwah, NJ: Erlbaum.

Shipka, Jody. 2011. *Toward a Composition Made Whole*. Pittsburgh, PA: University of Pittsburgh Press.

Sirc, Geoff. 2002. *English Composition as a Happening*. Logan: Utah State University Press.

Wardle, Elizabeth. 2009. "'Mutt Genres' and the Goal of FYC: Can We Help Students Write the Genres of the University?" *College Composition and Communication* 60: 765–89.

Warnock, Scott. 2009. "Methods and Results of an Accreditation-Driven Writing Assessment in a Business College." *Journal of Business and Technical Communication* 23 (1): 83–107.

Watkins, Robert. 2008. "Words Are the Ultimate Abstraction: Towards Using Scott McCloud to Teach Visual Rhetoric." *Kairos: A Journal of Rhetoric, Technology, Pedagogy* 12 (3). Online at http://kairos.technorhetoric.net/12.3/topoi/watkins/index.html.

Whithaus, Carl. 2005. *Teaching and Evaluating Writing in the Age of Computers and High-stakes Testing.* Mahwah, NJ: Erlbaum.

Wysocki, Anne Frances. 2005. "awaywithwords: On the Possibilities in Unavailable Designs." *Computers and Composition* 22 (1): 55–62.

Wysocki, Anne Frances, Johndan Johnson-Eilola, Cynthia L. Selfe, and Geoffrey Sirc. 2004. *Writing New Media.* Logan: Utah State University Press.

Yancey, Kathleen. "Made Not Only in Words." *College Composition and Communication* 56 (2): 297–328.

PART I

Multimodal Pedagogies That Inspire Hybrid Genres

CHAPTER 1

Genre and Transfer in a Multimodal Composition Class

Cheryl E. Ball, Tia Scoffield Bowen, and Tyrell Brent Fenn

In some other chapter, in some other collection, a teacher writes about how great her semester went teaching a new syllabus that seemed to have worked extraordinarily well. She details that syllabus and discusses how the assignments were sequenced; she concludes by providing quotes from the students' portfolio reflections to show that they learned a great deal from the class, from her. The reflections would say things like:

> When I was a child, I was fascinated by technology. I had an 8-bit Nintendo, built my own computer, and generally geeked out when it came to science and technology. But I wasn't always interested in this stuff. Personally, I blame Ender. I don't know who introduced me to the science fiction novel *Ender's Game*, but whoever it was inadvertently sparked my love for books, science, and technology. Working on the documentary in English 3040 reminded me of my early school years and my love of technology as a form of expression. As a kid I had a wild imagination, and as a senior in college [when I took 3040] I had a lot of ideas to express. Technology,

> writing, and good teachers gave me a way to do it. (Excerpt from Tyrell Fenn's design justification, December 2006)

Insert the teacher's glowing reflection of the class and the student. Then the teacher would insert another student reflection, this time moving the argument along toward the multimodal bit she was intending:

> Growing up, I was determined to be an inventor. What I wanted was for people to crowd my little cul-de-sac just to get their hands on the only "decorative mud-ball" in town. But since nothing I created had a significant impact on society, I quit the idea and my inventor dreams seemed to be doomed for good, until this class came along, giving me the option to dabble for a grade. My perspective of inventing has grown: Now my idea of invention is still tied to what's important to me right now, but how I invent something to fill that need has changed. For instance, unlike my older sister, who writes and writes and writes in her journal, I get overwhelmed by journal writing, but I love to reminisce and hold onto memories, so camcorders and pictures became my journals. Before I learned how to use programs that made slideshows, I would line pictures up next to each other on the floor, turn on a song in the background, make sure cell phones and pagers were turned down, turn on my parents' oversized camcorder, and record each picture manually. Watching them now, it's comical, but then I thought it was brilliant. (Excerpt from Tia Scoffield Bowen's design justification, December 2006)

That, however, is not this chapter. It would have been if written several years ago. Now, the then-brilliant reflections by the teacher seem comically naïve. She is not such a noob (newbie) anymore to think that that imaginary version of this chapter would still have been accurate. Instead, this chapter is about a once-upon-a-time, newish tenure-track teacher who misplayed a crucial teaching moment, which spiraled into a misuse of genre, and how she learned to recover and resituate her teaching-research with a genre studies approach. And the students (Tia Scoffield Bowen and Tyrell Fenn) are not trapped in some time-independent "student" status where their design justification statements represent a stagnant contribution to multimodal research. This chapter is now a coauthored piece written by two once-upon-a-time students and their somewhat nutty teacher. All three have moved on from the English 3040 course at Utah State University, and all three have continued to work in multimedia fields. This chapter synthesizes the experience of a multimedia composition course and asks how concepts of genre transfer across multiple boundaries.

A MULTIMODAL COMPOSITION CLASS

The course catalog description for English 3040, Perspectives in Writing and Rhetoric, is "an in-depth study of rhetoric and writing for non-majors" (Peterson 2009–10, 549). Over the three years Cheryl taught this course at Utah State University, she treated it like a special topics class in different forms of multimodal composition, and the genres that students produced were expansive:

(a) websites (i.e., religious travelogues of missionary trips, commercial sites promoting student-run businesses, genealogies, an intranet training site for a local veterinarian's office, and promotional sites for student clubs);

(b) literary hypertexts (poetic, prosaic, and imagistic); and

(c) videos (documentaries, poems, remediated research papers, visual argument slideshows, music videos, etc.).

The course topic—digital narratives—for the fall 2006 term in which Tyrell and Tia were enrolled was purposefully vague because Cheryl did not want students to have to choose from a narrow set of genres as they had done for the e-literature version of the course. Narrative left the generic option open, because Cheryl's hope was that students would produce a range of genres as well as multigenre texts.

Students sometimes resist open-ended assignments, which had been a staple and seemingly successful part of Cheryl's Happenings pedagogy repertoire. She chalked it up to the lack of incense.[1] But she had stuck with it because a Happenings pedagogy best explained what she did in her classes and why she did it, and it allowed her to change teaching directions suddenly if needed. This pedagogy is infused with a socio-epistemic critical lens (add Berlin 1988 to Sirc 2002, if you will). Geoffrey Sirc would probably approve despite his criticism of composition's epistemic turn and its formation of, in his words, "a compositional canon" where material restraints—that is, what we can and should be producing in writing classes and writing scholarship—are born (Sirc 2002, 7–8). Cheryl doesn't think, as James Berlin (1988, 485) has argued, that an expressive-ish Happenings pedagogy—as Sirc dreams it—is focused solely on "liberating students from the shackles of a corrupt society." It was Sirc's goal to examine and disrupt the space and materials of composition studies after its epistemic turn, and it is one of Cheryl's pedagogical goals to examine the material, rhetorical conditions in which we compose, while also asking students to produce texts that break out of traditional material restraints. Thus Cheryl combined socioepistemic and Happenings pedagogies, with a little critical, cultural, feminist, multimodal, and other pedagogies thrown in as needed.

As an early tenure-track faculty member in 2006, Cheryl worried that a Happenings pedagogy—one filled with wow and wonder and a want to write, to make meaning—was a thing she should leave to the tenured or the avant-garde. That worry is relevant to this story and yet she is a stubborn, mouthy daughter of Southern women, and she tends to do what she wants when teaching, if there's good justification for doing so. Sirc's pedagogical manifesto oddly justifies the brand of sustainability she was using in the teaching of writing: the recursive nature of teaching, learning, and writing as open, collaborative processes. Because she wants students to compose texts other than those that were typically found in first-year and other writing classrooms in 2006 (and, oh, how things have changed in those intervening years!), she needs to teach in a way so that students can relearn how to compose in media that is new to them as composers (not consumers), using modes of communication that are also new to their compositional wheelhouse.

To prepare students for the English 3040 course, Cheryl spent a good portion of the first day(s) convincing students that the course actually fulfills their writing requirement. In that discussion she didn't refer to the theoretical support for this work, such as the New London Group's *Multiliteracies: Literacy Learning and the Design of Social Futures* (Cope and Kalantzis 2000) or Gunther Kress and Theo van Leeuwen's (2001) *Multimodal Discourse: The Modes and Media of Contemporary Communication.* But that foundation is clearly evident in how she introduced students to the idea that none of us communicates only through writing and that written text itself is multimodal in that it carries visual, spatial, and sonic properties every time students type a new letter-character on the page. The course would then launch into a sequence of rhetorical analysis and production, each week covering a different medium. In relation to the 3040 class, here are some examples of modes, media, and genres used:

- *modes of communication*: linguistic, aural, visual, spatial, gestural, and combinations thereof (see Cope and Kalantzis 2000, 26).
- *media*: written text, static image, audio, video with only diagenic sound of the shot location, video with soundtracks, other audio, and writing.
- *genres*: blogged reading response, analog photograph, digital illustration, voiceover, soundtrack, vogs, and video documentaries.[2]

The syllabus was set up to step students through these progressively more multimodal and multimedia assignments. Although this metaphor was dated to her own process of learning to write before computers, she likened the shift from linguistic to aural to visual modes of communication in these assignments to how students at an early age first learn to write with crayons, then pencils, then pens (and now computers). This progression gave students hands-on practice with the increasingly complicated technologies they would need for their major projects. Once they got to the final project, students could readily see how the added, mediated components were sequenced to prepare them. But the main reason for using this assignment sequence was so that students could spend a week discussing how each medium (writing, audio, video) helped readers understand the text.

At the end of each semester, students indicated their raised awareness of critical and rhetorical (as well as technological) literacies—exhibited in portfolio reflective letters, in-class feedback to the instructor, and narrative course evaluations, as well as in the portfolio of work students submitted. For instance—and regardless that Cheryl promised just paragraphs ago not to rely on years-old student reflective writing to explain her coming to terms with the way she taught multimodal composition classes—Tyrell concludes the design justification of his video documentary about martial arts, "East Meets West," by hitting nearly all of the teacher's happy-dance words as possible:

> In the end, weaving a meaningful narrative using music, images, video, text, and voice really made the assignment worthwhile. The video editing and text creation were important aspects of that process, but it is the people who watch the film—those who may not already love martial arts or understand why or how it came to the States—whom I kept in the forefront of my mind during the composition process. The struggle to accurately represent the views of others forced me to think critically about the way the film would be received and therefore I had to think critically about the various media I was collecting and composing for the documentary. As part of being able to choose my own topic and interview people I knew (and some I didn't know that well), I learned that it's important to frame others' comments in ways that are fair to them while still choosing clips that are interesting to read or see. Ethics became a bigger concern when I knew the people whose words where being represented in my documentary. That's something that may be more difficult to relay (to students, to audiences) when you're dealing with impersonal texts. The creation of a research proposal for the

> documentary—while not a lot of people's idea of a good time—was a great learning experience that helped me foresee the ethical choices I had to make in the media I used. The proposal allowed me to put what were just ideas down on paper in a way that could be systematically useful to both my professor and me. Even in a narrative text, the research you do can and should change the direction of that text. If I had been unflinching in my drive to sell my message, it is likely that the significance of the message itself would be lost.
>
> One of the biggest lessons I took away from this project was that being given more power over my education (i.e., choosing the genre, focus, and media for my assignments) gives me more motivation to perform. It's something that I knew before but that was emphasized by this assignment. I liked all the other classes I took that semester, but I found myself worrying and working on the documentary in preference to other classes. Also, the assignments that led up to the documentary work focused on one aspect of the documentary process and were great preparation for the final project. For me, the introduction to technologies (such as the audio-editing software) was unnecessary because I've worked with them my whole life, but I can see how it was important to other members of the class, and I was able to help others who needed it if I already knew how to do a particular assignment or task. In the end, the sequence of individual media assignments leading up to our documentary research proposal, storyboard, interviews, and choices in editing the media clips provided me with a process in which I could understand how to ethically compose a multimedia text for a specific audience and purpose.

Tyrell's reflection, however, is not representative of the majority of the students who had been through that iteration of English 3040, nor of Cheryl's previous iterations of the class. Students indicated in their numeric and narrative evaluations that despite the teacher's enthusiasm for the course material, the syllabus lacked organization and focus. This is not an unusual critique for her teaching, and students don't always mean it negatively. One dedicated student referred to her teaching style as "controlled chaos," which Cheryl knew would not sound appropriate in the rhetorical situation of her impending, third-year tenure review. So she had crafted the digital narrative version of this class (which occurred the semester she was to have her teaching observed in preparation for her third-year review) to turn what students perceived as chaos into what they could recognize as a purposeful yet spontaneous series of events while also unintentionally clamping down on the opportunities

Cheryl thought open assignments provided for students. Here's what happened:

When the semester started, students were supposed to choose which genres, or combinations of genres, they wanted to use in their major projects. But the students and teacher discovered about four weeks into class that the experimental design of the syllabus was perhaps too grand in the making. The original syllabus had two major assignments: The first one was purposefully vague so that students could choose which combinations of media and genres they would use, which, as Julie Jung (2005, xi) noted, would help students disrupt their generic "expectations [and] result in expanded and revised points of view," helping students to "develop the epistemological pliancy one needs to negotiate responsibly in an ever-changing world."

The second project was an inquiry-based video. Cheryl had been speaking of this second assignment as a narrative documentary, in which she wanted students to use the storytelling techniques they'd learned in the sequenced assignments as a way to frame their documentaries. In negotiating a revised syllabus, students voted to remove the vague assignment in favor of the documentary. There were several reasons for their choice, including that the vague assignment was supposed to be composed in a software program that wasn't yet installed on the lab machines. That, and Cheryl knew it would be easier for the students and her as instructor to come to an understanding of the genre conventions of a documentary project. Since time was an issue, choosing a specific genre seemed to make sense. The students would still be able to use what they had learned regarding modes and media in fulfilling the video documentary assignment. In addition to the documentary, students would be required to produce a set of "supplementary materials," modeled on Jody Shipka's (2005) framework for multimodal composition. The purpose of this assignment was to ask students to reconsider the original rhetorical situation of their documentary and then to compose a different set of texts that would accomplish a related purpose for a different audience and through different media and genres, thus practicing their rhetorical and technological literacies through the practice of transfer (see, e.g., Russell 1995 and Smit 2004).

Partway through the semester, Cheryl noticed that half the students seemed to compose more naturally in different modes than the majority of students from previous semesters. For instance, Tia had told Cheryl that she made video projects all the time for her friends (a fact she elaborated on in her end-of-semester design justification), so Cheryl asked Tia to bring one of her videos to class for the group to analyze. Cheryl wanted students—especially those who were still leery of the narrative-documentary assignment—to see what she knew they were capable of completing and to reassure them that she wasn't expecting a professional History Channel documentary, the genre of which seemed to be a constant reference for them in class. A Happenings pedagogy allowed Cheryl to use Tia's video without having viewed it before class (a point we return to later in this chapter). Tia's video was about a group of friends reenacting a practical joke on another group of friends. It was a little crude in the storyline and editing (in both senses: coarse and awkward), but also fun, fast-paced, and full of subject matter that the students could relate to—a good example with which to draw students into the assignment.

The students adroitly analyzed Tia's video, and Cheryl realized as they mapped the sequence of scenes onto the dry-erase board that the students had picked up on the video's five-paragraph-like theme—it had an introductory scene, three supporting scenes, and a conclusion scene. It was an easy connection, but she was surprised that the students grasped it so quickly. She asked how many of them had produced homemade videos (or similar projects) before this class. Nearly half of the students raised their hands. She was shocked, dumbfounded that she had waited until midterm to ask about their new media literacies. In her previous two years of teaching video-based projects at that school, only one or two of the students had produced similar texts. Her expectations of the students hadn't changed from that—this was not her first mistake nor was it to be her last in this class.

THE MOVING TARGET OF STUDENTS' MULTIPLE LITERACIES

When that fall 2006 class began, YouTube was barely on folks' radar, Facebook was a month away from its public debut, and Twitter was not even a few months old. Cheryl was unsatisfactorily using a blog for the first time in a class. So it was still surprising to her when two students were vocal proponents for multimedia authoring. But it wasn't at all surprising when she found out how long they'd been working on creative media projects. Tyrell had helped start an after-school class on multimedia his sophomore year of high school. Much to that teacher's dismay, he and his fellow students were more interested in playing games than producing media. However, in the second year, when the teacher gave the class the opportunity to split into groups and work on creating their own educational multimedia projects, things turned around. Tyrell and two of his best friends, Joel Gillespie and David Eckels, started work on a space-themed project titled "Tour of Our Solar System." This small design group was in charge of every facet of the project, including photo manipulation, 3-D animation, sound, video, and a whole lot of storyboards and text.

In the mid-1990s, personal computer–based animation and editing had just emerged (the first fully 3-D animated film, *Toy Story*, was released in 1995). The scope and novelty of the media Tyrell and his friends wanted to use entailed a split in responsibilities. Tyrell worked on the 3-D animation and photo- and video-editing while David and Joel split written content and programming, respectively. Those responsibilities became blurred, and other important aspects like sound design were managed by all three of them. (Joel now has his master's degree in computer science, Dave graduated with an anthropology degree from an Ivy League college, and Tyrell got his undergraduate degree in liberal arts and sciences and is pursuing a master's degree in instructional technology.) In the end, the three students got a working program together and presented it at the Utah Multimedia competition, where they earned several design awards.

As for Tia, the video footage and pictures that she takes document her life. They record the people she's with, the activities they do, along with their personalities and memories. The manual slideshow-making ended when Tia discovered iMovie and learned to manipulate the footage even more to capture a mood or personality. The slideshows became more advanced with the time she took to learn different features, and the programs improved. It was exciting when Tia got a digital camera and could record tiny video clips—the pictures came to life, and Tia learned how to work with sound and do cropping. Every year of college, she made a new slideshow, advancing her techniques little by little. The final products were ending up more than forty minutes long, showcasing memories of that year in college. Producing these slideshows were her creative outlets: Tia could choose how to do them and what to include, reflecting her youthful desire to invent while also creating something her friends and family enjoyed.

Before the documentary assignment in Cheryl's class, however, Tia had never worked with that much video (she had used still clips juxtaposed to look like video or very short video clips), so she had to learn the basics of transferring from camera to computer. Tia felt confident that she could produce what was expected of her, even though this was her first documentary on camera. At this stage in the class, Tia seemed to appreciate her earlier experiences of writing, making slideshows, and inventing and understood that the documentary was not expected to be of professional quality, because of the introductory nature of the class. Cheryl had reassured the students that there were not any rigid guidelines for the project, which was encouraging to Tia and the other class members. (Preparation for this final project, both in and out of the classroom, enabled the documentary assignment to not be outside of the student's challenge zone. Instead, the culture of the class seemed to be excited and exploratory, making the hardest part just deciding what topic to actually choose. Few students, if any, seemed worried about how they would pull it off.) Carrying out the final project required a good amount of time, patience, and resources, but students could use anything they could rhetorically justify. This meant that the skills Tia already had with editing technology, combined with the possibility of creation, made the project exciting for her.

The assignment to create three supplemental texts, separate from the documentary, was yet another way to express herself through means besides writing. Tia's documentary project looked at why college-age people show interest in the supernatural. In keeping with that theme while producing three texts (two of which had to use different media than the documentary), Tia decided to compose a song—a dramatization of one of her documentary's scary stories—and create a batch of creepy candy with advertising. She chose to invent a candy because the other texts she had produced were fairly intense. The creation of candy offered a lighter experience in the form of comic relief while portraying a commercialized version of the supernatural. Here's how Tia described the candy-making process:

> My train of thought started with marshmallows because the tasty little things are a stereotypical staple at campfires. I couldn't just turn in marshmallows and claim them for my own. So I set out to the local grocery store and purchased the necessities: mini marshmallows, caramel squares, and hardening chocolate. (Not to say these were the only items that made their way into my inventing process.) After multiple burned fingers, a smoky kitchen, and a little of this and a little of that, I had something edible and justifiable to my theme. The wrappers would be advertisements meant to verbally relate the candy to my documentary. The one slogan I composed that did the most work for me was developed from a definition for "supernatural": "describing abilities which appear to exceed possible bounds." I

> didn't fit the definition within the documentary, so in the candy advertisement, I added to it. It read: "Your mouth will feel like it is describing abilities which appear to exceed possible bounds." Changing it into an advertisement gave the definition in a creative way that also promoted my treat. The best part was that at the end of the class open house, in which we got to present our final projects to classmates and faculty members, I went to collect my plate of creepy treats, and they were gone. So good, they disappeared!

Tia admits that when she first heard the word "rhetoric," she really had no idea what that meant for a class. Initially her motivation to take English 3040 was because a friend was taking it and as an English minor, it fulfilled a credit she needed. Some of her favorite classes so far had included fiction and nonfiction writing, because she not only could use but was required to use her imagination. During an in-class discussion a few weeks into the course, it really clicked that the slideshows, movie making, song writing, and creating of all kinds that she had done prior to this class did in fact have structure and development congruent to the essays she was writing for her nonfiction English class. This class, with Cheryl's guidance, took a portion of a slideshow Tia had made the year before and analyzed it until it was clear there was a theme, beginning, middle, and end, among much else. She began to see that what she had done—initially just trying to archive photographs, video clips, and music to give as gifts to her closest friends—was effectively communicating a message and a story.

The problem, however, is the way that the in-class discussion set up the entire class, most of whom were less experienced at multimedia authoring than Tyrell and Tia, to produce the equivalence of five-paragraph videos.

ACCIDENTAL HAPPENINGS

Cheryl's Reflection on "Wowlessness" and Transfer

To follow the genre conventions of (self-)reflection in design justifications, we switch from third to first person in the following sections.

Tyrell and Tia, as well as other students in the course, drew from their basic, critical, rhetorical, functional, ethical, and technological literacies in relation to new media production, which they indicated by describing instances of compositional processes (including hurdles and revisions) within a particular phase of production. For instance, Tia foregrounded the social aspects of invention when describing her need to create mud balls so that she could become famous, at least within the cultural context of her cul-de-sac. The design justification allowed her to make critical connections between that youthful experience and her adult invention (and revision) process for the ghoulish, yet yummy, snacks she made for the final project. Tyrell explicitly discussed the basic, functional, and technological literacies he brought to the class, but the design justification allowed him to address a topic that had been only briefly covered regarding ethnographic interviewing techniques—the ethical considerations that guided him through the video-composition process. The reflective documents made seeing these students' sophisticated connections possible (see Shipka 2005). Yet this is not an assignment that I have chosen to repeat because most students' discussions of their literacy practices were demonstrated better in the written design justification than in the final texts, and that runs counter to my purpose in teaching multimodal composition practices.

For instance, the documentaries for the fall 2006 class were "safe," as Patricia Sullivan (2001) would say. Nearly every student was successful at fulfilling the requirements of the video and supplementary projects, but I had to ask: Would the documentaries have been more rhetorically powerful, more aesthetically interesting, more "wowful" had the triangulation of mode-media-genre assignments been different? Tentatively, I believe the "wowlessness" is connected to the genre limitations I implicitly imposed on the documentary form, a form I persuaded the students to implement in a course that was really intended to be an introduction to digital, multimodal composition (not a course about documentaries).

As Jung (2005, 56–78) remarked in her book *Revisionary Rhetoric, Feminist Pedagogy, and Multigenre Texts*, using multigenre texts opens spaces for rhetorical listening and revision—not to correct or make students' texts perfect, but to "put the wrong words together" so that texts take on new, and before unseen, layers of meaning. In this case, "the wrong words" are substituted with the wrong modes, media, and genres. When juxtaposed, the wrong mix (or even the right one) can create breaks and silences, which in turn requires authors and readers familiar with linear genres (like these students' documentaries) to shift their expectations, to become attuned to making meaning from the unexpected, to potentially embrace the wow. Instead of allowing for the unexpected, which would have been a major benefit to my Happenings pedagogy, I was trying to make the students' texts perfect by assigning them a specific genre she had set up in a formulaic way that they could fulfill.

If I had to attribute the wowful breakdown to a particular moment, it would be the day I showed Tia's homemade video in class while my tenure chair was observing. Tia's video wasn't the cause, of course; it was my reaction to a situation much more complex than that one day of teaching. That day was the tenure chair's second visit to observe my teaching, which she would write up, and I would submit as part of my third-year review that fall. The chair's first visit to class had been unsuccessful because my lesson plan of having students sign up for free Wordpress blogs so that they could discuss the rhetorical nature of blog-theme options had turned into an unforeseen technology troubleshooting session. Students had not been able to retrieve their Wordpress passwords because their university e-mail accounts wouldn't allow any nonuniversity e-mail through. I would describe watching my teaching strategy on that first observation visit like watching a pink, squealing pig on the way to slaughter. Although Tyrell helped me out of that situation by figuring out how to bypass the e-mail restrictions on the students' accounts, the tenure chair decided it would be best for her to reschedule the observation.

The day of the chair's second observation—approximately a week before her letter and my tenure portfolio was due—the digital projector was unexpectedly not working and I wasn't going to waste another observation day trying to troubleshoot. In overcompensating with my newly thought-out Happenings pedagogy, I asked students to huddle around my computer screen to watch Tia's video. After viewing it, they discussed the video in a call-and-response, with students shouting answers that we scribbled on the board. In an "aha" moment that I was hoping would make me look smart and teacherly in front of the tenure chair, I pointed out that the students had applied the generic structure and conventions of a five-paragraph essay to Tia's video. Jackpot.

So I had done it. I had encouraged the students to map formulaic writing onto their new media texts, which the majority of their documentaries enacted to a T. There's not much unexpected or wowful about a traditional five-paragraph essay, whether it's composed in print or in multiple media. But it is relatively easy to complete, which is why I have seen this formulaic, expected writing happen even when undergraduate and graduate students are given open assignments to compose in any or multiple genres, modes, and media. Few students embrace the unexpected when fulfilling a project in which the only requirement I have given is to "produce a text that uses multiple modes and media."[3] What is more typical is for students to uptake, just like the majority of the 3040 students did, a familiar genre like the five-paragraph essay, or for graduate students the academic/research essay, onto a new medium such as video. The majority of those students do not engage in the critical and reflective revision strategies needed to understand the purposes and usefulness of new media composition; that lack of engagement is reflected in their design justifications, which often turn out thin and unsupported by effective rhetorical and aesthetic choices.

That is why I do not assign design justifications in my multimodal courses any more. I have come to see them as a school-based genre that doesn't have any context outside of a particular writing class. I am the sole audience for these documents, and my primary purpose in assigning them was to ask students to justify, literally, what their rhetorical decisions in a new media piece were. Although that goal isn't a bad one, it created a learning situation where the students had no responsibility for ensuring that the new media piece would speak to its audience clearly and on its own terms. In 2006 it made sense to accept that students were limited in their compositional techniques by technological literacy constraints, and thus having them write may have been a good substitute. However, I see years later, authors for the multimedial journal I edit—authors who are often first-time new media composers—struggling and succeeding, often with the same mentorship and guidance I provide students, despite their supposed technological constraints. If I expect authors of new media scholarship to succeed, and to have their work stand on its own upon submission, why should I expect students to self-assess their rhetorical intentions in writing?

This rejection of written justifications is not to say that others won't find it useful, or that I wasn't initially wowed by Tyrell's and Tia's (as well as other students') design justifications. I was. But that was because most of the justifications were so much better than the final videos, which I had ruined from the start by imposing a genre that had been uptaken in primarily dull ways, in an activity system of an advanced composition class. Elizabeth Wardle (2009, 774) has called these "mutt genres," which are assigned to "mimic genres that mediate activities in other activity systems, but within the FYC [first-year composition] system their purposes and audiences are vague or even contradictory." In speaking of these fake-audience, school-based genres, she wrote that "if students are taught decontextualized 'skills' or rigid formulas rather than general and flexible principles about writing, and if instructors in all classes do not explicitly discuss similarities between new and previous writing assignments, it stands to reason students will not see similarities between disparate writing situations or will apply rigid rules inappropriately. In other words, one reason for lack of transfer is instruction that does not encourage it" (ibid., 770).

The digital narrative class was the epitome of "instruction that does not encourage" transfer in new media compositional practices because the course assignments relied on the written documents to indicate that transfer. Sure, students were able to put together videos that worked and that made sense, which was more than many of them had done. But those projects weren't dexterous in their use of genre, primarily because students neither spent enough time analyzing a range of similar documentary genres nor understanding who the audience of their particular documentaries would be. I had simply allowed for the substitution of the medium of video for the medium of writing, as if documentaries were a flaccid, mutt genre.

Speaking of mutt genres, jump to my third-year portfolio, in which I had a nice letter about how enthusiastic a teacher I was (if a little disheveled in the lesson-planning department) and how obvious it was that my students were engaged in their learning. Tyrell and Tia had volunteered to write up their design justifications as their portion of a proposed coauthored book chapter, and I was able to include that information in my review as the first example of coauthoring with then-undergraduates, which would later become a significant thread in my research. (By the way, it was a positive review for a third-year tenure-tracker trying to push new media at a research university.) I have since left Utah State and have tenure, and Tyrell and Tia have graduated, but we three continued to correspond over e-mail about this chapter and on other life events. What struck me as most important to this coauthorship has been the paths that each author's life has continued to take with respect to their multimodal composing practices. These practices have built on previous passions and knowledge while also being composed within authentic rhetorical situations. The next two sections are recent reflections (from 2010) that Tia and Tyrell wrote about transferring their multimodal composition practices from that course to their everyday writing practices.

Tia's Reflections on Transfer

One aspect of the 3040 class and subject that has stuck with me the most is how multiple modes and media are powerful tools in expression. A lot of what I do now is videography. I use it fairly regularly to teach at-risk teenagers, and I'm watching it empower them to express their experiences and feelings in ways writing an essay does not. I have drawn reference to 3040 in efforts to design a syllabus for these teenagers to use videography as a new creative tool. I've learned to take my slideshows and video to a more professional level, now experimenting for a little money and not only a grade. I've continued to use a blog, which has been a very useful way to keep in touch with friends and family living all over the world. This was really important to me in October of 2009 when my mom, who was living in Tokyo with my dad, had a heart attack. I made a "get-well video card" to cheer her up and let her be able to see me. I posted it on my blog and a lot of other people added comments and sent pictures to make something really special for her. I don't know if this example is too personal, but it is one way that video and blogging have been really important to me lately. I feel like I draw reference to the 3040 class a lot, even if it's just to think about what I created while there, and it gives me pride. For instance, the supplementary song I wrote for the final project was the only song I've written, even though it's something I would love to do more. Having taken that class, where I got to successfully use some of my core passions and talents, has given me ideas about what direction I want to take those passions and talents further. And as of fall 2011, I am combining my multimodal composition and outreach interests by starting a masters degree in human development and family studies so that I can continue social work through personal connections in multimedia.

Tyrell's Reflections on Transfer

I'm not sure if it's by happenstance or design, but I've continued to be involved in "creative" literacies and media. In my job, or what many of my colleagues from my graduate program refer to as "the real world," I'm in charge of corporate technological initiatives. One of those has been the move away from more traditional business communication methods like e-mail (When did e-mail become traditional?) to micro blogging. It's been an interesting adventure. People are used to using micro blogging in a specific, very personal way. As we did our trial runs, I realized that there had to be a paradigm shift in thinking for people in the company to really get benefit out of it. The micro blog couldn't just be Twitter at work, where people sent companywide tweets about their dog or how much they like soda. There was an audience consideration, a concept that I first learned to apply outside of just written words in 3040. However, we also wanted to take full advantage of people's knowledge of this format and its more open nature. I ended up helping to craft a "best practices" document for our micro blogging. Even though it's a work in progress, there is a level of participation and information sharing happening now that we wouldn't have gotten had we not gone through the struggles of embracing a new media genre.

I'm also involved in a media-heavy project as part of my master's program in instructional technology and learning sciences. We are currently working on providing media as part of a quest to form an economic and cultural sister city relationship between Logan, Utah, and the Egyptian city of Faiyum. Our group is providing three types of media for Logan City to use. We've already produced a forty-five-minute PowerPoint presentation, with a unified design (thank you, graphic art majors!), that has tons of images and covers several important topics related to the proposed sister city relationship. We will also be working on a shorter video-style presentation as well as a short promotional YouTube video. It's an exciting project that has a lot of considerations. Unlike my project in high school and in 3040, this project has a real client, and that client has expectations. It's been a different experience trying to balance what I think looks and feels right for our message and the design and rhetorical limitations that get imposed for different groups on the client side. However, it looks like I will get the chance to pull out those old video-editing skills again!

HOW TO AVOID THE FIVE-PARAGRAPH VIDEO

Cheryl has learned numerous lessons from the English 3040 class and from repeated readings of Tia's and Tyrell's design justifications, as well as from the e-mail conversations they have had about writing this chapter and what each is currently working on. Here are the lessons learned:

- If you ask for five-paragraph videos, you will get five-paragraph videos. Focusing on a single, formulaic genre for the major project halts the critical progress of students who don't already come with multimodal composition experience.
- Assigning the opposite of five-paragraph videos—that is, offering students the opportunity to compose completely open-ended assignments—may not be the answer. In fall 2007, Cheryl taught a similar class, English 239, Multimodal Composition, at Illinois State. To test out her "avoiding five-paragraph videos" theory, she gave students an open assignment and their final videos included multigenre texts that were creative (poems, music videos, memoirs, etc.) and persuasive (documentaries, mockumentaries,

sports-newscast features, visual arguments, etc.). The videos weren't perfect, and they exhibited the kinds of breaks and silences that help foster critical thinking that Jung called for her in multigenre scholarship. Overall Cheryl was pleased with the students' engagement with the open-assignment texts, but she was not wowed enough to be satisfied that the students were deeply engaging with the modes, media, and genres in a way that would be transferable to other learning situations.[4] She felt the syllabus needed more depth.

- The syllabus outlined here, which used assignment sequences that transitioned from linguistic to aural to visual to multiple modes of communication, had two problems: (1) it assumed students came to class with zero basic literacies in multimodal composition and thus needed that step-by-step work; and (2) it was too hurried to allow them time to compose and revise the larger, multigenre texts in enough depth.
- Avoiding scholarship in multimodal theory in a class on multimodality (as Cheryl did in that English 3040 class and also in her first multimodal composition class at Illinois State) is stupid.

All of these points, but especially that last one, are not wowful, eureka notions; they are embarrassing realizations. But the teaching-as-process portion of a Happenings pedagogy has helped her realize her mistakes and moves her away from a naïve and chaotic interpretation of avant-garde pedagogy toward a critical, socioepistemic pedagogy that still incorporates the expressivism inherent in new media composing.

Several years have passed, and the major assignment has changed again based on the lessons learned. Her fall 2008 class focused on the recent history and purpose of multimodal composition in the humanities, with a particular look at how students are portrayed or are given voice in new media scholarship.[5] The students composed three group projects that were multivoiced, multigenre, multimodal, and multimedia (whew!), in whatever combinations they deemed necessary, for submission to a digital, peer-reviewed publication.[6] Three weeks into class, after analyzing sample video calls-for-papers (CFPs) available on YouTube, the students insisted on producing ones that could be used for the digital publication to which they were submitting. The students spent less than an hour learning how to complete this impromptu assignment, including grabbing video from YouTube, finding images and tips on analyzing the written CFP they'd pull content from, and using MovieMaker.

They had five days to complete the one-minute CFPs, and a majority of their first drafts were wowful. Those that didn't wow were still impressive, given the quickness of the project. Six weeks into class, Cheryl was amazed by their project pitches, which got at the heart of disciplinary conversations happening in digital-writing studies. By the end of the semester, the proposal the students submitted about their projects was accepted for publication. Cheryl has repeated that syllabus several times (with scholarly multimedia publication venues in rhetoric and composition being the primary audience), each time with similar success. While space limitations prevent detailing how this new syllabus is taught using a genre studies approach to multimodal composition (see Ball 2012), she can attest that the shifting nature of digital scholarship pushes students as authors to choose what modes, media, genres, and technologies they believe are needed to reach an audience of teacher-scholars invested in, but perhaps with much still to learn about, new media.

And there have been no more wowless, five-paragraph videos in her classes.

NOTES

1. The first line of Geoffrey Sirc's book *English Composition as a Happening* (2002, 1) reads: "I suppose the reason none of us burn incense in our writing classes any more is because of the disk drives."

2. Some terms must be defined at this point. I draw on the New London Group's (NLG) definition of "mode" (Cope and Kalantzis 2000), which they refer to as "modes of meaning" but which I more often refer to as "modes of communication" because it makes sense more quickly to those not familiar with this area of scholarship. The modes that the NLG discuss include linguistic, visual, aural, spatial, and gestural, with multimodal including combinations of the other five modes.

Next is "medium" or "media," which draws on Kress and van Leeuwen's (2001) *Multimodal Discourse.* Although generalizing their complicated distinctions between modes and media, I use "media" to indicate how modes of communication are produced and distributed for public consumption (reading). For example, a linguistic mode of communication might be enacted through the medium of writing, which can also be a visual mode and could be transformed into an aural mode when writing is spoken instead of read on a page or screen. (I should note that Kress himself has said publicly—at his keynote at the 2011 Writing Research Across Borders conference in Fairfax, Virginia—that trying to create distinctions between "mode" and "medium" has become useless.)

"Text" refers to any possible combination of modes or media used to communicate to an audience and is recognized through specific genres, which are texts that use flexible, social conventions in response to a particular rhetorical situation. "Genres" use multiple modes and may use multiple media (e.g., a research paper that includes a graph or illustration; a documentary that uses textual overlay and voiceovers, etc.). "Media," however, are genre-independent. The previous example of a linguistic mode of communication, writing, needs a generic container to hold it; otherwise, the writing remains a virtual text. The virtuality of the text thus requires an interface technology to display the medium, making it materially available to users (readers), which *can* be virtual—I am not intending to create a binary between virtual and material here; she simply does not have the space, or words, to get at what I am trying to say. Here's a quick example: The medium of writing, which is an example of the linguistic mode, can be placed into a genre such as a letter to the editor, and published on interface technologies, or materials, including newsprint or a webpage.

A question I will pose, but leave mostly for another time, is: When does a technology change from being a medium of production or distribution to a convention of the genre, and thus (in some cases) a genre itself? For example, when a student uses blogging software to host a personal website in which she is posting personal pictures, writing daily entries for her family, and posting course assignments (including written reading responses and multimedia elements such as MP3s created for class), one cannot accurately assign a specific genre to such a blog because it covers so many topics for different audiences; a writer is blogging, which seems to be a production method, but it is one, like word processing, that can encompass several genres (class posts, family posts) and media (writing, pictures, MP3s) at once. That is, a "blog" is not a genre. Although blogs tend to impose specific conventions on the texts they contain (including the design of the blog itself), blogs are also a technological distribution method. So maybe the better question is: What is the impact on meaning making of the layered genre conventions of distribution methods? And does the meaning of the contained text change when the interface changes? On video blogging (or "vogs," the term that the so-called father of vlogs, Adrian Miles, has called them), see http://vogmae.net.au/vlog/2011/06/the-vogma-manifesto-2000/.

3. Two examples of successful multigenre texts that students produced as part of coursework are discussed in Ball and Moeller 2007 and 2008.

4. One or two texts wowed me for sure—and in ways I wasn't expecting to be wowed: There was one student who, instead of following instructions to film and edit similar visual elements (based on an earlier version of the video motif assignment posted at the WritingWithVideo.net website; see http://www.writingwithvideo.net/curriculum/module-01), created a motif in which he

filmed different scenes through dirty windows—a high level of critical thinking from a student who already had video-production experience. His motif, called "Most Epic Battle," is available at http://www.youtube.com/watch?v=Ks8HLskwbJY. Or the student who I thought had dropped the course but showed up with a completed, and beautifully done, antiwar music video two weeks before the semester ended. The other students insisted that I allow his video into the showcase even though he'd missed the class-wide voting.

5. The topic of digital scholarship was in part gifted to me through my work with the hosts of the 2008 Thomas R. Watson Conference on Rhetoric and Composition. As coeditors for the digital book *The New Work of Composing* that came out of the conference, Debra Journet and Ryan Trauman wanted a video response to the conference itself in the book. The students attended the conference, conducted research, collected digital assets, and composed several pieces of digital scholarship for submission to the collection. Their submissions were reviewed by the editors (other than myself), accepted for publication, and peer-reviewed by the press's external review board.

6. The syllabi for my Multimodal Composition classes (since 2008) are available at http://www.ceball.com/classes/239. Although conceived more in relation to my work with *Kairos*, this project is similar to what Ohio State University's first-year writing program is doing in their Commonplace project (see http://www.commonplaceuniversity.com/). The major difference is that the peer-reviewers in my case are meant to be scholars, not other students.

REFERENCES

Ball, Cheryl E. 2012. "Assessing Scholarly Webtexts: A Rhetorical Genre-Studies Approach." *Technical Communication Quarterly* 21: 61–77.

Ball, Cheryl E., and Ryan M. Moeller. 2007. "Reinventing the Possibilities: Academic Literacy and New Media." *Fibreculture Journal* 10. Online at http://ten.fibreculturejournal.org/fcj-062-reinventing-the-possibilities-academic-literacy-and-new-media/.

———. 2008. "Converging the ASS[umptions] Between U and ME; or How New Media Can Bridge a Scholarly/Creative Split in English Studies." *Computers and Composition Online*. Online at http://www.bgsu.edu/cconline/convergence/.

Berlin, James. 1988. "Rhetoric and Ideology in the Writing Class." *College English* 50: 477–94.

Cope, Bill, and Mary Kalantzis, eds. 2000. *Multiliteracies: Literacy Learning and the Design of Social Futures*. New York: Routledge.

Journet, Debra, Cheryl E. Ball, and Ryan Trauman, eds. 2012. *The New Work of Composing.* Computers and Composition Digital Press at Utah State University Press. Online at http://ccdigitalpress.org/nwc.

Jung, Julie. 2005. *Revisionary Rhetoric, Feminist Pedagogy, and Multigenre Texts.* Carbondale: Southern Illinois University Press.

Kress, Gunther, and Theo van Leeuwen. 2001. *Multimodal Discourse: The Modes and Media of Contemporary Communication.* New York: Arnold.

Peterson, Sheri E., ed. 2009–10. *Utah State University General Catalog.* Online at http://www.usu.edu/generalcatalog/2009-2010/online/.

Russell, David. 1995. "Activity Theory and Its Implications for Writing Instruction." In *Reconceiving Writing, Rethinking Writing Instruction*, edited by Joseph Petraglia, 51–78. Mahwah, NJ: Erlbaum.

Shipka, Jody. 2005. "A Multimodal Task-Based Framework for Composing." *College Composition and Communication* 57: 277–306.

Sirc, Geoffrey. 2002. *English Composition as a Happening.* Logan: Utah State University Press.

Smit, David W. 2004. *The End of Composition Studies.* Carbondale: Southern Illinois University Press.

Sullivan, Patricia. 2001. Practicing Safe Visual Rhetoric on the World Wide Web. *Computers and Composition* 18: 103–21.

Wardle, Elizabeth. 2009. "'Mutt Genres' and the Goal of FYC: Can We Help Students Write the Genres of the University?" *College Composition and Communication* 60: 765–89.

CHAPTER 2

Back to the Future?

The Pedagogical Promise of the (Multimedia) Essay

Erik Ellis

> As I see it, our major responsibility is to help students become genre theorists in the true sense: to destabilize their often simplistic and sterile theories of texts and enrich their views of the complexity of text processing, negotiation, and production within communities of practice.
>
> —Ann M. Johns (2002, 240)

> Disallowing the pose of objectivity through which experts maintain their privileged status as "knowers," the essay dramatizes a process of negotiation and revaluation concealed by other genres, a process never wholly methodical or disinterested.
>
> —Kurt Spellmeyer (1993, 101)

When we think about new media and emerging genres in composition studies, it can be tempting to move full-speed ahead into the uncharted waters of the digital future, without pausing to look back at familiar shores and genres. The essay, of all things, might seem at first glance an implausible and dubious source of terra firma from which to launch the multimodal, multimedia genres of the future. Too stuffy. Too belletristic. Too old. But if we think about the essay as understood by historians and scholars of the genre and as practiced by essayists from Montaigne on, it shows tremendous potential to contribute to new, hybrid forms of composing. As Cristina Kirklighter (2002, 62) has argued in *Traversing the Democratic Borders of the Essay*, "the very act of exploiting genre boundaries is what the essay is all about and thus explains why it feeds into a democracy of writing forms." By blending such qualities of the print essay as its spirit of exploration and its embrace of ambivalence with new media such as digital video and audio, students can create complex, compelling multimedia essays that challenge and transcend conventional academic discourses.

In recent years I've been assigning multimedia essays in lower- and upper-division composition courses (the classes and assignments I write about refer to my work in the Program for Writing and Rhetoric at the University of Colorado at Boulder between 2005 and 2009). For example, in my upper-division Topics in Writing: Best American Essays course, students turn one of their written essays into a multimedia essay. By "multimedia essay" I mean a short multimedia composition that develops an original idea in an interesting way and that features such essayistic qualities as an underlying subjectivity, a reflective and exploratory spirit, and a flexible, often narrative structure. My students typically include digital video (often with special effects), photographs, music, sound effects, and voiceover. Sometimes they add hand-drawn images, animation, or computer graphics, and sometimes they omit voiceovers to tell their stories and make their arguments more visually. Of course, different rhetorical situations will yield different multimedia essays. Thematically, students in my courses have created multimedia essays that explore meaningful places in their lives, that examine the implications of their food choices, that debunk scientific myths, and that make counterarguments whose rhetorical power students go on to harness as concessions in their final, persuasive multimedia essays.

In one sense, my Best American Essays course follows a conventional, print-centric trajectory. First, students immerse themselves in the genre by reading, annotating, analyzing, and discussing a variety of exemplary essays by professional and student writers as well as a handful of scholarly works about the genre. Next, they write an original essay of their own, after which they transform it from page to screen (before writing more essays). By foregrounding the written essay, this sequence may appear to unequivocally privilege alphabetic literacy as ur-literacy and the print essay as the ur-genre without which even the most dazzling multimedia essays could not exist and under whose shadow they must forever languish. Of course, digital media did not emerge from a château in France in the 1500s, and the multimedia essay does not have a centuries-old tradition of genre development, so it only makes sense for students to learn about the written essay before re-visioning it in new media.

At the same time, though, an undue emphasis on the primacy of print literacy can be misleading. After all, humans have been seeing and hearing much longer than they have been reading and writing. As Stanislas Dehaene (2009, 8) has pointed out in *Reading in the Brain*, "our brain was not designed for reading, but recycles some of its circuits for this novel cultural activity." Furthermore, in "Metamedia Literacy: Transforming Meanings and Media," Jay L. Lemke (1998, 284) has argued that "all literacy is multimedia literacy: You can never make meaning with language alone; there must always be a visual or vocal realization of linguistic signs that also carries nonlinguistic meaning (e.g., tone of voice or style or orthography)." Some written genres are more visual and auditory than others. In terms of spirit, if not chronology, the relationship between the essay and the multimedia essay is not so much linear and hierarchical so much as fluid and symbiotic. The curricular progression from studying, writing, "multi-mediating," and then once again writing the essay ultimately helps students not only develop more thoughtful essays and more engaging multimedia projects but also helps them inhabit the flexible frame of mind that lies at the heart of both genres.

The secret behind the compelling, idea-driven multimedia essays that my students often compose—individually or collaboratively—is their knowledge of and experience writing the essay. This reasoning may sound tautological. That is, of course familiarity with a specific genre will help one reconstruct that genre in a new rhetorical context. This may be so, but it's worth noting that the essay's unique suppleness enables it to glide into new media, broadly speaking, in ways that other genres cannot. Whereas an abrupt shift from writing conventional academic discourse to creating ambitious multimodal discourse can threaten to disorient students and overburden them with the need to learn, simultaneously, not only new technologies and a new rhetorical situation but also a new genre (or combination of genres), the multimedia essay flows relatively smoothly from its print ancestor.

Of course, as Amy J. Devitt (2004, 146) has pointed out in *Writing Genres*: "Different genres exist with different conventions for different people in different contexts as well as for different purposes in different situations." If one's pedagogical purpose is to have students reproduce their print texts using new media in the most literal, least imaginative ways possible—as when I teach students in Writing on Business and Society to correlate video clips from their website usability tests to the recommendations in their written reports—then shifting from a more static genre to new media may suffice. Similarly, if one wants students to experience and navigate their way out of a kind of "genre shock," then switching from a conventional print genre to an experimental multimodal genre may be worthwhile. This approach, however, seems unrealistically ambitious for most undergraduates—if not a recipe for pedagogical frustration. As Cheryl E. Ball, Tyrell Fenn, and Tia Scoffield-Brown observe in chapter 1 of this edited volume, "Genre and Transfer in a Multimodal Composition Class," one's choice of genre(s) has significant rhetorical implications. "If you ask for five-paragraph videos," Ball reflects, "you get five-paragraph videos. Focusing on a single, formulaic genre for the major project halts the critical progress of students who don't already come with multimodal composition experience."

The move from (non–five-paragraph) essay to multimedia essay, by contrast, tends to be more organic and gratifying. Conceptually, students have less need to "translate" their original, written texts into new media forms. They don't need to radically "reinvent" their genres, their essays, or themselves onscreen to produce meaningful, often captivating projects. Of course, a degree of translation and reinvention is inevitable and desirable, and some students create multimedia essays that surpass their original essays by an order of magnitude. I simply wish to question the assumption that one must first teach students to write conventional academic genres and then ask them either to reinscribe or break the rules in multimodal or multimedia projects. When students write essays, they are already learning to break the rules of conventional discourses, to think from multiple perspectives, and to express their ideas and identities in narrative and cinematic ways. We shouldn't forget, in other words, that alternative antecedent genres exist, if only we're willing to recognize and embrace them.

By examining the serendipitous convergence of the essay and the multimedia essay, and by briefly considering how several students have handled the fusion, I hope to suggest the value of an essay-based multimedia pedagogy and to demonstrate how the two related genres can successfully overlap in the service of student learning. Why do they need to overlap? I believe the connection is important, because, as Carl Whithaus (2005, 131) has argued, "when digital elements are added as an afterthought, they are not fully valued by either students or teachers." As a result, "viewing multimedia literacy as a set of skills acquired after print-based literacy skills is detrimental to students' learning" (ibid., 131). This is not the case with the two genres students produce in my courses. For instance, the same spirit of intellectual exploration, the same willingness to embrace complexity, and the same inclination toward (simple or complex) narrative structure thrive in both forms.

GENRE SERENDIPITY: THE ESSAY AND THE MULTIMEDIA ESSAY

Unlike academic genres that faculty teach primarily as collections of discourse conventions and disciplinary "moves" or "gestures," the essay and the multimedia essay privilege students' original ideas articulated in original ways. Of course, the essay is hardly exempt from conventions, moves, and gestures, but within the genre these are much less rigidly defined and typically fall within the shadow of the writer's idea. John Gage (1995, 725) has made a good case that ideas should matter: "The difference between teaching writing as a strictly technical skill and teaching writing as the exercise of independent thought and the ability to reason can be found in the answer to a simple question: Is it possible to succeed fully in this writing task (whether from a textbook's or the teacher's directives) without having a good idea of one's own? If the answer is yes, then what is learned by performing the writing task can be said to exercise the student's competency at the expense of failing to exercise the student's judgment." Whereas students who write academic "papers" must follow a formula and construct good thesis statements—which may or may not contain original ideas—students who compose essays or multimedia essays need to contemplate how to develop original ideas in interesting ways.

What exactly is the difference between a thesis and an idea? This distinction puzzled me when I first taught composition as a graduate student in the Expository Writing Program at New York University, where I cultivated my love for the essay. I was surprised by what struck me as a very unorthodox and unnecessarily complicated pedagogy and curriculum. Why, I wondered, did the program's director, Pat C. Hoy II, make such a big distinction between "thesis" and "idea"? Why was the latter so much better? And why was it so important to call essay assignments "progressions"? As I began to teach the first progression—a sequence of reading, writing, thinking, and imagining exercises designed to help students discover an original idea and develop it into an essay—I had more questions. Why did I need to assign so many of these strange writing exercises, such as a dramatic scene or a letter to a friend? Why not just ask students to write a rough draft? What had I gotten myself into?

By the end of that first semester, I was exhausted from teaching, but

I was also excited because I was beginning to understand the program's philosophy and to see the fruits of my labors and my students' labors. "Idea" was an important concept after all. Unlike a thesis, which students often formulate too hastily by reducing invention to a token first step in an assembly-line writing process, an idea enables students to explore their thinking more gradually and intensely. In "The Outreach of an Idea" (2001a, 355), Hoy distinguished between an idea "deeply grounded in curiosity and discovery" and a thesis that "keeps us on safer ground." He elaborated on this distinction in "Requiem for the Outline" (Hoy 2001b, 23), in which he articulated his desire to move students toward "a supple idea, something more akin to notion than to thesis. Not a simple declarative sentence promising proof but a more digressive invitation to the reader to participate in an excursion, an exploration, an inquiry." Carefully constructed progressions, I realized, offer students the flexibility they need to discover and develop interesting ideas of their own. In many cases, students could draw upon an array of sources as evidence for their ideas—from print texts and films to art objects and stories from personal experience. Perhaps most impressively, students could structure their essays so that they took readers on a journey through their thinking process. Such essays were almost preposterously ambitious, and yet students consistently pulled them off—as have my students in the decade since at several large public universities.

I'm not claiming that the essay is easy to teach in its original, exploratory form. Far from it. Insufficient attention to the importance of students' ideas, for example, and the need for personal narrative to serve as evidence for those ideas, can yield unwieldy essays that ramble and make readers want to blush or sigh or give up on the genre entirely. Such loss of faith would be a mistake. Reading a batch of students' unimpressive personal essays (prompted usually by an unimpressive pedagogy) and concluding that the genre itself is therefore suspect makes about as much sense as reasoning that because you hated *Bonfire of the Vanities* you should give up on the genre of the novel. Another thing I'm not claiming is that students have a natural ability or even desire to write sophisticated, idea-driven essays. Although essays enable students to take advantage of their innate narrative sensibilities—as I will explain later in this chapter—they also require students to "unlearn" habits of composition and structure that have served them well in the past. The essay and the multimedia essay may very well lack institutional capital and be less convenient, less comfortable, and less obviously transferable to other composing situations, but I'm convinced that they are excellent genres for helping students to engage in authentic inquiry and to develop as creative, original thinkers.

Besides the need for an original idea, what other qualities do the essay and the multimedia essay share? For one thing, students who have studied and written essays can take advantage of their knowledge of narrative structure when approaching the multimedia essay. Some critics have questioned the "tacit privileging" of narrative in composition, with its "implied message to students that they should resist the temptation to learn to write traditional academic prose" (Bowden 1995, 184). I question whether most students find traditional academic prose "tempting," and even the term "traditional" suggests that such prose is privileged, not narrative. On a deeper level, humans do seem to favor narrative. "A good deal of the recent scientific work on consciousness," David Lodge (2002, 14) wrote in *Consciousness and the Novel*, "has stressed its essentially narrative character." According to Walter Fisher (1989, 24), "human beings are inherently storytellers who have a natural tendency to recognize the coherence and fidelity of the stories they tell and experience." In fact, as Peter Elbow (2006, 625) has observed, "good writers tend to heed, consciously or not, the fact that readers have an experience that is more temporal than spatial." As a result, "Successful writers lead us on a journey to satisfaction by way of expectations, frustrations, half satisfactions, and temporary satisfactions: a well-planned sequence of yearnings and reliefs, itches and scratches" (ibid., 626). By nurturing rather than suppressing students' narrative inclinations, the print essay not only helps students engage and persuade readers, but it prepares them to engage and persuade viewers of their new media projects.

In addition, both the essay and the multimedia essay highlight the importance of the visual, including the essay's use of vivid descriptions that appeal to multiple senses. As Charles A. Hill (2004, 303–1) has noted in "The Psychology of Rhetorical Images," "we commonly speak of readers constructing a 'mental image' while reading a narrative or descriptive text, and neurological studies show that this occurs quite literally—i.e., reading a descriptive text can actually activate the same parts of the brain used to process visual images [Howard et al.; Rebotier; Sinatra]." Students who learn to craft vivid essays, therefore, will already have experience appealing to an audience visually. As a result, they will have an advantage in bringing their "cinematic" visions to a literally visual realm.

Voice is another crucial shared element. Whereas students who have been shackled by the thesis-support structure will likely face major challenges in adapting their specific texts or their stylistic habits to media environments that often demand less formality and more creativity, student essayists will be able to draw upon their knowledge of voice, if not their specific conversational prose, to help craft voiceovers that resonate with an audience. Richard E. Mayer (2005, 207; emphasis in original) has cited "strong and consistent evidence for the *personalization principle*: People learn more deeply [from multimedia presentations] when words are presented in conversational style rather than formal style." Once again the essay fits the bill. "The conversational dynamic—the desire for contact—is ingrained in the [essay] form," Phillip Lopate (1994, xxv) wrote, "and serves to establish a quick emotional intimacy with the audience." Students who have dutifully worn masks of objectivity in their academic writing will naturally struggle more to achieve this kind of emotional intimacy in their multimodal texts.

Indeed, the way I organize the essay and multimedia essay assignments, many of the same assessment criteria flow from genre to genre—without privileging traditional, print-based literacy or expecting students' multimedia texts to be carbon/pixel copies of their essays. The overall success of both assignments is a testament, in large part, to the seamless connection between the two genres. In the end my argument for the value of the multimedia essay relies on the value of the essay, so I explore next the pedagogical advantages of the form before considering more specifically the parallel advantages of its twenty-first-century counterpart.

W(H)ITHER THE ESSAY?

As multimodal composition promises to emerge from the margins in rhetoric and composition, Thomas Newkirk's (1989, 6) question gains fresh urgency: "Do current approaches to teaching expository writing promote or do they actually foreclose possibilities for open-ended, conversation-like, exploration?" This question seems doubly important in the context of recent genre theory. In *Genre in the Classroom*, in her chapter "Destabilizing and Enriching Novice Students' Genre Theories," Ann Johns (2002, 237–38) has argued: "There are direct contradictions between what the theoreticians and researchers continue to discover about the nature of genres and the everyday requirements of the classroom. . . . Our curricular tendencies are to emphasize regularities and to search for stability so that students can learn some concrete facts about texts." Indeed, it is disingenuous to champion the complexities and paradoxes of genres in theory but then step into the classroom to serve students rules and formulas on a silver platter.

Of course, to embrace complexity in student writing is to accept a challenge with practical as well as theoretical implications. In "An 'Immensely Simplified Task': Form in Modern Composition-Rhetoric," Judith Goleman (2004) has reflected on the difficulty of responding to a student's particularly complex and ambivalent analytical essay. She wrote: "Teaching a non-unitary rhetoric, as we can see, produces writing that represents challenges so great for an instructor who must write a response to it that it might well make one wish for one of [late-nineteenth-century Harvard Professor Barrett] Wendell's 'immensely simplified tasks.' This, however, is a literacy issue for the instructor, not the student" (ibid., 67). As someone who has also taught "non-unitary rhetoric" for years, I agree that complex student essays require far more time and energy to respond to than traditional, thesis-driven articles, but ultimately I find the extra effort well worth it. Teaching the essay and the multimedia essay, in all their complexity, would go a long way toward resolving the embarrassing rift between genre theory and pedagogy.

Students in my Best American Essays course often seem shocked that I grant them so much artistic freedom in their writing—and later in their multimedia projects. They have been conditioned to think of artistic, literary works as products to critique, not texts to create. Steve Westbrook (2006, 469) has noted that "today, although we may demonstrate increasing interest in 'the visual,' we maintain a tendency to treat visual texts as if others will always be producing them while we and our students fulfill the role of viewer and respondent." In addition, as J. Elizabeth Clark (2010, 32) has pointed out, students do not always jump for joy when invited to practice rhetorical creativity: "Far from embracing digital rhetoric, many students reject it in favor of a more comfortable essayistic literacy." But if Kurt Spellmeyer (2003, 23) was correct in claiming that "a great secret of the academic humanities has been their quiet but consistent exclusion of the arts as an activity, as a practice," then I consider it my job to invite students to compose essays and multimedia essays as activities, as practices. Such a focus need not come at the expense of critical inquiry.

According to Lemke (2006, 13), "critical multimedia literacy needs to be taught as creation, as authoring, as production—in the context of analysis of existing models and genres." Students realize soon enough that, yes, I want them to question the mythologized supremacy of generic academic discourse. I want them to essay their original ideas in their own voices, not regurgitate or ventriloquize the voices of critics. I want them, ultimately, to take audiences on intellectual journeys, not presume to reveal mathematical proofs. Many students can write excellent proofs, and to an extent, I appreciate the neat, invisible bows they tie to their thesis statements, which sit predictably at the end of the first paragraph like apples placed on the edge of my desk. As comforting as such familiarity can be, I've always been more impressed by the risk-takers, the rebels—the students who let their imaginations run wild into the open spaces of the essay genre. Even if they stumble and fall short of their ambitions, I still admire these students for essaying, for attempting to preserve within the very form of their writing some semblance of their intellectual exploration, their motivating curiosity and wonder. Such essays, of course, lack the academic legitimacy of more formal, conventional texts that composition faculty routinely call essays. But perhaps such formal compositions should not be called essays after all. They might more accurately be called articles. What's the difference between the two genres anyway, and what are the implications for multimodal discourse? In "The Literary Essay and the Modern Temper," Mary E. Rucker (1975, 322) wondered "to what extent may a particular genre evolve before it becomes another genre? Or, to put it another way, just how far may the traditional essay as it was shaped by Montaigne adapt to a dynamic social order without becoming the polemic article?"

By and large, scholars of the essay see little room for such adaptation. In fact, the closer we examine the essay historically, the less it resembles the essay that composition faculty teach, write, and valorize in academia today. As far back as 1912, Maurice Garland Fulton, in his textbook *Expository Writing*, noted the peculiar mismatch between the genre's roots and its more modern incarnations. After describing the "familiar" nature of essays written by Charles Lamb, Richard Steele, Joseph Addison, William Makepeace Thackeray, and Robert Louis Stevenson, he explained: "It was this looser type of exposition which first gave vogue to the term essay, but the development of this form of literature has been so markedly away from a subjective, personal, and leisurely discussion towards an objective, concentrated, and unemotional method, that when we hear the word essay to-day we think rather of the scientific exposition than the familiar" (Fulton, as quoted in Brereton 1995, 405). Scholars of the essay repeatedly point out that such "scientific exposition" is antithetical to the genre. According to Kirklighter (2002, 6), "instead of working toward definitive conclusions, as in an article, the essay's spontaneity allows the writer to wander, to make connections in unusual places, to emphasize discoveries instead of conclusions." William Gass (1985) has also contrasted the essay with the article. He argued that "the article pretends that everything is clear, that its argument is unassailable, that there are no soggy patches, no illicit references, no illegitimate connections; its manners are starched, stuffy, it would wear a dress suit to a barbeque, silk pajamas to the shower" (ibid., 949). The essay, in other words, welcomes rather than shuns sustained, authentic inquiry and ambivalence.

After investigating what essayists themselves have had to say about the genre, Karl H. Klaus (1989, 65) concluded, "ultimately, most essayists simply do not recognize such a thing as the formal essay, presumably because it embodies the very antithesis of what they conceive an essay to be. . . . Most essayists, in fact, do not tend to classify essays at all." Thomas Recchio (1994, 273) offered a rationale for this resistance to classification, noting that "a formalist approach to the essay is misdirected because it ignores the dialogic quality of the essay. It ossifies a fluid form, turning it into a series of types: the narrative essay, the descriptive essay, the argumentative essay, and so forth."

But if we can't classify the essay without ossifying it, then what are some of its central characteristics—ones that we may be able to adapt to new media? Lopate (1994, xxxvii) has observed that the genre historically had "a notoriously flexible and adaptable form." Other scholars have similarly called the essay—not just the so-called personal essay—"reflective and exploratory and essentially personal" (Anderson 1989, ix); "essentially a peripatetic or ambulatory form" (Good 1988, 4); "an extraordinarily free form" (Pebworth 1997, 22); "kineticism incarnate" (Heilker 1996, 169); "impossible to define" (Core 1989, 219); and "an antigenre, a rouge form of writing in the universe of discourse" (Klaus 1989, 160). Theodor Adorno (1984, 171) went so far as to claim that "the law of the innermost form of the essay is heresy." Such characterizations of the essay, with their implicit invitation to writers—including student writers—to explore their ideas and identities, contrast sharply with the "eminently assessable" (Andrews 2003, 119) genre that many composition faculty privilege today.

Of course, we can't reasonably expect genres to remain static. We can't expect the essay in the early twenty-first century to mirror the essay of the sixteenth century. "Because users adapt genres to their purposes and make rhetorical choices in varying social situations," wrote Deborah Dean (2008, 14), "genres have flexibility—and flexibility can lead, eventually, to change." Still, one of the unique traits of the essay since its inception has been its flexibility. To erase what is arguably the genre's single most notable and persistent feature, to reinvent it completely for the sake of convenience and conformity in the context of academia, is to erase the genre itself. As disconcerting as the essay's original open-endedness may be for composition faculty accustomed to prescribing and following discourse conventions such as explicit thesis statements and topic sentences, I argue that what we gain in convenience by molding the essay into a procrustean formula, we lose in intellectual integrity. These discourse conventions are not inherently unwelcome, but they do tend to stifle, if not obliterate, the contingent nature of the form. As Jean Donovan Sanborn (1994, 122) has argued in "The Essay Dies in the Academy, circa 1900," "the ideals of the essay rooted in Montaigne that tried out ideas would be more valuable for learning, but this model has been squeezed out of the classroom in favor of a form still called the essay but antithetical to the intentions of essayists in the Montaigne tradition." By abandoning the essay, we deprive students of valuable opportunities to explore and share their original ideas in creative forms, including multimedia forms.

So why not just admit that we teach students to write articles and not essays? Such an admission, I suspect, would demand more than a simple change in vocabulary. It would force us to confront and reevaluate our professional identities. After all, would you really think about your teaching in the same way if you found yourself telling students, "Next week we'll workshop drafts of your articles"? Maybe I'm just projecting my own expressivist fears, but I would hope composition faculty of all pedagogical stripes would resist such a submissive "service" view of literacy. Even if "we have replaced the vitality of the essay with an externalized skeletonized rigid frame" (Heath 1987, 10), the fact that we still talk as if we teach essays enables us to preserve the illusion that we are deeply devoted to the progressive spirit of the humanities.

True, even the most conservative upholders of conventional academic writing scoff at the simplistic, formulaic nature of the five-paragraph essay. And yes, Elbow (2006, 648–49, emphasis in original) has made an intriguing argument that "we *can* in fact be riveted by the dynamic energy of an essay that starts off announcing its claim and structure." Still, our fundamental allegiance to discourse conventions such as explicit thesis statements and topic sentences suggests that the basic formula for a successful "essay" doesn't change much from high school to college. Most undergraduates will confirm that they've had the thesis-driven formula drilled into them since middle school at the latest. According to Paul Heilker (1996, 2), who has argued that the "thesis/support" form is "inadequate from developmental, epistemological, ideological, and feminist rhetorical perspectives":

> college-level writing instruction, it seems to me, should offer students something that is decidedly different from what they had in secondary school. That seems so obvious that I feel silly for saying it. Nevertheless, since an operational definition for insanity is "doing the same thing over and over again but expecting different results," we composition teachers may be insane: we have been pummeling students with thesis-driven writing in school for ten years, typically, before they come to college, yet we persist in the delusion that this time it will be different, that this time they will get it. But such an assumption is clearly flawed or terribly arrogant: Despite years of repeated previous attempts, our students obviously have not yet gotten it (because they otherwise would not be placed in our first-year composition classes), so how could another semester or two of almost exactly the same thing make any real difference? (Heilker 2006, 201)

From an essayist's point of view, there's an even deeper problem with this kind of formulaic writing. According to Robert Atwan (1998, xi), series editor of *The Best American Essays*, "what was especially maddening about the typical five-paragraph theme had less to do with its tedious structure than with its implicit message that writing should be the end product of thought and not the enactment of its process." Reflecting on his experience teaching the five-paragraph essay in college, he called the form "a charade. It not only paraded relentlessly to its conclusion; it began with its conclusion. It was all about its conclusion. Its structure permitted no change of direction, no reconsideration, no wrestling with ideas. It was—and still is—the perfect vehicle for the sort of reader who likes to ask: 'And your point is . . . ?'" (ibid., xii). To anyone who has recently asked a student "So, what's your thesis?," this question will no doubt sound familiar, perhaps with a suddenly dark and didactic overtone. As much as we might like to imagine that our students are taking intellectual journeys when they embark on their essays, our frequent demand for a thesis statement early in the writing process effectively slams the door shut on inquiry, asphyxiates invention, and makes it virtually impossible for students to essay their ideas, let alone to preserve the narrative trajectory of those ideas in a final draft.

Those of us who try to teach the essay in more of its original sense must do more than encourage students to sit at their keyboards and "let it all out." Skillfully written essays that burn always with a hard, gemlike flame can all too easily give students the impression of being brilliantly instinctive creations, when in fact they offer the artful illusion of spontaneity. Even Montaigne, the putative master of impulsive literary self-creation, was "a craftsman despite his claims to the contrary," according to Newkirk (2005, 313). Other essayists are more upfront about the arduous nature of the genre. As Klaus (1989, 166) pointed out, "though they oppose methodical discourse, the essayists are careful to make clear that they consider the essay to be a highly disciplined form of writing. Indeed, their insistence on its freedom from conventionalized form and thought probably makes them all the more intent on dispelling any notion that the essay is a free-for-all form of writing." Accordingly, anyone interested in teaching students to write essays, as opposed to articles masquerading as essays, has an obligation to help them embrace the form's freedom yet transcend the tempting self-indulgences of the solipsist.

TEACHING THE ESSAY AND THE MULTIMEDIA ESSAY

Fortunately, if we design and scaffold our essay assignments carefully, we can enable students to explore their thoughts, to give birth to interesting ideas, and to craft those ideas into what Hoy (2001b, 45) has called "one of the cherished gifts afforded to reader and writer alike: a picture of a mind thinking." On this note, Heilker (2006, 200) has offered the important insight "that students' identities are the most important texts they will ever read and write; that the exploring, composing, and expressing of their selves is the most important act of interpretation and writing they will ever undertake; and that the essay is a far better vehicle for this work than exposition."

The multimedia essay may be an even more engaging vehicle for students to explore their identities, in all their constructed complexity. Like written essays, multimedia essays offer abundant creative opportunities coupled with corresponding rhetorical challenges. In addition, they require students not only to understand various technologies but also to use them skillfully and with purpose. Teaching students to work effectively with multimedia can be a challenge, but if they are already familiar with the essay form, if they have practice writing in the genre, and if they have the freedom to explore their original ideas, then the transition to the multimedia essay can be surprisingly smooth. When students succeed, the results are exciting. They often take so much pride in their multimedia essays that they burn extra DVDs to share with their families. Their desire to archive and share their work—rather than deposit it into the "audience" of a recycling bin—is no small measure of the genre's success.

When they have a good idea of how the essay differs from the article, students in my Best American Essays course begin to write a reflective,

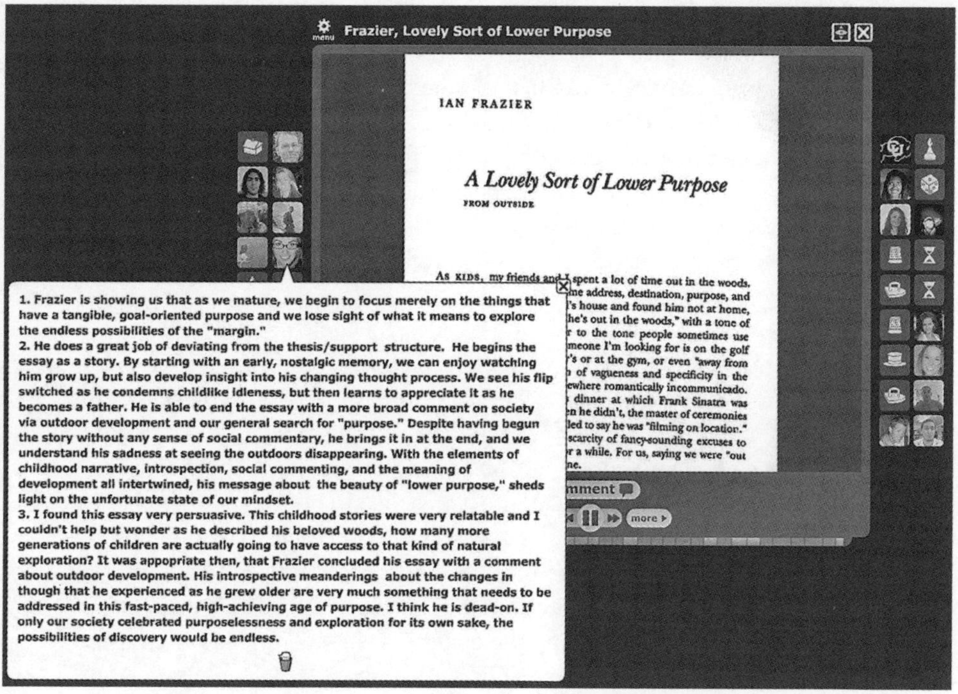
Frazier, Lovely Sort of Lower Purpose
IAN FRAZIER
A Lovely Sort of Lower Purpose
FROM OUTSIDE
1. Frazier is showing us that as we mature, we begin to focus merely on the things that have a tangible, goal-oriented purpose and we lose sight of what it means to explore the endless possibilities of the "margin."
2. He does a great job of deviating from the thesis/support structure. He begins the essay as a story. By starting with an early, nostalgic memory, we can enjoy watching him grow up, but also develop insight into his changing thought process. We see his flip switched as he condemns childlike idleness, but then learns to appreciate it as he becomes a father. He is able to end the essay with a more broad comment on society via outdoor development and our general search for "purpose." Despite having begun the story without any sense of social commentary, he brings it in at the end, and we understand his sadness at seeing the outdoors disappearing. With the elements of childhood narrative, introspection, social commenting, and the meaning of development all intertwined, his message about the beauty of "lower purpose," sheds light on the unfortunate state of our mindset.
3. I found this essay very persuasive. This childhood stories were very relatable and I couldn't help but wonder as he described his beloved woods, how many more generations of children are actually going to have access to that kind of natural exploration? It was appopriate then, that Frazier concluded his essay with a comment about outdoor development. His introspective meanderings about the changes in though that he experienced as he grew older are very much something that needs to be addressed in this fast-paced, high-achieving age of purpose. I think he is dead-on. If only our society celebrated purposelessness and exploration for its own sake, the possibilities of discovery would be endless.
more

FIGURE 2.1. A student's response to a sample essay on VoiceThread.

exploratory essay about a place or space in their lives that they consider meaningful—the Reflective Analysis of a Personally Meaningful Place, which I've since renamed Exploring an Idea through Place to foreground the importance of idea over place. To get a sense for how prizewinning essayists write about place, students read such essays as Ian Frazier's "A Lovely Sort of Lower Purpose," André Aciman's "Shadow Cities," Lawrence Otis Graham's "Invisible Man," and Jamaica Kincaid's "On Seeing England for the First Time." Through reading responses and class discussions of such essays, students acquaint themselves with the genre in the context of their rhetorical situation.

Figure 2.1 shows an online forum on VoiceThread in which students post their reflections on a sample essay. VoiceThread, which I later ask students to use for formative assessment of their storyboards and multimedia essay drafts—as well as for their director's commentaries and reflective portfolios—enables students to leave comments via text, audio, or webcam. With the system I set up, only students in the class could comment and view or hear one another's comments. Perhaps, in some small way, giving students this kind of initial interactive experience with text and technology—particularly the option to record audio comments and thus think more consciously and rhetorically about voice for an audience of peers—prepares them further to transform their essays into multimedia essays. My initial impressions of this powerful Web 2.0 application reinforce the idea that "computer-supported collaborative learning processes help students to achieve deeper levels of knowledge generation through the creation of shared goals, shared exploration, and a shared process of meaning making [Lipponen, Kakkarainen, and Paavola 2004]" (Khine 2007, 299).

As one student commented in her reflective audio portfolio on VoiceThread at the end of one of my Best American Essays courses: "I think VoiceThread was a good idea, because unlike CULearn [Blackboard], you could actually—it was more interactive, I guess, because you could see people's pictures and know who they were and what they were saying." Another student commented: "It was nice to just talk and really say what I thought. I think it was less stressful to just be able to record myself, and it was more honest sometimes." In addition, I noticed that students commented on one another's reading responses without any prompting from me, and they ratcheted up the quality of their comments from what past students had submitted to me in hard copy.

When I explain the first essay assignment to students—Exploring an Idea through Place—I emphasize that their essays, like the models we've been reading, should develop original ideas in interesting ways. Rather than write thesis-driven, five-paragraph "themes," they have the opportunity and challenge to write more flexible, thoughtful, narrative essays that draw upon personal experience as evidence. As they write the various exercises that will culminate in an essay, I encourage students to allow their thoughts to unfold and their ideas to emerge. Ultimately their essays should be compelling reflections or embodiments of their thinking that enable readers to experience their ideas as they have unfolded over time. The progression and pedagogy I outline in this chapter are adapted from Hoy's work at New York University.

When I first taught the "meaningful place" multimedia essay, two students in my Best American Essays course created projects that I have since shown as models of the genre. The projects are very different in purpose and technical ambition, yet they share an ability to draw audiences into their authors' perspectives. As a white, middle-class, Jewish woman who breakdances, linguistics major Katya Hott wrote her essay and made her increasingly dynamic DVD about the connection between her ambivalent subject position and the breakdancing website www.bboyworld.com—particularly the site's New Raw Footage section, where breakdancers post clips of themselves or others breakdancing. By contrast, Merced Perez-Hall used his essay and DVD to explore the psychological toll of "walking hours"—literally walking back and forth for hours as punishment for failing various inspections at West Point.

When Katya and Merced created their DVDs, my multimedia pedagogy was still in its infancy. I had not yet designed a full-fledged multimedia progression complete with voiceovers; storyboards; carefully orchestrated training and practice sessions devoted to the practical and rhetorical uses of programs such as iMovie, GarageBand, and iDVD; class time in the campus Media Lab; formative assessment; substantive self-reflection; and so forth. My students were more or less muddling through, seemingly inventing the genre through their experimental approaches. I say "seemingly" because their successful and creative DVDs correlated closely to their successful and creative essays—without being simplistic, literal adaptations. I have since developed a coherent yet ever-evolving multimedia pedagogy, but before I share some of its features and reflect on their importance, I want to spotlight Katya and Merced's outstanding multimedia essays, which illustrate some of the genre's rhetorical possibilities. By briefly profiling their projects, I hope to illustrate how a widely discarded, allegedly antiquated genre can snap vividly to life in the textual and digital realities of the twenty-first century.

As a preliminary task for the essay assignment, I ask students to list three potential places they might want to write about and to explain why each place might be a good choice. In small-group workshops, students help one another choose a place. In the past, people have chosen to write about places ranging from their trucks to their souls, from "the zone" to war zones in Iraq.

Below are the prompts I gave to Katya, Merced, and their classmates for their writing exercises. They are worth considering because, as Anis Bawarshi (2003, 128) has noted, "the prompt is a precondition for the existence of student writing, a means of habituating the students into the subject as well as the subjectivity they are being asked to explore so that they can then 'invent' themselves and their subject matter within it."

EXERCISE #1: Description of Place

> Write a one- to two-page (single-spaced) vivid description of your chosen place. Bring your place to life so others can get a good feel for it—e.g., appeal to multiple senses. Bring three copies to class.

EXERCISE #2: Summary and Dramatic Scene

Part 1: Write a one-sentence summary of a specific memory set in your chosen place that has meaning for you.

Part 2: Write a one- to two-page (single-spaced) dramatic scene (real, not fictional) set in your chosen place. This scene should be a dramatic account of your specific, meaningful memory (the one you summarized), told in a way that lets readers experience what you experienced. Bring three copies to class.

EXERCISE #3: Letter to a Friend

Write a two- to three-page (single-spaced) letter to a friend (a real friend; don't just write "Dear Friend,") in which you continue to explore and develop your emerging idea, drawing upon your earlier writing. Remember, you're not trying to "prove" a thesis; you're trying to create a record of your evolving thoughts about an idea—in a coherent way that will interest readers. Bring three copies to class.

EXERCISE #4: Account of New Evidence

Tentatively choose an idea that intrigues you and that you want to explore further in your writing and thinking. Don't let your emerging idea ossify into a closed-minded thesis.

Select an additional piece of evidence likely to support, enhance, or complicate your emerging idea—for example, a song or sound, a written text (book, essay, poem, story, ad, etc.), or a visual text (photo, film, TV show, painting, etc.).

Write a one- to two-page (single-spaced) account about the relationship between your emerging idea and your new piece of evidence. Bring three copies to class.

Katya's essay, which emerged organically from her writing exercises and which is the product of numerous revisions in light of peer and instructor comments, elaborates on her ambivalence about the seeming clash between her love of break-dancing and her identity as a middle-class, Jewish white woman. It explores an original idea in an interesting way and captures her experiences and insights as if they were unfolding before our eyes. Full of voice and curiosity, her piece is an essay in the best sense of the term.

FROM ESSAY TO MULTIMEDIA ESSAY

How did Katya turn her essay into a multimedia essay? The assignment asked her and her classmates to "create a compelling, rhetorically sophisticated multimedia version" of their essays on DVD. They could be no longer than five minutes. Table 2.1 shows the latest version of the critique form/grading criteria I've been using to assess multimedia essays. One key difference is that I now require students to use all original material. This requirement reduces the number of students who rely on Google Images, video clips from their favorite movies, and songs by their favorite artists—all of which tend to sap students' projects of their original energy. As it happens, even though Katya created her multimedia essay before this creative restriction, the overwhelming majority of her project consists of original material. This originality, I believe, is fundamental to her project's rhetorical power.

What were the logistics and limitations involved in creating Katya's project and in creating students' multimedia projects more broadly? To begin with, Information Technology Services at the University of Colorado–Boulder doesn't let students save work overnight on the computers in the labs where they learn iMovie, GarageBand, iDVD, and other relevant software, so students must work on their projects in the university's Media Lab, which is only open during regular business hours on weekdays. The Media Lab, however, offers students everything they need to create multimedia projects. Their facilities include five soundproof edit bays equipped with high-end Macs, software galore, media-conversion decks, and USB microphones for recording voiceovers and foley effects. The Media Lab also manages a pool of digital camcorders, tripods, and even portable Firewire hard drives that students can check out for free.

When Katya created her DVD, the Media Lab had more modest facilities, but it still had computers, camcorders, and a staff of professionals eager to help students with technical questions. Perhaps most important, students can create and store their work in the Media Lab for the duration of their projects. Increasingly I schedule class time in the Media Lab, especially as I emphasize more collaborative multimedia projects. In Katya's case, she already owned an Apple laptop, which she used to create most of her multimedia essay. (She did use the Media Lab for several tasks, such as importing clips from a breakdancing DVD and burning her final DVD.) Like her classmates, she used Apple's iMovie to create and edit her video. The class spent several days in a computer classroom on campus learning and practicing the basics of digital video editing. We

Table 2.1. Critique Form and Grading Criteria for Assessing Multimedia Essays

Grade	Feature of DVD	Comments and Suggestions
___/10	DVD menu (created using iDVD or similar program) matches content of DVD in terms of tone and psychic distance. This includes music/sound.	View all of the available menu "themes" in iDVD before choosing the one most appropriate for your essay. Remember that you can customize the music too—or choose silence or sound effects instead. • Choose specific fonts for a reason. Avoid overly bright colors, which make fonts hard to read. • If you use text in your DVD—e.g., for a title sequence or end credits—make sure all text is large, legible, and on screen long enough to be read twice.
___/10	DVD contains all original material.	• Reserve a digital camcorder for checkout ASAP from the ITS Media Lab. Likewise, call the Media Lab ASAP to schedule time(s) to work on your DVD outside of class. • If necessary, contact your parents or others ASAP to obtain potentially useful sources, such as family photos or home videos.
___/10	DVD explores an *idea*, transcending personal narrative for its own sake. The DVD provokes viewers to think about the idea, not just the writer's experience per se.	Remember the difference between description and analysis/argument. Don't just describe a place or series of events. Explain their significance and share your original idea.
___/10	DVD *explores* an idea, taking the viewer on a journey that reflects the writer's thinking process. The psychic distance is close.	As in your essay, avoid stating a "thesis" upfront. Your idea should unfold in a compelling way rather than be bluntly stated at the beginning.
___/10	DVD includes compelling and appropriate use(s) of *images*—e.g., photos, drawings, video clips, typography, etc.	• If you use photos, make sure they are high-resolution and will not look pixilated in your iMovie. Low-resolution images look amateurish, especially when you zoom in on

		them. (Of course, you can use pixilated images for a specific rhetorical purpose.) • When using the Ken Burns effect in iMovie, avoid monotony by varying how long photos stay on the screen and by varying the direction and distance of zooms (e.g., consider "panning" across a photo without zooming at all).
___/10	DVD includes compelling and appropriate voiceover.	• Record your voiceover first, so that you can edit the length of your images to match your words. • The tone and pace of your voice should match the tone and pace of your essay—e.g., don't sound cheerful while reading a sad part of your essay, don't read too fast out of nervousness, etc. • Remember the rhetorical power of silence—its power to let an image or sentence resonate. Choose pauses carefully.
___/10	DVD includes compelling and appropriate use(s) of *sound(s)* other than your voiceover.	• Keep in mind the sound effects available in iMovie. Also, please consider recording original "foley" sound effects. • Always use sound effects and music for a good reason. • To edit images to match music (e.g., the beat), import your music first, then edit your images.
___/10	DVD's style and pacing are compelling and appropriate.	A slower pace can have a more reflective, contemplative quality. To create this quality using photos, let them stay on the screen longer.
___/10	Transitions between images (photos, video clips, etc.) are compelling and appropriate.	Abrupt cuts between photos can look unprofessional, unless you want to create a disjointed effect. Also, avoid using every transition available, which can look amateurish.
___/10	Ending is compelling and appropriate. DVD is five minutes or shorter.	Take the time limit seriously. This restriction is a major rhetorical challenge.

also discussed the rhetoric of multimedia. For example, under what circumstances and for what purpose would you want to use black and white, slow motion, dissolve transitions, and so forth?

Katya created a powerful multimedia essay that did justice to her written essay while at the same time giving viewers a deeper, more visceral understanding of her experiences and ideas. Her voiceover is a well-edited, well-read 511-word version of her 2,482-word original essay. She recorded some passages, such as the following one, verbatim from her writing exercises or essay: "That's what bboyworld does: It breaks barriers. You are judged on your skill and not your background or your color. I can post a clip of me that's called 'Bgirl from Massachusetts,' and people will reply about whether they think I'm a good dancer or not. I bet no one will reply, 'How much money does your dad make a year?' That would be whack."

In some cases, Katya's multimedia essay directly parallels the storyline from her essay. In the opening sequence of her DVD, for example, we see her walk home from training, open the door to her apartment, struggle up the stairs, and sit down in front of her laptop to browse bboyworld.com (see fig. 2.2). The music that accompanies this sequence is an understated, rumbly hip-hop groove. We also hear ambient sounds such as her keys jingling and the sound of her footsteps. Her voiceover adds another layer of meaning. As she enters her apartment, we hear her read a quotation from her essay—one of four posts by people visiting bboyworld.com that punctuate her essay at key intervals: "it knows no language boundries, it knows no color boundries, it knows no national boundries, it knows no religious boundries, it knows no age boundries, it knows no sex boundries, it knows no economic boundries, it knows no boundry on this planet. nothing, nada, zip, zero, nothing can contain or hold up hiphop. the only other thing on this planet to do such a thing is the human spirit and its will to survive and grow" (Chicano322, registered user, Los Angeles). When Katya opens her laptop, the camera zooms in on the screen, which shows the title of her DVD, "Bboyworld." As viewers, we are being invited to enter her perspective and to share her enthusiasm. As the title screen cuts to a montage of breakdancers in action, the music picks up.

Katya uses a variety of images in her project, including a photo of a big house that represents her well-off upbringing, as well as screenshots from bboyworld.com. But most of her multimedia essay consists of original photos and video footage that show her and other breakdancers in action. This material, much of which Katya allows to play without any voiceover,

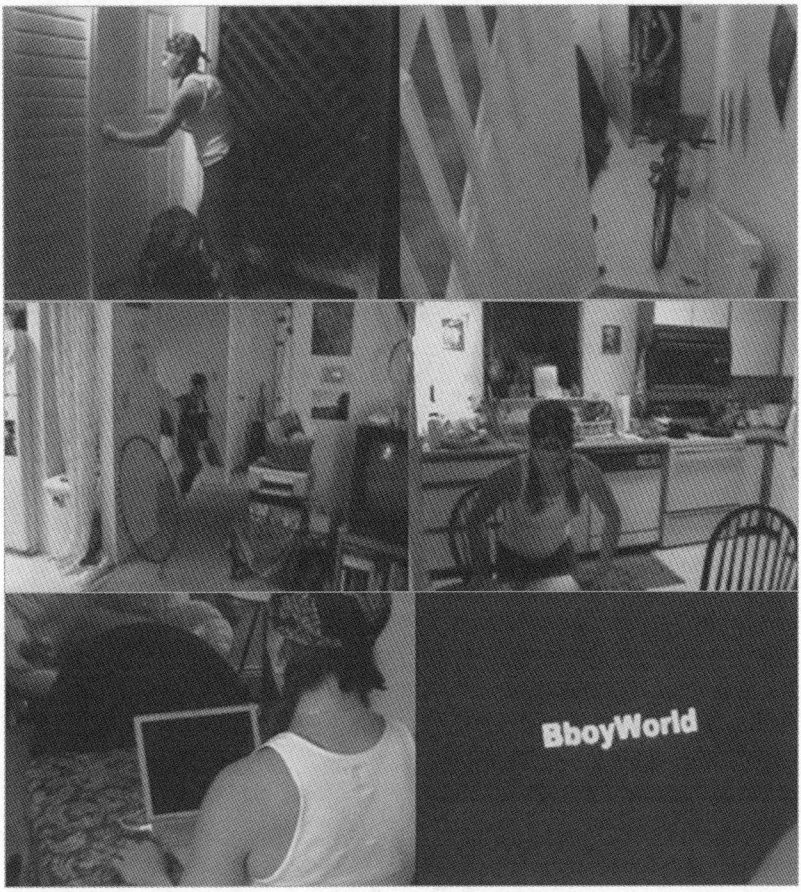

FIGURE 2.2. The opening sequence of Katya Hott's multimedia essay "Bboyworld" mirrors yet uniquely dramatizes the beginning of her essay.

vividly reinforces her idea that, as she says at the end of her DVD: "It's all about the dancing, really. It's comforting to know that my race matters only as much as I make it matter. But it's just as discomforting to accept that I am my biggest critic. My race and background matter more to me than to anyone else." The final shot of her project shows her training at the gym, moving her arms and legs so fast that it's hard to keep up with her (see fig. 2.3). She finishes her complex routine, stands with a flourish of well-earned confidence, and smiles. A freeze-frame captures the moment, and the move from essay to multimedia essay feels complete.

Perhaps Katya's most impressive rhetorical accomplishment is to structure her multimedia essay so that it cleverly mirrors, in both image

FIGURE 2.3. Katya dancing.

and sound, her cultural metamorphosis from a powerless and insecure outsider for whom breakdancing was initially "beautiful, intimidating, and extremely foreign" to a conflicted yet confident insider. Early in her video, for example, we see six still photographs of the first "crew" she encountered. Katya is noticeably absent, reflecting her lack of agency. On her voiceover, which has no background music at this point as if to further reinforce her alienation, she says, "I learned my first six-step from a kid named Kevin. Kevin was from Florox crew, from Boston. Well, originally they were from Hong Kong and Taiwan. Kevin was from Korea. When I first started training with them, in a forgotten studio outside of MIT, Kevin told me not to be offended if some of the breakers didn't talk to me. They were not used to white kids training with them—especially white girls."

As we see more photos—this time featuring Katya and Kevin in non-dancing situations, plus the men from Florox dancing—Katya explains that she's "probably only one of ten white, Jewish, middle-class bgirls in the country. Sometimes I want to hide that from other dancers—not that I'm ashamed of being white or Jewish, but because it makes me not as raw as the rest, not as hard, not as worthy of the dance." The voiceover pauses here as we watch original video footage of a tall, black, and presumably "raw" breakdancer "popping" in the street to the accompaniment of a mellow hip-hop beat. This shot is followed by screenshots from www.bboyworld.com as Katya explains that the website is her "number-one proof that I'm overthinking the role of race in my dancing."

Katya's DVD ends with a dynamic montage of her breakdancing. The montage opens with several still images of her executing acrobatic maneuvers. Then, following a hip-hop artist's exclamation "Soon as the beat is felt, I'm ready to go!," we go into a one-minute sequence of Katya dancing on Boulder's Pearl Street Mall, in clubs, and in the campus gym—all without voiceover. Whereas the background music in her opening sequence was muted and anticipatory—the soundtrack of an observer—this final groove, which is by far the most upbeat, puts her unequivocally in center stage. Her account of how she acquired agency in spite of her apprehension and self-criticism—a process that she articulated so well in her original essay—now dances before our eyes and rumbles in our ears with powerful new immediacy.

Of course, the rhetorical techniques and strategies that work well for one student are likely to fail for others. As with the essay, there are no formulas. Katya's progressively dynamic editing and hip-hop soundtrack, for example, would have done nothing for another student in the same class, Merced Perez-Hall, whose moving essay "Walking Hours"—about the verbal abuse and punishment he experienced at West Point—has an almost suffocating immediacy.

As with Katya, Merced used much of his original writing in his voiceover. For example, he says (as he writes): "Walking hours for me was the worst thing I've ever done. I've been physically exhausted until I can't even lift my arms out in front of me. I've been deprived of food. And I have had people get under my skin so bad I thought I might begin to cry. None of those things I experienced at West Point were as bad as walking hours." He goes on: "Some people think of hell as a molten lake of fire. Others think of it as freezing cold. To me, hell is a 50- x 100-yard stretch of black tarmac called Central Area where walking hours takes place." Only with a genre as flexible as the essay can students take an invitation to write about a "meaningful place" and tailor it so powerfully to their individual lives and so smoothly to new media.

What did Merced do for his multimedia essay? How did he capture the mental anguish of walking hours? For one thing, he chose to turn his video footage into black and white—an excellent rhetorical choice that further reflects the dreariness and monotony of walking hours. Another of his main techniques was to videotape himself walking. Rather than show his whole body, however, he chose to show only his legs—first from his perspective looking down at the ground, then from various angles, including a 360-degree close-up of his polished shoes (see fig. 2.4). The effect, with long fade-outs and fade-ins, is to increase the audience's experience of identification—to put viewers, literally, in his shoes. Earlier in the semester we had analyzed the visual rhetoric of the title sequence of *To Kill a Mockingbird*. We noted that we see a child's hands but not the whole child, and we discussed the power of tight close-ups to reflect the intensity of children's playful imaginations—the large presence of small things. In addition, we talked about how each shot is filmed with the unrushed fluidity of a summer afternoon, a sensation furthered by the choice of transitions—slow dissolves that give the impression of one moment melting into the next.

Did our analysis influence Merced? Perhaps. Either way, this example highlights the potential importance of visual analysis as part of a multimedia-essay progression—an insight I've taken to heart. Interspersed throughout Merced's original video footage are photos of West Point. For instance, when he talks about Central Area, we see a grainy, black-and-white image of it. A picture of an officer yelling at a cadet is accompanied by voiceover: "I think about the upperclassman who screamed that he was ashamed that he came from the same district as me. I think about how powerless I felt when I couldn't hit him."

Another rhetorically savvy use of multimedia that helps viewers identify with Merced is his selective use of an entirely black screen. At key moments in his DVD, his voiceover demands our full attention. We are forced to absorb the blackness and experience Merced's inability to escape his thoughts when he says: "It's a horrific thing when you become your own enemy. Then, not only does everyone around you hate you, but you do too. You hate yourself for being a failure. You hate yourself for being weak. You hate everything, because it's the only emotion that you've allowed yourself not to turn off." The combined effect of Merced's emotional voiceover and his choice of introspective darkness forces you out of your comfort zone as a viewer yet pulls you into his emotional landscape in a powerful way.

NEW PEDAGOGICAL DIRECTIONS

I continually refine how I teach and evaluate multimedia essays. Although I respect those who invite their students to use and purposefully

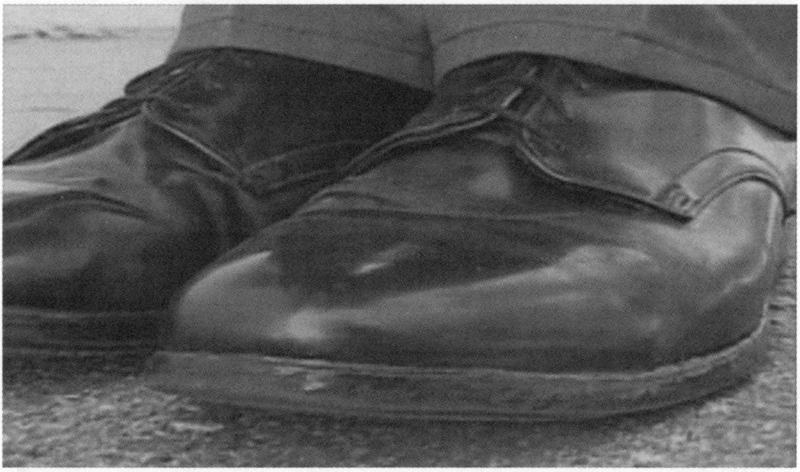

FIGURE 2.4. A close-up shot in Merced Perez-Hall's multimedia essay "Walking Hours."

manipulate and remix existing media—whether commercial or Creative Commons—I've found that the best student multimedia projects are inevitably the ones that contain all, or nearly all, original material. When students know they can't borrow, their creativity increases tenfold. Their instinct to plop down in front of their computers to find images and videos that others have produced is immediately replaced by their need to go out and create suitable material themselves. For example, a student reflecting on the significance of the Boundary Waters Canoe Area went to a nearby lake and filmed close-ups of lapping waves, which in his video transported viewers convincingly to Minnesota. A group of students working on a collaborative multimedia essay about the U.S. industrialized food system took a road trip to Greeley, Colorado, and hopped a fence to film a massive feedlot, complete with stunning close-ups of steam snorting from a black cow's nostrils. Another group of students, exploring myths about the American West, filmed one of their hands drawing various stereotypical Western images on separate pieces of paper. They sped up this footage to match their voiceover. In the next shot, they played the same sped-up footage in reverse before stating—over a slowly panning, sepia-tinted original image of two figures gazing across a mountain vista—"Then again, perhaps the West isn't any one of these. Perhaps the West is simply what we need it to be. Perhaps that's what any place is." Could this group have created a montage of mythic images of the West

Figure 2.5. Storyboard presentation.

from popular media? Certainly. Would the effect have been as beautiful, as rhetorically perfect, and as reflective of the students' own visual imaginations and personal investments? I doubt it.

If you plan to require all original material, though, don't be surprised if students seek your permission to make exceptions. I used to give in to these requests, but I usually regretted it in the end. The sudden appearance of a Hollywood-quality film clip in an otherwise compelling low-budget production tends to be more jarring than enlightening. If you're unequivocal about original material, students will usually rise to the challenge. One student, who was creating a multimedia essay about the gap between media stereotypes of Iran and his own experiences visiting relatives there, asked me if he could include YouTube clips of biased TV news coverage of Iran. Literally within seconds of my saying no, he had the idea to film himself and his friends dressed up as "terrorists" for a simulated newscast.

When students devote more creative energy and ambition to their multimedia essays, not only do they feel more invested in them, but the essays also require more time to complete. I typically devote five or six weeks to a multimedia essay project. Faculty unfamiliar with how long it takes to plan, film, edit, score, and distribute a multimedia project can easily underestimate how big a chunk you need to carve out of your syllabus to accommodate everything. Many faculty assume that "students these days" are such digital natives that they can dash off short films as easily as they can skateboard across campus. Nothing could be further

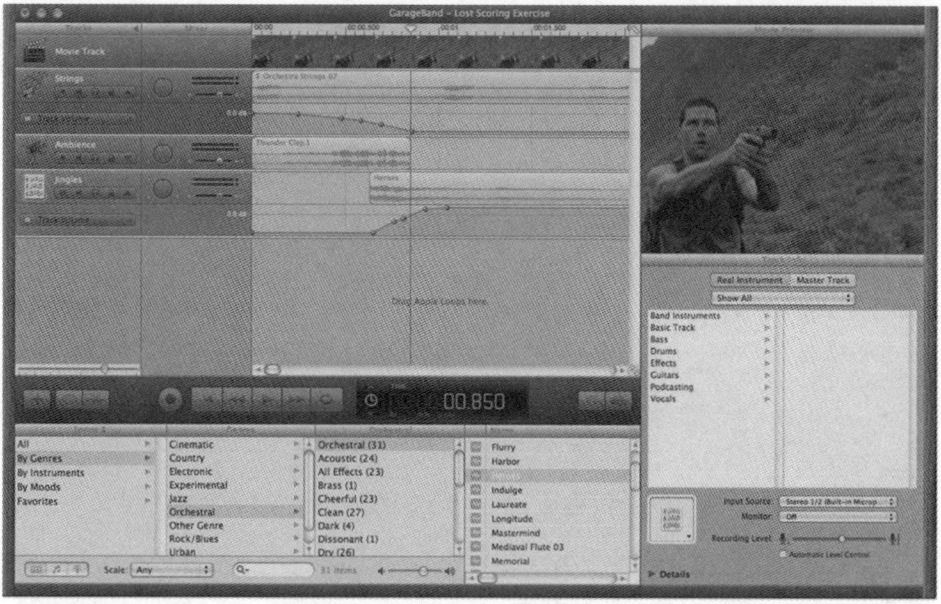

FIGURE 2.6. The interface of Apple's GarageBand showing a clip from *Lost*.

from the truth. My informal surveys in class reveal that even the students with the fanciest Apple laptops seldom have experience using the included software to edit video or create audio, let alone with rhetorical finesse. (Curiously, some of the most confident and experienced students have created the least impressive projects.) Fortunately, Apple's iLife applications are intuitive, but even assuming fluency with iMovie, finetuning thirty seconds of video can still take hours. Accordingly, students will feel (deservedly) cheated if you don't value their multimodal assignments as a significant percentage of their grades. Once I learned to overcome my own print-centric insecurity about grading such projects substantially, I actually felt more invested in them and their success.

Another pedagogical adjustment is that I now begin multimedia projects with even greater attention to multimodal rhetoric. For instance, I invite a knowledgeable guest speaker to introduce students to the language of film and the art of storyboarding. During this class session, Dave Underwood, manager of Academic Media Services at the University of Colorado–Boulder, shows clips from various films. For example, he shows a scene from *Taxi Driver* to illustrate the cinematic and psychological significance of camera angles, slow zooms, and foley effects (see fig. 2.5). Besides arranging training in iMovie and iDVD, I now also

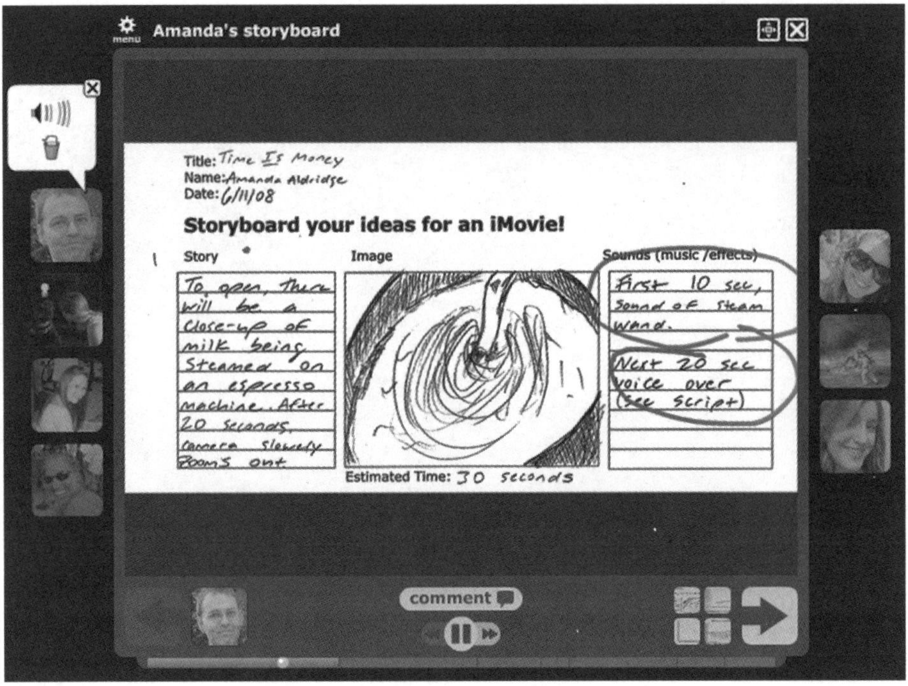

FIGURE 2.7. A student's storyboard with peer and instructor comments in VoiceThread.

invite students to think more about the rhetoric of sound. We might listen to and discuss audio essays on NPR, listen for subtle, hilarious sound effects in clips from *America's Next Top Model*, or even workshop drafts of students' voiceovers, paying attention to such issues as tone and pacing. I also set aside class time for students to explore the creative potential of Apple's royalty-free music-composition software GarageBand, which lets them score iMovie projects with astonishing precision. Sometimes I use a clip from the TV show *Lost*, with the audio extracted, to give students an opportunity to practice adding and editing appropriate music and sound effects (see fig. 2.6).

Another of my pedagogical priorities in recent semesters has been to devote more class time to workshops on storyboards, VoiceThread comments on draft storyboards (see fig. 2.7), and drafts of students' multimedia essays (see fig. 2.8). After all, it seems irresponsible to neglect the importance of formative assessment and revision when switching media. Finally, to emphasize the importance of reflection, I ask students to record a director's (or directors') commentary, to write a Memo to Future

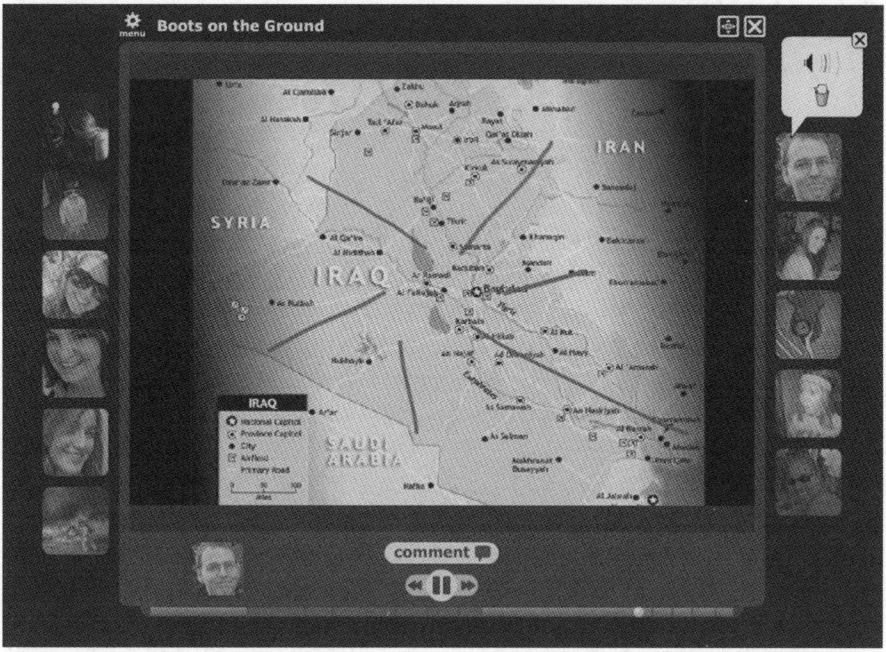

FIGURE 2.8. Draft of multimedia essay in VoiceThread.

Multimedia Collaborators, to submit a DVD self-critique in which they justify the rhetorical choices they've made, and sometimes to create a reflective VoiceThread portfolio (see fig. 2.9). At the end of the course I give students the option to share their written assignments and multimedia essays with future classes. They almost always say yes, so I often find myself in the Media Lab creating new "greatest hits" DVDs. To reach even larger audiences, students in some of my courses have posted less personal multimedia essays to YouTube and other websites—for instance, a video promoting Rocky Mountain Riding Therapy featured on that organization's homepage.

Of course, the scope and even the possibility of an original multimedia essay is determined by access—to digital camcorders or cameras, to easy-to-use editing software, to computers or hard drives on which students can save huge digital files long term, and to people with the expertise to train students and troubleshoot their technical problems. Fortunately, even cell-phone quality photographs and video clips can suffice, and digital camcorders are becoming increasingly affordable, as are Flash drives with ever greater storage capacities. Ultimately, though,

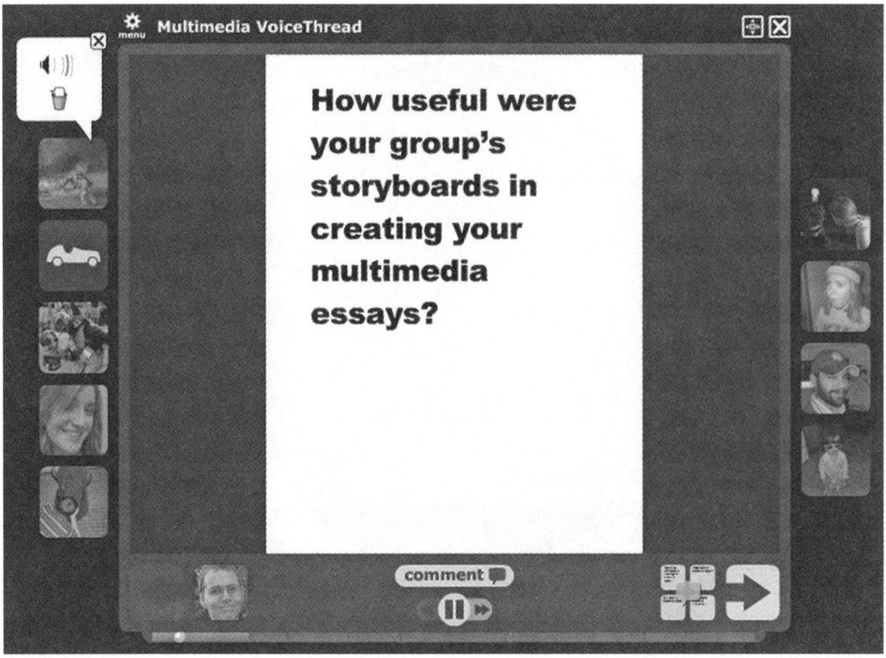

FIGURE 2.9. Portfolio VoiceThread. Students use audio comments on VoiceThread to respond to prompts as part of their online reflective multimedia portfolios.

institutions that see the value of new genres such as the multimedia essay will need to invest in the necessary equipment, facilities, and staff to help student see their projects through to completion.

In addition, if we are to admit the essay and the multimedia essay, as discussed in this chapter, into composition curricula, we need to reconsider our assumptions and expectations as readers and viewers. Jane E. Hindman (2003, 14) has expressed a legitimate concern that "our [reading] practices undermine, if not censure, innovative textual production." Claire de Obaldia (1995, 33) has written: "Instead of leading the passive reader 'step-by-step, in a logical and orderly manner to an already established point of certainty and clarity,' the essayist requires the reader's active participation in the form of a constantly renewed evaluation, deduction, and interpretation of the matter at hand." In the classroom a failure to clarify and justify this shift in rhetorical situation and responsibility—in syllabi, assignments, readings, and class discussions—does students a disservice and can provoke students to write in course evaluations, "I don't know why we were making videos in a writing class."

Beyond institutional pressures to privilege more conservative and predictable genres, are we flexible enough thinkers to consider such a shift in our ways of reading? In "Interrupting the Conversation: The Constructionist Dialogue in Composition," Joseph Petraglia (1991, para. 38) noted that "social constructionists do not explain how a minority's knowledge can exist in the face of consensus, much less alter that knowledge. From where do individuals derive unconventional ideas, and how can the expression of this 'abnormal' discourse be tolerated?" He pointed out that "consensus-building may not always be a progressive, 'liberatory' process, that it could involve coercion instead" (ibid., para. 39). Similarly, Alan W. France (1994, 102), in *Composition as Cultural Practice*, argued that "the conversation metaphor [writing as joining an ongoing conversation, per Burke] disguises not only who may speak but also what may be spoken." He observed: "To equate knowledge with conformity to an institutional discourse is ideological as well as epistemological, and the rhetoric of consensus is most handy to those whose oxen are not being gored" (ibid., 104).

As first-year writing faces increasing scrutiny about its relevance beyond itself (Bawarshi 2003; Devitt 2007; Downs and Wardle 2007), can we afford not to consider a broad range of alternative pedagogies and genres at different curricular levels? The essay and the multimedia essay may not guarantee obviously transferable composition "skills," and although Devitt (2007, 216) has argued that "any skills so generalized as to be transferable from one situation to another would be so generalized as to be virtually meaningless," focusing on the genre of the essay does have the potential to give students a valuable ability to think not only critically but originally. If we truly value innovation in rhetoric and composition, shouldn't we be receptive to new multimodal genres—and old, antecedent ones—that offer such potential?

REFERENCES

Adorno, Theodor. 1984. "The Essay as Form." Translated by B. Hullot-Kentor. *New German Critique* 11: 151–71.

Anderson, Chris, ed. 1989. *Literary Nonfiction: Theory, Criticism, Pedagogy*. Carbondale: Southern Illinois University Press.

Andrews, Richard. 2003. "The End of the Essay?" *Teaching in Higher Education* 8: 117–28.

Atwan, Robert. 1998. Foreword to *The Best American Essays 1998*, edited by Cynthia Ozick and Robert Atwan. New York: Houghton Mifflin.

Bawarshi, Anis. 2003. *Genre and the Invention of the Writer: Reconsidering the Place of Invention in Composition*. Logan: Utah State University Press.

Bowden, Darsie. 1995. "The Rise of Metaphor: 'Voice' in Composition Pedagogy." *Rhetoric Review* 14 (1): 173–78.

Brereton, John C., ed. 1995. *The Origins of Composition Studies in the American College, 1875–1925: A Documentary History*. Pittsburgh: University of Pittsburgh Press.

Clark, J. Elizabeth. 2010. "The Digital Imperative: Making the Case for a Twenty-First-Century Pedagogy." *Computers and Composition* 27: 27–35.

Core, George. 1989. "Stretching the Limits of the Essay." In *Essays on the Essay: Redefining the Genre*, edited by Alexander J. Butrym, 207–20. Athens: University of Georgia Press.

Dean, Deborah. 2008. *Genre Theory: Teaching, Writing, and Being*. Urbana, IL: National Council of Teachers of English.

Dehaene, Stanislas. 2009. *Reading in the Brain*. New York: Viking.

de Obaldia, Claire. 1995. *The Essayistic Spirit: Literature, Modern Criticism, and the Essay*. Oxford: Clarendon.

Devitt, Amy J. 2004. *Writing Genres*. Carbondale: Southern Illinois University Press.

———. 2007. "Transferability and Genres." In *The Locations of Composition*, edited by Christopher J. Keller and Christian R. Weisser, 215–27. Albany: State University of New York Press.

Downs, Douglas, and Elizabeth Wardle. 2007. "Teaching about Writing, Righting Misconceptions: (Re)Envisioning 'First-Year Composition' as 'Introduction to Writing Studies.'" *College Composition and Communication* 58, 4: 552–84.

Elbow, Peter. 2006. "The Music of Form: Rethinking Organization in Writing." *College Composition and Communication* 57 (4): 620–66.

Fisher, Walter R. 1989. *Human Communication as Narration: Toward a Philosophy of Reason, Value, and Action*. Columbia: University of South Carolina Press.

France, Alan W. 1994. *Composition as a Cultural Practice*. Westport, CT: Bergin and Garvey.

Fulton, Maurice Garland. 1995 [1912]. "Expository Writing." In *The Origins of Composition Studies in the American College, 1875–1925: A Documentary History*, edited by John C. Brereton, 392–406. Pittsburgh: University of Pittsburgh Press.

Gage, John T. 1995. "Why Write?" In *Rhetoric: Concepts, Definitions, Boundaries*, edited by David Jolliffe and William Covino, 715–33. Boston: Allyn and Bacon.

Gass, William H. 1985. "Emerson and the Essay." In *Habitations of the Word*. New York: Simon.

Goleman, Judith. 2004. "An 'Immensely Simplified Task': Form in Modern Composition-Rhetoric." *College Composition and Communication* 69: 51–71.

Good, Graham. 1988. *The Observing Self: Rediscovering the Essay*. London: Routledge.

Heath, Shirley Brice. 1987. "The Literate Essay: Using Ethnography to Explode Myths." In *Languages, Literacy, and Schooling*, edited by Judith A. Langer, 89–107. Norwood, NJ: Ablex Publishing.

Heilker, Paul. 1996. *The Essay: Theory and Pedagogy for an Active Form*. Urbana, IL: National Council of Teachers of English.

———. 2006. "Twenty Years In: An Essay in Two Parts." *College Composition and Communication* 58 (2): 182–212.

Hill, Charles A. 2004. "The Psychology of Rhetorical Images." In *Defining Visual Rhetorics*, edited by Charles A. Hill and Marguerite Helmers, 25–40. Mahwah, NJ: Lawrence Erlbaum.

Hindman, Jane E. 2003. "Thoughts on Reading 'The Personal': Toward a Discursive Ethics of Professional Critical Literacy." *College English* 66 (1): 9–20.

Hoy, Pat C. II. 2000–2001. "The Disarming Seduction of Stories." *Writing on the Edge* 12 (1): 41–48.

———. 2001a. "The Outreach of an Idea." *Rhetoric Review* 20 (3/4): 351–67.

———. 2001b. "Requiem for the Outline." *Writing on the Edge* 12 (2): 19–27.

Johns, Ann M. 2002. *Genre in the Classroom: Multiple Perspectives*. Mahwah, NJ: Lawrence Erlbaum.

Khine, Myint Swe. 2007. "Video Annotation in Online Collaborative Discussion: A Constructivist Tool for Computer-supported Learning." In *Advances in Computer-supported Learning*, edited by M. M. Neto and F. V. Brasileiro, 298–314. Hershey, PA: Idea Group.

Kirklighter, Cristina. 2002. *Traversing the Democratic Borders of the Essay*. Albany: State University of New York Press.

Klaus, Karl. H. 1989. "Essayists on the Essay." In *Literary Nonfiction: Theory, Criticism, Pedagogy*, edited by Chris Anderson, 253–70. Carbondale: Southern Illinois University Press.

Lemke, Jay L. 1998. "Metamedia Literacy: Transforming Meanings and Media." In *Handbook of Literacy and Technology: Transformations in a Post-typographic World*, edited by David Reinking, Michael C. McKenna, Linda D. Labbo, and Ronald D. Kieffer, 283–301. Mahwah, NJ: Lawrence Earlbaum.

———. 2006. "Toward Critical Multimedia Literacy: Technology, Research, and Politics." In *International Handbook of Literacy and Technology*, edited by

Michael C. McKenna, Linda D. Labbo, Ronald D. Kieffer, and David Reinking, 3–14. Mahwah, NJ: Lawrence Earlbaum.

Lodge, David. 2002. *Consciousness and the Novel: Connected Essays*. London: Secker and Warburg.

Lopate, Phillip. 1994. *The Art of the Personal Essay: An Anthology from the Classical Era to the Present*. New York: Anchor Books.

Mayer, Richard E. 2005. "Principles Based on Social Cues: Personalization, Voice, and Presence Principles." In *Cambridge Handbook of Multimedia Learning*, edited by Richard E. Mayer, 201–12. New York: Cambridge University Press.

Newkirk, Thomas. 1989. *Critical Thinking and Writing: Reclaiming the Essay*. Urbana, IL: National Council of Teachers of English.

———. 2005. "Montaigne's Revisions." *Rhetoric Review* 24 (3): 298–315.

Pebworth, T.-L. 1997. "Not Being, but Passing: Defining the Early English Essay." *Studies in the Literary Imagination* 10: 17–27.

Petraglia, Joseph. 1991. "Interrupting the Conversation: The Constructionist Dialogue in Composition." *JAC* 11 (1). Online at http://www.jacweb.org/Archived_volumes/Text_articles/V11_I1_Petraglia.htm.

Recchio, Thomas E. 1994. "On the Critical Necessity of 'Essaying.'" In *Taking Stock: The Writing Process Movement in the Nineties*, edited by Lad Tobin and Thomas Newkirk, 219–35. Portsmouth, NH: Boynton/Cook.

Rucker, Mary E. 1975. "The Literary Essay and the Modern Temper." *Papers in Language and Literature* 11 (3): 317–35.

Sanborn, Jean Donovan. 1994. "The Essay Dies in the Academy, circa 1900." In *Pedagogy in the Age of Politics: Writing and Reading (in) the Academy*, edited by Patricia A. Sullivan and Donna J. Qualley, 121–38. Urbana, IL: National Council of Teachers of English.

Spellmeyer, Kurt. 1993. *Common Ground: Dialogue, Understanding, and the Teaching of Composition*. Englewood Cliffs, NJ: Prentice Hall.

———. 2003. *Arts of Living: Reinventing the Humanities for the Twenty-First Century*. Albany: State University of New York Press.

Westbrook, Steve. 2006. "Visual Rhetoric in a Culture of Fear: Impediments to Multimedia Production." *College English* 68 (5): 457–80.

Whithaus, Carl. 2005. *Teaching and Evaluating Writing in the Age of Computers and High-Stakes Testing*. Mahwah, NJ: Lawrence Erlbaum.

CHAPTER 3

Including, but Not Limited to, the Digital

Composing Multimodal Texts

Jody Shipka

> Under this new definition, neither is it "new media" simply to have a text that incorporates texts and sound and graphics and animation and photographs and illustrations in some combinatorial ratio other than that of a traditional academic or literary text. . . . I am trying to get at a definition that encourages us to stay alert to *how* and *why* we make these combinations of materials, not simply *that* we do it.
>
> —Anne Wysocki (2004, 19)

In "Part 1: Thinking out of the Pro-Verbal Box," Sean Williams (2001, 23) suggests that composition is a "largely conservative" discipline because it tends to "cling to the idea of writing about representation systems in verbal text because that's what we do in composition." According to Williams, while ideas about appropriate subject matter for writing courses have broadened, form has remained fixed as students are still often expected to compose linear, print-based texts. For Williams and others, the goal has been to work toward the destabilization of form by highlighting how "meanings are made, distributed, received, interpreted and remade . . . through many representational and communicative modes—not just through language" (Jewitt and Kress 2003, 1).

In the years since Williams's "Part 1" was published, there has been an increase in scholarship providing readers with ways of, and further justifications for, extricating ourselves from the "pro-verbal box" (see, for instance, George 2002; Hocks 2003; Sorapure 2006; Wysocki et al. 2004; Yancey 2004; Zoetewey and Staggers 2003).

Although I value scholarship that underscores the importance of providing students increased options for engaging with course materials, the first concern I would highlight here is how a tendency to equate "multimodal" or "multimodality" with digitized, screen-mediated (i.e., "new/digital media") texts may severely limit the kinds of texts and communicative strategies or processes students explore in our courses.[1] When it is suggested time and again that "new media writing affords students new opportunities to reassemble the world outside the linear constraints of the print paradigm and make things fit in new ways" (Zoetewey and Staggers 2003, 135), I have to wonder whether, in attempting to resist the pro-verbal bias, we have allowed ourselves to trade in one bundle of texts and techniques for another: pro-verbal becomes pro-digital. Beyond seeming to assume that students have already exhausted every affordance associated with linear print paradigms, the suggestion is that students would not be able to or would simply not want to demonstrate how they have thought to "reassemble the world" and "make things fit in new ways" *without* necessarily taking that work online.

Connected to this first concern is that a tendency to identify or label as "multimodal" only certain kinds of *texts*—whether they are digitally based or comprised of a mix of analog components—works to facilitate a text-dependent (or textually overdetermined) understanding of multimodality, thereby limiting potentials for students to consider the scope, complexity, and pervasiveness of multimodal practice. Following Paul Prior (2009, 16), I argue that multimodality is not some special feature of certain texts, objects, or performances, but a "routine dimension of language in use." As Prior (ibid.) explains: "Multimodality has always and everywhere been present as representations are propagated across multiple media and as any situated event is indexically fed by all modes present whether they are focalized or backgrounded. . . . Through composition, different moments of history, different persons, different voices, different addresses may become embedded in the composed utterance."

The problem, as Prior and others have noted, is the field's tendency to "freeze" writing, to treat it as a noun rather than a verb, and to privilege the static text—what Prior (ibid., 8) refers to as the problem of "composed utterances." In her critique of "strong-text conceptions of literacy," Deborah Brandt (1990, 104) compares the analysis of static artifacts—searches for stable "patterns in language-on-its-own"—to "coming upon the scene of a party after it is over and everybody has gone home, being left to imagine from the remnants what the party must have been like" (ibid., 76).

Prior's point, and the point I'd like to echo here with Brandt's party metaphor in mind, is that texts—like parties, objects, and other events or performances—have a history and are connected to, or informed by, other processes and systems of activity. Pedagogical and methodological frameworks that allow for the extraction, and with this, the decontextualization of a text, object, or performance "from the messy ground of the life world" (Prior 1998, 146) fail to provide students with an understanding of the messy, multimodal, historied dimensions of all communicative practice. It then becomes far too easy to overlook (or to underestimate the import of) the role other texts, talk, people, perceptions, semiotic resources, motives, activities, institutions, and so on play in the production, reception, circulation, and valuation of those "finished" texts, artifacts, or events. Otherwise put, when we fail to consider (or when our practices do not ask students to consider) the complex and highly distributed processes associated with the production of texts (or parties), we miss opportunities to explore how writing functions as one "stream within the broader flows of semiotic activity" (Prior 1998, 12; see also Medway 1996).

For example, in the case of a student working to produce a linear, print-based argumentative essay, the student spends time "writing," to be sure, but throughout the process of completing her text, she will also likely consult as well as construct other kinds of texts (i.e., the assignment description, outlines, notes, diagrams, to-do lists). She may draw on—to remember or recruit—prior memories or experiences of producing similar kinds of texts using these as an aid in accomplishing this particular task. She may discuss the assignment (i.e., how she feels about it, what she plans to do in response to it) with family members, classmates, friends, or with her teacher, and she may consult models of the kind of argument she wants to make. She might reread on her own or share with others portions of her text as it develops, perhaps gesturing toward or otherwise marking passages she believes are working particularly well or could use revisiting. She may experiment with different ways of layering or structuring her argument, moving bits of text from one place to another, trying out different font styles and sizes, tweaking line spacing and margins, deciding whether to place page numbers bottom center, upper right corner, and so on. Provided she has not begun working on the essay an hour before it is due, she will also need to decide when, where, and for how long she will devote herself to this task, determining when she will set the task aside to manage other of her life's interests and obligations: eating, sleeping, working, working out, cleaning, visiting with friends, having hobbies, preparing for and attending other classes, and so on.

If we are committed to providing students with opportunities to become increasingly cognizant of the ways texts and various kinds of technologies (both new and old) provide shape for, and take shape from, the historied environments in which they are produced, circulated, valued, and consumed, I think we need to resist equating multimodality with digitally based or screen-mediated texts. Following Anne Wysocki (2004), I'd suggest that what matters is not simply "*that*" students in our courses learn to produce a specific kind of text (i.e., whether linear, print-based texts, digital texts, object- or performance-based texts, or some combination thereof) but that students leave our courses exhibiting *a more nuanced* awareness of the various choices they make throughout the process of accomplishing that work and the effect those choices might have on others.

We also need to begin creating opportunities for students to attend to the highly distributed and fundamentally multimodal aspects of all communicative practice, to treat, in other words, communicative practice—whether the end result is a digital text, a print-based essay, an object-as-argument, or a performance—*as multimodal accomplishment*. One way that we might facilitate this kind of metacommunicative/multimodal awareness involves asking students to assume more responsibility for determining the representational systems that best suit the work *they* hope to accomplish and, with this, to ask them to closely attend to and share with others details of their composing practices.

FACILITATING METACOMMUNICATIVE AWARENESS THROUGH AN ACTIVITY-BASED MULTIMODAL APPROACH TO COMPOSING

Advocates of curricula that privilege metacommunicative awareness have underscored the limitations of pedagogical frameworks that privilege, instead, the acquisition of discrete skill sets, skill sets that are often and erroneously treated as static and therefore universally applicable across time and diverse communicative contexts (see, especially, Devitt 2004; Downs and Wardle 2007; Petraglia 1995; Russell 1995). Instead of perpetuating the myth that writing is a general/generalizable skill that, once successfully acquired, will serve students equally well irrespective of what they are attempting to accomplish, many scholars have suggested that we focus instead on increasing genre awareness, stressing, as both Amy Devitt and Anis Bawarshi have, the importance of flexibility, adaptation, variation, and metacommunicative awareness. If we acknowledge that writing is "a way of being and acting in the world at a particular time, in a particular situation, for the achievement of particular desires," we gain more, Bawarshi (2003, 156) persuasively argues, "by teaching students how to adapt as writers, socially and rhetorically, from one genred site of action to the next."

Although they focus primarily on the written texts circulating within and between what Bawarshi calls "genred site[s] of action," I find Devitt's and Bawarshi's work extremely valuable, invested as it is in helping students to "understand the intricate connections between contexts and forms, to perceive potential ideological effects of genres, and to discern both constraints and choices that genres make possible" (Devitt 2004, 198). I do find potentially limiting, however, the way Devitt's and Bawarshi's frameworks tend to treat the production of texts. For example, after spending time "practicing genre analysis," Bawarshi's (2003, 168) first-year writing students are "at times" asked to write some of the genres they have been analyzing, "thereby moving [students] from the analysis to production of texts." This is not to say that "practicing genre analysis" does not involve the production of written texts. Rather, students seem not to be spending as much time practicing the genres they are analyzing as writing *about* those genres. And while I value the emphasis Devitt places on asking students to consider alternative ways of achieving similar rhetorical purposes (i.e., considering, for instance, alternative ways of announcing a wedding and to think about how the various choices one makes might impact announcements, or more broadly, the practice of announcing), the instructor ultimately assumes sole responsibility for determining the genres students will employ in their work. "To keep genres from being part of the hidden curriculum," Devitt (2004, 203) writes, "we need to choose deliberately the genres we have students write and need to help students succeed at performing within those genres.

An activity-based multimodal framework for composing provides an alternative to pedagogical approaches that facilitate metacommunicative awareness *without* having teachers predetermine for students the specific genres, media, and modes with which they will work. As I have detailed elsewhere (see Shipka 2006, 2011), the framework is engineered to underscore the interconnectedness of systems of production, distribution, reception, circulation, and valuation and to encourage students to recognize and make explicit how the "conventional forms they employ work strategically" (Coe, Lingard, and Teslenko 2002, 6). Informed by theories of mediated activity, particularly so by James Wertsch's (1998, 94 and

124) toolbox approach and discussions of semiotic privileging, the framework places primary emphasis on having students attend to "the array of mediational means to which people have access and the patterns of choice they manifest in selecting a particular means for a particular occasion"—especially when others are, "in principle, imaginable."

Instead of being provided with assignments that result in the production of "like" texts (i.e., where the goal is to have each student produce the same or similar types of text such as a webpage or a podcast or a research-based essay), students are provided with tasks that function largely as communicative problems to be solved—and that can, in fact, be solved in a variety of ways as I will illustrate shortly—and that require students to consider how the contexts in which texts participate shape the way those texts are received and responded to. In contrast to frameworks that have students focusing primarily on the production of screen-mediated or visual-verbal texts or, conversely, on the production of linear print-based texts, an activity-based multimodal framework requires they spend the semester attending to how language, *combined with still other representational systems*, mediates communicative practice (see Appendix A later in this chapter for a list of questions students are asked to consider when producing and analyzing texts throughout the semester).

As a crucial aspect of the framework involves having students come up with different ways of accomplishing the tasks I provide them with, I have found it helpful to draw on a concept that communications professors Roderick Hart and Don Burks, in 1972, termed "rhetorical sensitivity." Originally offered as a way of theorizing verbal interactions, Hart and Burks maintained that the "rhetorically-sensitive individual":

1. accepts role-playing as part of the human condition
2. attempts to avoid stylized (i.e., rigid) verbal behavior
3. is willing to undergo the strain of adaptation
4. seeks to distinguish between all information and information acceptable for communication
5. understands that an idea can be rendered in multi-form ways. (Hart and Burks 1972, 76)

Perhaps because they were most interested in face-to-face verbal interactions, Hart and Burks do little to address the way people work with (or, as is often the case, *work against*) the agency of nonhumans, of things. Rather, the environment, the "stuff" of the material world is, quite literally, backgrounded here as they focus instead on the ways individuals employ spoken language while interacting with, resisting, persuading, and so on, "the [human] Other" (Hart and Burks 1972, 83).

Yet given the emphasis it places on flexibility, variation, and adaptation, Hart and Burks's "rhetoric-in-action" still proves useful in thinking about what other representational systems require of participants/users—writing in relation to writers, as one example. This said, Hart and Burks's "rhetoric-in-action" proves to be *still more useful* when issues of materiality are factored in as well. In this way, to understand that "an idea can be rendered in multi-form ways" (ibid., 76) is not only to recognize, to use an example used by Hart and Burks, the constraints and affordances associated with saying this versus saying that versus opting to remain silent. Rather, with materiality added to the mix, students might *also* be asked to consider what difference it might make to "render" an idea through the production of a webpage, a live in-class performance, a series of memos, a speech, a travel guide, and so on.

To facilitate the metacommunicative dimensions of the framework, students are required to compose a statement of goals and choices (SOGC) for each of the tasks they complete. In these highly detailed statements, students catalog their goals for their work and describe how the specific choices they made and strategies they employed throughout the process of completing that work facilitated, or as is often the case, *significantly altered* their goals and ways of approaching a task. Here, students are asked to highlight the various actors, both human and nonhuman, that played a role in helping them accomplish work for the class and to detail how both people and things (i.e., objects, deadlines, workspaces, access to resources, belief systems, past experiences, future goals) function to "authorize, allow, afford, encourage, permit, suggest, influence, block, render possible, forbid, and so on" (Latour 2005, 72) certain actions and outcomes (see Appendix B later in this chapter for the questions students are asked to respond to in their SOGC).

To be sure, adapting to the framework can prove challenging for some students. Those who enter the course expecting that it will provide them with the magic formula for writing "right" for all time and every occasion may find frustrating (or may outright resist) an approach to communicative practice that asks him or her to take the time to consider how a piece of writing (or a way of writing) that may well have been deemed successful at a particular point in time, that was particularly well suited for a particular purpose, audience, occasion, and so on might not be successful (or even appropriate) if one or more of those variables were to change. Students who have grown accustomed to successfully negotiating school-based writing tasks by running a specific "generic routine" (Medway 2002, 135) (i.e., producing a five-paragraph essay "just because" it is a form they come to associate with academic writing or because it has worked successfully in other courses) may also struggle with the metacommunicative aspects of the framework—specifically so, having to take the time to think about and to articulate exactly how, when, why, for whom, and for what ends those particular routines may or may not work. To illustrate how an activity-based multimodal framework facilitates metacommunicative awareness by asking students to consider how a communicative objective might be approached "in multi-form ways," I draw on the two students' SOGCs, describing briefly how each reported negotiating a task entitled "A History of 'This' Space."

DOCUMENTING "A HISTORY OF 'THIS' SPACE"

Like each of the tasks they receive over the course of a semester, the history task presents students with a number of "non-negotiable objectives," or specific criteria that must be met for them to earn a passing (C) mark on the task. An ethnographically inspired task, the history requires, first, that students locate or define a space they would like to research. As a goal, the task has to do with coming up with ways of re-presenting for an audience of their choosing the data they collect on their spaces. Therefore students must also determine the methods they will use while researching their spaces. At the end of the semester, students turn in their history (in whatever form it takes) along with an SOGC.

Trashed: A History about All the Histories She Didn't Do

When students in sections of my first-year composition courses receive the history task, they are advised to spend time considering the various ways they might approach the task before settling on a specific plan of action. While students often spend at least a week or two deciding on a plan of action, Katie, a member of my 2004 first-year composition (FYC) course, spent the better part of the semester trying to devise a way of successfully completing the task. Katie's struggles were not a result of her failing to understand what the task was asking her to do or being unable to come up with ideas that interested her—ideas that she also believed would be of interest to her audience. Rather, Katie reported that her frustration had more to do with having too many ideas, some of which ultimately proved untenable, others of which she found herself losing interest in, ideas she would write off as "stupid" or "not good enough" shortly after coming up with them.

Working in her favor was that Katie had determined, shortly after the task was assigned, what, generally speaking, she hoped her history would accomplish. Having struggled greatly with the task herself, she wanted to provide future students—those who would someday be asked to accomplish this same task—advice on how they might approach the task and avoid struggling with it. She had also decided, early on, that the space she would be researching would be the space of the 2004 FYC classroom, specifically so, the backgrounds, interests, and experiences of her peers.

Katie visited office hours and emailed me frequently over the semester to discuss and define further her ideas for the task. Initially interested in researching when, how, and why people in the class dyed their hair, she considered creating surveys or conducting interviews with her classmates.

After losing interest in that idea, Katie decided to research the differences between what her classmates valued versus what they considered disposable. To this end, she considered conducting interviews with her classmates as well as taking photos of each of them holding, in one hand, a valued object, and, in the other, something they were poised to throw away. Losing interest in that idea too, she decided to document what her classmates (all of whom were living on campus) missed most about living at home. She asked her classmates to list, on a class discussion board, five things they missed most about home. Assuming that people would list food items, her plan was to bring to class some of the food items people missed and record their reactions. Discouraged to find that most people listed things that she could not bring into the classroom (i.e., pets, beds, significant others, cars), Katie abandoned that idea as well.

Katie thus generated a number of ideas for the history and started the data collection process for a number of them. Then I suggested that she consider creating a history about all the histories she *didn't* do. Surprised that I was suggesting an alternative that seemed "too easy" (i.e., she was still hoping that she'd come up with a new and better idea for the task), she eventually warmed to the idea and chose to document her history of false starts and stops, reasoning that this history might prove more helpful for her intended audience than would one that suggested that she had had a far easier time negotiating the task than she had.

On the day histories were due, Katie turned in a black trash can (see fig. 3.1) containing twenty crumpled-up texts of various types, many of which had been written by hand on lined notebook paper. Included in the

Figure 3.1. Katie's history.

collection were Katie's handwritten project notes for each of the histories she had considered pursuing, notes taken during class discussions, to-do lists, printouts from the course discussion board, a three-page typed, single-spaced letter from Katie addressed to future students, and a number of journal entries in which she documents her frustration with the task. Handwritten text appeared on the surface of the trash can as well.

The phrase "Don't give up" (a reference to one of her classmate's histories) had been written twenty times on the inside of the can. On the outside of the can appeared an assortment of quotes taken from class readings and handouts, quotes that Katie felt most accurately represented her experience in the course, including this from Linda Brodkey (1996, 57): "To see writing anew, to look at it from yet other vantage points, we must tear ourselves away from an image that we have come to think of as the reality of writing."

Take 20: An Undergraduate Perspective

When he received the history task in the spring 2007 section of my Language and Society course (a 400-level required course for rhetoric and composition majors), Adam had already taken two other upper-level courses with me, and so, was familiar with what the history task required. During the spring 2007 semester, Adam was also enrolled in another of my courses, Theories and Practices of Teaching Composition (a 400-level course that English education majors are encouraged to take the semester before they begin student teaching). He decided, early in the semester, to focus on the space of the theories and practices course as he was interested in learning more about, and documenting for others, the thoughts and expectations of people who were about to begin their teaching careers. Although he had a pretty clear idea of what he hoped his history would accomplish, and, with this, an idea about both who and what he would focus on (i.e., people preparing to begin student teaching), Adam still needed to come up with a plan for collecting data. He also needed to begin generating ideas for ways he might go about arranging and representing his findings.

As luck and timing would have it, midway through the semester Adam was able to obtain a copy of Todd Taylor's *Take 20: Teaching Writing*. Believing strongly that *Take 20* would make an excellent model on which to base his history, Adam began adapting the list of twenty questions Taylor had asked of his participants (all of whom were experienced teachers of writing), and set to work on plans for creating his own version of *Take 20*, entitling it *Take 20: An Undergraduate Perspective*. In describing Adam's experience as I have here, I do not mean to suggest that he had an easier time with this, the third history he would produce for me, than he had with his other histories or than Katie did with her history. In fact, even as the discovery of Taylor's work helped Adam solve some of the problems he had been having with his history (i.e., Adam now knew he would conduct videotaped interviews of members of the course and create a DVD modeled after Taylor's), it also presented him with a series of material, methodological, and rhetorical challenges he had not anticipated and for which he had not been especially prepared.

In addition to having to adapt or alter many of Taylor's questions (i.e., he couldn't ask people who hadn't taught before what they remembered about their first day of teaching; he would need instead to ask them what they *expected* their first day would be like), Adam needed to begin soliciting the participation of his peers. To this end, he needed to create a document that briefly described his study and what would happen during each interview, how long interviews would take, how the data would be used, and so on. After securing the participation of eight members of the course (only five of which were able to complete interviews), Adam needed to find a place to conduct the interviews and to begin scheduling times and days for the interviews to take place. Finally, he needed to make sure that the room where he'd be conducting interviews was set up properly and in time for each of his (increasingly time-challenged) interviewees. Taking on the dual role of interviewer and tech support, he needed to ensure the equipment was properly working throughout the course of each interview.

Complicating matters still further, although Adam had prior experience creating, shooting, and editing video footage, he didn't have experience shooting and editing video shot with more than one camera. But for this project, he chose to use three cameras for each interview, two of which would record directly to computer hard drives, the other to tape. Having three cameras (each of which had been set up to capture the interview from a slightly different perspective) would provide him with backup footage in case something malfunctioned, but it would also provide him with the option of editing the video in ways that would make it more interesting, visually speaking, than would be a video shot with a single-source feed.

By the time histories were due, Adam was only able to complete a forty-five-minute-long "rough cut" of his version of *Take 20*. Adam was flattered by his peers' reception of the piece and confident that what he was able to produce by the semester's end more than satisfied the task requirement. Yet given all that he had hoped to accomplish by the semester's end (i.e., he had hoped to do more with multiple camera angles, and he planned on including a track featuring interview outtakes and bloopers as well as one that dealt with "the making" of the history), Adam couldn't help but feel a bit disappointed with how his history turned out.

If he had it to do all over again, he said he might have arranged the interviews sooner than he had, giving him more time to tinker with the look and sound of the final product.

MAKING THINGS FIT IN (ANY NUMBER OF) NEW WAYS

Toward the end of *Writing Genres*, Amy Devitt (2004, 206) suggests that "the genres students acquire—or do not acquire—in writing courses will also shape how they view new situations and contexts," underscoring again the importance of "choosing our genres carefully in order to serve our students best" and reminding readers that what "we assign today may appear in new guise tomorrow." Although this may be true, I also recognize how the kinds of learning experiences and challenges students are afforded—or, conversely, may not be afforded—in our classes might also play a role in determining how, as well as *how well*, students are able to negotiate new situations and to forge connections across contexts. I cannot say with any measure of certainty, of course, whether Katie or Adam will ever be asked to (or will ever want to) produce the kinds of texts they produced for the history. I can say, however, with a bit more certainty that they will likely be required again to conduct research (whether on scholarly, workplace, or "everyday" phenomena), to approach and solve problems, and to re-present their findings and solutions to others. Like Devitt (2004, 202), I believe that "conscious awareness of anything makes mindful living more possible than it would be otherwise." Yet to assume sole responsibility for determining the specific genres, media, and modes with which students work might ultimately work against the goal of facilitating metacommunicative awareness, especially when we might, instead, provide students with communicative objectives that they might be encouraged to satisfy in any number of ways.

APPENDIX A

Students in my first-year composition courses receive this handout, created in 2001, on the first day of class. I bring in a collection of "social" texts (i.e., a calendar, a dental chart, food packaging, an obituary, a takeout menu, a greeting card, a phone book, a play by Shakespeare, a letter, a recipe, an email, a crossword puzzle, a wallet containing photos and receipts), and we spend time analyzing these texts using some of the questions below.

READING SOCIAL TEXTS: Some Frequently Asked Questions

Throughout the semester we will be responding to a wide range of "social" texts—those typically encountered in certain academic spaces as well as those found in a variety of "everyday" spaces. While we will be asking the following questions of the texts we begin examining the first week of class, please hang onto this list as it will come in handy as you consider all the texts you encounter and produce throughout the semester. This list of questions is far from complete. Feel free to add to your list and to share your questions with others. Also, I'd encourage you to bring in (and share with others) any interesting, confusing, and "suspect" social texts you come across during the semester.

- What is the text? How would you classify and/or describe it? In other words, what aspects about the text help you identify it as a certain type of text? If there is any variation between "like" texts, what does each text have to have in common for us to group it as a "type"?
- On issues of materiality, what is the text made out of? If words appear on the text, are they handwritten, printed, stitched, embossed, etched, and so on? Does the text have visuals? If so, what are they made of? What difference does it make if a text is just words versus a combination of words, colors, visuals, and so on? Could the text be other than it is? In other words, could it be made out of other materials and have the same impact?
- What "work" does the text do? What needs does the text fulfill? How is the text "supposed" to be (or "normally") used? Consider design.
- Does the text come with direction for specific uses? Does it have multiple uses? What other things could one do with the text (for example, to doodle on, to tape things to, to annotate, to hold open doors or windows, to use it as a calendar, and so on)?
- Who, specifically, might have access to the text? What does one have to have, own, or use to even come in contact with the text?
- Is the text necessary, or can we live without it? How would life be different if the text did not exist? If the text is not necessary, what needs/wants does it capitalize on to create a space for itself?
- How does one read the text? Out loud? With emphasis? Silently or to oneself? Does one read the text left to right and top-down, or does one read it in another manner?

- Is the text credited with having an author? Why or why not? What difference does that make? What does it say about the relationship of words/texts to authors?
- Related to the previous question, who produces the text? Does it have coauthors or coproducers? How many people might be involved in the production, distribution, and reception of the text?
- Is the text pretty much the whole thing, or does it, instead, introduce or otherwise illustrate the use of the object it is affixed to?
- Does the text expect a response from readers? If so, how would you classify that response: emotional, intellectual, behavioral, other? Does one write on the text, save/collect the text? Pay extra for the text? Is the text socially valued? Seen as a nuisance? Saved or disposed of?
- What does the existence of the text say about the values of the culture that produces it? What are the conditions (economic, historical, cultural, technological) that make this text possible? Is the text expressly associated with the United States? With this moment in history? Would people living in other places or at other times have had use for such a text?

APPENDIX B

Students are asked to address the follow questions in their SOGC:

1. What, specifically, is this piece trying to accomplish—above and beyond satisfying the basic requirements outlined in the task description? In other words, what work does, or might, this piece do? For whom? In what contexts?
2. What specific rhetorical, material, methodological, and technological choices did you make in service of accomplishing the goal(s) articulated above? Catalog, as well, choices that you might not have consciously made, those that were made for you when you opted to work with certain genres, materials, and technologies. [Note: The bulk of your response should be devoted to answering this question.]
3. Why did you end up pursuing this plan as opposed to the others you came up with? How did the various choices listed above allow you to accomplish things that other sets or combinations of choices would not have?
4. Who and what played a role in accomplishing these goals?

NOTE

1. At a session held at the 2006 Computers and Writing conference in Lubbock, Texas, Dan Anderson, Anthony Aktins, Cheryl Ball, Cynthia Selfe, and Richard Selfe reported the findings of a CCCC Research Initiative Grant to gather information on teachers who had students produce multimodal texts in writing classes. When asked to define or describe the term "multimodality," Ball reported that the majority (85 percent) of the survey's forty-five respondents described digital texts, such as digital audio, video, and websites. The sample, admittedly small, reflects a tendency to use terms like "multimodal" and "multimedia" to indicate digital texts.

REFERENCES

Bawarshi, Anis. 2003. *Genre and the Invention of the Writer: Reconsidering the Place of Invention in Composition.* Logan: Utah State Press.

Brandt, Deborah. 1990. *Literacy as Involvement: The Acts of Writers, Readers, and Texts.* Carbondale: Southern Illinois University Press.

Brodkey, Linda. 1996. *Writing Permitted in Designated Areas Only.* Minneapolis: University of Minnesota Press.

Coe, Richard, Lorelei Lingard, and Tatiana Teslenko. 2002. "Genre as Action, Strategy, and Difference: An Introduction." In *The Rhetoric and Ideology of Genre*, edited by Richard Coe, Lorelei Lingard, and Tatiana Teslenko, 1–12. Cresskill, NJ: Hampton Press.

Devitt, Amy J. 2004. *Writing Genres.* Carbondale: Southern Illinois University Press.

Downs, Douglas, and Elizabeth Wardle. 2007. "Teaching about Writing, Righting Misconceptions: (Re)envisioning 'First Year Composition' as 'Introduction to Writing Studies.'" *College Composition and Communication* 58: 552–84.

George, Diane. 2002. "From Analysis to Design: Visual Communication in the Teaching of Writing." *College Composition and Communication* 45: 11–39.

Hart, Roderick P., and Don M. Burks. 1972. "Rhetorical Sensitivity and Social Interaction." *Speech Monographs* 59: 75–91.

Hocks, Mary E. 2003. Understanding Visual Rhetoric in Digital Writing Environments. *College Composition and Communication* 54: 629–56.

Jewitt, Carey, and Gunther Kress. 2003. Introduction to *Multimodal Literacy*, edited by Carey Jewitt and Gunther Kress, 1–18. New York: Peter Lang.

Latour, Bruno. 2005. *Reassembling the Social.* New York: Oxford University Press.

Medway, Peter. 1996. "Virtual and Material Buildings." *Written Communication* 13: 473–514.

———. 2002. "Fuzzy Genres and Community Identities: The Case of Architecture Students' Sketchbooks." In *The Rhetoric and Ideology of Genre*, edited by Richard Coe, Lorelei Lingard, and Tatiana Teslenko, 123–54. Cresskill, NJ: Hampton Press.

Petraglia, Joseph. 1995. "Writing as an Unnatural Act." In *Reconceiving Writing, Rethinking Writing Instruction*, edited by Joseph Petraglia, 79–100. Mahwah, NJ: Lawrence Erlbaum.

Prior, Paul. 1998. *Writing/Disciplinarity: A Sociohistoric Account of Literate Activity in the Academy*. Mahwah, NJ: Lawrence Erlbaum.

———. 2009. "From Speech Genres to Mediated Multimodal Genre Systems: Bakhtin, Voloshinov, and the Question of Writing." In *Genre in a Changing World*, edited by Charles Bazerman, Adair Bonini, and Deborah Figueredo, 17–34. Fort Collins, CO: WAC Clearinghouse and Parlour Press.

Russell, David. 1995. "Activity Theory and Its Implications for Writing Instruction." In *Reconceiving Writing, Rethinking Writing Instruction*, edited by Joseph Petraglia, 51–78. Mahwah, NJ: Lawrence Erlbaum.

Shipka, Jody. 2006. "Sound Engineering: Toward a Theory of Multimodal Soundness." *Computers and Composition* 23: 355–73.

———. 2011. *Toward a Composition Made Whole*. Pittsburgh: University of Pittsburgh Press.

Sorapure, Madeleine. 2006. "Between Modes: Assessing Student New Media Compositions." *Kairos* 10. Online at http://english.ttu.edu/Kairos/10.2/binder2.html?coverweb/sorapure/index.html.

Taylor, Todd. 2008. *Take 20: Teaching Writing*. DVD. 65 minutes. Boston: Bedford/St. Martin's.

Wertsch, James. 1998. *Mind as Action*. New York: Oxford University Press.

Williams, Sean. 2001. "Part 1: Thinking out of the Pro-Verbal Box." *Computers and Composition* 18: 21–32.

Wysocki, Anne F. 2004. "Opening New Media to Writing: Openings and Justifications." In *Writing New Media: Theory and Applications for Expanding the Teaching of Composition*, edited by Anne F. Wysocki, Johndan Johnson-Eilola, Cynthia L. Selfe, and Geoffrey Sirc, 1–41. Logan: Utah State Press.

Wysocki, Anne F., Johndan Johnson-Eilola, Cynthia L. Selfe, and Geoffrey Sirc, eds. 2004. *Writing New Media: Theory and Applications for Expanding the Teaching of Composition*. Logan: Utah State Press.

Yancey, Kathleen. 2004. "Looking for Sources of Coherence in a Fragmented World: Notes toward a New Assessment Design." *Computers and Composition* 21: 89–102.

Zoetewey, Meredith W., and Julie Staggers. 2003. "Beyond Current-Traditional Design: Assessing Rhetoric in New Media." *Issues in Writing* 13: 133–57.

CHAPTER 4

Something Old, Something New

Integrating Presentation Software into the "Writing" Course

Susan M. Katz and Lee Odell

> Power corrupts. PowerPoint corrupts absolutely.
> —Edward Tufte (2003)

As the chapter title suggests, we think that oral presentation should play a role in writing courses, but we recognize that this assertion may meet with some resistance. If we take a look at the objectives for the typical first-year writing course, we frequently find something similar to this statement from the University of Minnesota: "The primary purpose of first-year writing at the University of Minnesota is to provide incoming students with the fundamental skills and knowledge about writing demanded in university study." Although the wording is not always this direct, other programs echo the general idea that students need to be prepared for the work that will be expected of them in the college setting. (See, for example, the course descriptions for first-year writing courses at North Carolina State University.)

Traditionally, this preparation has focused on writing—witness the long-standing interest in Writing across the Curriculum or Writing in the Disciplines. In recent years, however, the emphasis has begun to shift to include both oral and written communication. Consider, for example, the schools where we teach. At North Carolina State University, Writing across the Curriculum has morphed into a Campus Writing and Speaking Program; at Rensselaer Polytechnic Institute, a campus "writing requirement" has been replaced by a requirement that all students successfully complete two "communication intensive" courses that require both written and oral communication. An even more ambitious program appears at Iowa State, where the WOVE program seeks to develop students' skills in written, oral, visual, and electronic media. And even conventionally labeled writing centers (at Rice University, for example) may offer tutorial work in oral presentations.

This sort of change seems especially important given the demands of communicating effectively, whether in other academic subjects or in professional careers. A quick scan of the first twenty results from a Google Scholar search of the phrase "formal oral presentation" reveals that this type of assignment is a regular feature of courses in more than a dozen disciplines, including such disparate fields as accounting, industrial engineering, public health, higher education, and chemistry. And a survey of Rensselaer alumni showed that they make—on average—five presentations each month. The plethora of self-help books, websites, and short courses on how to make presentations suggests that individuals recognize that they need to hone these skills if they are going to succeed.

Some may argue that students need to focus on writing in the writing course and take separate courses on public speaking. However, public speaking courses frequently focus on form and delivery, the "presentation" aspect of the task, with minimal emphasis on the rhetorical principles that form the basis for effective communication. Furthermore, if we think of the oral presentation as a text rather than as an event, we can find that it comfortably fits within the writing course and serves to enhance students' understanding of those principles and shows them how they can transfer skills from one situation to another.

So if we are to integrate oral presentation into the writing classroom, we have to expand our understanding of appropriate media for assignment submissions. While new communication technologies seem to be developed with an almost frightening frequency, presentation software (most notably PowerPoint) has been in use for long enough that it is widely used and readily accessible, both inside academia and in a wide variety of workplace settings.[1] However, the familiarity that students have gained with this software, either as viewers of lectures given via PowerPoint in classrooms or online or as producers of PowerPoint presentations for various classes, can actually be somewhat problematic in the writing classroom.

In writing courses the two of us teach, most students either begin our courses with a high degree of technological proficiency with presentation software or manage to acquire it through some sort of technological osmosis. They create slides with color, still images, moving images, and sometimes even sound. Objects or texts emerge, vanish, or move across the screen in the most dazzling ways. Having developed the ability to do all this, they conclude they are proficient with the software.

But, of course, they are not. Their technological expertise far outstrips their rhetorical judgment. In too many instances images are simply adornment that has nothing to do with the substance of a presentation; color choice is inept (e.g., red type on a blue background); neither print text nor images have any discernable relationship to what a speaker is saying; moving images compete (often successfully) for attention with what the speaker is saying; and screens are so densely packed with words that the presentation consists solely of the presenter's reading aloud information that the audience could more easily—and more quickly—read for themselves. Even more significant is the fact that when they make their oral presentations, students seem to forget what they have been learning about writing. For example, by the time students in our courses come to the oral presentation assignment, they know they need to begin their essays by providing an engaging introduction to their topic, one that provides readers with a context that lets them see how the topic relates to their concerns and existing knowledge. But this knowledge does not automatically carry over to their oral presentations. At least in their initial presentations, students are likely to begin not with an engaging introduction but rather with a simple announcement of the topic: "OK, today I'm going to talk about . . . " While this phrase may "introduce" a topic, it does nothing to establish a connection between audience members and either the speaker or the topic itself.

Given the potential for misuse, presentation software confronts writing teachers with a series of challenges. Writing instructors must find some way to challenge students' assumptions, too often well grounded in what they see in professors' and classmates' work, about what using this software entails. (Some variant of "Today I'm going to talk about . . . " routinely begins class lectures and other oral presentations.) Instructors may also have to change some of the assignments they often give, not only requiring students to make oral presentations but also finding the class time to devote to these presentations. In addition, instructors will have to find some way to incorporate these assignments seamlessly into their conventional work on writing—helping students not only to observe the conventions of Standard Written English, but also to achieve more complex rhetorical goals of engaging their audience, developing and organizing their ideas, and creating an appropriate voice. And, of course, instructors will have to have some way to show how these rhetorical goals are achieved through the use of visual communication that this software enables.

In meeting these challenges with our own students, we have drawn heavily on an understanding of the "given-new contract," a concept drawn from several scholarly fields. The basic assumption in all of these disciplines is that in order to understand anything, people must be able to integrate new information into their existing knowledge, attitudes, and values—all of which constitute a given. This concept, explained more fully in the next section, enables us to accomplish two basic goals: seamlessly integrating work on visual and oral communication into the routine work of our writing courses and helping students develop the metacognitive ability to assess visual, oral, and written elements in their own work. To justify these claims, we will briefly explain the given/new contract and then present slides from an oral presentation created by an undergraduate student, whom we refer to as Dave.

THE GIVEN-NEW CONTRACT

The phrase "given-new contract" rarely appears in composition texts, but it has a solid foundation in studies of reading as well as in linguistics, technical communication, visual semiotics, and rhetoric. For all practical purposes, we can assume that "readers" (a term of convenience we apply to audiences of any type, listeners and viewers as well as readers of print text) never approach any text as a blank slate. Instead, they come to a text with a set of givens—an existing a body of knowledge, preconceptions, prior experiences, values, and questions. The job of a "speaker" (another term of convenience) is to identify those givens and use them as a basis for introducing new information that will expand or enhance readers' understanding of or reactions to a given text.[2]

This idea of moving the audience from something already known, or given, to something new is a well-established mechanism for structuring sentences to make text cohesive. Linguist Joseph Williams (2007) has explained how sentences in cohesive written texts are likely to begin with some sort of given: something the reader was aware of before beginning to read a text, an idea or detail mentioned in a preceding sentence or a theme introduced earlier in the text. These sentences move to new information, usually displaying it at the end of the sentence, a position Williams describes as "emphatic," since readers are especially likely to remember information in this position of a sentence.

Although Williams (2007) focuses on sentence-level structure, theories from rhetoric and linguistics support moving from given to new as an effective, successful method of improving communication and learning on a macro level. For example, Kenneth Burke's (1969) discussion of identification in *A Rhetoric of Motives* is essentially describing the need for the creation of common ground between speaker and audience—the establishment of a given as a starting point. In linguistics, the given-new contract stems from the early work of Herbert Grice (1957, 1975) on how communicators cooperate to derive meaning. One of the most thorough discussions of the given-new contract remains Herbert Clark and S. E. Haviland's (1977) essay, which explains that when speakers begin with information that they believe is familiar to the audience, they are attempting "to ensure reasonably efficient communication."

Although much of the research that led to these theories focused on oral communication, the application to other contexts has been well established (see, for example, Kent 1984). References to the "given-new contract" are cited as an important component of designing websites on "Web Writing That Works!" (Price and Price 2004). Visual semioticians Gunther Kress and Theo van Leeuwen (1996) illustrate ways the given-new contract applies to visual information, such as ads, classic paintings, and TV. They point out that the left-hand side of an image is likely to contain given information, while the right-hand side often contains new information. They note, for example, that in a television or film interview, the interviewer often serves as a given, the person whom the viewer is likely to recognize or who is likely to pose questions that comprise givens for the viewer. The interviewee—the source of new information the interviewer is hoping to elicit—appears on the right-hand side of the screen (ibid., 191).

INTEGRATING MEDIA EFFECTIVELY: ONE STUDENT'S POWERPOINT PRESENTATION

As their final assignment in a science writing class (taught by one of us), students were asked to create a multimedia presentation on a scientific topic. These presentations ranged from a podcast to a website to a documentary. Most typically, however, students chose to do PowerPoint presentations that entailed both still and moving images. One of these students, Dave, created a PowerPoint presentation titled "Warm Weather Conditions: Heat Exhaustion and Heat Stroke." In the audience analysis he produced for this assignment, he identified his target audience as "parents with children still living in the house."[3] After talking with selected members of his audience, Dave identified a number of givens—the knowledge, values, and questions with which his audience would, consciously or tacitly, approach his presentation. Specifically, he identified his audience as people who:

- live in the northeastern part of the United States
- are likely to be active in the outdoors year round
- are aware that there is danger in becoming overheated in the summer, but assume it is more of a problem in the Southwest than in the Northeast
- do not know the difference between heat exhaustion and heat stroke
- are familiar with news reports on the deaths of football players due to hot weather
- are familiar with the tired feeling associated with spending time in the sun
- are concerned for the well-being of their children
- encourage their children to participate in outdoor activities
- believe the global climate is warming

In addition, Dave noted that his audience was likely to want answers to several questions.

- How do heat-related injuries happen?
- How do I treat them?
- How do I prevent them?

In this detailed audience analysis, Dave is able to articulate the givens—the existing knowledge, assumptions, questions—that his audience will bring to his presentations and that he must build upon in introducing them to new insights into his topic. We see this movement from given to new in the way Dave goes about engaging his audience, selecting content, organizing his material, and creating an appropriate voice. We discuss three of these topics (engaging audience, selecting information, and creating a voice) in separate sections of this chapter. However, the forms of organization we are concerned with—specifically, sequencing information and creating and fulfilling expectations—are so closely tied to the substance of what students have to say that we address organization as we discuss engaging the audience and selecting content.

ENGAGING THE AUDIENCE

Given his audience's concern for health and their interest in having their children remain active during the summer, Dave could assume that his topic was likely to be of at least potential interest to his audience. But he also knew that parents in the Northeast might be less concerned about his specific topic—dangers of heat exhaustion and heat stroke—than would parents in, say, the Southwest, where summers are longer and hotter than those in the Northeast. Thus his problem was to move his audience from a given—a potential interest—into something new: a serious health concern that would get his audience to pay attention to what he had to tell them.

USING VERBAL CUES

Dave opens his presentation by briefly relating a story about a high school student from Texas who "was killed by the hot sun in an August football practice" (script). Dave believed that the incident, which had been recently reported in news media, would constitute a given for his audience, a piece of information with which they were already familiar. Yet he could also assume that, because the incident occurred in the Southwest rather than the Northeast, his audience might think the incident had no direct implications for themselves or their children. Thus, having reminded his audience of this story, Dave makes the following claim: "Whether we've been aware of it or not, most of us have probably experienced some degree of heat exhaustion. You may have experienced it while jogging in the midday sun, or seen it in your children after spending too much time walking around at the county fair" (script).

This information is new: heat exhaustion may occur in activities that might otherwise seem innocuous. And at least tacitly, this claim raises a couple of questions: How serious is heat exhaustion? What can be done about it? These questions create the expectation that they will be answered in the introduction and throughout the rest of Dave's presentation. He meets this expectation with some new information that also helps the audience understand what to expect from the remainder of the

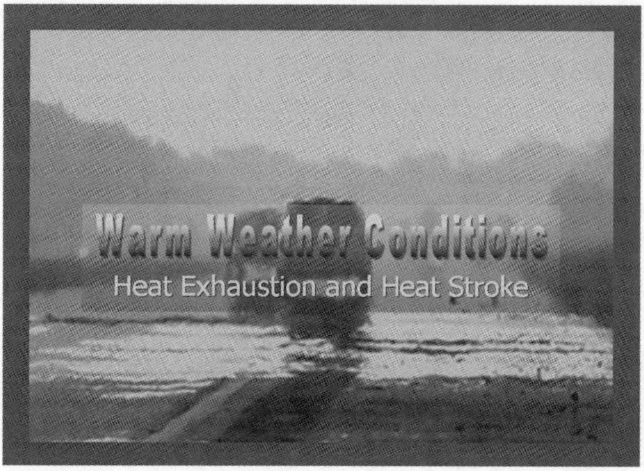

FIGURE 4.1. Dave uses an image and color to create common ground with his audience.

presentation: "Heat exhaustion is not life threatening and can be treated easily, but it's important to do so immediately and not let it progress to heat stroke" (script).

USING VISUAL CUES

Dave knew that even though his audience of adults lived in the northeastern part of the United States, they would be familiar with the mirage effect that occurs on highways during periods of extreme heat. Thus he begins his presentation with a visual (fig. 4.1) that complements the givens established in the verbal text. In this image, apparently a desert highway, heat waves shimmer up from the road, partially obscuring some sort of object—a bus? a truck?—that is vaguely discernable in the background. The main heading ("Warm Weather Conditions") is printed in colors that suggest heat rising: the lowest 25 percent of each letter is dark red, with upper portions of each letter appearing in a continuum of colors, ranging through two shades of orange to yellow at the top—a progression of color reminiscent of fire.

The second slide (fig. 4.2) continues with an image from the highway, but the camera has panned back, and the vehicle from the first slide can now be seen as a follow vehicle supporting a long line of cyclists trailing well off into the background, all of them miniscule in comparison to the vast desert expanse that surrounds them, all of them presumably

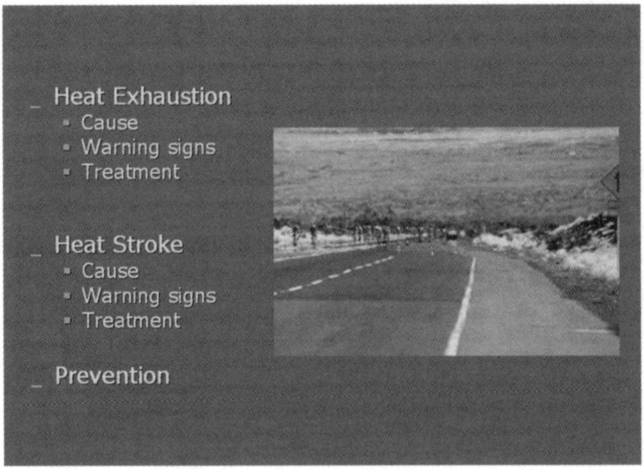

FIGURE 4.2. Dave uses words and an image to create expectations for his audience.

suffering from the heat suggested by the first image. These visuals let Dave assume that his audience is readily able to identify with the weather conditions he wants to talk to them about.

In addition to the photograph, Dave presents a bulleted list on the slide, creating expectations as to what he will talk about with respect to this slide and establishing a pattern the audience can expect him to follow on all subsequent slides.[4] These bullets are, as he notes, "succinct and intuitive," consisting of "terms that the audience is familiar with." Both visual and verbal information in this slide work to move the audience from the previously established "given" of problems related to excessive heat and the "new" information about causes, warning signs, and treatments that will be the focus of the presentation. This combination of visual and verbal elements also creates the expectation that Dave will provide the same type of information about both types of heat-related health conditions.

SELECTING CONTENT

Just as Dave used his audience analysis to make decisions about how to engage his audience, he also used this analysis to help him select the content to include and organize that information. In selecting content for his presentation, Dave knew he could work with at least two givens: (1) his audience was not especially well informed about heat exhaustion and heat stroke, and (2) the potential seriousness that he has established at the outset of his presentation should prompt them to ask the questions around which he built his presentation: How do heat-related injuries happen? How do I treat them? How do I prevent them? Once introduced, these questions constitute givens, and their answers constitute the new information Dave wants to convey.

VERBAL CONTENT

Throughout the verbal portions of his presentation, Dave answers these questions with details drawn not from medical textbooks (which would not constitute a given for his audience) but from the practical experience of someone who appears to have observed and treated heat exhaustion and heat stroke. Here's the portion of the script in which Dave explains how to treat heat exhaustion:

> If you suspect that somebody is experiencing heat exhaustion, your first action should be to move them to a cooler environment. An air-conditioned building would be the best, but even the shade of a tree is better than nothing. Next, remove any excess clothing. The victim doesn't need to go through the humiliation of lying naked under a tree, but wearing long heavy pants and a jacket isn't going to help them get any cooler. Try to cool them further by any means possible. Fanning their body or spraying them with water will help to remove heat. Another effective treatment is applying a cool washcloth to the forehead. The head has many blood vessels close to the surface; this makes it a prime area to lose heat. Finally, keep the victim hydrated and take note of any special medical conditions. If they especially are weak from an existing condition, or have a history of heart problems, they may be more likely to progress into heat stroke.

This passage shows Dave simultaneously moving from given to new and creating and fulfilling expectations. The first sentence acknowledges the limitations of his audience's knowledge: lacking extensive information, they may only suspect that someone might have heat stroke. In that sentence the word first leads his audience to expect exactly what Dave provides: a chronological sequence of steps (remove excess clothing, fan body/spray with water, etc.). Each step is marked by a clear transitional word ("next," "further," "another") and each consists of a familiar (i.e., given) action that is new in response to this situation. And, of course, each step constitutes new information that builds on the preceding information. Dave also anticipates a different sort of given, a possible misunderstanding about the amount of "excess clothing" the audience would need

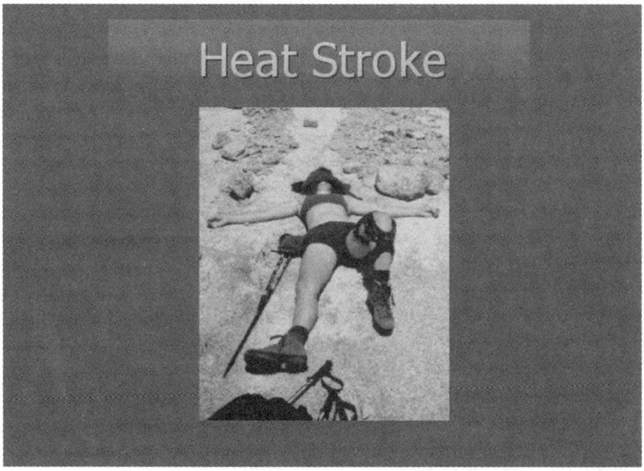

Figure 4.3. Dave uses photographs to emphasize the severity of heat stroke.

to remove, accompanied perhaps by some discomfort at seeing a person stripped naked. He moves his audience beyond this given, reassuring them that they don't need to remove all of a victim's clothing.

VISUAL CONTENT

Although Dave could assume that the visuals we mentioned earlier would constitute givens for his audience, he also could assume that his audience of Northeasterners might not fully appreciate the severity of heat-related injuries. Consequently, he complements his verbal information with images that demonstrate different levels of severity of heat-related conditions—from activity in the hot sun to heat exhaustion and heat stroke. Although the visuals are also depicting extreme heat, as described earlier, there at first is no sign of any heat-related problems. But as Dave progresses from his introduction to his discussion of heat exhaustion and heat stroke, the photographs begin to show scenes depicting increasingly severe problems, such as a woman possibly unconscious along a desert trail (fig. 4.3).

In his audience analysis Dave made it clear that he would be speaking to people who were vaguely aware of the dangers of being overheated but who didn't really understand the actual conditions of heat exhaustion and heat stroke. He reasoned that it was important for his audience to be able to recognize the warning signs, and that a video would do a better job of demonstrating those warning signs than still photographs. Consequently,

FIGURE 4.4. Sample visuals from the YouTube video.

he complements his verbal information about warning signs with a video clip from YouTube, in which a marathon runner in the 1984 Olympics stumbles toward the finish line. While Dave thought that the most important information in the presentation was the information about preventing heat-related injury, he recognized that the material on warning signs needed to be memorable. The videos, from which we have selected only three frames (fig. 4.4), combine sight, sound, color, and motion to provide the most sensory input and are therefore likely to be the most memorable. Images from an Olympic competition will surely be a given, but these specific images move beyond that given, introducing dramatic new information about the way a competitor might suffer and, by implication, the consequences of heat exhaustion his audience might suffer.

The final photograph of the presentation (fig. 4.5), which accompanies the suggestions for preventing heat exhaustion and heat stroke, is the "coolest" photograph, fulfilling the expectation that Dave would talk about prevention by suggesting a resolution to the difficulties described earlier in the presentation. This visual consists of a close-up of a person

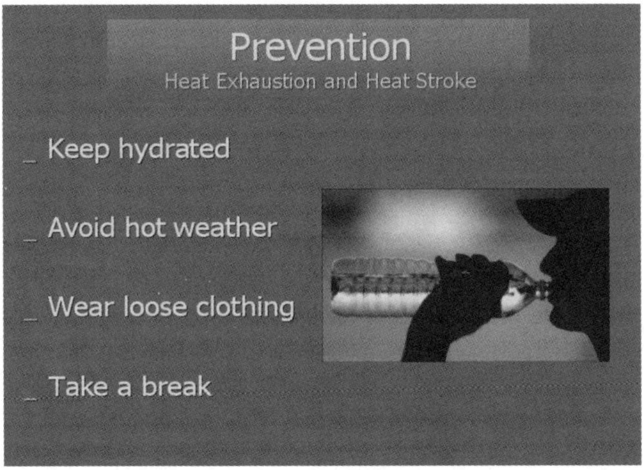

FIGURE 4.5. Cooler colors reinforce preventive strategies.

drinking from a water bottle. The individual is shown in silhouette, suggesting shade. The silhouette is set against a green background, and both the water bottle and the water in it have a bluish cast, with both green and blue echoing the coolness of shade. Overall, this visual contrasts sharply with the "hot" reds, yellows, and oranges that have dominated the other photographs, most of which show people in direct sunlight.

CREATING AN APPROPRIATE VOICE

At the very beginning of his presentation, Dave speaks as someone who is highly knowledgeable about the topic and is able to convey the seriousness of the topic without seeming melodramatic. He also comes across as someone who can present information about a medical topic in straightforward, audience-friendly terms.

Using Verbal Cues to Create Voice

As suggested in the earlier passage concerning treatment for heat stroke, Dave's knowledge of his topic is sufficient to let him not only explain basic information about heat exhaustion and heat stroke, but also to anticipate difficulties and concerns members of his audience might encounter in treating heat stroke. If people are not able to get the victim to an air-conditioned building, "the shade of a tree is better than nothing." If people are concerned about how much "excess clothing" should be removed, Dave points out that "the victim doesn't need to go through the humiliation of lying naked under a tree, but wearing long heavy pants and a jacket isn't going to help them get any cooler."

Dave's technical knowledge also shows he is someone who can acknowledge and rectify his audience's likely preconceptions about the conditions under which heat stroke can occur. In describing these conditions, Dave returns to the example with which he began his presentation: the high school football player who died from heat stroke. Because the player died during a summer football practice in Texas, his audience might assume that the death was caused by the extremely hot summer weather one associates with the Southwest. But Dave points out that this is not the case: "At the time of his death, [the player] showed a temperature of 106 degrees." However, [the outdoor temperature] was only in the mid-nineties during that football practice." Although this fact might be construed as challenging, Dave presents the challenge gently, as a reminder rather than a statement of a fact that someone fails to know or a refutation of a careless assumption: "Remember, the air temperature does not need to be 106 for somebody to have a body temperature that high."

This knowledge, of course, shows Dave's awareness of the seriousness of heat stroke and heat exhaustion. He continually emphasizes the consequences of both conditions. Dave points out that even in the relatively less serious condition of heat exhaustion, people can experience excessive fatigue and muscle cramping, symptoms that can presage heat stroke, which in turn can cause confusion, nausea, organ or brain damage, and even death. But even in describing these serious consequences, Dave is careful to modulate his voice, choosing language appropriate for the level of concern he hopes to raise at different points in his presentation. When he is discussing heat exhaustion, he uses words and phrases such as "difficult," "vulnerable," and "susceptible" (script). He provides commonsense guidance for how to treat heat exhaustion, providing a bulleted list of simple suggestions, such as "move to a cooler environment" and "remove excess clothing." This guidance is supported with his oral commentary and additional information.

However, when Dave moves on to his discussion of heat stroke, he uses what he calls (in his self-assessment) "alarming language"—words such as "deadly" and "fatal"—to arouse the concern of the audience and make sure that they pay attention. In talking about heat stroke, he tells the audience that "very bad things start to happen": sweat glands will "fail," "body temperature will soar," and there can be "both organ and brain damage." Yet even though he is determined to make his audience realize the seriousness of heat stroke and heat exhaustion, Dave is often reassuring. Early in the presentation, he promises his audience he will explain "simple methods to prevent both afflictions. Heat exhaustion and heat stroke start the same way, and it's very simple to stop both from happening" (script). Subsequently, he fulfills this promise, laying out simple actions nonmedical personnel can take to treat and prevent both conditions. He even ends his presentation with this reassurance:

> There are some very easy steps you can take to avoid ever dealing with heat exhaustion or heat stroke. In the summer, do most of your work in the mornings and evenings and leave the afternoon for relaxing. If at all possible, avoid the hottest days altogether. Keep hydrated at all times. Water will help to cool your body and allow your sweat glands to do their job. Loose clothing will allow for air circulation next to your skin. You never see people in the deserts of the Middle East wearing tight clothing. They know what they're doing; long loose clothes protect you from the sun and let your body breathe. Finally, when working or playing outside take a break. If you feel yourself becoming fatigued, or see it in your children, take a moment to rest and cool off.

Drink lots of water, wear loose clothing, take breaks—reassuringly simple, straightforward advice that should equip anyone to avoid the serious medical conditions Dave has described in the verbal elements of his presentation.

Using Visual Cues to Create Voice

As was the case in the verbal component of his presentation, Dave shows he is able to articulate the seriousness of his topic in varying degrees of emotion. The images with which the presentation begins evoke feelings of discomfort but not of direct threat to the audience. The scene of the desert mirage does not show anyone suffering from the heat that produced that mirage. And even if we can assume that the cyclists in the second image are suffering from the heat and physical exertion, the camera never moves in close so we can see the sweat, straining muscles, or grimaces.

Several slides later, when Dave gets to the video clip described earlier (see fig. 4.4), he chooses visuals that suggest more concern. The young woman shown in the video is suffering from heat exhaustion, and the warning signs of that condition are obvious in her stumbling, labored breathing, and sweating. Dave is not yet ready to frighten the audience,

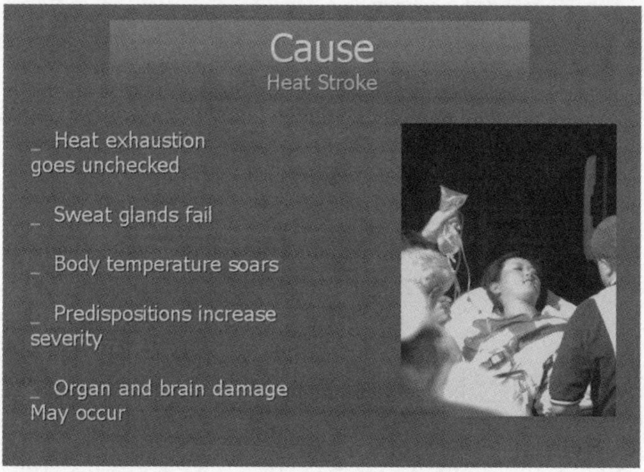

FIGURE 4.6. Serious images help create a more serious voice.

so the voice does not move beyond seeming concerned. The video ends with the runner being allowed to complete the race after being examined by medics, so the voice is optimistic about the outcome of heat exhaustion: with appropriate caution and recognition of the warning signs, heat exhaustion need not be a serious problem. However, Dave knows that heat exhaustion can lead to heat stroke, and that heat stroke can be fatal. When he transitions to his discussion of heat stroke, the voice created by the images changes abruptly. The first slide in the heat stroke section (see fig. 4.3) shows a woman who could be in distress. Other slides in this part of the presentation depict a woman on a stretcher being given IV fluids (fig. 4.6) and an ambulance with lights flashing. These photographs create a serious voice and demonstrate that Dave is not exaggerating his concern.

BENEFIT OF MULTIMODALITY IN DAVE'S PRESENTATION

As is obvious by now, Dave has three different modes of communication working together: the words that he is saying (and which he wrote to be spoken aloud), the words that he put on his slides (which he wrote to be read silently), and the visual features of those slides: images, color, layout, font choice, and so forth. Although a detailed discussion of the many theories pertaining to adult learning styles is beyond the scope of this chapter, we all know that individuals can be divided into groups based on their preferred method of learning: some prefer visual information, others prefer verbal—and those in the latter group can be further subdivided between those who will learn better from reading and those from listening. (For an excellent discussion of several major theories of learning styles, see Felder and Brent 2005.) Dave's decisions about words and images are so well aligned with his understanding of his audience that each can very nearly stand alone to create common ground with that audience and introduce them to his topic.

- The photographs and color choices in the opening remind viewers of a hot summer day and establish "heat" as a topic.
- The words on the slides explicitly provide information about the topic and outline the presentation.
- The words Dave says while these slides are being shown expand on the visual presentation of information by incorporating a brief narrative (about the football player) and adding detail about what is to follow.

As the presentation progresses, the photographs typically provide supplementary information to the verbal presentation—the bulleted lists and accompanying talk convey the meaning, but the photographs and videos dramatize the condition.

By using a multimodal approach, Dave increases the chance that his audience will retain the information that he is presenting to them. The modes work together to help him produce an effective presentation, a presentation that can hold the attention of his audience, provide relevant information—both visually and verbally—in an easy-to-follow format, and create a credible, trustworthy voice that will make his message memorable.

IMPLICATIONS FOR "WRITING" TEACHERS

In analyzing Dave's multimedia text, we have been guided by one basic question we use in helping students create any sort of text at any stage of the composing process: How well has the author integrated visual and verbal information in attempting to move readers from the givens they bring to the text to the new insights the author hopes to convey? More specifically, we ask—and teach students to ask—the following questions.

- At the beginning of the text (written or oral), how well do words or images establish common ground with the audience and provide a basis for introducing new information?

- Throughout the text, how do visual and verbal elements present new information that will answer the questions that are, for a particular reader or group of readers, the givens they bring to the text?
- How is material organized? More specifically, how does the text create expectations and then fulfill those expectations with new information?
- How do words and visuals create a voice that seems appropriate, given what we know about the intended audience?

We use these questions to guide class discussions of model texts, whether student or professional. We raise them as students create their own texts. And we use them—and show students how to use them—in evaluating their own and their classmates' work.

Having seen more than our share of inept multimedia presentations, we have some sympathy with Edward Tufte's (2003) point about the harmful potential of presentation software. If presentations using such software may not actually be evil, they too often are tedious and mind numbing. But Tufte's claim, which we take to be an assertion of fact, does not have to be a self-fulfilling prophecy—not if we show students how to integrate visual and verbal information in ways that move from given to new. If, like Dave, they can identify key points that create a bridge to the audience, produce succinct visuals with engaging and relevant images, and elaborate orally with appropriate detail, then presentations can be informative and perhaps even entertaining. If Tufte is right, he is only partly right. His point does not always need to apply—not for our students, not in our classrooms.

APPENDIX: Instructions for Producing and Using an Audience Analysis

Establish your purpose for the presentation.

- Decide what you hope to accomplish with the presentation.
- Choose an appropriate target audience for the presentation.

Think about your audience.

- Identify what your audience knows, values, and believes about this topic.
- Predict the kinds of questions your audience will find interesting about this topic.

Use your audience analysis.

- When you write your first slide and the introduction to your talk, use something your audience already knows and/or cares about to create a given, or create a given by providing background your audience will need to understand the new information that follows the introduction. These givens should engage the attention of the audience and encourage them to read what you have written and listen to what you have to say.
- As you organize your presentation, sustain the interest of your audience by providing
  - » headings for groups of slides that the audience can connect with—either givens that they will recognize and want to know more about or new information that follows logically from a previous given.
  - » succinct phrases in bulleted lists that anticipate the main points of your talk.
- As you choose content for your presentation,
  - » select material (both visual and verbal) that will connect with what you know about your audience's knowledge, values, and beliefs about the topic.
  - » select information that will answer the questions that you think your audience is most interested in.
- In structuring slides, as a rule,
  - » begin with given or old information and move to new (and more important) information.
  - » incorporate visual/audio information that has a specific function; that is, choose material that, for example, engages or sustains the interest of your audience, helps to create a particular tone, or makes a memorable impact that will help you achieve your purpose.

NOTES

1. We recognize that students have a variety of options when it comes to presentation software, including free software such as SimpleSlide and zooming presentation programs like Prezi. However, in our experience PowerPoint is still the most commonly used application in the classroom. Our discussion is not intended to promote the use of PowerPoint per se, but to demonstrate the

rhetorical strategies that can help students develop effective oral presentations with appropriate visual accompaniment regardless of the specific tools used to create that presentation.

2. Janice Redish (1993) has described this process as it pertains to readers of technical documentation. Gunther Kress (2003) and Charles Bazerman (1985) have drawn on work in two very different areas to suggest that readers will approach other documents in similar ways.

3. We require students to produce a detailed audience analysis before all major assignments. Because most students are unfamiliar with this type of analysis, we spend a good bit of time showing them how to do this sort of work. You can see our instructions for producing and using an audience analysis in the appendix at the end of this chapter.

4. Granted, Kress and van Leeuwen (1996) would have advised Dave to put the image on the left-hand side of the slide and the bullet points on the right. The instructor should have explained this aspect of visual semiotics to the science writing class—a lesson learned for the next time the class is offered.

REFERENCES

Bazerman, Charles. 1985. "Physicists Reading Physics: Schema-Laden Purposes and Purpose-Laden Schema." *Written Communication* 2: 1–23.

Burke, Kenneth. 1969. *A Rhetoric of Motives*. Berkeley: University of California Press.

Clark, Herbert H., and S. E. Haviland. 1977. "Comprehension and the Given-new Contract." In *Discourse Production and Comprehension*, edited by Roy O. Freedle, 1–40. Norwood, NJ: Ablex.

Felder, Richard M., and Rebecca Brent. 2005. "Understanding Student Differences." *Journal of Engineering Education* 94: 57–72.

Grice, Herbert Paul. 1957. "Meaning." *Philosophical Review* 64: 377–88.

———. 1975. "Logica and Conversation." In *Studies in Syntax*, edited by P. Cole and J. L. Morgan, 3: 253–65. New York: Seminar Press.

Iowa State University. ISUComm. "What Is WOVE?" Online at http://isucomm.iastate.edu/node/267.

Kent, Thomas L. 1984. "Paragraph Production and the Given-New Contract." *Journal of Business Communication* 21: 45–66.

Kress, Gunther. 2003. *Literacy in the New Media Age*. London: Routledge.

———, and Theo van Leeuwen. 1996. *Reading Images*. London: Routledge.

North Carolina State University. Campus Writing and Speaking Program. Online at http://www.ncsu.edu/cwsp/.

North Carolina State University. Department of English. English 101 Academic Writing and Research, Learning Objectives. Online at http://english.chass.ncsu.edu/undergraduate/first_year_writing/fy_eng101_course_description.php.

Price, Lisa, and Jonathan Price. 2004. "Web Writing That Works!" Online at http://www.webwritingthatworks.com/DGuideCHUNK4c.htm.

Redish, Janice. 1993. "Understanding Readers." In *Techniques for Technical Communicators*, edited by Carol M. Barnum and Saul Carliner, 14–41. Boston: Allyn and Bacon.

Rice University. Rice Online Writing Lab. Online at http://riceowl.rice.edu/.

Tufte, Edward. 2003. "PowerPoint Is Evil." *Wired* 11 (9). Online at http://www.wired.com/wired/archive/11.09/ppt2.html.

University of Minnesota. First Year Writing. Online at http://www.fyw.umn.edu/.

Williams, Joseph M. 2007. *Style: Lessons in Clarity and Grace*, 8th ed. New York: Pearson Longman.

CHAPTER 5

Thinking outside the Text Box

3-D Interactive, Multimodal Literacy in a College Writing Class

Jerome Bump

For more than twenty years now print has been steadily replaced by electronic media, words by images, and literature by movies, television, computers, and video games. Hence, as Richard Lanham (1993, 264) put it, "we can neither preserve the educational system unchanged nor throw out the 'literate' ways of thinking. We have, in some way, to move the humanities from the old to the new operating system." Many of us have embraced the "digital humanities" and hailed the move of literature to the Internet in sites such as Jerome McGann's *Rossetti Archive*. But what about the more basic and essential teaching of writing? Gunther Kress (2003, 1) has stated: "One might say the following with some confidence. Language-as-speech will remain the major mode of communication; language-as-writing will be increasingly displaced by image in many domains of public communication, though writing will remain the preferred mode of the political and cultural elite." More recently, Alan Liu (2011) has stressed that this will be an "ever smaller elite." Some of us have been trying to salvage writing for a wider audience by designing a new verbal/sensory rhetoric that supports hybrid genres of multimodal "writing." McGann's move from the *Rossetti Archive* to the *Ivanhoe Game* suggests a promising operating system for teaching hybrid genres to today's students: the virtual world, often considered a kind of video game.

Video games "are a *push* technology, providing people entrée into other important technologies, such as computers," and "the online affinity groups that emerge around games function as a kind of *push community*, engaging members in identities, values, and practices, markedly similar to the intellectual and social practices that characterize high level, conceptual communities of innovation in fields such as science, technology, and engineering" (Steinkuehler 2005; see Gee 1999). These communities are growing rapidly in India and China but conspicuously absent among most young learners in this country. Many are attracted to video games, however, and "beneath the veneer of fantasy and seeming childishness . . . videogames are sites for socially and materially distributed cognition, complex problem-solving, identity work, individual and collaborative learning across multiple multimedia and multimodal 'attentional spaces' (Lemke n.d.), and rich meaning-making. . . . massively multiplayer online games (MMOGs) are the quintessential example of such communities" (Steinkuehler 2005, 4). Hence the question arises: Would a use of an MMOG virtual world enable us to *push* the boundaries of English, rhetoric, and composition curriculums, providing these students entrée into truly multimodal composition and the communities of innovation related to it?

ANTIVERBAL BIAS IN NEW WRITING ENVIRONMENTS

For more than ten years this question has driven much of my teaching, but I have encountered two fundamental problems I had not anticipated: increasing antiverbal bias in the "new operating systems" and their instability. As Julia Flanders (2011) has pointed out, scholars have become increasingly dependent on a media structure that has become as invisible as an ideology—until it breaks down. We all assume that electricity will always be available for us, like a force of nature. Even when it is, we are still at the mercy of the kinds of problems Howard Besser (2011) enumerates: failures of display devices, of servers, of network connections; data or application corruption; copyright restrictions; link rot; embedded video content that is multiple hops away; and, of course, rapid disappearance of the content itself (about half a million YouTube videos have already been taken down). All this is exacerbated by the exponential pace of change in the media itself.

I anticipated some of these problems but not the uncertainty of institutional support for research on the new operating systems caused by ever-changing security, disability, privacy, and financial issues. For example, the computer programs English graduate students developed at my institution in the eighties for the teaching of English (the Daedalus system) came under fire by the intellectual property committee; the MOO (multiuser object-oriented) virtual world we then created was shut down for institutional security and disability access concerns; and finally our extensive teaching site on our university's island in the *Second Life* (*SL*) MMOG was torn down almost as soon as it was constructed, apparently for financial reasons.

Ironically, electronic media like these are said to be "persistent." Alex Games (2009), the expert who evaluated our MOO, explained that "'persistence' is a common term used in the computer disciplines to refer to the permanence in computer memory of software entities even when they are not in immediate use." He believed at the time that in our MOO student projects "will remain available even after they have left the university," that it was a place where "a multitude of experiences and perspectives" came together "in a single, shared space over long periods of time," a place where "future generations of students can enter and participate," "a place to both give permanence and historical context to their experiences," ultimately a "virtual public space for humanistic writing on the internet" (ibid.). In fact, not long after this statement was made, the MOO was removed by the systems analyst on the grounds of security and access issues, never to be seen again, with nothing effectively archived.

A similar fate met even my students' electronic portfolios, which facilitated more effective letters of recommendations and better job applications. Even though my institution, the University of Texas at Austin, has a goal of electronic portfolios for all students, the institutions' lawyers and my department, terrifed by FERPA (Family Educational Rights and Privacy Act) guidelines, demanded that all the portfolios that had been published by my students on the Web over the past fifteen years be deleted. Even if this massacre of the innocents had not occurred, with no secure institutional commitments to maintaining student electronic portfolios, such a fate becomes almost inevitable when the instructor of the students is no longer on the faculty.

The lesson seems to be that "software entities" and "computer memory" are not "persistent" but volatile, ephemeral, even evanescent. After participating in the MOO "space," one of the students saw campus buildings in a new way and "wondered how many more generations of people would have the chance to utilize and respect them." The answer for the MOO's virtual space was "none," but the answer for the campus buildings, including the library, remains "many." In other words, it may be that at this time some of the new operating systems are too unstable even to sustain experiments, much less replace the old humanities. There is still no true digital equivalent of a library: electronic media can and often do vanish almost as soon as they appear, leaving no record, no archive of their existence (other than verbal accounts such as this one). In other words, though we can still go to Harvard to study the contexts of the writing assignments of the 1830s, possibilities for more research on the use of programs cited earlier (Daedalus, the MOO, and our *SL* buildings) have already vanished without a trace into cyberspace. Even when librarians try to archive such materials, the obstacles prove enormous. Besser (2011) has pointed out that in the case of e-mail and social media, we barely can deal with archiving messages, much less their social connections; in fact, *Facebook*'s terms seem to forbid such preservation. Student access can be blocked or restricted by other corporations as well, such as *SL* or *Blackboard* (Rumsey 2011).

People also vanish. New faculty members who plunge wholeheartedly into the digital humanities, leaving the old print ways behind, such as books and articles, may soon disappear themselves. Even if one's work in the field persists long enough to be considered for tenure or promotion, the instability of the digital humanities remains a concern for those who evaluate new faculty members.

ANTIVERBAL BIAS IN DESIGNERS AND USERS OF VIDEO GAMES

The other problem I had not fully anticipated was increasing antiverbal bias in designers and users of video games. There are currents flowing stronger and stronger it seems in these new media toward the rejection of not just print literacy but verbal media and the thinking processes associated with them. The goal at times seem to be the death of words altogether, language replaced entirely by technological imagery. This attitude was evident in the sandbox virtual world, *Second Life*. When my students found themselves alone in *SL*, they found a world of very few words. Indeed, at times it seemed to me that *SL*, like video games, was not only basically nonverbal but even antiverbal. After all, the basic method of learning in the computer world seems to be trial and error, on your own. If you get effective help, it is usually someone showing you, by example, how to do a task, not putting the process into words. In any case, without someone to show them how to build in *SL*, my students seemed lost in that virtual world.

In the eighties, adventure games such as *Zork* were based entirely on textual communication, but the quest for the "no-typing interface" soon began (Moberly 2008). Images, in the form of icons, soon began to replace many of the text elements and the text windows began to shrink. The latest development is the rise of voice chat to replace the last remaining uses of writing in games and virtual worlds. The text boxes in virtual worlds such as *World of Warcraft* and *SL*—essential for hearing-impaired players, for those seeking a different "voice," and for teachers using virtual worlds to teach writing—have long been regarded as obstacles to greater "immediacy" and more "immersive" experiences. Voice chat proponents describe text boxes as unreal, inauthentic, "primitive," "outdated," "bizarre," and "irrelevant" vestiges of the "dark ages of communication." Conversely, they describe voice chat as a revolutionary "improvement," an "economic and technological imperative" required for "efficient communication and collaboration." One voice chat company, Vivox, equates typing with "an in-game death sentence for players" (Moberly 2008).

Other designers state explicitly that verbal thinking itself must die. One of the primary critiques of the effects of multimedia on us is our declining attention span, our inability to concentrate for any length of time (Birkerts 1994, 27; see Postman 1985; Healy 1990; Kernan 1990; Stoll 1995; Sanders 1995). This tendency is accelerating in the current generation, partly because of their increasing use of the Internet. The result seems to be that at times mindlessness has replaced mindfulness. The normative word in one classic of web design is indeed "mindless" (Krug 2006, 41). The "first law of usability" in *Don't Make Me Think!* is "I should be able to 'get it'—what it is and how to use it—without expending any effort thinking about it" (ibid., 11). The author concedes that sometimes, "particularly if you're doing something original or ground-breaking, or something very complicated you have to settle for *self-explanatory* . . . it takes a *little* thought to 'get it'—but only a little" (ibid., 18). "Reading" has become anathema: "we don't read pages. We scan them [because] we're usually in a hurry"; looking "at most Web pages," the author of this web design book says, "I'm struck by the fact that most of the words I see are just taking up space, because no one is ever going to read them" (ibid., 22, 48).

This "refusal to read" is said to be typical of what has been called "the Dumbest Generation": until now, "no generation trumpeted *a-literacy* (knowing how to read, but choosing not to) as a valid behavior of their peers" (Bauerlein 2008, 40). Admittedly, this generation is not "dumb" in its own world of short communications such as texting and Twitter, which move us toward new definitions of literacy, and some employers may hire them just to skim data sets and reduce them to charts, tables, and other visual formats.[1] However, this new "literacy" increases impatience with the kind of time-consuming, careful, critical, "close" reading and writing genres that are traditionally the capstones of the college experience and crucial to the advance of civilization.

READING AND CONCENTRATION IN THE AGE OF MASSIVELY MULTIPLAYER ONLINE GAMES

The impatience of practitioners of the new "literacy" extends even to reading relatively short, practical texts, such as directions. The rule is "Instructions must die" (Krug 2006, 47). If we supply detailed directions to the current generation of students, what happens? Do most of the students read them? Would we? Many of us clearly have a strong tendency to do rather than to read. "Faced with any sort of technology, very few people take the time to read instructions. Instead, we forge ahead and muddle through" (ibid., 26). For example, how many of us, when given the task of assembling something we have purchased, have the patience to really take the time first to read the directions carefully? How many of us just skim them or skip them and plunge instead into the assembly process as fast we can, carefully reading the directions only when we discover that part left over?

Employers usually expect college graduates to be able to read, analyze, and follow directions, but in multimedia, the rule is "Instructions must die" (Krug 2006, 47). Apparently instructions must die also in many ordinary writing assignments. We assume that "writing will remain the preferred mode of the political and cultural elite" (Kress 2003, 1), but even my advanced honors students disliked reading directions for assignments. If they were not multitasking or rebelling against being told what to do, they were in a hurry, had other priorities, and no patience for any but the simplest directions. Although they were highly verbal, like other college students, they seemed to prefer someone showing them what to do, an instant fix, rather than "reading" detailed directions.

Technical writers are now taught that instead of providing detailed instructions, they should provide good training sessions and video tutorials (with previews and screen shots), showing users how to do it, and set up expert support sites as well as user forums where the clients can help each other and suggest changes to the developers (formerly known as "writers"). These suggested changes in turn lead to additional usability testing, focus groups, attitudinal surveys (do students like it?), formative evaluation (tests in classrooms), think-aloud protocols, and more identification of the "affordances" or capabilities of the technology (Spiro 2011). Simple, easily accessible instructions with many examples are to be provided for them to turn only to as a last resort. Moreover, these instructions have to at least appear to be brief, organized hypertext documents with details hidden, to be supplied only as needed. Even when it comes to directions, apparently the fewer the words the better.

EXPERIMENTS WITH POSSIBLE FUTURES FOR THE TEACHING OF WRITING

What does this say about the future of teaching writing? Obviously, we cannot simply assume that pedagogical gaming is a good way to teach writing to the Internet generation, for games and virtual worlds are not only unstable, their antiverbal messages are all too obvious, undercutting our attempts to salvage at least some aspects of print literacy. Is reserving writing for the elite the only solution? For the moment that seems to be the case. Hopefully some day there will be stable electronic libraries for preserving the history of electronic research in writing and we can reduce and even counter some of the antiverbal messages, including those coming from the surrounding culture. Perhaps we could remove the live chat option from a virtual world, liberate words from the tiny text boxes to which they have been relegated, and make them essential to success in that game. If and when that day comes, we will be able to build on the experiments such as the following, conducted in virtual worlds like MOOs and *SL* before live chat was introduced.

Both of these worlds are known as "sandbox" games. The focus of K–12 game research was in a fairly traditional genre: the narrative. However, Edward Miller (2007, 17), senior researcher at the Alliance for Childhood, criticized K–12 educational games because they fail "to teach higher-order thinking and encourage creativity and imagination in the classroom." These abilities are especially important at the college level, of course. So we turned to "sandbox" MMOGs. Instead of providing a set narrative like most of the other video games, a sandbox game invites members not just to write their own narratives, but to invent new

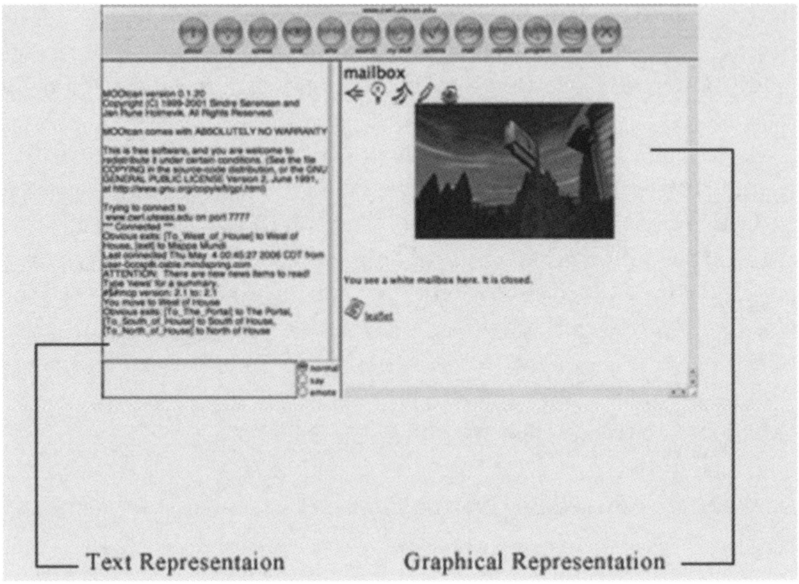

FIGURE 5.1. EnCore MOO interface.

hybrid genres by creating their own objects as well as their own avatars, thereby participating in the construction of a new virtual world. Their "objects" could be scripted actions or characters ("bots") as well as buildings, rooms, landscapes, sculptures, paintings, and so on.

While the first MOOs were composed almost entirely of text, with only ASCII drawings serving as images, and were quickly adapted for English courses, they were soon competing with Internet "hypermedia"—words, graphics, sounds, animation, and video integrated by hyperlinks—which addressed both sides of the brain and invited multiple intelligences (Gardner 1993; Bump 1999). Hence the EnCore MOO, out of the University of Dallas, was developed, which allowed access to the Web and thus to Internet multimedia. The first sandbox virtual world that we tested at our institution was called "*Mappa Mundi*, an Educational MOO for writing and composition." This MOO interface was divided fairly equally between a text box and a multimedia space, representing for us the ideal balance of verbal and visual rhetoric (fig. 5.1).

We tested the capacity of this multimedia MOO to facilitate virtual place-based education because many of my writing courses were based on semiotics: reading the world as text, thus educating the right as well as the left side of the brain. Whenever possible, I lead students out of the classroom to places, usually on campus, that invite the questions and answers of our curriculum. My aim is to counteract the tendency of multimedia and Internet use to cause "an estrangement from geographic place and community" (Birkerts 1994, 27). Another way to do that perhaps is to use the Internet itself to increase the sense of place in students. I began by expanding the meaning of the word Cynthia Haynes and Jan Holmevik applied to MOOs: "archi*textural*" (Haynes and Holmevik 1998, 4). The leader of the research, Alex Games, began by observing our campus excursions that he decided were "experiential activities reminiscent of what Lewis Mumford calls the *regional survey*"; ultimately he observed the students learning "what Paulo Freire would call *reading the world*" (Orr 1992, 10, emphasis in the original; Freire and Macedo 1987, qtd. in Games). As the students learned that each building represented not only an individual architect's vision but centuries of European traditions, they discovered, as Games put it, "what Freire called the *colonizing nature* of discourse and by questioning it" began that liberation that Freire associated with literacy (Freire and Macedo 1987, qtd. in Games, emphasis in the original).

We attempted to transfer that experience to a virtual world and in some ways succeeded: our MOO embodied "a *sense of place* uncommon in most other electronic media" (Meyrowitz 1985, qtd. in Games, emphasis in the original). At first the goal was to give ordinary students a sense, however primitive, of what it was like to experience study abroad. Because our English department had a summer program at Oxford, students were asked to re-create Oxford and its people. Eventually, the focus shifted to adding a similar version of our own campus. In both cases, in the MOO the students soon became designers of their own worlds, building interconnected "rooms" in which they placed "bots": programs that could carry on very simple "conversations" with the MOO reader. As "the students came to see architecture as a form of writing," they practiced a radical version of "archi*text*ural" writing to explore "Freire's *ways to write and rewrite the world* in dialogue with each other" (Orr 1992, 10, emphasis in the original; Freire and Macedo 1987, qtd. in Games). They transformed "*knowledge through new constructions and representations of reality*" (Chandler-Olcott and Mahar 2003; New London Group 1996, qtd. in Games). The result was a wide variety of "*hybrid texts*" (New London Group 1996, qtd. in Games, emphasis in the original): new forms created by integrating different ways of reading and writing the world. However, because of a fear that the open-source MOO software could be penetrated by hackers, and a fear that the MOO could not be very well adapted to vision-impaired users, the system analyst was ordered to destroy these hybrid texts and the MOO that produced them.

We had to move our project to another environment. The sandbox MMOG that had received the most publicity at this point was the "3-D" virtual world *SL*. One obvious advantage was that by adding the three dimensions of virtual worlds to multimodal pedagogy we could enhance not only engagement by both sides of the brain, but also active learning, the kind of learning that enables college students to retain what they learned longer than the average of two weeks after the course is over. As one of our team members put it:

> Three-dimensional virtual worlds such as *Second Life*, *Active Worlds*, and *There* [provide] experiential learning opportunities unavailable in traditional learning environments (Gee 2003; Kirriemuir and McFarlane 2003; Dede et al. 2005; Prensky 2006). Additionally, some have suggested that there exist positive effects specific to virtual worlds, such as creating a sense of social presence in interactions. Hence 'virtual worlds . . . are expected to have a large impact on teaching and learning within higher education in two to three years (EDUCAUSE 2007b). [Yet] to date, relatively few . . . pioneering studies have initiated inquiry into how to use virtual worlds in instructional settings. (Trapaghan 2007)

This is especially true of English studies. While it is said that "a plethora of literacies congregate around the ever-expanding subject English as the prime site for innovation and development" (Matthewman, Blight, and Davies 2004, 153), rarely attempted was teaching English *in* virtual worlds, requiring writing not just in a small text box but in hybrid genres created *in* and *for* that 3-D world. Although Harvard Law already offered a course entirely in *SL*, English, rhetoric, and composition were conspicuous by their absence in Megan Conklin's (2007) "101 Uses for *Second Life* in the College Classroom." A few teachers had their students write about cyberculture in traditional academic genres after they explored *SL*, but I know of none who asked students to write *in* the virtual world itself. Our specific hypothesis was that by requiring the use of words in hybrid genres *in* the virtual world itself, we could better test the appeal of massive, multimedia, multiplayer, interactive, 3-D social virtual worlds to facilitate the teaching of multimodal composition, especially hybrid genres, putting students on the cutting edge of the visual-verbal, print-online divide.

From 2006 to 2008 we tested our hypotheses in two kinds of first-year writing courses at a large American state university. We began in 2006–7 with a two-semester, required, honors first-year English course.[2] In 2007–8 we compared a new section of this honors course with a first-year

FIGURE 5.2. The main building on our island in *Second Life*.

seminar that met the university's basic requirements for substantial writing. The honors students in the fall of 2006 were more verbal than the first-year seminar students, but in a survey that featured the question, "Do you feel more skilled about technology skills than other students your age," 93 percent answered "yes"; 86 percent felt confident playing virtual world games such as *SL*; 76 percent liked the use of games in class; and 70 percent liked playing video games.[3]

The first step was to create a *place* for us in *SL*, a virtual campus of our university, thereby helping students "create a sense of place" for their university experience, a recommendation of the Boyer Commission on Educating Undergraduates in the Research University (1998). Therefore, during the summer Alex Games built the main building of our university in painstaking detail on our new island in *SL* (fig. 5.2):

Games also created a version of the campus creek, with trees, and added a Greek amphitheater for debates. (This area, with the students' buildings, is the section that was demolished soon after we built it.) In the fall the students were given their first assignment: to "write" their "road maps" *in* this world. The "road map" is a visual-verbal-musical presentation of the most important places in the student's life. In first-year courses it is also a relatively painless transition from one genre of high school hypermedia "writing" to college "writing." Even the weakest students are able to make impressive PowerPoint presentations and many students often spend inordinate amounts of time on it, producing very creative and effective autobiographical works. Most students are also able to transform their road maps into movies or websites. All the students then make brief in-class presentations of their road maps and thus get to know each other and create a sense of community. (This road map assignment also triggered the FERPA complaint that led to the demolition of all student portfolios.)

The challenge in this particular class was to put the road map *in SL* somehow. One of the most obvious ways was to convert one's PowerPoint presentation into a website, then somehow link that website to a location in the virtual world. It is not difficult to make a limited web version of a PowerPoint presentation, but putting the link in *SL* was the challenge. The students discovered that the easiest way to put multimodal text into *SL* was to embed a "webloader" script in an object. When a user discovered and then selected such a visual sign in the virtual world, an Internet browser screen opened with the usual 2-D mix of multimedia and text enlarging the message of the sign. For most students this *SL* object was essentially a billboard that presented the first picture in a series. *SL* provided many opportunities to go beyond the multimedia and interactive potential of the Encore MOO. For example, one student, Brad Barry, actually made a series of boardwalks in *SL* from one webloader picture to the next, at one point over the creek. In this hybrid genre one's avatar had to virtually walk through his life (fig. 5.3).[4]

Another student, Mauro Caffarelli, added a third dimension to his hybrid "writing" genre when he used an *SL* note-writing script to embed texts about his life *in* four 3-D objects. First there was a billboard on the creek with the text (fig. 5.4): "As you walk down the river towards the horizon, you shall find four distinct objects that symbolize four great aspects of my life: religion, academics, athleticism, and music. Within each of the objects are two or three notes with concise narratives explaining how I have evolved in the four subjects over the course of my life. Some of them start from when I was of a young age, others begin at a time only three years ago. In order to access the notes, right-click on the object."

Figure 5.3. Brad Barry's boardwalks in *Second Life*.

Mauro sculpted four very difficult objects, a very complex, time-consuming process in *SL* that required not only creativity and imagination, but also higher-order thinking, including knowledge of geometry. He actually embedded text in the objects themselves, creating a true 3-D hybrid writing genre. Like Brad, Mauro also incorporated the interactive motions of a "reader" who had to learn to walk or fly along the creek (or walk in/under its water) to find the objects as well as "select" them to read the text. By forcing the reader to "walk the talk" to briefly experience someone else's life, Mauro, like Brad, helped us cross the divide between self and other. They helped us move toward another pedagogical goal of my courses: stretching the sympathetic imagination, "the ability of a person to penetrate the barrier which space puts between him and his object, and, by actually entering into the object, so to speak, to secure

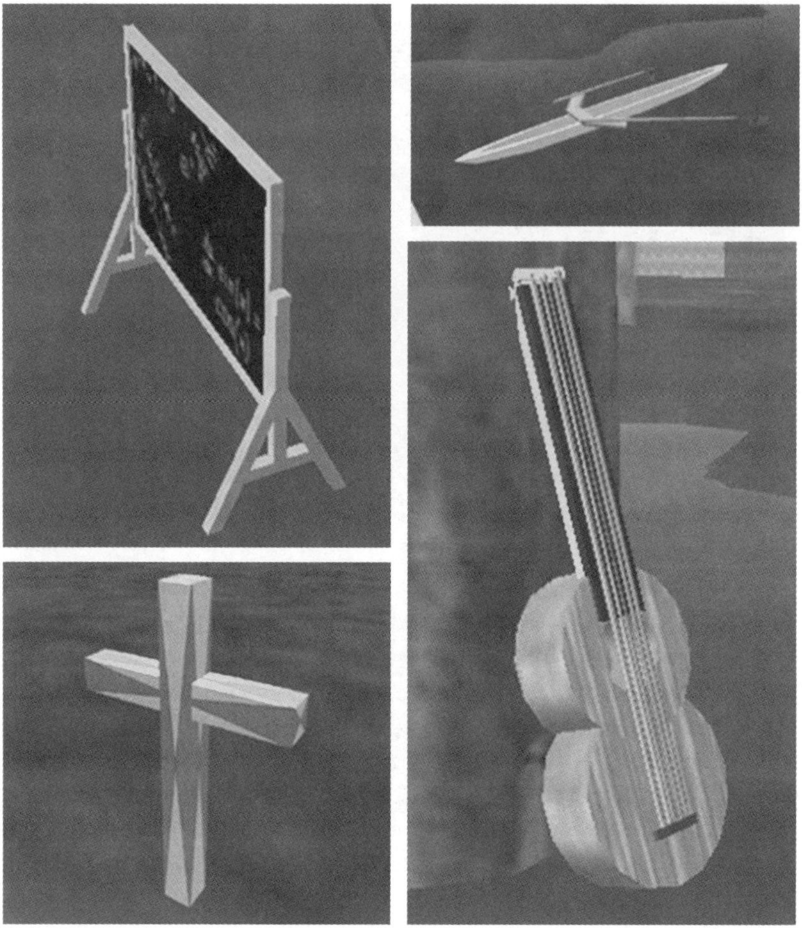

Figure 5.4. Mauro's objects.

a momentary but complete identification with it" (Bate 1945, 144). By connecting the sympathetic imagination to another of the course goals—multicultural understanding—this exercise helped us meet some of the diversity goals of our university.

These road maps prepared the students for their first major formal "writing" project. They were to design their own campus master plan and then communicate it in a truly "architextual" hybrid genre: simultaneously composing essays and buildings in *SL*. Their rhetorical task was to integrate their verbal arguments for their own campus master plan into the virtual buildings that exemplified their master plan's style of architecture, to somehow fix their arguments *onto* or *into* the buildings

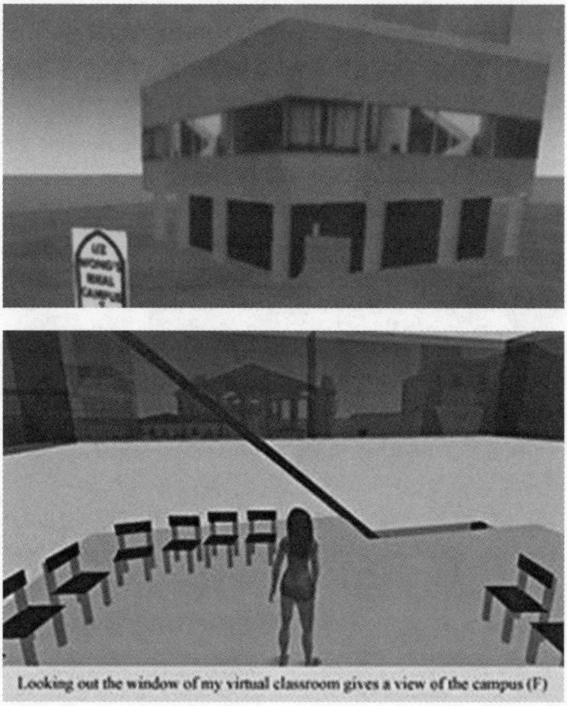
Looking out the window of my virtual classroom gives a view of the campus (F)

FIGURE 5.5. The breakthrough.

themselves. In other words, they were to construct in *SL* models of the kinds of buildings they wanted to see on campus and embed words in these structures to persuade others to adopt these edifices as models for their campus architecture master plan.

We knew that for our liberal arts students (as opposed to gamers and architectural engineers), advance planning is obviously crucial to meet such a challenge. Our preparation seemed to be fairly thorough, but a month before the course was to begin, our *SL* adviser, Games, transferred to a different university. At first, in the absence of our building expert, constructing true 3-D buildings that one could walk into and "inhabit" in *SL* seemed impossible. However, one student, Elizabeth Wong, stayed up all night and was able to construct such a building (fig. 5.5).

The other students gained confidence and went on to produce some extraordinary buildings of their own (fig. 5.6). This process of creating radically hybrid genres by constructing buildings and embedding texts was very time-consuming, and I doubt these students would have succeeded if they had not been a special class of very advanced, extremely

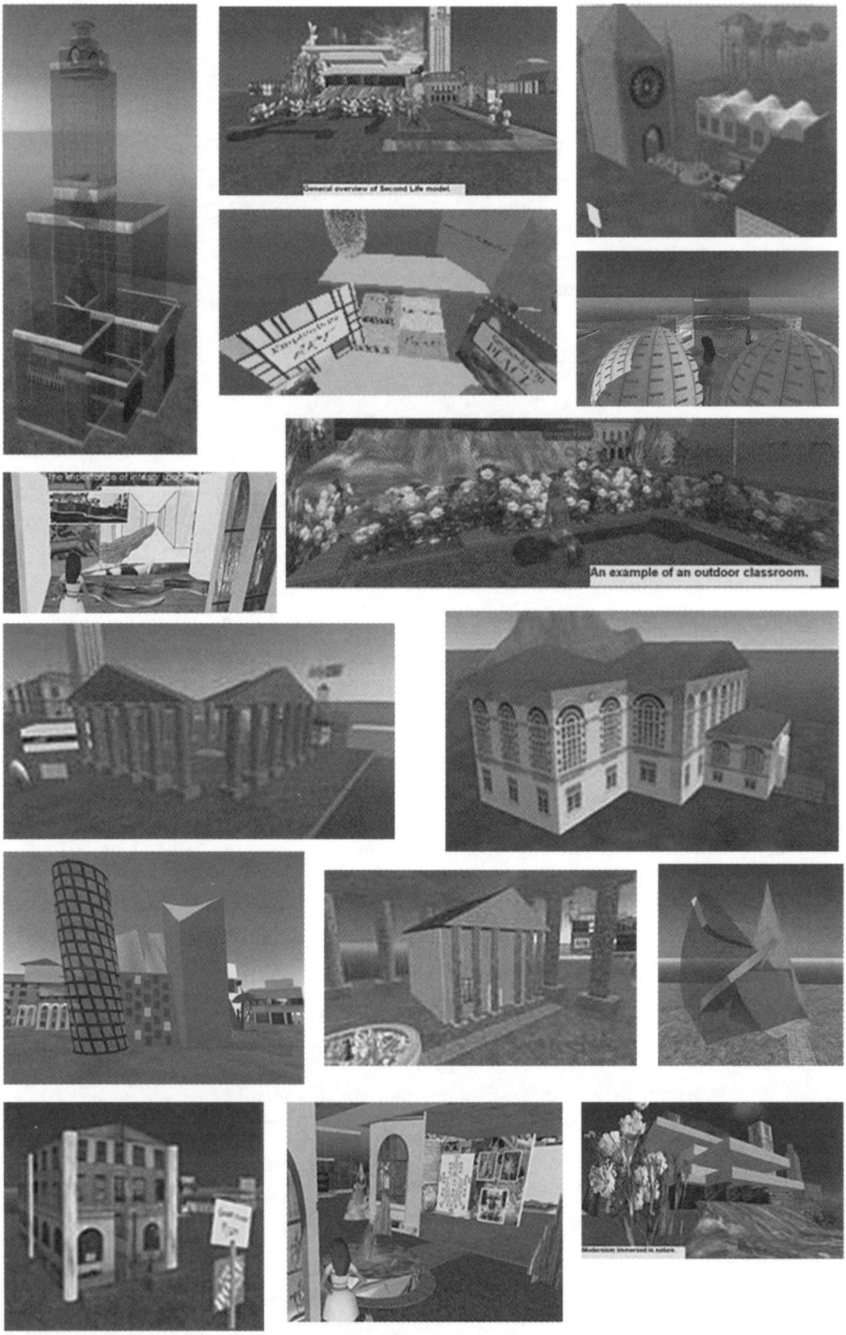

FIGURE 5.6. The result, a virtual campus.

competitive students. As Mauro had shown, in the *SL* virtual campus the most visual but in some ways most difficult way to integrate text and architecture was to embed the text itself in part of a building. Another option was a "Thincbook," a virtual simulation of a book, with covers, pages that turned, and so on. When the students added them to their projects, they thus seemed to resurrect print literacy in the new virtual world. Though the atavistic Thincbooks were difficult to master, some students were able to put their entire multimedia projects in them. In other words, the 2-D mix of words and images they would have put on the Internet was now inserted into the pages of these virtual books, which were then put on or near their buildings. The "reader" was able to "turn" the pages of the books and "read" the project and get an overview of it before exploring further. Often the "writer" also provided more embedded texts in the buildings.

There is no doubt that these archi*text*ural assignments stimulated the creativity of the students and helped them embrace multiple modes: linguistic, visual, spatial, and many added aural on their own. They were forced "to assume responsibility for determining the representational systems that best suit the work they hope to accomplish" (see Jody Shipka's chapter in this collection) and to "stay alert to *how* and *why* we make these combinations of materials" (see Shipka in this collection; Wysocki 2004). Ultimately, they discovered building as a valuable model of composing and how to write from inside the object one has created, as in "L's" comment in the interview below about how she was able "to feel what I think."

This campus building project was clearly successful in three other respects: 100 percent of the students agreed that their "awareness of campus architecture has increased because of SL"; they had created "a sense of place" for their university experience, as recommended by the Boyer commission. The campus they created helped them overcome the divide between the individual and the group; like Charles Soukup (2004, 20), they "discovered that the ability to collectively construct the environment enhanced participants' sense of social community." More than 80 percent felt that a virtual campus of their university in *SL* would be "a good recruiting tool"; "good for freshman orientation"; and "good for retaining alumni interest." A full 77 percent found that their "sense of U.T. as my alma mater increased because of *SL*."

The relation of *SL* to multimodal writing was more complicated, however. The interviews conducted during the first semester by Michael Mayrath—like Games, a graduate student in educational psychology, revealed that the goals of discovery learning and increased engagement by both sides of the brain had been achieved by some of the students. Indeed, the result seemed to be a new hybrid rhetoric of persuasion and important changes in point of view:

MM: How is *SL* influencing how you write?

L: It let me talk from the inside about architecture.

MM: Is it making writing easier or more difficult?

L: I think it makes it easier.

MM: Does having a virtual identity in *SL* make a difference in the way that you wrote your assignment?

L: Sort of. When I'm talking about my virtual pictures, I can really describe the view from a person. Like being inside it. Coming from my *SL*, I can say I took my avatar up into the building I can look out and see. It changes the perspective I can write from.

MM: It sounds like it's more of a first-person experience rather than a third-person experience. Is that right?

L: Yeah. . . . It's really cool to take your avatar and be able to walk into the building and then you can take the camera and look up and look out the windows. It's a lot easier to feel what I think.

MM: Do you think what you are doing in *SL* is related to composition and rhetoric in world literature?

L: Definitely, in the description of the class he said we will be looking at world literature as the world around us rather than actual books.[5] So learning about iconography has made me aware of stuff; then building in *SL*, where you're actually creating a world with its own symbols and stuff.

MM: How has *SL* affected your interest level in this course?

L: For our class I'm definitely more interactively involved.

As this interview reveals, at least some of the students were aware of our goal of a new 3-D visual-verbal rhetoric.

There is also no doubt that *SL* activated the students' imaginations. When the evaluators came at the end of the first semester of the experiment to do focus groups, the students responded on note cards that were then assembled and discussed. The students emphasized how much their creativity was stimulated (fig. 5.7). But they also vented their frustration (fig. 5.8).

Figure 5.7. The creativity.

There were various causes of this aggravation, many related to the steep learning curve and maintenance and security problems in *SL*. *SL* was a rapidly growing site with hundreds of thousands of users, and permissions and other matters were difficult to resolve at a distance. For example, as Mauro had shown, in the *SL* virtual campus the most visual but in some ways most difficult way to integrate text and architecture was to embed the text itself in part of a building. Some students were able to do this, but the results were usually not visible to others because of the complex *SL* layers of permissions. In addition, *SL* was often down for maintenance and even when it wasn't, almost every time the students logged

FIGURE 5.8. The frustration.

onto the program, they had to download and install a new desktop client. One time it was shut down completely for days to deal with a security breach and a change of passwords.

Hence, at the end of the first semester, 53 percent revealed that they did not "really" enjoy the experience of building in *SL* and 65 percent were "glad that we are using *SL* less next semester." This experience is congruent with the research of Sasha Matthewman (Matthewman, Blight, and Davies 2004, 158), who "collected and analysed data which showed frequent instances of English and technology clashing uncomfortably. . . . The main themes were: technological hitches, lack of technical support, . . . tension between the need for coverage of curriculum content against the time taken up by technology, as well as the time taken by pupils in their exploratory and often time-consuming uses of technology." When the *SL* experiment failed most obviously, as in the building experiment, the basic problem was apparently a gulf between two cultures. The student responses to the *SL* building/writing assignments were ambivalent. Our primary goal of integrating visual and verbal rhetoric was achieved in one respect: in the first semester 71 percent felt that their "understanding of how to integrate visuals and writing improved because of *SL*." Yet only 56 percent agreed that "it is a good idea to use *SL* in a literature and writing course." Most remarkably, only 24 percent agreed that their "writing skills have improved because of *SL*." (During the second semester the numbers were even lower, but there was no *SL* writing assignment that semester, except for an extra-credit informal analysis of our avatar chat transcript.)

A second-semester comment summarized the basic problem: "This program taught us about implementing visual rhetoric, but did not improve our writing." All of the respondents to this survey were first-year honors students who, like English majors, had already mastered print literacy and thus did not easily see the need to add on multimodal composing. Although these very verbal students were no doubt aware on some level that the visual was replacing the verbal in public communication, they were also probably aware that writing was still the key to success in the elite class to which they aspired.

What about the more typical students in the first-year seminar? I had assumed that because of their use of Facebook and multimedia websites in general, most of these students arrived with a sense of multimodal rhetoric, an assumption supported by the unqualified enthusiasm of many of the articles on the subject and by the demands of groups of true believers (see Bauerlein 2008). We assume there is a "growing percentage of students who believe that their ability to communicate using new media will be critical to their futures" (Faigley 2003, 179). Obviously, outside of the classroom the students do prefer visual-verbal rather than merely verbal rhetoric, although they may not be fully aware of this preference. Indeed, it has been said that "more and more students come to college with years of experience writing online and now with publishing on the web . . . we do not have to introduce them to the conversation. They are already in it" (Faigley 2001, 419). However, we need to be more conscious of what "writing online" and "publishing on the Web" means to most students arriving from high school. In other words, we need to ask, what are they already *in* exactly?

With the exception of a few students like Tia Scoffield Bowen, they are certainly not *in* the world of PowerPoint and other programs they are asked to use in high school.[6] Rather, as Shari Dinkins (2008) has observed: "Outside of class, my young students' lives seemed to be a whirl of online relationships, virtual 'lives', and constant reliance on the same two or three friends through instant messaging, text messaging, e-mail, and phone calls; indeed, 'keyboard bravery,' combined with a lack of modesty produced shocking revelations on social communication sites like MySpace and Facebook." Some students are *in* not only sites like these, but also in "Quake tournaments" (see Cheryl Ball's chapter in this collection) and other 3-D virtual-world multimedia video games.[7] In the future, apparently they will be *in* 3-D hybrids that combine the best of Facebook and *SL*.

However, even though Lester Faigley's *Picturing Texts* (2004) and *Little Penguin Handbook* (2006) were ordered for the class, and the first reading assignment focused on how the new multimedia literacy connects the right and left sides of the brain (Bump 1999), many students did not even identify the integration of text and image in their road maps as "writing." Even after their formal writing *in SL* for the building assignments, some students still did not accept the premise that "writing," meaning writing like that assigned in high school, includes visual as well as verbal rhetoric. In other words, appearances to the contrary, print versus digital literacy, like the left versus the right side of the brain, remains one of the more debilitating antitheses in the university classroom.

In short, students' perceptions and understandings of their own visual and verbal literacies do not always match the teacher's. This is true even of PowerPoint. Matthewman (Matthewman, Blight, and Davies 2004, 157) summarizes experiments in England: when teachers asked their "high school" students to convert a PowerPoint story into a written text, the teachers all agreed "that the translation from multimodal story into written language had proved very problematic," and they agreed with Richard Andrews's (2001, 125–26) conclusion, in his overview of prior research, that the result was "two quite separate sets of creative activity rather than . . . a liberating interaction." The divide is even greater when we move to more adventuresome multimodal composing. Most students do not agree with the statement made by Cheryl Ball, Tyrell Fenn, and Tia Scoffield that "none of us communicate *only* through writing and that written text itself is multimodal in that it carries visual, spatial, and sonic properties every time we type a new letter-character on the page" (see their chapter in this collection). A few students do know this, to some extent, as the interview between "MM" and "L" (earlier in this chapter) reveals, and no matter what problems arose, those of us conducting these experiments have, as Ball and her coauthors argue, "raised awareness of critical and rhetorical (as well as technological) literacies, [because] difference in teaching modes of communication that students have never 'written in' before requires them to rethink their basic literacies."

RECOMMENDATIONS FOR WRITING AND BUILDING IN A VIRTUAL WORLD

As Tomoko Trapaghan (2007) wrote: "Because the virtual-world environment is not pre-defined, creating effective learning environments in virtual worlds poses substantial demands for instructional design and technical skills with virtual worlds. As yet, there is little empirical literature that addresses how to effectively design instructional activities for use in virtual worlds." So what are the possibilities for more "empirical literature" on multimodal composing in virtual worlds? Where can we take this? Assuming the current instability and antiverbal bias of electronic media can be addressed in the future, more research on hybrid genres that appear when students write *in* the games themselves would be valuable, especially to explore the possibility of a new multimodal rhetoric in which abstractions and examples are more fully integrated.

For this new research on writing and building in a virtual world, my specific recommendations are:

1. choose a virtual world more user-friendly and easier to use than the original *SL*;
2. understand the differences between gamers and the general population;
3. know the differences between teachers' and students' perceptions of visual and verbal literacies;
4. know the limits of discovery learning, especially concerning directions;
5. "provide training, support, and clear directions" for virtual world activities (Trapaghan 2007).

First, we need to choose a stable virtual world that is not based solely on the video game model, does not have a steep learning curve, nor the kind of maintenance, permissions, and security problems that plagued *SL* at that time. In other words, we need to begin with a virtual world designed for general populations rather than gamers. Such a virtual world must offer the stability, training, support, and clear directions novices need.

The second recommendation is based on interviews: "Interviewees said that students' difficulties in using *SL* were related to their lack of experience as gamers" (ibid.). Much of the research on the pedagogical use of MMOGs at the college level is based on courses that attract gamers rather than the average students. If we are to tap into the power of virtual worlds for, say, first-year English, we need to acknowledge the important differences among these populations. The average student has played board games, of course, but the directions in such games are fairly clear. In video games, however, most of the rules of the system are withheld from the player, who must learn by playing, testing hypotheses against the physics of the virtual world (Johnson 2005, 42–45). Needless to say, this is not the world most students want to *be in* to find the directions for a major project in a required first-year English class the night before it is due.

Third, according to Shipka's contribution to this edited volume, we must help students "adjust to a framework that explores the communicative potentials of materials, genres, technologies, and rhetorical strategies that are, more often than not, 'new' to them—at least insofar as they are being taken up, explored, and analyzed in a classroom context." To do this, we must first be aware of what their Internet experiences mean to our students. Take, for example, the differences between teachers' and students' perceptions and understandings of visual and verbal literacies. We need to acknowledge that, whatever we think we know about their online activities outside the classroom, inside the classroom "students are accustomed to taking courses where writing is treated as separate from other representational systems (i.e., where the visual design of the page, font choice, and spacing are not discussed)" (Shipka, this collection). In other words, perhaps we should begin with the assumption that many students will not already see that verbal rhetoric is, to some extent, also visual rhetoric. We will have to make more time in our schedules to practice both thinking in general and transcending this dichotomy in particular.

To challenge simplistic dualisms, we can begin by tapping into the students' awareness of the Internet outside the classroom, for it has predisposed them to prefer complexity to simplistic antitheses: "For the TV generation, things are black and white. . . . no middle ground. But this is not the N-Gen world. [The Net's] half-tone, complex world of information, pointers, judgment, and interpersonal connection is the antithesis of the good guys/bad guys world of adults" (Tapscott 1999, 297). We need to draw on this Internet experience to make them more aware of the limits of either-or logic *in* the classroom as well as outside it: helping them see that each pole of antitheses, such as print versus online literacy or verbal versus visual rhetoric, is dependent on the other and that most successful communication combines elements of both. By choosing both-and rather than either-or logic inside the classroom, students will then be able to apply it to rhetoric and writing as well.

Fourth, at times we must accept the limits of discovery learning. Some students want to be told what to write and how to think. As Shipka put it, "this is especially true for students who enter the course expecting that it will provide them with the magic formula for writing 'right' for all time and every occasion" (Shipka, this collection). Even students who are masters of discovery learning in traditional academic settings may feel lost in *SL*.

Fifth, what can we do about directions? What happened in the honors class? A few students figured out how to build in *SL* and they helped the others. This process would have been greatly facilitated if, from the start, we had set up user forums where they could help each other and encouraged them to do so. And, of course, the frustration would have been greatly diminished if we had good training sessions and video tutorials, showing them how to do it, and, finally, provided, as a last resort, hypertext documents clearly organized with details hidden and supplied only as needed.

We hope that some day other students will benefit from what we learned from the honors students' experiments in salvaging print literacy in *SL*, and designers and researchers will be able to adapt features of educational games that not only encourage creativity, imagination, and higher-order thinking in the college classroom, but do so in multimodal formats that integrate the verbal and the visual. However, we must first deal with the instability and antiverbal bias of the "new operating systems" we are being asked to adopt.

NOTES

A brief preview of this chapter appeared in the e-zine *Currents in Electronic Literacy*. See "Teaching English in *Second Life*," *Currents in Electronic Literacy* (spring 2007), http://currents.cwrl.utexas.edu/spring07/bump.

1. Alan Liu (2011) adds that we are moving from close to "distant" reading in many senses of the word, including toward more and more "distance" learning as budget-cutters impose business models of assembly-line efficiency. Amy Earhart (2011) cites one Texas A&M regent who prefers the feedlot model. She traces this business efficiency model to Bill Gates, who argued that technology should be able to reduce the cost of college education to two thousand dollars. Amanda French (2011) suggests that the goal of the total-distance-learning budget-cutters is to reduce the university to a collection of powerful portals that also offers a little physical space for those who desire human contact now and then, something like the building housing the national digital library of Korea.

2. "Composition and World Literature," http://www.cwrl.utexas.edu/~bump/E603/. The use of *SL* in this course was cited in the *Horizons Report* (EDUCAUSE and the New Media Consortium 2007a, 19).

3. See http://secondlife.com/. These surveys, along with interviews and other evaluations were administered by a team that had been assigned to the project by the university's Division of Instructional Innovation and Assessment (DIAA). The team included Joe Sanchez (information studies); Michael Mayrath (educational psychology); Dr. Tomoko Trapaghan (educational psychology); Dr. Linda Dickens and Dr. Joel Heikes (DIIA); and Kyung Huh (systems analyst). Originally the team also included Alex Games (educational psychology), the chief architect of the course, before he moved to the University of Wisconsin.

4. One website can be seen at http://www.cwrl.utexas.edu/~bump/E603/web06/maps/Brad/Brad%20Barry%20-%20Road%20Map/.

5. "Actual books" apparently means here "complete novels" as there was a 720-page course anthology in the first semester, as one can see in the schedule, see http://www.cwrl.utexas.edu/%7Ebump/E603/scheduleFall06.html. The complete novels were deferred to the second semester, see http://www.cwrl.utexas.edu/~bump/E603B07/schedule.html.

6. See Cheryl Ball's chapter, written with Tyrell Fenn and Tia Scoffield Bowen, in this collection.

7. As Tyrell puts it: the reference is to the multiplayer online game Enemy Territory Quake Wars, which requires an Xbox.

REFERENCES

Andrews, Richard. 2001. *Teaching and Learning English: A Guide to Recent Research and Its Applications*. London: Continuum.

Bate, Walter Jackson. 1945. "The Sympathetic Imagination in Eighteenth-Century English Criticism." *English Literary History* 12 (2): 144–64.

Bauerlein, Mark. 2008. "Research Funds for Technophiles." *Inside Higher Education.* Online at http://insidehighered.com/views/2008/05/20/bauerlein.

Besser, Howard. 2011. "Large Datasets of Visual Daily Culture: Why They're Important; Who's Studying Them; and the Challenges for Scholars, Scholarship, Pedagogy, and Stewards." The Digital and the Human(ities) Symposium, Texas Institute for Literary and Textual Studies, University of Texas at Austin, March 12.

Birkerts, Sven. 1994. *The Gutenberg Elegies: The Fate of Reading in an Electronic Age.* Boston: Faber and Faber.

Boyer Commission on Educating Undergraduates in the Research University. 1998. *Reinventing Undergraduate Education: A Blueprint for America's Research Universities.* Online at http://www.cwrl.utexas.edu/~bump/Boyer_Report.pdf.

Bump, Jerome. 1999. "Left vs. Right Side of the Brain: Hypermedia and the New Puritanism." *Currents in Electronic Literacy* 1 (2). Online at http://www.cwrl.utexas.edu/currents/fall99/bump.html.

Chandler-Olcott, Kelly, and Donna Mahar. 2003. "'Tech-savviness' Meets Multiliteracies: Exploring Adolescent Girls' Technology Mediated Literacy Practices." *Reading Research Quarterly* 38 (3): 356–85.

Conklin, Megan. 2007. "101 Uses for *Second Life* in the College Classroom." Online at https://ctle.northgeorgia.edu/ctlen/index.php?option=com_remository&Itemid=95&func=fileinfo&id=1.

Dede, C., J. Clarke, D. Ketelhut, B. Nelson, and C. Bowman. 2005. "Fostering Motivation, Learning, and Transfer in Multi-User Virtual Environments." Paper presented at the American Educational Research Association Conference, Montreal.

Dinkins, Shari. 2008. "Academic on Track: Learning to Teach Tech-Savvy Students." *Inside Higher Education.* Online at http://insidehighered.com/views/2008/03/20/Dinkins.

Earhart, Amy. 2011. "Back to the Land: Using the Digital to Create a Smallholding within the University." The Digital and the Human(ities) Symposium, Texas Institute for Literary and Textual Studies, University of Texas at Austin, March 12.

EDUCAUSE and the New Media Consortium. 2007a. *The Horizon Report.* Austin: New Media Consortium.

———. 2007b. *Learning Initiative.* Austin: New Media Consortium.

Faigley, Lester. 2001. "They Are Already In It." In *New Worlds, New Words: Exploring Pathways for Writing about and in Electronic Environments*, edited by John F. Baber and Dene Grigar, 417–20. Cresskill, NJ: Hampton Press.

———. 2003. "The Challenge of the Multimedia Essay." In *Composition Studies in the New Millennium: Rereading the Past, Rewriting the Future*, edited by Lynn Z. Bloom, Donald A. Daiker, and Edward M. White, 174–87. Carbondale: Southern Illinois University Press.

———. 2006. *Little Penguin Handbook*. Boston: Longman

Faigley, Lester, Diana George, Anna Palchik, and Cynthia Selfe. 2004. *Picturing Texts*. New York: Norton.

Flanders, Julia. 2011. "What's in the Black Box? Technology and Intellectual Responsibility in the Humanities." The Digital and the Human(ities) Symposium, Texas Institute for Literary and Textual Studies, University of Texas at Austin, March 12.

Freire, Paulo, and Donald Macedo. 1987. *Literacy: Reading the Word and the World*. Headley, MA: Bergin and Garvey.

French, Amanda. 2011. "Plied with Cheese No More: New Metaphors for the University in a Digital Future." The Digital and the Human(ities) Symposium, Texas Institute for Literary and Textual Studies, University of Texas at Austin, March 12.

Games, I. Alex. 2009. "Promoting Dialogic Writing through Videogame Character Dialog Design." Conference on College Composition and Communication, San Francisco.

Gardner, Howard. 1993. *Multiple Intelligences*. New York: Basic Books.

Gee, James Paul. 1999. *An Introduction to Discourse Analysis: Theory and Method*. New York: Routledge.

———. 2003. *What Video Games Have to Teach Us about Learning and Literacy*. New York: MacMillan, Palgrave.

Haynes, Cynthia, and Jan Rune Holmevik. 1998. *High Wired, On the Design, Use, and Theory of Educational MOOs*. Ann Arbor: University of Michigan Press.

Healy, Jane M. 1990. *Endangered Minds: Why Our Children Don't Think*. New York: Simon and Schuster, Touchstone, 1990.

Johnson, Steven. 2005. *Everything Bad Is Good for You: How Today's Popular Culture Is Actually Making Us Smarter*. New York: Riverhead Books.

Kernan, Alvin. 1990. *The Death of Literature*. New Haven: Yale University Press.

Kirriemuir, John K., and Angela McFarlane. 2003. "Use of Computer and Video Games in the Classroom." *Proceedings of the Level Up Digital Games Research Conference*. Utrecht, Netherlands: Universiteit Utrecht.

Kress, Gunther R. 2003. *Literacy in the New Media Age*. London: Routledge.

Krug, Steve. 2006. *Don't Make Me Think: A Common Sense Approach to Web Usability*. Berkeley: New Riders Publishing.

Lanham, Richard. 1993. *The Electronic Word: Democracy, Technology, and the Arts*. Chicago: University of Chicago Press.

Lemke, Jay. N.d. "Why Study Games? Notes toward a Basic Research Agenda for Education." Online at http://jaylemke.squarespace.com/.

Liu, Alan. 2011. "The University in the Digital Age: The Big Questions." Keynote address. The Digital and the Human(ities) Symposium, Texas Institute for Literary and Textual Studies, University of Texas at Austin, March 10. Online at http://tilts.dwrl.utexas.edu/content/media#Liu.

Matthewman, Sasha, Adrian Blight, and Chris Davies. 2004. "What Does Multimodality Mean for English? Creative Tensions in Teaching New Texts and New Literacies." *Education, Communication, and Information* 4 (1): 153–74.

Meyrowitz, Joshua. 1985. *No Sense of Place: The Impact of Electronic Media on Social Behavior.* New York: Oxford University Press.

Miller, Edward. 2007. "Gaming the System." *Newsweek*, April 16, p. 17.

Moberly, Kevin. 2008. "Composition, Computer Games, and the Absence of Writing." *Computers and Composition* 25: 284–99.

New London Group. 1996. "A Pedagogy of Multiliteracies: Designing Social Futures." *Harvard Educational Review* 66 (1): 60–92.

Orr, David. 1992. "Place and Pedagogy." *Ecological Literacy*. Albany: State University of New York Press.

Postman, Neil. 1985. *Amusing Ourselves to Death: Public Discourse in the Age of Show Business*. New York: Penguin.

Prensky, Marc. 2006. *Don't Bother Me Mom—I'm Learning!* St. Paul: Paragon House Publishers.

Rossetti Archives: The Complete Writings and Pictures of Dante Gabriel Rossetti. Online at http://www.rossettiarchive.org.

Rumsey, Abby Smith. 2011. "Response to Panelists. A Googleplex of Books: Changing Libraries and Archives." The Digital and the Human(ities) Symposium, Texas Institute for Literary and Textual Studies, University of Texas at Austin, March 12.

Sanders, Barry. 1995. *A Is for Ox: The Collapse of Literacy and the Rise of Violence in an Electronic Age*. New York: Viking Books.

Soukup, Charles. 2004. "Multimedia Performance in a Computer-Mediated Community: Communication as a Virtual Drama." *Journal of Computer-Mediated Communication* 9 (4). Online at http://jcmc.indiana.edu/vol9/issue4/.

Spiro, Lisa. 2011. "Good Is Useful?: Towards a Humanities Tools Portal." The Digital and the Human(ities) Symposium, Texas Institute for Literary and Textual Studies, University of Texas at Austin, March 12.

Steinkuehler, Constance A. 2005. "Cognition and Literacy in Massively Multiplayer Online Games." Online at http://website.education.wisc.edu/steinkuehler/papers/SteinkuehlerNEWLIT2005.pdf.

Stoll, Clifford. 1995. *Silicon Snake Oil: Second Thoughts on the Information Highway.* New York: Doubleday.

Tapscott, Don. 1999. *Growing Up Digital: The Rise of the Net Generation.* New York: McGraw-Hill.

Trapaghan, Tomoko. 2007. "Evaluation of a Pilot Use of Second Life in an English Course: 2006–2007." University of Texas at Austin Division of Instructional Innovation and Assessment. Online at http://www.cwrl.utexas.edu/~bump/TrapaghansecondLife.pdf.

Wysocki, Anne F. 2004. "Opening New Media to Writing: Openings and Justifications." In *Writing New Media: Theory and Applications for Expanding the Teaching of Composition*, edited by Anne F. Wysocki, Johndan Johnson-Eilola, Cynthia L. Selfe, and Geoffrey Sirc, 1–41. Logan: Utah State Press.

PART II

Multimodal Literacies and Pedagogical Choices

CHAPTER 6

Invention, Ethos, and New Media in the Rhetoric Classroom

The Storyboard as Exemplary Genre

Nathaniel I. Córdova

> If English is to remain relevant as the subject which provides access to participation in public forms of communication, as well as remaining capable of providing understandings of and the abilities to produce culturally valued texts, then an emphasis on language alone simply will no longer do. English will need to change.
>
> —Gunther Kress (1999, 67)

> For who does not know, except them, that the art of using letters is fixed and unchanging, so that we always use the same letters for the same purposes, but in the art of discourse the case is entirely the reverse?
>
> —Isocrates, *Against the Sophists*

What might it mean to be multimodally literate today, and what would it take to sustain such literacy in an age of rapidly changing cultural and technological innovation? To be sure, the question is not original, many have asked it before me, but it is a persistent question precisely because any possible answer, like the conditions that give rise to such rapid change, must perforce constantly evolve. In a very Darwinian sense then, *adaptation* is the key. To say, however, that culture and technology change rapidly and that we must adapt if we want to remain "literate," is as obvious as it is unhelpful and unclear. The question after all is not about change per se, but about agency: what can we do to cope effectively with not just evolutionary but revolutionary change that shapes the cultural, political, and economic life of a people? As educators, the corollary follows, how might we teach not just adaptation but a liberatory praxis that provides an inclusive, democratic, and existential framework for, in the words of the New London Group (NLG 1996), "designing social futures?"

In their ground-setting article in the *Harvard Educational Review*, the NLG (1996, 9) attempted an answer that centered on extending "the idea and scope of literacy pedagogy." Their article, "A Pedagogy of Multiliteracies: Designing Social Futures," (and the chapter by the same title in their subsequent book (NLG 2000) grounded such a multiliteracies pedagogy as a response to two main cultural trends captured succinctly in this formulation: "First we want to extend the idea and scope of literacy pedagogy to account for the context of our culturally and linguistically diverse and increasingly globalized societies; to account for the multifarious cultures that interrelate and the plurality of texts that circulate. Second, we argue that literacy pedagogy now must account for the burgeoning variety of text forms associated with information and multimedia technologies" (ibid., 61). This explanation rightfully connected rapidly changing global conditions, with the plurivocality we increasingly experience in our society, and the need to effectively negotiate the multiplicity of discourses and discursive forms that technological innovation generates. In particular, the New London Group's concern was with how new technological innovation and changing cultural life produced unprecedented waves of information that significantly affected people's working, public, and personal lifeworlds.

The NLG's effort found motivational impetus in how new information technologies reshape the kind of literacies needed to lead working, public, and personal lives, and how a refurbished educational practice ought to respond to such demands. These concerns are tightly integrated as new communication and information technologies, coupled with the rapid cultural change we've experienced as a result of such development, have generated an emerging digital culture in which traditional notions of text, reading, composition, and understanding are differently realized. Alongside such changes comes the realization that meaning making in our contemporary world is not a linear proposition, tied only to an alphabetical literacy, but that it is increasingly multimodal and interactive. In effect, the NLG called us to a pedagogy responsible for developing an "epistemology of pluralism" focused on the metaphor of design as "metalanguage of multiliteracies" (ibid., 73). Such a pedagogy of design was broken down into three main categories: available design, design, and the redesigned. In the vocabulary of discourse analysis this metalanguage of multiliteracies translates "available design" as the cultural and symbolic resources at our disposal, and the structures in place already constituted and available for our use, manipulation, and consumption. In a fortuitous turn of phrase, the NLG refers to available design as the "grammars of various semiotic systems" (ibid., 74). It follows from this that "design" accounts for the actual agentic capacity to construct and reappropriate such cultural resources, the weaving together of cultural texts. The redesigned thus becomes the cultural outcome of such creative design processes (ibid., 76).

The NLG's efforts, not unlike many other poststructuralist or postmodern interventions that have followed, assume what Norman Denzin (1995) has called the three crises facing a contemporary world: a crisis of representation, legitimation, and praxis. While Denzin focused on the inability, given our lack of representational fidelity, to legitimate particular narratives, and thus to choose particular courses of action (praxis), the NLG's vocabulary focused on designing a critical pedagogy practice that sought to foster design as the ability to formulate and reformulate interventions within the malleable cultural symbolic resources at our disposal. Embedded within this assumption is not just a deep recognition of the multimodal nature of meaning making, but of what Manuel Castells (2000, 469) reports as the morphological changes to our society brought about by new technological innovation, in particular by a networking logic that gives "pre-eminence" to "social morphology over social action": "dominant functions and processes in the information age are increasingly organised around networks. Networks constitute the new social morphology of our societies and the diffusion of networking logic substantially modifies the operation and outcomes in the processes of production, experience, power and culture. While the networking form of social organization has existed in other times and spaces, the new information technology paradigm provides the basis for its pervasive expansion throughout the entire social structure." Hence, the NLG recognized that information technologies, by giving centrality to the networking logic of global connectedness, change flows of power and alter the way in which we organize our working, public, and personal lives. The challenge, they noted, was to "make space available so that different lifeworlds can flourish; to create spaces for community life where local and specific meanings can be made" (NLG 1996, 70). These are indeed questions that go to the core of what can be represented, how particular narratives obtain legitimation, and how we might choose particular courses of action.

Among these considerations, perhaps an evident, if not explicit, assumption in the NLG's foundational essay is that meaning making has always been a rhetorical endeavor. In fact, with a few changes their initial essay can be profitably read as a call to rhetorical arms, to a pedagogical practice that recognizes the significance of rhetoric and a rhetorical hermeneutics as foundational for critical citizenship and democratic participatory culture. What's more, the attitude that surrounds the effort can be read as an attempt to "understand the transformations in perspectives that the symbolic action of text initiates," where such texts are not merely alphabetical and unmediated, but instead are quite frequently the result of digital encounters, the outcomes of new media processes (Stillar 1998, 11). It is then rather unfortunate that the NLG's founding essay neglected careful parsing of those rhetorical considerations that animate the design process as a negotiation of cultural agency—a task I take up in this chapter.

A reengagement with rhetoric can help us extend our understanding of the multimodal nature of meaning making and strengthen our development of a critical pedagogy and multimodal literacy. I have organized the chapter by framing it around three main interrelated themes:

1. the challenge that new media and technological innovation pose for notions of ethos, and suggesting that a reengagement with an understanding of ethos as dwelling place (Hyde 2004) can enhance a pedagogy of multiliteracies disposed toward the praxis of designing liberatory social futures. This reinvigorated notion of ethos is of central relevance to the NLG's vision of enhancing the working, personal, and public lives—the lifeworlds—of people;
2. proposing a rhetorical model that gives texture to a pedagogy of multiliteracies by focusing on a set of rhetorical relationships hitherto obscured but that animate the NLG's understanding of design as negotiation of cultural agency. These relationships are captured in the terms fragmentation, articulation, circulation, convergence, and interface; and
3. briefly describing a storyboard assignment as a potential way to enhance students' understanding of multimodality.

This chapter then extends more than challenges any of the NLG's findings, by reasserting the significance of the notion of ethos that is often lost in the conversation about new media and multimodal literacies, and by suggesting a rhetorical framework that cuts across ways of making meaning within student work.

"MAKING SPACE AVAILABLE": ETHOS AS DWELLING PLACE

For all their commitment to "make space available so that different lifeworlds can flourish; to create spaces for community life where local and specific meanings can be made," the NLG does not devote explicit attention to the philosophical issues that underpin such claims to human existence. I'm thinking in particular of how such claims to human existence, lifeworlds, and being with others, open up the domain of responsibility and thus ethics. Avidly discussing civic space, citizenship, membership in multiple lifeworlds, the increased texture of identity, and recognition of the other, the NLG relegates exploration of the starting points of such human existence, its ontology, to the margins. Such treatment is unfortunate because, as Heidegger (1996, 51) reminds us, determinations about how we ought to live follow from questions concerning who we are. Moreover, such reflections naturally lead us to the notion of dwelling, or to borrow the NLG's language, of the spaces that not only we inhabit but can craft together. In short, an emergent pedagogy of multiliteracies stands to be enhanced by a direct engagement with the notion of ethos as dwelling place, with the ethics of dwelling.

Explicit attention to matters of human existence and lifeworlds would require that we reconsider the notion of ethos as the essential character of human being-in-the-world. This view of ethos, however, is not the traditional understanding of the concept. In the rhetorical tradition, for example, ethos has customarily been understood as "credibility" and thus moral character or ethics, which along with logos and pathos form Aristotle's three artistic proofs (*pistis*) as central components to argumentation. As Michael Hyde (2004, xiii) notes in *The Ethos of Rhetoric*, however, ethos has a primordial meaning as dwelling place, different from its familiar use by rhetoricians: "Abiding by this more 'primordial' meaning of the term, one can understand the phrase 'the ethos of rhetoric' to refer to the way discourse is used to transform space and time into 'dwelling places' (ethos; pl. ethea) where people can deliberate about and 'know together' (con-scientia) some matter of interest. Such dwelling places define the grounds, the abodes or habitats, where a person's ethics and moral character take form and develop." This primordial meaning, Hyde reminds us, gives presence to the architectonic nature of rhetoric, which helps us understand it best as art of invention, or the *design* of dwelling spaces and landscapes of being with others: "the ethos of rhetoric . . . mark out the boundaries and domains of thought that, depending on how their specific discourses are designed and arranged, may be particularly inviting and moving for some audience" (ibid., xiii). Hyde further locates this understanding of ethos in Heidegger's consideration of Aristotle's *Rhetoric* as the 'the first systematic hermeneutic of the everydayness of Being with one another" (ibid., xvii; Heidegger 1962, 178).

As I noted earlier, it was indeed fortuitous that the NLG relies on the notion of design to refer, albeit not explicitly, to a rhetorical hermeneutics, to the understanding of the formative power of public discourse to shape our lives, and thus our lifeworlds. A pedagogy of multiliteracies in its recognition of the multimodal ways of meaning making perforce understands the classroom as a collaborative space that seeks to transform the way in which participants dwell and construct their dwelling in their working, personal, and public lives. This is the prevailing sense of the NLG's desire to change the present and future by redefining our vision for work, citizenship, and lifeworlds. The pedagogical process envisioned thus is one that "transforms the spatial and temporal orientation of an audience, its way of being situated or placed in relationship to things and others" (NLG 1996, xviii). It follows that a multimodal literacy must attend to the rhetorical quite explicitly as the architectonic art through which ethos is understood as revealing the "open region in which [humans] dwell" and thus from which he or she launches such transformative ethical projects (Heidegger 1977a, 233). This "re-cognition" of ethos gives primacy to the multiple layered activities of building and cultivating the ontological relationships essential to designing social futures.

As it attends to technological innovation and emergent forms of establishing connectivity, a multimodal literacy needs to keep in mind that it must not understand technology and new media as the effective use of computational machinery. Rather, as Japanese philosopher Kiyoshi Miki noted, technology mediates the confrontation between "the active subject and the environment" (Miki 1968, 202). Yoko Arisaka reminds us that already in the 1940s Miki conceptualized technology not as the "sophisticated manipulation of tools," but as a form of action. As a result, Miki understood the power of technology as its "ability to make our imagination concrete" (Arisaka 2001). Heidegger points to the same relationship in two ways. First, in his famous essay "The Question Concerning

Technology," Heidegger (1977b) challenges the traditional and everyday understanding of technology as instrumentality, a mechanism for getting things done. In place of such an understanding, he espouses a renewed examination of the ancient Greek concept *techne* as a related precursor to the word "technology." In this formulation "technology" ought to be understood in light of the concept of *techne* as creative bringing-forth, a disclosing or revealing. For Heidegger, then, the essence of technology properly understood, lies with *poiesis* (ibid., 295). In his account, *techne* or technology refers to both the doing and the artistic impetus or creative act of imagination, what Miki referred to as the "ability to make our imagination concrete." At this juncture, the NLG's fortuitous choice of the notion of design for this creative process becomes even more readily apparent.

Second, Heidegger (1971, 146) also reminds us of this relationship with his distinction between building, a technical endeavor, and dwelling: "These buildings house man. He inhabits them and yet does not dwell in them, when to dwell means merely that we take shelter in them . . . do the houses in themselves hold any guarantee that dwelling occurs in them?" This is of critical importance because it has been precisely that conception of literacy as technical mastery of skills necessary to operate software or equipment that renders ethos and the relationships with others secondary to the cult of technical expertise, and to a narrow circumference as moral injunctions about the uses and abuses of technology.

A RHETORICAL FRAMEWORK FOR MULTIMODAL LITERACY

The challenges to our understanding of ethos as the "open region of the abode" wherein we design, build, and sustain our lives together, stem from a network culture that gives "pre-eminence" to "social morphology over social action" (Castells 2000, 469). According to Castells, such networking logic suffuses global connectedness by expanding to take over all forms of associational and economic life, and is a distinctive characteristic of the information economy mode that he calls the "technical-economic paradigm." The resulting "informationalism" is "the attribute of a specific form of social organization in which information generation, processing and transmission become the fundamental resources of productivity and power" (ibid., 21). The pervasive effects of that informationalism indeed require a new multiliteracies pedagogy, one that challenges the gravitational pull that the multimedia industry, as the driving engine of this information and communication industry, exerts toward the consumption of technical wizardry, the spectacular, and the dispersal of the critical faculties of the subject to establish nourishing human relationships. An initial step in cultivating rhetorical sensibility and multimodal literacy lies with emphasis on how, "in this society, individuals consume a world fabricated by others rather than producing one of their own" (Best and Kellner 1999, 131). A reaffirmation of rhetoric as architectonic practice of lifeworlds emphasizes the centrality of ethos as dwelling terrain from which a liberatory praxis of design can be launched, one "crucial for reading Available Designs and for Designing social futures" (NLG 1996, 81).

If one aspect of reaffirming a rhetorical framework for a multimodal literacy is to reinstitute ethos as dwelling as foundational for a liberatory multiliteracies pedagogy, another is to focus on salient elements that characterize contemporary semiotic flows. If, as Gunther Kress (2000, 153) tells us, "theories of language will simply not serve to explain the other semiotic modes," we must turn to an account "which deals adequately with the processes of integration/composition of the various modes in these texts: both in production/making and in consumption/reading." Kress (ibid., 154) calls for an adequate theory that can account for the "description both of the specific characteristics of a particular mode and of its more general semiotic properties which allow it to be related plausibly to other semiotic modes." Furthermore, a deficit in contemporary theories of semiosis that renders them unable to account for the semiotic changes that characterize our current mode of existence are the result of those explanations' reliance on supposedly stable systems of signification rather than on "remaking and transformation" (ibid., 154). Kress tell us that dominant theories of semiosis do not help us make sense of the changing landscape we face. Kress's argument can be fruitfully connected to both Yoko Arisaka's and Andrew Feenberg's arguments about the pressing need for a more robust critical theory of technology that can account for "the real changes technology makes in material conditions and its long-term impact, as these are clearly existential manifestations of our cognitive grasp of the world" (Arisaka 2001, 155; Feenberg 1999).

As this suggests, the prospects for a strong multimodal literacy practice rests with the adoption of a theory that focuses on invention, is highly contextual, is deeply concerned with the hybridity of cultural and the intertextuality of semiotic or symbolic flows, and is explicitly self-conscious about its own contingencies. This theory moves away "from explaining interpretation in terms of isolated readers and isolated texts to discussing rhetorical exchanges among interpreters embedded in discursive and other social practices at specific historical moments" (Mailloux 1989, 134). As I have already asserted, we are looking at a rhetorical hermeneutics, a critical rhetoric (McKerrow 1989, 1993) savvy to the changing conditions of the technological juggernaut our global society has become. Such a rhetoric, unlike its traditional conceptualization as an art of representation, is conceived as a mode of cultural production and reproduction. Most important, such a theory is highly provisional, operating "on the level of performance rather than on the level of a universally applicable theory" (Haskins 2003).

Finally, the point is to insist on a theory or theories that can respond not just to changing conditions, but that recognize, as Hyde (2004, xxi) explains, that "we are creatures who dwell on this earth and who are thereby destined to hear and answer a call that, among other things, requires a capacity for practicing the art of rhetoric. The ontological structure of existence is such that we must learn to dwell rhetorically. This artful way of being, as Richard McKeon reminds us, is 'architectonic.' . . . The call of human being, of conscience, calls on us to be rhetorical architects whose symbolic constructions both create and invite others into a place where they can dwell." Developing or extending such a theory is beyond the scope of this chapter. Moreover, along with Bill Cope and Mary Kalantzis (2000, 211), I believe that multimodal meaning is truly a sensitivity to various modes of meaning making working together. No one theory will contain the explanatory power to deal with all that is required. With that in mind, I offer five dimensions that underscore what has already been said, and that are indicative of the kinds of relationships a multimodal, or multiliteracies, pedagogy might ask itself in order to be truly responsive to the needs specified above.

A multimodal literacy pedagogy should focus on the formative power of public discourse—in particular, five relations that exemplify the way in which texts circulate, the malleability of symbolic resources, and the ways in which technological relations shape the emergence, articulation, circulation, and connectivity of multimodal texts. I refer to these relations as: (1) fragmentation, (2) articulation, (3) circulation, (4) convergence, and (5) interface. Given limitations on length and scope of this chapter, I only provide a brief sketch of each element.

Fragmentation and Modularity

Texts are multimodal in nature, and they are composed of various pieces that have been woven together that in turn mask that process. One of the illusions of texts is that they give the appearance of wholeness, of unitary origin, of not being a pastiche of cultural and symbolic resources. Fragmentation reminds us that texts are not solidly iconic but are woven together of various fragments, pieces, ideas, and other texts themselves. As a result, texts can travel in fragments, dissected, partitioned, and mediated, only to be put together as particular cultural logics and mediations might dictate. Frequently, parts of a text take lives of their own ostensibly separate from the conditions of its production (McGee 1990). Reminiscent of memes, these fragments can be picked up and connected to others, and thus texts can be said to engage in a kind of promiscuous intertextuality. Hence it is here that a multimodal literacy can begin by exploring the nature of texts, alphabetical or multimodal, as constructs following particular articulatory logics. Yet another related notion here is that of mobility. Not only are texts increasingly mobile, so are we, and thus mobility and its continued decentering of texts and subjects reaffirms the increased fragmentation of everyday life and calls us to examine how we bring these pieces together.

Articulation

The notion of articulation hearkens back to the work of Ernesto Laclau and Chantal Mouffe (1985) in *Hegemony and Socialist Strategy*, where they describe how dominant structures and political struggles are best viewed not as emerging out of historical necessity but out of hegemonic articulations that help us frame those same struggles. Articulation is a process by which different discursive elements or fragments are combined to form a new element that can in turn gain social primacy. Multimodal meaning making is inherently a process of various articulations, the "non-necessary connections of different elements that, when connected in a particular way, form a specific unity" (Slack 1989, 331). These elements are never permanent but can obtain partial fixity. In fact, it is the aim of articulatory logics to stabilize meaning making to establish the basis for a social order that obtains dominance (hegemony).

Thus articulatory logic is exactly what lies behind the NLG's notion of a pedagogy of design: social actors articulate and rearticulate social elements and symbolic resources to create identity and meaning, where a social actor is "any element which bends space around itself, makes other elements dependent upon itself and translate their will into a language of its own" (Slack and Wise 2002, 489). The effect of introducing the concept of social actors is that it emphasizes the complexity and rich texture of the process of meaning making, as it is part of discursive processes larger than single individuals. In effect, then, the critical discernment of articulatory logics ought to be an integral part of a multimodal literacy as a pedagogy of design.

Circulation and Dissemination

The notions of fragmentation and articulation are tightly connected to the notion of circulation in that much of the power of discursive elements or fragments, of texts, resides in the way in which they enter, pass, and travel through a circuit, a discursive economy, and are put together with such circulatory potential, and mobility, in mind. The process of articulation does not only create texts but places them within a discursive economy, within a network flow. As Kenneth Rufo (2006) artfully reminds us, to understand the value of texts, we must look beyond "particular texts in and of themselves," or their emergence. Rather, "what matters increasingly is the circulation of the texts, the manner in which a text is broken into fragments (and, in fact, written for the express purpose of controlling which fragments will achieve the highest circulation), and the spin with which these fragments will be disseminated/circulated" (ibid., blog post).

Texts are cultural forms that serve as carriers of cultural meaning, but as Dilip Gaonkar and Elizabeth Povinelli (2003, 387) note when speaking about technologies of circulation, the "dynamics of national, transnational, and subnational public life cannot be truly engaged without understanding flows and forms as integrally related." Gaonkar and Povinelli (ibid., 388) highlight the work of Benjamin Lee and Edward LiPuma (2002) on cultures of circulation, as the "enabling matrix within which social forms, both textual and topical, emerge and are recognizable when they emerge." Rather than reading these elements of fragmentation, articulation, and circulation on their own as discrete steps in an assembly-line model of discursive production, a multimodal literacy must strive to attend to the discursive economy that establishes the context not just for meaning making but for cultural intelligibility.

Convergence

Convergence, while particularly difficult to parse as a concept given its multiplicity of meanings across various domains, points to the coming together, the fusion of various technologies of dissemination, technical means, and media forms into an increasingly seamless web of information and culture. Calling convergence "a new paradigm for understanding media change," Henry Jenkins (2006, 2), in his recent book *Convergence Culture*, posits convergence as the site "where old and new media collide, where grassroots and corporate media intersect, where the power of the media producer and the power of the media consumer interact in unpredictable ways." Media convergence, according to Jenkins (ibid., 26), "enables communal rather than individualistic modes of reception." In other words, convergence is the coming together of the demands of a dynamic technical-information mode, with the demands of cultural forms for dissemination.

At the same time, we can think of convergence through the lens of the postcolonial concept of hybridity. Although also a disputed term, "hybridity" refers to "the creation of new transcultural forms within the contact zone produced by colonization" (Ashcroft, Griffiths, and Tiffin 2003, 118). Quite transparently, within the contact zone of globally mediated cultural relations new transcultural forms that seek to sustain the dominant status of particular configurations and flows of power are generated. In terms related to composition, this hybridity heralds the significance of new multimodal genres such as digital storytelling. In short, the remediating power of convergence has facilitated the emergence of multimodal genres such as mash-ups, digital storytelling, and transmedia narratives. A potential new genre lies with opportunities to reflect on our digital lifestream, our appearances and interventions in various social networks such as Twitter, Facebook, MySpace, Delicious, LinkedIn, and others. Such reflection highlights not just our presence but self-theorizes about our digital selves beyond the confines of individual multimodal activity and pushes us to understand multimodality as social practice.

A marked difference, however, is that while colonial or postcolonial hybridity emerges out of, and relishes, difference, convergence as the creation of new transcultural forms strives toward smooth cultural integration. A telling example of this convergence mode is Apple's iPhone —ostensibly a multimodal device that facilitates consumer personal and professional lives, yet one that is designed to level hybridity for the smooth cultural integration, the convergence, and thus the rearticulation of the basis for the hegemony of the technical-economic paradigm of which it is a part. A multimodal literacy perforce looks at processes of convergence in the overall communication environment of globalized societies and ought to keep a critical eye on the potential bureaucratization of emerging multimodal genres.

Interface

If convergence smoothes out and levels the hybridity that accompanies cultural and linguistic diversity, and the deep plurality of text forms in circulation, it does so increasingly and specifically through the logic of the interface. The convergence of multiple diverse forms must take place within a zone or terrain that facilitates the transmission and reconciliation of cultural messages. Such reconciliation, however, carries its own dangers since, as a non-neutral mechanism, any encoding process shapes the way the message is transmitted, disseminated, and understood. Because most such transformations take place through the computer, interfaces "shape how the computer users conceives the computer itself" and "determines how users think of any media object accessed via a computer" (Manovich 2001, 64). The interface is a virtual site where people engage in the process of design within the distinct models of the mediated world. The key move is the transformation of the computer from tool to medium. Consequently, much more than a layer of interaction, interfaces constitute the way in which culture and information technology converge to facilitate the "plugging in" of people into culture itself: "we are no longer interfacing to a computer but to culture encoded in digital form" (ibid., 70). The distributed systems of global capitalism that drive the information economy need cosmopolitan cultural forms and interfaces that reduce cultural dissonance and make recognizable its knowledge and information consumption demands.

As I noted at the outset of the chapter, these five dimensions do not aim for hegemony as sole model nor comprehensive theory for a liberatory multimodal literacy praxis. These dimensions are more properly understood as rhetorical considerations that animate NLG's design process as understanding of cultural agency. What's more, these dimensions need to be supplemented with careful examination of critical understandings of the power of mobility, multimodal interaction, and individual and social creative expression. In particular, a critical examination of how mobility and corollary practices of location-aware technologies, and augmented reality, generate new hybrid storyspaces, shape interactivity with multimodal texts and mobile/displaced subjects. This facilitates the emergence of new multimodal genres and a logic of connectivity that works powerfully in tandem with the constitutive logics we've come to understand. These five dimensions, however, can facilitate the understanding of both the location of rhetorical power in our increasingly mediated global societies and the points of resistance that a multiliteracies pedagogy seeks to overcome. It remains for educators the practical task of developing critical engagements that can bring to life these dimensions.

THE MODIFIED STORYBOARD AS EXEMPLAR

Given the preceding understanding, new assignments and critical work are needed to address the literacy demands posed in "the context of the ever more critical factors of local diversity and global connectedness" (Cope and Kalantzis 2000, 3). Although by now we in the academy have made significant incursions into the realm of technology and new media, perhaps even receiving specialized training and requiring special assignments from students, we must admit that the primary exploratory experience for university students is that of writing. Writing, and the adjoining conversations regarding writing across the curriculum, as well as how to teach writing, is indeed the dominant way through which we teach students how to use their voice, how to develop and craft cogent arguments. In my own field of rhetoric, where courses in visual rhetoric are few and far between, the moniker "visual rhetoric" itself reveals a kind of incredulity about the possibility of rhetoric being other than primarily a logocentric pursuit. The public speaking courses offered in many departments of speech communication, or communication studies, and the rhetoric-based composition curriculum of many English departments across the nation further expose the centrality of alphabetical linear and propositional argument as the primary tool of discovery.

To be fair, many educators have explored and continue to explore alternative pedagogies for composition. From visual brainstorming, outlining, note cards, and conceptual mapping, various technologies and approaches have proven helpful in rendering composition a multidimensional, and nonlinear process. All such approaches point to the growing realization that increasingly our students' experience of invention and composition is multifaceted and processual, and that the focus on the verbal as a privileged way to access or discover the contents of consciousness has shifted. As the NLG's original essay makes clear, however, we need a shift to multimedia and the newer understandings of literacy that it makes possible in our changing global and technological climate. An example of just such an important modification is Gregory Ulmer and Talan Memmott's (2000, online interview) refashioning of the term "literacy" itself into "electracy" or the kind of literacy most appropriate for the nonprint world and a term "to give a name to the apparatus of the emerging digital epoch." The increasing reliance on digital storytelling assignments, including Ulmer's own "Mystory" form, reveals a desire to craft a unique learning experience that in its use of multimedia resources also aims for a reconceptualization, a shift in consciousness of what it means to be literate and engage in composition as design of meaningful and evocative communication.

That consciousness shift encompasses far more than our understanding of how to write cogent arguments and reveals seismic changes in the nature of associational life and communication in our society. A multimodal literacy would do well to explore the nontraditional inventional resources of new media and new forms of cultural production, keeping in mind that inventional resources, as meaning-making resources, always extend well beyond the capabilities provided with multimedia technologies. Another way of saying this is that, approaches to multimodal literacy must take into account that such literacy is not about simply understanding but about design as performance and that a primary consideration for educators ought to be the level of awareness a student might have of his or her own performative relationship to technology. Technological innovation shapes our performance of life as well as of learning. In my own practice I have found that a modified storyboard assignment is particularly helpful in instilling recognition of a "grammar" of design, of the importance of fragmentation, articulation, circulation, convergence, and interface, and of literacy as an interpretive performance in the process of meaning making, of cultural production.

A modified storyboard assignment, as a precursor to a digital storytelling project, requires that students craft a comprehensive visual representation of a narrative. Although traditionally put together by hand, students nowadays rely on Microsoft PowerPoint or other computer software to organize their storyboards. I have found the dedicated storyboard software Storyboard Quick (Power Production Software, Inc.) a wonderful resource for a storyboard assignment. Storyboard Quick provides a simple "stage" interface and multiple resource palettes from which students can select characters, backgrounds, objects, and other artifacts and place them onto the stage as they craft scenes (fig. 6.1). These resources can then be modified and manipulated so that the created scene matches the narrative flow. The benefit of dedicated software that gives presence to the visual is the opportunity for students to quite literally visualize narrative and the process of narrative emplotment instead of thinking about it in a linear and propositional fashion. Students can also import their own creations or photographs as a way to further personalize their storyboards.

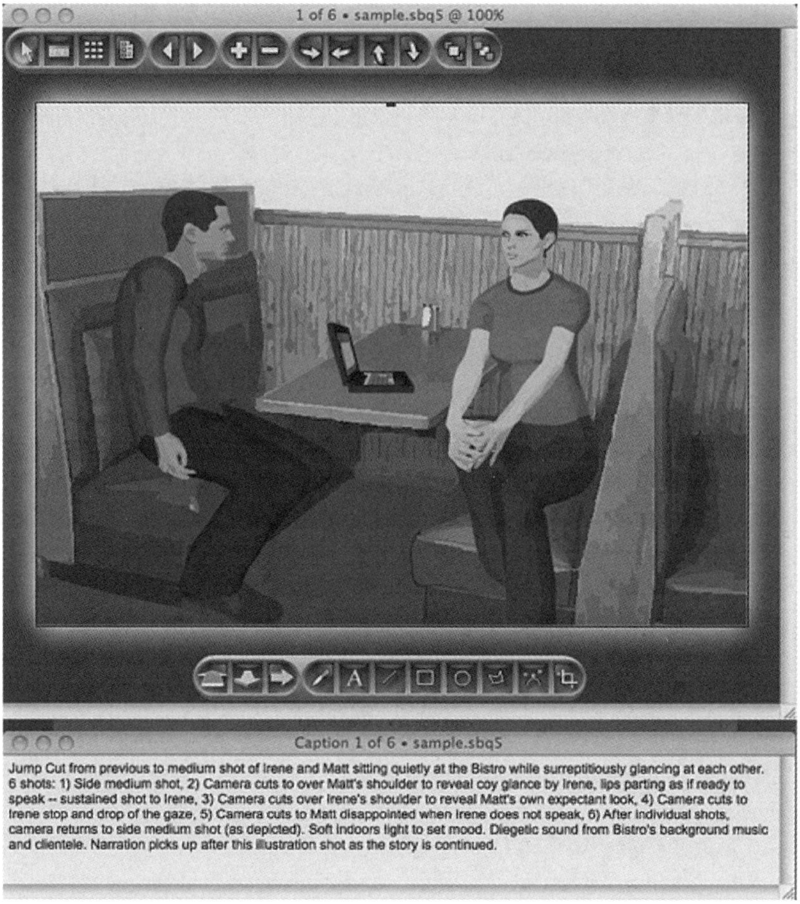
1 of 6 • sample.sbq5 @ 100%
A
Caption 1 of 6 • sample.sbq5
Jump Cut from previous to medium shot of Irene and Matt sitting quietly at the Bistro while surreptitiously glancing at each other. 6 shots: 1) Side medium shot, 2) Camera cuts to over Matt's shoulder to reveal coy glance by Irene, lips parting as if ready to speak -- sustained shot to Irene, 3) Camera cuts over Irene's shoulder to reveal Matt's own expectant look, 4) Camera cuts to Irene stop and drop of the gaze, 5) Camera cuts to Matt disappointed when Irene does not speak, 6) After individual shots, camera returns to side medium shot (as depicted). Soft indoors light to set mood. Diegetic sound from Bistro's background music and clientele. Narration picks up after this illustration shot as the story is continued.

FIGURE 6.1. *Storyboard Quick.*

A distinct focus on the storyboard, as part of a digital storytelling project, features the process of cultural production, helps students visualize narrative, reinforces the fragmentary nature of texts, and the importance of the articulations drawn through every frame of their project. Moreover, the storyboard, as precursor to a unitary product to be made ready for circulation, reminds the student of the project's placement in a flow of cultural products. Including a clear component for its dissemination through other mediums and media forms emphasizes the importance of understanding convergence, and how others will interact and thus interface, with their product. A collaborative storyboard project gives prominence to the dialectical and dialogical nature of invention and ethos. Discourse analyst Glenn F. Stillar (1998, 5) has made this point well when he notes that discoursal practice, "peers, Janus-headed, at two dynamic and ever-evolving horizons: one way, toward the other actual discourses and discourse conventions it relies on for relevance; the other way, toward the multiple, only semi-stable systems of resources it draws on to construct relevance." A noteworthy outcome of this recognition of the dialectical and dialogic nature of cultural production is the resurgence of the importance of situation as standpoint "that limits the possibility of vision," a horizon of interpretation (Gadamer 1989, 301–2). The benefit of giving stark presence to situation as horizon of interpretation is the challenge it presents to informationalist attempts to disperse the critical faculties of the student. To be most effective, however, the storyboard assignment emphasizes visuality and multimodality over an alphabetical text logic. This approach must balance both the individual aspects of composition, with the supra-individual totality that multimodality and emerging genres bring forth as social practices, in short, with an understanding of literacy as a stylized performance.

Lest we assume that a storyboard assignment or a multimodal literacy approach is free from snags and frustrations, I hasten to add that the "increasing multiplicity and integration of significant modes of meaning-making" (NLG 1996, 64) that such a multimodal perspective brings present considerable challenges. Taking seriously the notions that our students inhabit multiple lifeworlds and are "members of multiple and overlapping communities" demands considerable reflection on how to take such differences into consideration when crafting critical assessment rubrics. In addition, multimodal complexity means far more coaching time in and out of the classroom, a variety of equipment, and sample projects for students to explore. A multimodal literacy perspective means that we must take seriously questions that traditionally have not been part and parcel of instruction in composition. For example, the question of production value looms large with digital storytelling projects, and a balance between the freedom of exploration and final products that reveal care and understanding is imperative. Aside from the technical challenges associated with these projects, if we want to live up to the interdisciplinary nature of a multimodal literacy, we must enrich ourselves and our classrooms with discourses and concepts that help us integrate such multiple perspectives. Quite often those discourses and concepts might originate away from our own intellectual and disciplinary domains. Finally, a multimodal literacy that takes seriously the NLG's call for a pedagogy of design must attend to the importance of our students recognizing their role as critical producers, and performers, of cultural content. Hence, assignments are best when they do not remain confined to the classroom or the technological tools at our disposal but when students fully assume the role of critical participants in their community.

Storyboarding gives presence to the process of invention itself and thus can elucidate a critical understanding of composition. Much like a literacy narrative, a storyboard assignment can enhance reflection on how technological innovation and emergent meaning-making practices shape our interaction with others. It can also open doors for exploration of the significance of the ubiquity of technology and the roles it might play, not as sophisticated tool, but increasingly as limited social actor in its own right (see the earlier definition of social actor). As such, storyboards and other such assignments, as ways to explore multimodal literacy, seem to resonate with Grant Kien's (2009) notion of a "technography," a way to evince human meaning-making activity within an increasingly ubiquitous technological context.

The ideal and promise of a multiliteracies pedagogy rests with a refurbished and reinvigorated engagement with a semiotic landscape that is constantly evolving in fundamental ways. The changes we are experiencing do not remain solely in a single realm but cut across economic, political, cultural, and social domains. Hence such a pedagogical practice aims to make the classroom not a tool of traditional power but an incubator of a multimodal literacy that will open up the possibilities of access and critical engagement in the design of liberatory social futures. It has been my contention that the efforts of multimodal literacy ought to refocus on what the NLG and other scholars in this field have not explicitly articulated—the role of rhetoric as crucial to the engagement with contemporary historical realities. In particular, I have suggested the adoption of the concept of ethos as dwelling place as a way to underwrite the philosophical basis of the effort to "make space available so that different lifeworlds can flourish." It is in this spirit that I proposed the rhetorical framework that, albeit limited, stresses five dimensions that push us further in exploring the kind of questions a multimodal literacy needs to ask as essential to the NLG's notion of design.

On the whole, the changes brought about by the "burgeoning variety of text forms associated with information and multimedia technologies" in a networked culture, not to mention the cultural and linguistic diversity present in a global society, are best understood as highlighting the essential formative character of human relationship (NLG 1996, 61). Citing Leslie Paul Thiele's notion that a proper abode for humans cannot be constructed except as a set of relationships, Nicholas Dungey (2007, 240) notes, in his essay "The Ethics and Politics of Dwelling," that "because the character of human being-in-the-world is nothing other than the webbing of its social and cultural relations, the building of things must be directed in light of the cultivation of these essential relationships." It is my strong contention that rhetoric has always been the art of inventing, constructing, and cultivating these essential human relationships of dwelling. In my chapter opening I pondered what it might mean to be multimodally literate today, and what it might take to sustain such a state given rapidly changing cultural conditions. A multimodal literacy practice approximates an answer when it keeps at its center the task of enhancing the construction, cultivation, and maintenance of such human relations of dwelling in a multimodal world.

REFERENCES

Arisaka, Yoko. 2001. "Women Carrying Water: At the Crossroads of Technology and Critical Theory." In *New Critical Theory: Essays on Liberation*, edited by Jeffrey Paris and William S. Wilkinson, 155–71. New York: Rowman and Littlefield.

Ashcroft, Bill, Gareth Griffiths, and Helen Tiffin. 2003. *Post-Colonial Studies: The Key Concepts*. London: Routledge.

Best, Steven, and Douglas Kellner. 1999. "Debord, Cybersituations, and the Interactive Spectacle." *Substance* 28 (3): 129–56.

Castells, Manuel. 2000. *The Rise of the Network Society*. Oxford: Blackwell Publishers.

Denzin, Norman. 1995. "Lessons James Joyce Teaches Us." In *Postmodern Representations: Truth, Power, and Mimesis in the Human Sciences and Public Culture*, edited by Richard Harvey and Ed Brown, 38–59 . Champaign: University of Illinois Press.

Dungey, Nicholas. 2007. "The Ethics and Politics of Dwelling." *Polity* 39 (2): 234–58.

Feenberg, Andrew. 1999. *Questioning Technology*. New York: Routledge.

Gadamer, Hans Georg. 1989. *Truth and Method*. Translated by Joel Weinsheimer and Donald G. Marshall. New York: Crossroad.

Gaonkar, Dilip P., and Elizabeth Povinelli. 2003. "Technologies of Public Forms: Circulation, Transfiguration, Recognition." *Public Culture* 15 (3): 385–97.

Haskins, Ekaterina V. 2003. "Embracing the Superficial: Michael Calvin McGee, Rhetoric, and the Postmodern Condition." *American Communication Journal*

6 (4). Online at http://www.acjournal.org/holdings/vol6/iss4/mcmcgee/haskins.htm.

Heidegger, Martin. 1962. *Being and Time.* Translated by John Macquarrie and Edward Robinson. New York: Harper and Row.

———. 1971. "Building, Dwelling, Thinking." *Poetry, Language, Thought.* Translated by A. Hofstadter. New York: Harper Row.

———. 1977a. "Letter on Humanism." In *Basic Writings.* Translated by David Farrell Krell. San Francisco: Harper Collins.

———. 1977b. "The Question Concerning Technology." In *Basic Writings.* Translated by David Farrell Krell. San Francisco: Harper Collins.

———. 1996. *Being and Time.* Translated by Joan Stambaugh. Albany: State University of New York Press.

Hyde, Michael, ed. 2004. *The Ethos of Rhetoric.* Columbia: University of South Carolina Press.

Jenkins, Henry. 2006. *Convergence Culture.* New York: New York University Press.

Kien, Grant. 2009. *Global Technography: Ethnography in the Age of Mobility.* New York: Peter Lang Publishing.

Kress, Gunther. 1999. "'English' at the Crossroads: Rethinking Curricula of Communication in the Context of the Turn to the Visual." *Passions, Pedagogies, and Twenty-First Century Technologies*, edited by Gail E. Hawisher and Cynthia L. Selfe, 66–88. Logan: Utah State University Press.

———. 2000. "Design and Transformation: New Theories of Meaning." In *Multiliteracies: Literacy Learning and the Design of Social Futures*, edited by Bill Cope and Mary Kalantzis, 149–58. London: Routledge.

Laclau, Ernesto, and Chantal Mouffe. 1985. *Hegemony and Socialist Strategy: Towards a Radical Democratic Politics.* London: Verso.

Lee, Benjamin, and Edward LiPuma. 2002. "Cultures of Circulation: The Imaginations of Modernity." *Public Culture* 14 (1): 191–213.

Mailloux, Steven. 1989. *Rhetorical Power.* Ithaca: Cornell University Press.

Manovich, Lev. 2001. *The Language of New Media.* Cambridge: Massachusetts Institute of Technology Press.

McGee, Michael Calvin 1990. "Text, Context, and Fragmentation of Contemporary Culture." *Western Journal of Speech Communication* 53 (3): 274–89.

McKerrow, Raymie E. 1989. "Critical Rhetoric: Theory and Praxis." *Communication Monographs* 56: 91–111.

———. 1993. "Critical Rhetoric and the Possibility of the Subject." In *The Critical Turn: Rhetoric and Philosophy in Postmodern Discourse*, edited by I. Angus and L. Langsdorf, 51–67. Carbondale: Southern Illinois University Press.

Miki, Kiyoshi. 1968. *Miki Kiyoshi Zenshu* [Collected Works of Kiyoshi Miki]. Volume 7. Tokyo: Iwanami Shoten.

New London Group (NLG). 1996. "A Pedagogy of Multiliteracies: Designing Social Futures." *Harvard Educational Review* 66 (1): 60–93.

———. 2000. "A Multiliteracies Pedagogy: A Pedagogical Supplement." In *Multiliteracies: Literacy Learning and the Design of Social Futures*, edited by Bill Cope and Mary Kalantzis, 239–49. London: Routledge.

Rufo, Kenneth. 2006. *Teaching Rhetorical Criticism*. Online at http://www.ghostinthewire.org/2006/04/teaching_rhetorical_criticism.php.

Slack, Jennifer Daryl. 1989. "Contextualizing Technology." In *Rethinking Communication, Volume 2: Paradigm Exemplars*, edited by Lawrence Grossberg, Brenda Dervin, Barbara O'Keefe, and Edith Wartella, 329–45. Thousand Oaks, CA: Sage.

———, and J. MacGregor Wise. 2002. "Cultural Studies and Technology." In *Handbook of New Media: Social Shaping and Consequences of ICTs*, edited by Leah A. Liewrouw and Sonia Livingstone, 485–501. Thousand Oaks, CA: Sage.

Stillar, Glenn F. 1998. *Analyzing Everyday Texts: Discourse, Rhetoric, and Social Perspectives*. London: Sage Publications.

Ulmer, Gregory L., and Talan Memmott. 2000. "Toward Electracy: A Conversation with Gregory Ulmer (Interview)." *Beehive Hypermedia Literary Journal* 3 (1).

CHAPTER 7

Multimodal Composing, Appropriation, Remediation, and Reflection

Writing, Literature, Media

Donna Reiss and Art Young

In his 2004 talk at the Conference on College Composition and Communication, Gunther Kress described a "revolution in modes of representation" in which images dominate writing and the medium of the screen is dominant over the book. Concerned that current literacy theories and practice are incomplete, Kress (2003, 35) wrote in *Literacy in the New Media Age*, that "language alone cannot give us access to the meaning of the multimodally constituted message; language and literacy now have to be seen as partial bearers of meaning only." We have been exploring Kress's notions of "incompleteness" and its presumed corollary "completeness" of multimodal messages—what Kress (ibid., 116) calls "ensembles of modes, brought together to realize particular meanings"—together with our students. Although we don't think of any learning strategy as "complete," we have discovered through our students' work with multimodal compositions and accompanying reflections an important access to meaning making that words alone cannot provide.

Developed in collaboration with Dickie Selfe, our 1998 collection *Elec-*

tronic Communication Across the Curriculum promoted a communications-intensive approach to teaching disciplinary courses with a wide range of media and communications technology. We suggested then and continue to suggest now, thirteen years later, a pedagogy where students' messages are comprised of both words—sometimes analytical, reflective, or personal, especially reflections on their own learning experiences—and alternative expressions in a modality or multiple modalities of their choice. Giving students a wide range of options for developing and publishing their compositions enhances their engagement with the subject matter and empowers them to make creative and rhetorical decisions, to be what Anne Wysocki (2004, 15) has described as "composers who are aware of the range of materialities of texts and who then highlight the materiality; such composers design texts that help readers/consumers/viewers stay alert to how any text—like its composers and readers—doesn't function independently of how it is made and in what contexts." Thus central to our approach are not only innovative ways of combining and composing texts but rhetorical and multimodal ways of thinking about form and content, genre and purpose.

Vital to our pedagogical approach are several precepts:

- In the twenty-first century, students' experience, both scholarly and social, is multimodal, and we are committed to engage them as communicators in writing and other media in ways that relate to and expand their experience of the world. They regularly compose and represent themselves with both words and images on their blogs and social network websites; they connect with each other aurally, orally, textually, in person, and online. They combine collage-like their own compositions with words, images, and movies appropriated and remediated from other sources. At Clemson University, where we teach, laptops are required and the campus is networked wirelessly; a text messaging system alerts students to dangerous weather and to dangerous incidents. As a result, students are always connected by mobile devices, and we strive for our courses in writing and other disciplines to be included in that network.

- We welcome creativity and innovation not limited by our own skills and practices. We admit that we cannot ourselves do everything we invite our students to do—make videos and Flash movies, for example—as ways to express their learning or to teach us and classmates. By composing in ways not available to us, some students provide us and their classmates with insights into the subject matter that would have been otherwise unavailable to us. Giving students choices of modes and media often increases their motivation to learn and to communicate and enables them as both composers and audience to make rhetorical as well as creative decisions, as Cheryl E. Ball and Ryan M. Moeller (2008) have emphasized: "Aesthetic and rhetorical choices, or (as we call it) creative and scholarly choices, must be made in every text. Moreover, the meaning that those creative and scholarly choices engender should be made available for interpretation in every reading of every text."

- We respect the various ways students represent what they think, what they learn, and why they express themselves as they do. Significantly, we seek to understand their perspectives in response to course material, and we value the rhetorical choices they make to persuade, to enlighten, to entertain, and to combine such purposes to engage readers and viewers. These choices have included original performances such as dances and music as well as photographs and collages. As teacher-facilitators, we must be an attentive audience in responding to students' productions. For us as for our students, "multimodal meaning is truly a sensitivity to various modes of meaning-making working together," according to Nathaniel I. Córdova (in chapter 6 of this collection), citing the work of Bill Cope and Mary Kalantzis (2000, 211), who say that "multimodal meaning is no more than the other modes of meaning working together. And they always do."
- We expect reflective practice where students not only present and represent their thinking and learning but also are aware of their rhetorical and design choices. Most of our multimodal assignments include a substantial written reflective text where students articulate their choices of topics, words, and media so that they recognize the relationship between their rhetorical purposes and their productions. Our emphasis on these reflections grows out of a communication-across-the-curriculum pedagogy founded on the theories of James Britton (1970) and Janet Emig (1977), among others, on "writing to learn" and other functions of language. We appropriate and accommodate "*composing* to learn" in the context of communication technology and new media.

During the past decade as the modalities of composition available to our students have increased, so have the options we encourage them to use. Danielle Nicole DeVoss, Joseph Johansen, Cynthia L. Selfe, and John C. Williams Jr. (2003, 169–70) have reminded us that "if we continue to define literacy in terms of *alphabetic practices only*, in ways that ignore, exclude, or devalue new-media texts, we not only abdicate a professional responsibility to describe accurately and robustly the ways in which humans are now communicating and making meaning but we also run the risk of our curriculum holding declining relevance for students who are communicating in increasingly expansive, networked environments."

Our focus in this chapter is on communication-intensive literature classes, where in past decades students have read and written primarily formal critical analyses, but where new or mixed or hybrid genres that incorporate visual, aural, and media expressions now may substitute for or complement traditional scholarly essays. Literature classes have not always given students the opportunity to be writers as well as readers of the very genres they are studying. The personal computer has expanded opportunities for students to create and produce as well as consume and critique. As Janet Murray (1997, 8) wrote in *Hamlet on the Holodeck* about the dramatic changes in literary studies, "computers can present the text, images, and moving pictures valued by humanistic disciplines with a new precision of reference." In addition, for many of our undergraduates who will be engineers, architects, or information technology specialists, using computers and a range of media to develop and demonstrate knowledge in literature classes echoes their experience in their scientific and technical courses. Our graduate students often will teach English in high school or college; they will make rhetorical choices about genre and media for various audiences, including students, parents, and administrators. As citizens, when they attempt to make a difference in their communities and the wider world, all our students will read, view, and write for an even wider and increasingly networked public.

Thus we suggest a more "complete" (as in Kress's view) or reinforcing learning experience where students develop multimodal expressions as one possible alternative to a formal essay. This approach recognizes the pedagogical value of incorporating academic writing as an essential component of multimodal compositions and at the same time recognizes that remediations, appropriations, reflections, and performances often deepen students' learning and develop a fuller range of their communicative abilities. The examples of student work we present in this chapter demonstrate how students' poems and multimodal expressions enhance their interpretations of assigned texts—for instance, a computer-generated animation in response to Henry David Thoreau's "Resistance to Civil Government" or a slide show critical analysis of Marge Piercy's "The Secretary Chant" (fig. 7.1).

This slide from a PowerPoint presentation, selected as the development tool for the accessibility and simplicity of the technology, demonstrates how easily a student can create in multiple modalities even when

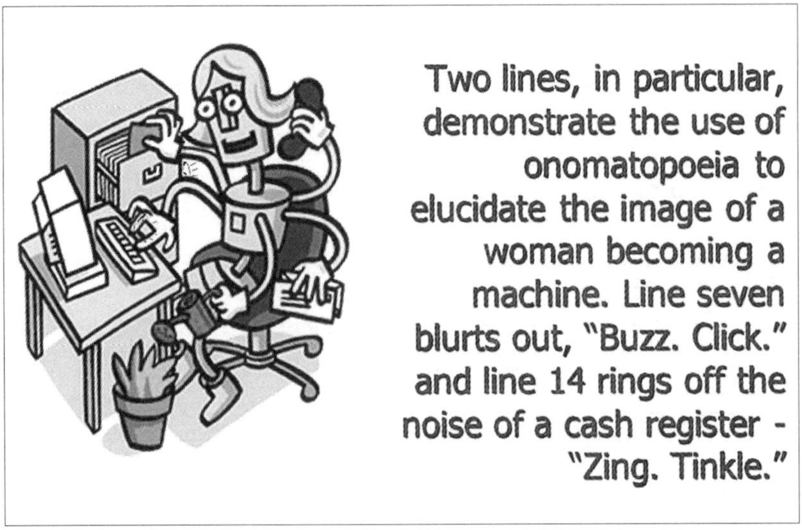
Two lines, in particular, demonstrate the use of onomatopoeia to elucidate the image of a woman becoming a machine. Line seven blurts out, "Buzz. Click." and line 14 rings off the noise of a cash register - "Zing. Tinkle."

FIGURE 7.1. Slide from Beau's audiovisual PowerPoint with his commentary on onomatopoeia in Marge Piercy's "The Secretary Chant."

there's no opportunity to learn new equipment or software. Computer slide programs facilitate the use of supporting words, images, sounds, and video, as Beau has done with his analysis of the onomatopoetic elements of Piercy's "The Secretary Chant." Beau—a biology and chemistry major taking a required general education introduction to literature—incorporated sound effects and a clip-art drawing that reflect his understanding of the mechanistic elements of Piercy's (1982, 77) poem, which is rich with the sounds of the office environment and includes these words:

> My head is a switchboard
> where crossed lines crackle.
> Press my fingers
> and in my eyes appear
> credit and debit.
> Zing. Tinkle.

Beau's written analysis was chunked into slides, many of them illustrated with appropriate sound effects and found visuals. To further underscore his awareness of the importance of sound to Piercy's poem, he cites a scholarly essay by Alexis Tadiė (2001, 110), "From the Ear to the Eye": "an emphasis on sound suggests that the reader must be aware of the materiality of the world and its acoustic properties." Indeed, the materiality of the world in Piercy's poem, where a woman is represented as just another machine in the modern workplace, is conveyed by Beau's choice of images, sounds, and scholarship. This recognition of the auditory elements of poetry in general and the Piercy poem in particular, along with the "found" or appropriated sound effects and visuals, gave Beau a simple but meaningful way to analyze the poem and to compose multimodally as well as to demonstrate that he understands the importance of the poetic use of sound. Beau and his classmates did not abandon traditional text when they composed their slides, altered books, and digitized collages; a reflective essay submitted with each project provided an opportunity to identify the rhetorical and material choices they had made and to expand verbally on their research and analysis. Our students do not create new genres but rather mix, merge, and remediate familiar genres and modes of communication to express their academic insights and knowledge. They do sometimes use new electronic tools. What may be new is the presence of multimodal expressions as legitimate critical responses to literature in writing and literature courses.

Language alone may not always represent best our students' thinking and understanding, even when we are teaching language-dependent courses in writing (composition) or reading (literature) or any academic course where reading and writing are important to learning. Fortunately, thanks to computers and the Internet, students have an opportunity to make meaning and demonstrate their intellectual growth in multiple modalities. In fact, one of the most compelling aspects of writing in online environments is the opportunity to include and exchange a variety of verbal, nonverbal, and mixed modes of expression that enrich and clarify communication by appealing to many senses at the same time. Although the integration of text and image is not unique to the era of the personal computer—for example, the embellishments in illuminated manuscripts—digital technologies make it possible for all of us to both decorate and communicate with multiple media and modes. The computer-generated animation of Sloan, another student, in response to Henry David Thoreau provides an example (fig. 7.2).

A physics major with an interest in politics and computers studying Thoreau in an American literature survey class, Sloan offered a contemporary perspective on the meaning of "resistance to civil government." Posting his poetic response and reflective essay online and presenting the work orally in class added a performative dimension and shared intellectual engagement with his classmates. His animation unfolds against a black brushed-on background: varicolored individuals appear like flowers

FIGURE 7.2. Final scene of Sloan's animation of "Citizens Be Anarchists."

blooming in a garden followed by grayish corporations, golden arches, and rays of government influence that the crowd protests (colors reversed here for black-and-white display). In his original poem "Citizens Be Anarchists," Sloan writes: "Anarchists hear me / listen indeed, and open your mind / self reliance is a rare commodity in this modern world." Although the poem and animation would stand alone to explain Sloan's understanding of and engagement with Thoreau's essay as well as disseminate his own political views, an accompanying reflective essay invites both the author and the audience (teacher, classmates, others who find the website) to share that understanding and perhaps even challenge his views.

In his reflection, Sloan writes, "the consumerism of Thoreau's time has only increased and the government has become quite good at distracting the public in order to silence unpleasant voices." Thus in Sloan's animation large corporations are challenged by crowds that the composer hopes will be nonviolent but not silent. He adds, "I think that both the poem and the cartoon help with my exploration of objective criticism of society through the elimination of dependence of society upon our structured bureaucracy." With his multimodal composition, Sloan has digitally published his contemporarily relevant understanding of Thoreau. Although we expect students' multimodal compositions to speak for themselves, we require a reflective text to encourage articulation of their own rhetorical choices and to be able to transfer and adapt such knowledge in new rhetorical situations.

Words that seek to represent meaning in more than one way may be enhanced with a visual image, a song, a dance, an animation, or a video. Students engaged in such composing activities become inquirers not only by interpreting Thoreau's essay but by becoming imaginative composers and resourceful thinkers seeking to discover original expression through appropriation, remediation, critical analysis, and creative play. Indeed, computers and the Internet increase opportunities for our students to participate in the ancient practice of ekphrasis as defined for the digital age by Jay David Bolter (1996, 264): "Ekphrasis is the description in prose or poetry of an artistic object or striking visual scene; it is the attempt to capture the visual in words. Today, as the visual and the sensual are emerging out of verbal communication, images are given the task . . . of explaining words, rather than the reverse." Such artful remediations, where one mode of expression is revisited by another—like the poetic representations of W. H. Auden's or William Carlos Williams's interpretations of a Bruegel painting or the poet Anne Sexton revisiting the oral narrative of Icarus—may well inspire our students to compose words and images that deepen their thinking and more broadly reveal to others their understanding of the intellectual and cultural concepts in their college classes. In addition to studying the disciplinary content, in this case literature, students also become creators and critics as did Auden and Sexton.

In "Musee des Beaux Arts," W. H. Auden (1976, 146–47) responded to *Landscape with the Fall of Icarus* by Pieter Bruegel the Elder, a sixteenth-century painting that included allusions to ancient Greek legend, Christian tradition, and Dutch narrative painting. Literature textbooks of a decade or so ago included few graphics; however, many did include a black-and-white or grayscale reproduction of this painting so that students could have an impression of the visual that inspired the poet. Teachers with access to slides of paintings and slide projectors could display a color reproduction, or they could bring in an art book and pass it around. Today, many textbooks include color plates of Bruegel's painting so that students can more readily see the red shirt of the farmer plowing his field, the tiny naked legs of Icarus descending into the sea. Students can conduct additional research, visiting the museum home of this painting online, perhaps enlarging the image to see the grazing sheep, the wooden ship, and the bright sunny sky whose heat melted the wax of the wings of Icarus.[1] As a result, they will generate fresh insights about the works under study. For example, they might be struck by "the dreadful martyrdom" that "must run its course" and wonder who if not Icarus is the martyr. If they are Christians, students might wonder about the "miraculous birth" and the speaker's statement that "there always must be / Children who did not specially want it to happen." Perhaps they will want to know more about Bruegel or Auden or painting or poetry. They may turn to the more accessible, more secular, but no more optimistic words of William Carlos Williams, who wrote about that same painting:

> unsignificantly
> off the coast
> there was
> a splash quite unnoticed
> this was
> Icarus drowning (Williams 1962, 385)

Students can compare these different poetic readings of the same painting and create their own poetic renderings and visual representations, and in doing so collaborate in a conversation about ambition, art, poetry, and culture that has continued for millennia.

Or consider another poem about the Icarus legend, not about Bruegel's painting although we may think of the painting when we read Anne Sexton's (1999, 53) tribute to the young Icarus, "larger than a sail, over the fog and the blast / of the plushy ocean, he goes. Admire his wings!" In "To a Friend Whose Work Has Come to Triumph" (recalling Yeats's poem "To a Friend Whose Work Has Come to Nothing"), Sexton finishes:

> Who cares that he fell back to the sea?
> See him acclaiming the sun and come plunging down
> while his sensible daddy goes straight into town. (Sexton 1999, 53)

Students who have previously read Auden and Williams can now consider how the phrase "sensible daddy" may problematize their understanding of the Icarus myth, the painting, the poems, and perhaps their own poem and those of their classmates.

In our composition and literature classes, where words have been the primary mode of expression, students can expand their thinking and knowing and their communication of their understanding by remediating their own compositions just as Auden did with his response to Bruegel's painting. Because not all students have the equipment or skills for making their own media, we suggest a pedagogy of choice that encourages students to compose both words and other modalities in ways that appeal to their interests and abilities. We design assignments where multimodal expression is required and the media vary, sometimes permitting appropriation and remediation of the works of others, sometimes permitting only "original" creative expressions. We recommend that students receive credit for multimodal academic work and "expanded essays" for reasons that W. J. T. Mitchell (1990, 36) promulgated with his University of Chicago class Literature and the Visual Arts, to "foster both verbal and visual literacy so that students will discover the intimate connections and conflicts between these sorts of literacy."

An early proponent of multimodal compositions in literary studies, Mitchell influenced our thinking about assignment design; as a result, our assignments provide options for students to experiment and to make choices about how much time and energy they will invest in the writing or the nonverbal elements of these projects. Some students take a photograph with the camera they carry around campus or they make a quick pencil drawing. Others spend many hours considering how to best express their thinking, motivated by the opportunity to be creative and to share their creativity with others. They paint or they sculpt or they use their computer graphics software to design visual or video representations. The choice of modalities and media is a decision each student makes after considering the contextual and rhetorical possibilities of the assignment.

For some students, selecting from the creative expressions of others rather than composing their own alternative modalities of expression can effectively dramatize their thinking. Collages or mash-ups are like found poems with their combination of the works of others along with students' own words and ideas. When students lack the confidence or materials, or time and energy, to compose original creative expressions or media, such appropriations and remediations can be powerful multimodal expressions that support their explanations and bring them confidence in their creative abilities. Many of these "found" works of art can be incorporated into word-processed documents, websites, or electronic slides, as with Beau's analysis of Piercy's "The Secretary Chant." Another example, an altered book, enables students to construct their own analysis of a short story or play as they build their own book. For her analysis of Susan Glaspell's play *Trifles*, Aiken, a biology major in a general education introduction to literary genres, composed not with a computer but with a paperback book, rope, colored inks, and pieces of paper. To provide a rendering of her interpretation of *Trifles*, she purchased a used copy of *Portrait of a Lady* by Henry James as the frame for her critical analysis. Although

Aiken had not read James's novel, the idea of "portrait of a lady" dramatized her reading of Glaspell's play in which a turn-of-the-twentieth-century "lady" is locked in an unhappy marriage and where the other "ladies" in the play make an ethical decision that challenges the social roles of women.

Aiken's appropriation of Henry James's novel based on its title alone underscored some of the ironies of Susan Glaspell's play; Aiken's remediation of the physical book as a collage-critique of *Trifles* may seem on the surface simple. However, the intelligence and creativity of her composition are complex and relevant; she demonstrated the "greater rhetorical sensitivity" described by Nathaniel I. Córdova in his contribution in this collection. Aiken composed her text with her word processor and cut the text into units, which she dispersed throughout the book and decorated to illustrate elements of the narrative and characterization. Readers, like the detectives and the women in the play, had to solve a mystery/puzzle to find some of the text, opening envelopes or unfolding pages. In this example a blood red–spattered page is tied with rope like the one used in *Trifles* to murder John Wright (fig. 7.3).

The choices Aiken had to make to bring her composition to life included analysis of the play, research on Glaspell and women's roles at the turn of the twentieth century, design of the project, selection of materials, construction of the altered book, and performance and reflection when she presented the project and her purposes to the class. Aiken had not only demonstrated a unique perspective on *Trifles*, but she created to the delight of her audience of classmates a three-dimensional sculpture in book form. A greater challenge for students, but a valuable opportunity for them to demonstrate their creativity in any class, is to require original verbal and multimodal compositions to enhance their written expressions and have these compositions published for an audience beyond the classroom, such as web pages, electronic portfolios, blogs, books, or poster displays in building hallways. When we give students a variety of options for an authentic audience, they respond in sometimes surprising ways that reveal their interests and talents along with their learning.

Multimodal compositions can also enhance international understanding and collaboration as the following blog discussion shows. Writing letters online within interactive groups of ten students, a PhD class called Fiction for Engineers at Chalmers University of Technology in Gothenburg, Sweden, and two classes at Clemson University in South Carolina (one master of art's class in Victorian poetry and one a sophomore survey of American literature) discussed "The Love Song of J. Alfred Prufrock"

FIGURE 7.3. "Blood-spattered" page from Aiken's altered book and critical analysis of *Trifles* by Susan Glaspell.

by T. S. Eliot. In addition to their prose personal responses and critical analyses, students were asked to give their readers alternative expressions of their understanding of Eliot's poem, such as paintings, drawings, and photographs available online that students could link to. Through their choices and their explanations of how those choices contribute to our understanding of the poem, students furthered their own and their correspondents' thinking about the language, meaning, and experience of "Prufrock." Marigrace, a sophomore literature student at Clemson, chose Salvador Dali's *Persistence of Memory* as a visual complement to Prufrock's perspective of time. In addition, she offered some lyrics from "Time," a song performed by South Carolina rock-and-roll band Hootie and the Blowfish: "Time, why do you punish me? Like a wave bashing into the shore, you wash away my dreams." These choices added a visual and auditory dimension to her analysis, as Marigrace explains: "The entire poem ['Prufrock'] reflects on time in some form. The word is seen eleven times in lines 23–48. . . . The song personifies time and its overwhelming presence. Time, in a sense, controls everything and we must learn to make the best of what little we have. Prufrock does not understand this—he is unable to take a stand and do something about his situation."

Erin, a Clemson graduate student, pointed to M. C. Escher's *Relativity* to highlight the indecision and repetition in Prufrock's life. She explains her choice: "Figures are wandering around in a maze of a house. The house is kind of Mediterranean in terms of architecture, with trees and light (like the pleasant homes of Eliot's Victorian England), but the figures are faceless, moving about in the house without destination or visible purpose. I feel the painting connects with the theme of bleakness and flatness that is conveyed through Prufrock/Eliot's apparent disparity over himself. Prufrock/Eliot, like the figures in Escher's *Relativity*, wander without destination or purpose, barely aware of each other and alone in their own little seemingly pleasant world."

Another Clemson student echoed these motifs in Eliot's poems with her original painting that portrays Eliot himself as his character Prufrock with the women who "come and go" in the background. Melody's critical reflection on her choices explains that "Eliot's coat is highlighted by places painted grayish-blue, indicating moods of private melancholy and poetic sensitivity, similar to Pablo Picasso's Blue Period." Melody's continued analysis of her own creative process indicates to us that she has read Eliot's poem thoughtfully and imagined the possible contrast between an author's worldview and that of his fictional character. About using a muted two-tone palette for her painting (fig. 7.4), Melody continues: "Typically in art, the color blue is associated with the emotions, particularly with feelings of misery and gloom." She added: "I wanted to picture Eliot in Prufrock's places 'scrutinized, criticized, and avoided' but, simultaneously, elsewhere. The Eliot I painted has a slight smirk on his face, as if though recognizing society's scrutiny he has determined

FIGURE 7.4. Melody's painting of T. S. Eliot as J. Alfred Prufrock.

to focus his gaze beyond. Perhaps he mulls over the thought that, unlike Prufrock with his indecisions and revisions, his life as both a writer and a poet has been worth it after all."

This reading of Prufrock demonstrates that through the interplay of visual representation, color, light and shadow, and language, Melody was able to express her attitude toward both poet and poem. A written reflection on both process and product gave Melody further opportunity to explain to herself and her audience—classmates as well as teachers—her engagement and understanding. Melody concludes her message on a personal yet playful and complicating note: "I added a personal touch to

Eliot/Prufrock by placing my eyes in the place of Eliot's own, to suggest that the face that I prepared, the face that was 'murdered' was my own and 'created' in its place was Eliot's."

Using words along with music (made available to blog participants by a link to a sound file) to convey his auditory expression, Jacob from Chalmers in Sweden interprets the situation confronting J. Alfred Prufrock:

> In 1937 Sergej Prokofiev wrote a piano suite from his ballet "Romeo and Juliet." In the beginning the feelings portrayed are of pure love, but gradually the theme moves closer to death and pain of lost love. So this could be related to Prufrock . . . the feeling has grown very eerie and tragic. If you listen closely you can hear the time running in the first bars. . . . In Prufrock this can be related to him remembering moments of "tea and cakes." . . . It's interesting to see that some ways of expressing evolved their counterparts in different types of art at approximately the same time. . . . As you notice, I am quite fanatical about this piece, and I am practicing it now.

Jacob's choice of music as an alternative expression to his verbal analysis of "The Love Song of J. Alfred Prufrock" not only illuminates his understanding but also enhances the way readers in Sweden and the United States perceive the poem. Most students, like the three teachers, had never heard this music before. Other students listened to the excerpt from *Romeo and Juliet* and responded thoughtfully to Jacob's musical contribution, which enriched our experience as part of "studying" and discussing Prufrock. From the students' visual and oral linked selections, we all discovered personal, intercultural, literary, and historical connections no single one of us could have made on our own.

Here are the various options we present to our classes: original drawing or painting scanned as an image file, photograph taken with a digital camera or with a film camera and then scanned and manipulated, three-dimensional construction or sculpture photographed and scanned as an image file (using any materials such as clay, play dough, popsicle sticks, coat hangers, metal, or other craft materials), graphic narrative (otherwise known as a comic) with at least four frames, computer-generated image composed with drawing or painting software, animation, video, or altered or embellished text. Given so many options, most students are able to compose an original expression in a medium other than or in combination with words. Results have included original poems in the style of Puritan poet Anne Bradstreet written from the point of view of her absent husband, Tom, printed on paper made to look like antique parchment and decorated by "his" hand; social satires on contemporary issues written in the style of William Blake and decorated to resemble the engravings on Blake's originals; modern dance interpretations of Victorian poems; and graphic narrative remediations of American short stories. Students also have appropriated works intended for one purpose to serve another purpose—for instance, a Dali painting and a rock-and-roll song or a Prokofiev ballet to interpret T. S. Eliot's "The Love Song of J. Alfred Prufrock."

We encourage students to be playful and creative within the parameters of an assignment, and we let students know our expectations and how we will assess their work. Crucially, we require a written reflection in which students critically examine their own learning and compositions, and where they explain their purposes and processes and tell us how their multimodal compositions achieve their goals and the assignment's expectations. Evaluating and grading student work is often difficult for many teachers, so we do not underestimate the challenge of assessing students' multimodal expressions. A teacher who struggles to decide whether a student's scholarly essay or final grade is a B+ or an A– often feels ill equipped to judge the creative and critical aspects of a student's original video clip or mixed-media presentation—genres and modes in which the teacher may have little or no formal training. But accepting this challenge, without denying its difficulties, is what teachers must do, else we risk denying our students experiences in a robust range of rhetorical and communicative expressions, narrowing their choices to only the ones we teachers know best. Accepting the challenge involves placing trust in students and trust in ourselves as teachers. We assess creative or innovative contributions in the context of other work included in a student's course portfolio, in the context of the student's critical reflection about such contributions, in the context of our course and assignment-specific criteria, and in the context of the engaged learning and participation of the student in the collaborative knowledge-making class community.

In "Between Modes: Assessing Students' New Media Compositions," Madeleine Sorapure (2006) writes, "rather than assessing individual modes in a multimodal work, I suggest an assessment strategy that focuses on the effectiveness with which modes such as image, text, and sound are brought together or, literally, composed." Along with that evaluation of the interrelation of the elements, we consider a student's reflective analysis important for her or his intellectual and creative growth, whether it appears as a formal essay accompanying the multimodal composition or elsewhere—for instance, an entry in a final course portfolio. Performance and publication to classmates or wider audiences are essential as well. We don't require expertise in video production or painting from our students; we do require commitment, critical thinking, engagement with content, and thoughtful composing where multiple communicative elements interrelate.

"Students are using rich and varied ICTs [information and communication technologies] and drawing on equally rich and varied concepts of the genres of writing valued in multimodal environments," write Tracey Bowen and Carl Whithaus in the introduction to this volume. We invite students to create, to appropriate, to remediate, and to reflect during the composing process. Undeterred by the fact that we don't (can't) teach multimedia development, we give students opportunities to learn about both language and literature by composing with the tools they already know or want to learn, such as a carefully selected series of available images, an original painting or drawing or audio or video presentation, a computer-generated animation, or an expanded essay that communicates with more than words alone.

NOTES

We are grateful to our students for their creativity and enthusiasm for multimodal projects and for their permission to quote them and to showcase their work. We also thank our colleagues Dickie Selfe of Ohio State University, our coeditor for *Electronic Communication Across the Curriculum* (http://wac.colostate.edu/books/ecac/), and Magnus Gustafsson of Chalmers University of Technology in Gothenburg, Sweden, our collaborator on *Cross-cultural Collaborations* (http://wordsworth2.net/projects/crossculturalcollabs), a series of online discussions among students in Sweden and the United States.

1. At Artchive (http://www.artchive.com/artchive/B/bruegel/icarus.jpg.html) or the WebMuseum site (http://www.ibiblio.org/wm/paint/auth/bruegel/), students may be tempted to spend time with this painting and poem and to think about the ways these modalities relate to each other and to them as viewers and readers, engaging in activities of a scholarly habit of mind.

REFERENCES

Auden, W. H. 1976. "Musee des Beaux Arts." In *Collected Poems*, edited by Edward Mendelson, 146–47. New York: Random House.

Ball, Cheryl E., and Ryan M. Moeller. 2008. "Converging the ASS[umptions] Between U and ME; or How New Media Can Bridge a Scholarly/Creative

Split in English Studies." *Computers and Composition Online* (spring). Online at http://www.bgsu.edu/cconline/convergence/.

Bolter, Jay David. 1996. "Ekphrasis, Virtual Reality, and the Future of Writing." In *The Future of the Book*, edited by Geoffrey Nunberg, 253–72. Berkeley: University of California Press.

Britton, James N. 1970. *Language and Learning: The Importance of Speech in Children's Learning*. Harmondsworth: Penguin Books.

Cope, Bill, and Mary Kalantzis. 2000. "Designs for Social Futures." In *Multiliteracies: Literacy Learning and the Design of Social Futures*, edited by Bill Cope and Mary Kalantzis, 203–34. London: Routledge.

DeVoss, Danielle Nicole, Joseph Johansen, Cynthia L. Selfe, and John C. Williams Jr. 2003. "Under the Radar of Composition Programs: Glimpsing the Future through Case Studies of Literacy in Electronic Contexts." In *Composition Studies in the New Millennium: Rereading the Past, Rewriting the Future*, edited by Lynn Z. Bloom, Donald A. Daiker, and Edward M. White, 157–73. Carbondale: Southern Illinois University Press.

Emig, Janet. 1977. "Writing as a Mode of Learning." *College Composition and Communication* 28 (May): 122–28.

Kress, Gunther. 2003. *Literacy in the New Media Age*. London: Routledge.

Mitchell, W. J. T. 1990. "Against Comparison: Teaching Literature and the Visual Arts." In *Teaching Literature and Other Arts*, edited by Jean-Pierre Barricelli, Joseph Gibaldi, and Estella Lauter, 30–37. New York: Modern Language Association.

Murray, Janet H. 1997. *Hamlet on the Holodeck: The Future of Narrative in Cyberspace*. Cambridge: MIT Press.

Piercy, Marge. 1982. "The Secretary Chant." In *Circles on the Water: Selected Poems of Marge Piercy*. New York: Knopf.

Reiss, Donna, Dickie Selfe, and Art Young. 1998. *Electronic Communication Across the Curriculum*. Urbana, IL: National Council of Teachers of English. Full text online at http://wac.colostate.edu/books/ecac/.

Sexton, Anne. 1999. "To a Friend Whose Work Has Come to Triumph." In *The Complete Poems: Anne Sexton*. Boston: First Mariner Books.

Sorapure, Madeleine. 2006. "Between Modes: Assessing Student New Media Compositions." *Kairos: A Journal of Rhetoric, Technology, and Pedagogy* 10 (2). Online at http://kairos.technorhetoric.net/10.2/coverweb/sorapure/.

Tadiė, Alexis. 2001. "From the Ear to the Eye: Perceptions of Language in the Fiction of Laurence Sterne." In *Sensual Reading: New Approaches to Reading in Its Relations to the Senses*, edited by Michael Syrotinsky and Ian Maclachlan, 106–26. London: Associated University Presses.

Williams, William Carlos. 1962. "Landscape with the Fall of Icarus." In *The*

Collected Poems of William Carlos Williams: Volume 2, 1939–1962, edited by Christopher MacGowan. New York: New Directions.

Wysocki, Anne. 2004. "Opening New Media: Openings and Justifications." In *Writing New Media: Theory and Applications for Expanding the Teaching of Composition*, edited by Anne Wysocki, Johndan Johnson-Eilola, Cynthia L. Selfe, and Geoffrey Sirc, 1–42. Logan: Utah State University Press.

CHAPTER 8

Writing, Visualizing, and Research Reports

Penny Kinnear

THIS CHAPTER EXAMINES WHAT HAPPENS when an instructor attempts to correlate two theoretical frameworks to conceptualize and practice instructional goals and activities in an undergraduate research and writing class. Literacy and writing have been theorized as multimodal design activities by the New London Group (Cope and Kalantzis 2000). Language and other signs were theorized as mediational means in learning by Lev Vygotsky and subsequent sociocultural theorists. Together these ideas could inform the development of a course to take advantage of signs and tools in addition to text to conduct and present research. This chapter focuses on a visualization activity used in a class to facilitate data analysis and research conceptualization (fig. 8.1).

Vygotsky (1978) argued that human experience is always mediated. It may be mediated by signs, tools, or experiences. Signs and tools are developed and produced by people. These can be both material and symbolic. The symbolic tools include language, symbol systems such as numbers, musical notation, formal aesthetic principles, and various writing systems

Figure 8.1. Consumer savvy: developing brochures and online campaigns in a professional writing research course.

and images. With regard to reading and writing, material tools can include various writing implements, computers, brushes, inks, paper, and books. This mediated activity can be the basis of learning.

It is imperative to understand mediation and mediational means, as these are the terms through which I theorize writing. According to Alex Kozulin (1996, 105), Vygotsky, in his 1978 treatise "The Prehistory of Written Language," "brought together such seemingly disparate phenomena as gesture, symbolic play, and children's drawing and writing in an attempt to show that they all are but steps in the process of mastering symbolism and conventionalism, which are essential for the development of written language." The child's or learner's experiences and thoughts thus are mediated by all of these material and symbolic tools. This process intertwines with the concept of *Tätigkeit*, or socially meaningful activity where symbol systems and their conventions "are imposed on an individual's behavior, shaping it, and reconstructing it along the lines of the sociocultural matrix. The concept of activity thus was perceived as an actualization of culture in individual behavior, embodied in the symbolic function of gesture, play, and speech systems" (Kozulin 1996, 106).

The actions of writing and speaking engages an individual in the activity of expressing thoughts. According to Vygotsky (1986 [1934], 251), this is not merely a transfer of completed expressions from the mind to an externally expressed form—oral or written—but rather "in his mind the whole thought is present at once, but in speech [or writing] it has to be developed shedding a shower of words. Precisely because thought does not have its automatic counterpart in words, the transition from thought to word leads through meaning. . . . thought does not express itself in words, but rather realizes itself in them." Most people have had the experience of searching for words to express something that seems so clear "in their heads." The language(s) an individual has access to mediates the meaning he or she attempts to make and it is only in this mediated process that the thought is realized, that the meaning is made. That meaning takes a form in words, sentences, a discourse, or in a visual grammar and syntax. It becomes concrete and public, an artifact. One of the goals of the course was to have students understand that research meant creating new meanings from the data which they collected and that using language in their research journals, in their note taking, in their analysis notes, created those meanings not just recorded a reformulation of someone else's meanings/words.

The mediational means used in this process is also a product, an artifact of social interactions. Language is a systematic, codified artifact of a culture that is continually being reshaped and reformed. Mikail Bakhtin (1981, 277) described this eloquently when he wrote: "The way in which the word conceptualizes its object is a complex act—all objects, open to dispute and overlain as they are with qualifications, are from one side highlighted while from the other side dimmed by heteroglot social opinion, by an alien word about them. And into this complex play of light and shadows the word enters—it becomes saturated with this play, and must determine within it the boundaries of its own semantic and stylistic contours." Within all cultures different discourses have shaped and been shaped by different contexts and interactions.[1] One of these is academic discourse and its accompanying written genres. By the time most students arrived in the third-year university course, Research and Writing, they had participated in at least fifteen years of instructional activities that privileged certain texts and genres. Although students used and participated in multimodal communication activities outside of the classroom, they appeared to see no valid connection between academic genres and their multimodal communication systems.

The historical relationship of words and visuals in writing classrooms must be examined and dealt with in this push to imagine alternative presentations of research material. Although most of my students were experienced as consumers of multimodalities and were often quite adept and creative in their personal use, especially of various electronic technologies, they had difficulty bringing that experience and skill into their academic, classroom-based work. It seems the value for this knowledge, the anticipated profit in Pierre Bourdieu's terms, is low in an academic setting. I found that the Professional Writing Communication (PWC) students frequently changed their approach to writing when they put on academic prose. The writing withered as the students, rather than make meaning, tried as Cinderella's step-sisters did, to fit their research experience into the perfectly formed glass slipper: the research report.

Diana George (2002, 13), in a historical review of the relationship between writing instruction and visual elements, asserts that when acknowledged, the visual has been seen as a lesser, incomplete element most useful as the carrot-on-the-stick to pull student interest and attention to the more serious and worthy business of composing: "visual and written communication continue to be held in a kind of tension—the visual figuring into the teaching of writing as a problematic, something added, an anomaly, a 'new' way of composing, or, somewhat cynically, as a strategy for adding relevance or interest to a required course." Visual elements and expressions ranging from television, comic books, advertising, and picture books have also been seen as a threat to "real" literacy as represented by books and essays. As hooks to capture student interest, the use of visual design has been equated with unflattering assumptions about reader intelligence. George (ibid., 19–20) quotes Robert Connors's critique of a standard university composition textbook: "Robert Connors points to the visual design of the fifth edition as indicating a 'lowered evaluation of its audience's abilities' signaled by 'wide margins and a two-color format to open up the text's appearance.' . . . [The 1976 edition] goes in deeply for the 'visual observation' invention methods. . . . It is filled with photos, cartoons, illustrations, all meant to add spice to the text." Visual elements are seen only as spice rather than examined for ways in which they may work with text, or against text, to mediate meaning making. There have been some exceptions to this general pattern in technical writing and in science writing. In these areas visual elements can play important roles in clarifying meaning or more efficiently communicating complex ideas such as multistep processes.

Another part of the history that positions other modalities as mere accessories, hooks, or threats to literacy and meaning making involves the conceptualization of the visual as a consumable rather than something to be produced. In the use of visual as prompts, hooks, or objects of analysis, the need to think about how to teach students to produce visuals and the underlying criteria for making those kinds of decisions has not developed in the same way students were and are taught how to make rhetorical decisions about their writing (George 2002).

I had two motives for including modalities other than text in the Research and Writing course I taught in the PWC program. First, images, symbols, diagrams, and pictures along with text could be additional mediational means students might use to make sense of their research data. Second, multimodal presentations could be used to present their research findings to audiences outside of the academy. I hold that researchers, be they students or tenured professors, have an ethical responsibility to share the knowledge, insights, and questions they produce. In the social sciences, where people act as participants and informants, this requires a presentation that respects the participants' and informants' world. In other types of research, researchers can (and should) contribute their knowledge to public intellectual discussions. Susheela Varghese and Sunita Abraham (2004) provide an excellent analysis of an emerging genre, the book-length scientific essay written by researchers about their own research. This contrasts with more traditional popularizations of science most often written by journalists. Multimodal presentations of research by researchers, even student researchers, would fit within this developing genre.

What this means to me as a teacher of writing is that writing is a socially meaningful activity that depends on the relationship between the individual and the social context(s) the individual participates in (in this case a university undergraduate class) mediated by both material and symbolic means. The material means may be pen and paper or a computer or poster paper, glue sticks, images, Post-its, and markers. The major symbolic means are the language(s) of the student, the language(s) of the authors the student uses as references, the language the professor uses, the language peers use when editing the writer's work, as well as the hybrid symbol systems of drawing, images, and mark-making they create within their research notebooks and coding activities. The research activity produces artifacts that in turn can mediate the production of other artifacts—for example, the first draft becomes a mediational means for further understanding.[2] One of the strengths of Vygotsky's conceptualization of meaning making is its dynamic quality and that means that language can be simultaneously a mediational means *and* an activity.

Thus the Research and Writing students entered a particular context and engaged in a socially meaningful activity that was mediated by oral, written language(s), and various symbols, images, and gestures. The individual was neither isolated from nor dependent upon the interpsychological interactions that he or she used in the process of making meaning with written and visual signs and symbols. The Research and Writing course, in this way of thinking, became yet one more context for the development of written and visual communication concepts.

THE RESEARCH AND WRITING COURSE

In Research and Writing, a professional writing course at the University of Toronto at Mississauga, students had thirteen weeks to choose a site and a topic to "research," to collect and analyze data, and to present their findings from that data in two forms. The course focused on the writing of research using the principles students had learned and practiced in other PWC writing courses. In addition to a basic text about doing research, I required students to read research from journals, from books, from newspapers, and from technical or professional magazines. I wanted them to become connoisseurs of the diverse ways in which the results of doing research could be presented to other interested audiences.

For most of the students, this course provided their first opportunity to do more than report on information they had gleaned from other sources. Comprehending the difference between producing a report of someone else's research and analysis and collecting and analyzing their own data challenged most of the students throughout the course. Given the word "research," the students tended to think of a term paper or an extended essay on an assigned topic. They saw the task as a matter of gathering sufficient information from a designated minimum number of reliable sources that met the professor's formatting and content requirements. One of the course goals was to facilitate the reconceptualization of the notion of research to include the generation of questions and analysis of original data and information from secondary sources to create new knowledge—in Vygotskian sociocultural terms, to integrate the everyday (or spontaneous) and scientific concepts.[3]

To introduce the idea that writing mediated the production of meaning (as well as practice observation and field note skills), students completed a four-hour authoenthnography before beginning their research projects. The students had to keep detailed field notes, produce a narrative based on those field notes and then a reflective piece that examined the process of moving from field notes to narrative in this initial exercise. Employing the sociocultural concepts of mediation and mediational means, I tried to keep the question of how writing mediated their understanding of experience central in their thinking.

Once the students settled on a research topic, they plunged into data collection with a great deal of enthusiasm. The importance of field notes and a research journal became increasingly apparent as the process of collecting, recording, and reflecting on data became more complex. Before students began to analyze their data, I used a series of in-class exercises to practice the skill of repeatedly reading data for themes or concepts, writing definitions, and then coding data with those definitions in mind. Approximately five weeks before the end of term, students produced a first draft of the academic version of their report. This would provide the basis of the alternative version, produced for a nonacademic audience. Students were asked to consider who might be interested in their research question and what form would be most appropriate for that audience.

Early in the course, the "alternative" versions prompted questions from the students. I sensed a certain tension between what students had learned counted as research, what counted as academic writing, and where an alternative version of that activity fit. The students mostly aimed their queries at extracting a description of "what the prof wants." Much to their consternation, I replied with questions: who else might enjoy, benefit from, or appreciate the research they have conducted? Once students answered those questions, I asked what kind of document or report that particular audience would best respond to. At the same time, I insisted that students respect the integrity of their research findings and the intelligence of their intended audience. They could not simplify or "dumb down" what they had found. Changing the form should not compromise the content.

DEFINING RESEARCH IN THE AGE OF MULTIMODALITY

Students entered the classroom with a variety of everyday conceptualizations of the research process gleaned from their various experiences with "research" in various educational contexts. Their conceptualizations were specific to the experiences they had had. The weakness of these everyday concepts showed in the students' inability to apply them beyond the confines of the experiences that formed them. Students also entered the class with a number of pseudoscientific concepts. These, according to Vygotsky, are sets of abstractions that have been learned in school but are not connected to concrete, empirical experience. True concepts are characterized by their relational system. True concepts are also consciously used as problem-solving tools. Someone who has yet to develop scientific concepts can solve a problem but cannot explain the process by which he or she solved the problem.

Marianne Hedegaard (2007) has used the term "conceptual competence" to describe the goal of concept development. She (ibid., 249) writes in the context of early childhood development that "it is only when the scientific concepts become integrated with the child's everyday concepts that they become a competence in the child's life outside the classroom." It is the dialectic between a student's everyday concepts and the concepts encountered in the formal, systematized body of school knowledge that can facilitate the development of conceptual competence, the transformation of everyday and scientific concepts. This process is by no means confined to early childhood but continues throughout an individual's life. Some contexts better facilitate this dialectic than others, some students take up the dialectic more readily than others. For the students in the Research and Writing course, I had the goal (which they may or may not have shared) of developing this conceptual competence of research. Thus one of the goals was to systematize the process of doing research, to reconceptualize research as a scientific concept.

Language, meanings, and other sign and symbol systems all mediate both the problem-solving process and the development of the conceptual competence. When I asked students in the first class, "What is research?" I got answers that described the various activities a student engaged in before deciding on which stereo system, cell phone plan, or car to invest in. Other students recited the steps in the "scientific method"—form a hypothesis, design a test or experiment of the hypothesis, conduct the experiment, measure the results of the experiment, draw a conclusion, and report the findings. The first can be categorized as an everyday concept and the latter a pseudoscientific concept learned in a formal instructional setting. Students used the same words and mimicked the actions of this form of scientific investigation but worked with a very different set of meanings and map of reasoning than most scientists. Most students practiced this method with predetermined hypotheses, experiments, and results in their high school science courses, thus only mimicking the concepts. As Vygotsky (1986 [1934]) wrote, the everyday concepts develop upward toward abstraction and the scientific concepts develop downward toward concreteness. I would argue that this is evidenced in the students struggle to analyze the data they had collected. Many students leapt to conclusions that may have been valid but had no idea of how they got there. Other students became mired in specific examples or instances unable to abstract from them, unable to see paradoxes or develop relationships among the data collected. This motivated me to search for additional mediational means, to include more than written and oral language.

USING MORE THAN JUST WORDS

In conversations with my colleague, we explored the idea of mapping data to break the dominance of text and provide alternative ways of seeing and experiencing the data students had collected. The use of images, diagrams, pictures, and symbols mixed with text is not an entirely new idea but perhaps one that more accurately has reentered our field of vision (all puns intended). Kristie Fleckenstein (2007) provides an insightful examination of the way visual elements were once part of our literacy practices, faded, and have emerged again in the first chapter of *Ways of Seeing, Ways of Speaking.* Certainly, from my sociocultural perspective, all of these nonword elements are potential mediational means that may be used to realize thoughts. A graph often more clearly sets out certain kinds of statistical data than a paragraph, and for some readers the paragraph makes much more meaning than the statistical tables. The meanings a reader (and the writer) can possibly make change when different textual elements appear on the page.

My writing students grew to understand that they had some but not complete control over how a reader understands what they have written. A writer who writes to be read by others has a concern for how much the reader will "get," what the reader will comprehend, how much of what the writer intended to say gets picked up by a reader. That knowledge can guide a writer's choice of words, sentences, paragraphs, and the choice of details. A writer has a number of rhetorical strategies and techniques to use, depending on what the writer wishes to accomplish, what kind of response the writer hopes to spark in the reader. Moving from the standard, word-centric research report format provides another set of mediational means for writers—and readers. Using something other than written definitions, categories, and descriptions of data could provide additional mediational means for the student researchers to make sense of their data. As my colleague and I planned the visualization activity, we hoped that it would literally help students re-vision their research and the knowledge they could construct from it.

Both the social nature and the neurobiological basis of our meaning making have been acknowledged, although not as fully explored as more traditional educational cognitive psychological assumptions. From the field of technology and writing, Jim Porter (2003, 388) wrote: "We need a theory that focuses on writing as not simply the activity of an individual writing or the isolated writing classroom (where the field of computers and writing has been strong, but also limited), but that looks closely at the socialized writing dynamic and the conglomerate rhetorical dynamic of readers, writers and users and their impact on society. The revolution, if there is one, is in the social one of interconnectivity." Arguing for more research-based curricular decisions, Shirley Brice Heath (2000, 122) introduced recent physics and neurobiology contributions to our understanding of visual literacy: "Simply put, what amounts to visual perception carries meaning because the imagistic character of neural activity manages to link up stored up experience that gives coherence and embeddedness to primary sensory images."

This information points to a relationship between visually perceived images and thought, and because they are simultaneously processed, it would not be unreasonable to expect an interaction between the language and visual dimensions. That interaction mediates the meanings a reader or a writer builds. Nor would it be unreasonable to expect that visual or linguistic interactions alone would produce different meanings. Indeed, researchers drawing on the work of the cognitive scientist Aneta Paivio (1986) and his dual-coding theory began to investigate how people learn in multimedia environments. Although work by Paivio and others explicitly addresses vocabulary learning and the use of visual and verbal information, the dual-processing theory that emerged from those investigations certainly seems to support the idea that it is in the interaction of verbal and visual that learning (and I would add meaning making) is most likely to happen. Paivio argues that it is because students have access to two different channels, but if I adjust the metaphor away from a completely mechanistic one to an interactive one, I think it is possible to argue that it is the interaction of the two sources that reinforce and prompt the recall and the comprehension, which makes sense in the context of verbal and visual information as mediational means.

Pushing in that direction, Richard Mayer (1997) describes his research that explores the effectiveness of multimedia learning—specifically, combinations of visual, oral, and textual explanations of scientific principles. Mayer's (ibid., 17) research is constrained to specific sets of information, and he is careful not to overgeneralize his findings, but he found that "according to this [generative theory of multimedia learning], coordinated presentation of explanative words and pictures is effective because it helps guide learners' cognitive processes." Russell Carney and Joel Levin (2002) reviewed research conducted throughout the 1990s and concluded that the use of pictures in texts as decorational, representational, organizational, interpretational, or transformational helps students learn from texts. I believe this research supports the interpretation of these "aids" as mediational means that provide affordances which students have access to. Susan Hagan (2007) explores the relationship between the visual and the verbal in more detail. She sees it as a collaboration and "an untapped rhetorical opportunity" (ibid., 49).

Hagan has identified, labeled, and categorized the kinds of meaning-making relationships possible between visuals and texts. Unlike many explications of the visual elements in text, her work assumes the perspective of learning to use the relationships between visual elements and text in much the same way rhetorical strategies are explicitly taught. The PWC students had all learned a number of rhetorical techniques and strategies to help them use words to complete their thoughts. Now, we would challenge them to use more than words, as they often did unconsciously in their lives outside of the classroom, in an academic setting for academic goals.

MAKING MEANING

For many of the students the visualization exercise clarified the relationship between the discrete bits of data they had collected, the information they had gathered, and their own analysis or lack of analysis and interpretations. It pulled them away from the idea of organizing all the discrete bits and pieces they had amassed through a linear outline and allowed them to explore relationships. In sociocultural terms, this means moving upward from the everyday, direct experience toward the more relational field of concepts. The week before the first draft of the academic report was due (and after I had done in-class exercises that practiced reading data for patterns, themes, and categories), my colleague and I instructed students to bring images, charts, drawings related to their research, and their research journals to class. In class we gave the students large pieces of blank paper and the instructions to lay out their findings. They could use words, signs, pictures, and space to explore relationships and identify concepts. In her instructions to the group, my colleague was adamant that the students were *not* making a collage (which many of them had assumed they would be doing). Students have certain assumptions about collages. They seem to think of collages as expressive art pieces and so bring aesthetics to the production of a finished "picture."

We wanted students to focus on ideas and a variety of possible relationships of ideas through multiple signs and symbols rather than a picture. We also instructed them not to glue anything down until they had tried several permutations. We instructed them to work individually for a minimum of thirty minutes. After thirty minutes we let students glue their bits and pieces down and add arrows, circles, boxes, or whatever other marks they wished to add. We collected the papers, redistributed them, giving students about ten minutes to "read" the paper to themselves and then to "read" the paper to the class. After the paper was "read," students discussed the meanings that had been made, comparing what the "author" had intended and what the reader had read. This is where we began to see evidence that some students appeared to be changing their understanding of the research process and product. Not everyone took advantage of the activity in this way. In other words, this activity, for whatever reason, did not mediate research and the research process in the same way.

Several responses bear examination. In these cases the students discovered something new about their research questions. For the first of these students, Paul, it was the manipulation of the images and snippets of text that mediated relationships he had not been able to see through written text alone. He had worked quietly shuffling pictures of the two musicians he had observed and interviewed, titles of songs, representations of music styles, other rappers, and excerpts from his field notes around on his paper. He grouped and regrouped the pictures and the other different elements before fixing them to the paper and adding his own organizing and relational symbols. He came to my office the next day for an editing appointment, excited to tell me what he had figured out. By moving the different elements around, he had seen what the musicians shared in experiences, in influences, and in goals. Until he had physically grouped the pictures of the musicians with the names of the songs, music genres, and other artists, he had been unable to make meaningful relationships among the bits and pieces of his observations, interviews, and the musical influences his participants had cited. The text of his field notes had not provided the vision he needed to see relationships.

I believe this is an example, in contrast with Shelley's use of the activity, where image, symbols, and the instructions to move the elements into different relationships aided Paul in breaking from a linear interpretation of his interviews and observations. Even though Paul had read through his notes, rearranged them, highlighted, or underlined sections, the observations, interviews, and images had never been juxtaposed. In preparing for the activity, Paul had found images of artists, images from some of the music, musical notations of beats, images of the "sense" of the hip-hop culture and history. He had moved from literal text to a different abstraction of his observations and knowledge. The combination of physically playing with relationships represented through images and symbols had provided Paul with a mediational means that helped him move from those everyday concepts of amassing and reporting data toward a more systematized, relational scientific interpretation. Research no longer was confined to the "term-paper" he had experienced in high school and first-year university classes. That realization had him so excited when he came into my office that he barely had sat down before he pulled out his poster and started explaining how the visualization had mediated his restatement of his initial very broad and abstract research question: "How does the environment, political climate, relationships, and religion surrounding a musician (in this case Critical Mood and 6th Militant) shape creative process, recording, and ultimately the final product?"

The combination of images and the ability to freely reconfigure them into a variety of relationships, including paradoxes, mediated the transformation of that question to: "The following research intends to investigate how Hip Hop artists learn. In addition, to interrogate how artists construct a creative process, formulate strategies and tools that can be defined, and ultimately affect the music that is created." Paul had connected his data in ways that helped him conceptualize his research query. He went on to interpret his data through the conceptual lenses he developed from his second, slightly more focused question.

Chris experienced the visualization exercise as much more of a dialogue, first with himself and then when his visualization (fig. 8.2) was read to the class. This young man had begun his project with a straightforward, or so it seemed, question about how music and memories seem to be connected. His reading and interviews had taken him off into brain research, music theory, emotional memory research, even music programming. His poster shows some of this plethora of information and his attempts to draw connections and make meanings out of everything. When his poster was "read," it sparked a flurry of comments and suggestions about what it might all mean. No one, it seemed, read it the same way and this sparked more and more focused questions both to Chris and to other class members. Chris took notes, answered and asked questions

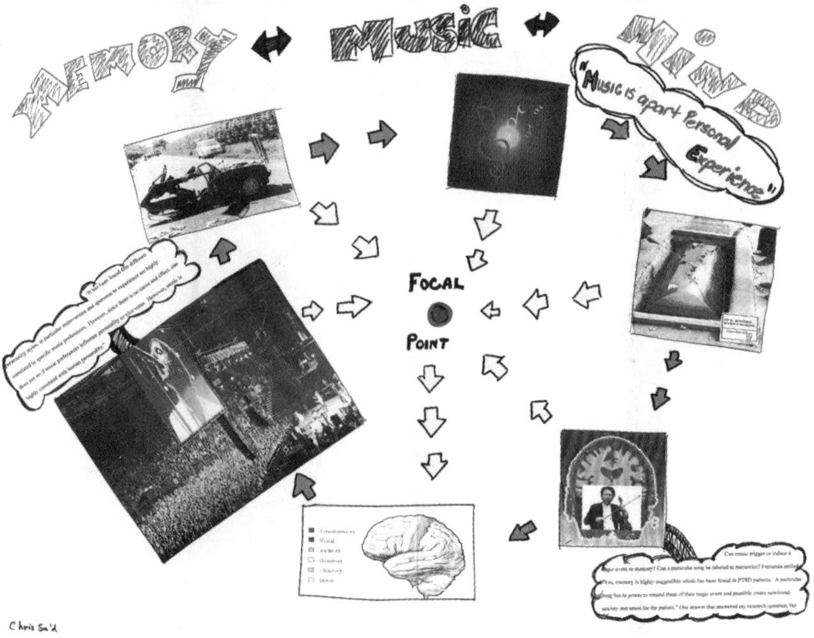

FIGURE 8.2. Chris Sa'ad's visualization.

of his own. In this case, I believe, the visualizing activity had mediated an intense discussion that mediated a focus Chris took with him. What had been a sprawl of tangential information eventually focused on an understanding of the role of chance (e.g., what was popular and being played at that time, repetition of a song, and the bond that produced with the dominant emotion in memory).

Another way in which the posters played an important step in students' development of their final multimodal reports was to represent their current research process more than their final conceptualization of the project. Andrea's poster was a visualization not of her final product but of the messy process she was engaged in. She had conducted surveys, interviews, done observations, even conducted a controlled experiment, yet her poster shows a dynamic thought process that plays with her ideas, including the conceptualization of a book cover as a performance and a billboard. She used a combination of directional symbols, arrows, question marks, large chunks of printed text, her own questions, images, pictures, and color to mediate her thinking. It appears that this visualization exercise afforded her the opportunity to try out her ideas about performance, something that had not yet emerged from her analysis of her

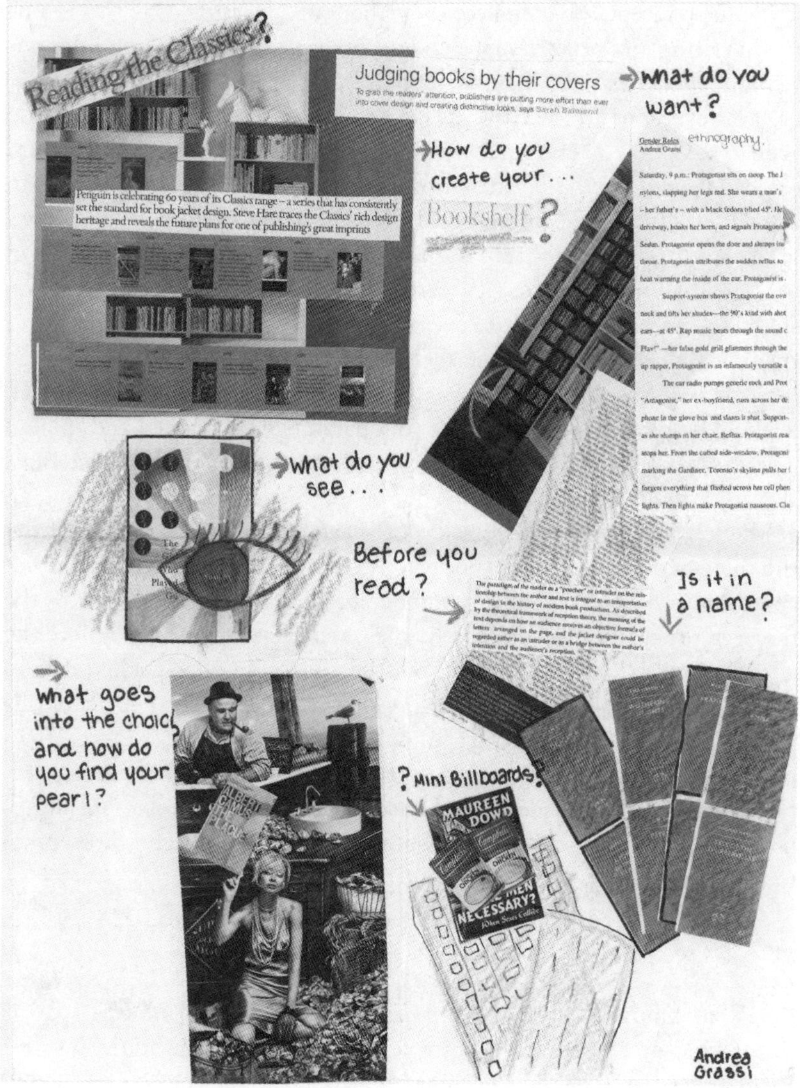

Figure 8.3. Andrea's visualization.

data until the visualization exercise. She continued to play with these two ideas as she drafted and revised her academic paper (fig. 8.3).

The cases of Paul, Chris, and Andrea illustrate that mediational means are not used the same way by each student in a class; they are only part of a complex set of interactive elements that students use (or not) to understand, to make links between everyday experiences and formal academic concepts, to complete their thoughts. Writing does this in one way. Writing and other visual elements on large papers without lines potentially mediates thinking differently.

However, not all the students used the mediational means to develop their concepts. For example, one student (Shelley) laid out the artifacts she had brought with her (including a cigarette and a cigarette box) in an attractive, literal, and linear representation of the results of her survey with supporting quotes from her interviews. She had been interested in how health-care professionals, particularly dental hygienists, felt about smoking. She had surveyed several hygienists and interviewed two of them. It appeared that she used the paper to create a poster that presented her findings. She did not juxtapose different pieces of data—for example, a dental hygienist's observations about patients who smoked and the hygienist's battle to quit smoking—to explore what other interpretations she might find in her data. Instead, Shelley concentrated on creating an aesthetically pleasing presentation of survey numbers and quotes from the interviews that echoed those survey numbers. The activity did not appear to have mediated any new understandings of either her data or the research process itself. Why? Why did Shelley either resist or ignore the affordances of the exercise? Without the collection of additional data to bring into the analysis the students' histories and contexts outside of this particular classroom activity, I cannot analyze her specific response. However, her response raises questions about what kinds of experiences, explicit instruction, and mediational means have shaped student meaning-making processes and what may be done to alter or expand those practices.

ALTERNATIVE REPORTS

What kinds of alternative research reports did all of this spawn? What kind of understanding of research did the visualizations inspire? In all honesty, not nearly what I had hoped for. Perhaps it was a function of time—most students carry full course loads, many work at least part-time, and many commute between two campuses. Then again, perhaps it was also a function of our presentation of the task and the follow-up support I provided. I also think we needed to develop our visual vocabulary. Without the visual vocabulary—I include both the words to talk about the visual elements and the elements themselves—text remained privileged in the reports and in the ways students worked with their data. Most of the students remained firmly based in text and text alone. I do not think this came from any lack of technical skill, as most of these students were adept with web design, desktop publishing, and photo and drawing computer software. Rather, I think it partly comes from what students have been taught to value and continues to be valued in an academic setting. The Dean's Essay prize has never been awarded to a multimodal composition. The writing program, with the exception of this and one other course, deals exclusively in the production of word text.[4] None of the courses explicitly address the meaning-making functions either in composition or in presentation of nontext elements beyond layout for ease of reading.

Most of the alternative reports re-presented their "findings" as newspaper or magazine articles. Some of these involved revision of the language to cut down on the use of technical terms, cutting the explicit citation of researcher names and details in an attempt to change the level of formality—the popularization of research findings that Varghese and Abraham (2004) described. With only two or three exceptions, none of the writers attempted to use other modalities to create opportunities to make meaning.

The exceptions ranged from a text-based piece on shyness that utilized an airbrushed background in pastel colors with the word "shyness" barely discernable from the background and several pieces of clip art that acted as adjuncts to the words; a set of short stories that more or less chronicled the author's investigation and used photographs placed in juxtaposition to the narrative to an ad campaign complete with storyboarded public-service announcements, posters, and a brochure. The clip art worked only through what Hagan called proximity to set up affordances for meaning making. The set of short stories used the proximity of text and photographs or scanned images of government documents to provoke meaning making. The cohesive ties were quite loose in both instances. The text in both cases had undergone only superficial revision from the academic piece.

REVISING AND RE-VISIONING THE RELATIONSHIP OF MULTIMODALITIES AND RESEARCH

The College Composition and Communications Conference has addressed visual/multimodal composition instruction in its conferences, journals, and online journals and communications. The issue raises questions about the definition of the discipline, about definitions of multimodality, of visual grammar, visual literacy, and the place of these elements in a writing or rhetoric curriculum. This issue also raises the question of the place of technology, as in some people's minds at least—including students'—information technology and multiliteracies and multimodalities are conflated. But they are not the same even though they are related and certainly technology has made it much easier for anyone with a computer and a willingness to fool around to include and use visual and aural modalities when composing written texts. Jay Lemke (2002, 300) differentiates between hypermodality and multimodality: "Hypermodality is more than multi-modality in just the way hypertext is more than plain text. It is not simply that we juxtapose image, text, and sound; we design multiple interconnections among them, both potential and explicit.

I believe my goal is closer to hypermodality, in both my pedagogy and in the work I expect from students. I understand the use of visual (and other modalities, although they were not part of this exercise) as simultaneously mediational means students and I can use to produce new interpretations and understandings as well as tools we can use to produce artifacts—assignments.

Why is it important for students to experience this multimodal process (more than just appealing to learning styles) in both understanding their own research process and in the production of alternative presentations of that research? I hoped to stimulate the students to recognize how the meanings they make change as they go through different writing tasks using different mediational means: framing a research rationale, a question; taking field notes; taking notes or responding to secondary sources; recognizing relationships in data, defining coding categories; drafting a first report of their research. I hoped that students would develop their conceptual understanding of the research process, linking everyday and scientific conceptualizations of doing, writing, and reading research. I also hoped to stimulate and expand the mediational tools they feel confident in using within the academic setting to include multiple modalities, not just as hooks and decorations in written and oral presentations.

Despite the students' familiarity with visual and aural modalities, I find the academic context with its privileging of plain text, the assumed symbolic value attached to a narrow definition of research and research writing still constrains student ventures into understanding and presenting their own research experiences, at least in this particular university context. But it is not enough to look only at the dominant values. It was and remains my responsibility to develop and use multimodalities in my teaching, in the way I present and develop ideas in the classroom. The deliberate inclusion of visual elements in both the way material is presented as well as in assigned "readings" and eventually the assignments students must complete may make a difference in the way students respond to and make use of activities such as the research visualization exercise. I, like my students, had not yet made links between the scientific concepts and everyday concepts of multimodalities in research.

NOTES

1. James Gee (1999) provides an accessible introduction to this concept of discourse in his *Introduction to Discourse Analysis*.

2. Gordon Wells (2002, 2007), David Russell (1997, 1999), and others have begun to think of language or discourse as an activity and not just as a mediating means.

3. Vygotsky (1986) identified a continuum of development between spontaneous and scientific concepts. These concepts are important as tools for solving problems. The spontaneous or everyday concepts are loosely equivalent to "rules of thumb"—unsystematic collections of ideas about how things work grounded in specific, everyday experiences. Everyday concepts are not always useful when applied to contexts other than the original experience. Scientific concepts are systematized, formal statements of principles applicable across multiple contexts. Vygotsky valued both. Everyday concepts grounded and enriched scientific concepts; scientific concepts systematized and broadened everyday concepts.

4. Students use diagrams, charts, maps, and pictures in some of the assignments they produce for other courses; however, to the best of my knowledge, the rhetorical opportunities, in Hagan's words, are not explicitly addressed.

REFERENCES

Bakhtin, Mikail M. 1981. "Discourse in the Novel." In *The Dialogic Imagination*, edited by Michael Holquist, 259–422. Translated by Caryl Emerson and Michael Holquist. Austin: University of Texas Press.

Carney, Russell N., and Joel R. Levin. 2002. "Pictorial Illustrations *Still* Improve Students' Learning from Text." *Educational Psychology Review* 14 (1): 5–26.

Cope, Bill, and Mary Kalantzis. 2000. "Multiliteracies: The Beginning of an Idea." In *Multiliteracies: Literacy Learning and the Design of Social Futures*, edited by Bill Cope and Mary Kalantzis, 3–37. London: Routledge.

Fleckenstein, Kristie S. 2007. "Testifying: Seeing and Saying in World Making."

In *Ways of Seeing, Ways of Speaking: The Integration of Rhetoric and Vision in Constructing the Real*, edited by Kristi S. Fleckenstein, Sue Hum, and Linda T. Calendrillo, 3–30. West Lafayette, IN: Parlor Press.

Gee, James P. 1999. *An Introduction to Discourse Analysis: Theory and Method*. New York: Routledge.

George, Diana. 2002. "From Analysis to Design: Visual Communication in the Teaching of Writing." *College Composition and Communication* 54 (1): 11–39.

Hagan, Susan M. 2007. "Visual/Verbal Collaboration in Print: Complementary Differences, Necessary Ties, and an Untapped Rhetorical Opportunity." *Written Communication* 24 (1): 49–83.

Heath, Shirley Brice. 2000. "Seeing Our Way into Learning." *Cambridge Journal of Education* 30 (1): 121–32.

Hedegaard, Marianne. 2007. "The Development of Children's Conceptual Relation to the World, with Focus on Concept Formation in Preschool Children's Activity." In *The Cambridge Companion to Vygotsky*, edited by Harry Daniels, Michael Cole, and James V. Wertsch, 246–75. Cambridge: Cambridge University Press.

Kozulin, Alex. 1996. "The Concept of Activity in Soviet Psychology: Vygotsky, His Disciples and Critics." In *An Introduction to Vygotsky*, edited by Harry Daniels, 99–122. London: Routledge.

Lemke, Jay L. 2002. "Travels in Hypermodality." *Visual Communication* 1 (3): 299–325.

Mayer, Richard E. 1997. "Multimedia Learning: Are We Asking the Right Questions?" *Educational Psychologist* 32 (1): 1–19.

Paivio, Aneta. 1986. *Mental Representations: A Dual-Coding Approach*. New York: Oxford University Press.

Porter, Jim. 2003. "Why Technology Matters to Writing: A Cyberwriter's Tale." *Computers and Composition* 20 (4): 375–94.

Russell, David. R. 1997. "Rethinking Genre in School and Society." *Written Communication* 14 (4): 504–54.

———. 1999. "Activity Theory and Process Approaches: Writing (Power) in School and Society." In *Post-Process Theory: Beyond the Writing-Process Paradigm*, edited by Thomas Kent, 80–95. Carbondale: Southern Illinois University Press.

Varghese, Susheela A., and Sunita A. Abraham. 2004. "Book-Length Scholarly Essays as a Hybrid Genre in Science." *Written Communication* 21 (2): 201–31.

Vygotsky, Lev S. 1978. *Mind in Society: The Development of Higher Psychological Processes*, edited by Michael Cole. Translated by Michael Cole, Vera John-Steiner, Sylvia Scribner, and Ellen Souberman. Cambridge: Harvard University Press.

———. 1986 [1934]. *Thought and Language.* Translated by Alex Kozulin. Cambridge: MIT Press.

Wells, Gordon. 2002. "The Role of Dialogue in Activity Theory." *Mind, Culture, and Activity* 9 (1): 43–66.

———. 2007. "The Mediating Role of Discoursing in Activity." *Mind, Culture, and Activity* 14 (3): 160–77.

CHAPTER 9

Multimodality, Memory, and Evidence

How the Treasure House of Rhetoric Is Being Digitally Renovated

Julia Romberger

The New London Group (NLG 2000) has discussed extensively the need to teach multimodal composing in our computer-mediated, communication-oriented society. Each of the modes of meaning the NLG (ibid., 26) has identified—audio, spatial, linguistic, visual, and gestural—can be found in digital media compositions. The NLG advocates that these design elements be integrated into curriculum so that students of all backgrounds are at a greater advantage in societies whose communication is dominated by computer-based tools. This group of scholars recognizes that there is a wealth of information being distributed through audio, video, and interactive means that challenge our notions of what is valid, how and if the book will retain its primacy as conveyor of information for the advancement of knowledge and creation of active civic participation, and what cultural impact these shifts will have globally. Many of the chapters in this collection are working toward developing means of applying the call of the New London Group toward composition pedagogy.

In this chapter I begin to interrogate two issues that are important to the work of developing multimodal composition within academic settings—evaluation of the content and authority of what the New London Group would call "available designs"—or evidence—and the coherence of argument.[1] It is my goal to further open the questions of how we teach students to evaluate sources that are not traditional academic sources that are disseminated in nontraditional academic modes and how we teach them to develop cohesive arguments when they are bringing together various modalities into one rhetorical act. Utilizing the canon of memory for multimodal composing processes is one entry point into thinking about these questions, certainly not the only one, but as a starting place, memory has the advantage of being linked to invention and delivery. These two canons encompass the two questions being posed. I argue that some of what students wish to bring to the table as evidence is fundamentally built on social memory, memory built by groups—a factor that necessitates that instructors draw students' attention to the rhetorical situation and power dynamics involved in the creation of such evidence.

The second issue is how these pieces of evidence, while promising to draw argument structures into new territories, must also fit within argument strategies that rhetoric and composition teachers and others in academia can recognize. To locate possible metadiscursive strategies for arguments that take into account spatiality and interactivity, I call upon the architectural mnemonic—particularly the less well-known trope of the theater. This chapter concludes with a call for further work to be done to discern how argument structure will be changed by multimodal composing and to identify strategies to address new argument structures for our students who are engaged in such work.

MEMORY AND AVAILABLE DESIGN

To better teach students how to work within these digital communication spaces, the NLG's (2000, 21) scholarship emphasizes available designs, the design conventions that "take the form of discourses, styles, genres, dialects, and voices, to name a few key variables." These discourses are a "configuration of knowledge" (ibid., 21). This emphasis is important as it defines as critical the need to allow students to incorporate all types of available designs into their designing process. The designing process is intellectual engagement for the growth of student knowledge, "the process of shaping emergent meaning" through transformation to accomplish the redesigned, an outcome that is more than just "reinstantiation of one Available Design" or even recombination of available designs (ibid., 22–23). The redesigned are new resources produced through the transformative processes of design (ibid., 23). The New London Group have developed a metadiscourse for analysis of these outcomes (see NLG 2000, 26–27, for an example).

However, they have not dealt with two important questions. First, they haven't addressed the question of how these available designs operate as various configurations of knowledge. The modes that the resources are presented in impacts how the content can be understood as evidence based on traditional academic criteria. Different modes carry different academic weight depending on how they are vetted, and this can influence how the information delivered by these modes is perceived in academic texts. The redesigns that are such an important outcome of multimodal work are also texts embedded in the academy. The goal of this multimodal pedagogy with its focus on the goal of redesign may aim to teach students how to operate in more broadly in a society where technology proficiency is key to advancement because so much discourse is happening through, with, and in it—however, the primary context in which this work occurs is still a critical part of the rhetorical situation.

EVALUATION: SOCIAL MEMORY AND DIGITAL SOURCES

The field of rhetoric and composition has for some time now been rethinking all of the canons for a multimodal pedagogy to open up the very type of composing modes that the New London Group has advocated. Memory held great importance among the canons for the ancients because it was inextricably bound up with both the first act of invention and the last act of delivery. Memory was called the "treasure house of eloquence" into which the rhetor must store information from repeated readings in an orderly fashion along with what had been said by their opponents (Quintilian 1998, XI.11.1–2). Memory is the "transmitting agent and hands on to the delivery what it has received through the imagination" (ibid., XI.11.3). According to Winifred Horner's (1998, 338) *Rhetoric in the Classical Tradition*, students learn that the traditional canon of classical memory must be expanded past the traditional memory (artificial and natural) of the rhetor to include information stored in computers and libraries—the latter making up the bulk of what was available to students in 1988.

Today, however, the situation has changed dramatically with a wealth of information of varying value available on the Internet as well as through library databases, government sites, and so forth. As Sharon Crowley and Debra Hawhee (2004, 328) note: "Software is now available that serves the heuristic function of ancient memory—something that literate storage could not do." Such software and search engines have the ability to call up information based on a wide variety of schemes, including cross-references, natural language processing, and Boolean operator logic. The information that this software can reference isn't confined to just traditional text but can include video, audio, image, and interactive modes as well.

If we accept the premise that memory has been externalized into digital treasure houses, then we need to discuss how this memory—created by entities other than the rhetor—may actually complicate the invention process and the choices made concerning delivery. Integrating the artifacts of this memory as it is archived in many different modalities (such as video, audio, image, and traditional text) forces the rhetor to think about delivery in concert with invention. The ties between the canons have never been more overt. Another assumption is that within multimodal texts, the rhetor who originates the pieces is composer and reader, as are all audiences for the piece. This puts a strain on the canon of memory in that, although any multimodal composition relies on memory from a variety of sources (which I'll speak about in more detail later), it also must, if it is civic discourse, find a way to make itself memorable to the audience and enter into the larger stream of social memory that is increasingly digitally available.

Wikipedia, Digg, Slashdot, and Complications of Social Memory

The quantity and kind of information available for student digital compositions, from PowerPoint to wikis, digital video and discussion boards, has expanded exponentially. The arbitration of these spaces as loci for memory often uses a different process than that which determined memory for Horner's students, although it might be built on a similar infrastructure, such as the required use of sources in Wikipedia. Academic peer review as such does not exist on YouTube, Wikipedia, Slashdot, and Digg, although these sites do have systems for monitoring and approving (with varying degrees of passivity) what is and is not acceptable to their audience and their perceived mission. Instructors who are in a position to deny legitimacy to this evidence need to make their perceptions about the modes explicit either through direct discussion or through student inquiry, as there is likely to be wide variation based on institutional policy, the instructor's familiarity with such sources, and instructor bias.

Value and Contextual Appropriateness

Often times, institutionally, there is little for an instructor to rely on for either advancing his or her own knowledge or helping students learn how to evaluate evidence found in various modes other than text. I examined three large university library websites and one online writing lab to see what type of information literacy instruction they had. Neither the Penn State (2005), Johns Hopkins (2010), nor University of Illinois (2009) libraries have anything specific about assessing video or audio tracks, nor about evaluating information on a community weblog like Slashdot or a news aggregate site like Digg. Advice given was limited to assessing the author, source of origination, bias, and currency of the information. Wikipedia is mentioned only in prohibitions about its use. The Purdue Online Writing Lab (OWL) (2010) has no advice on integrating such evidence into research papers, despite the fact that they mention such media as possible texts for developing arguments.

If the treasure house of digital memory is to include such evidence within multimodal compositions, then students need to be able to go beyond the common rubrics of assessing the author's credibility through institutional affiliation, academic credentials, and bibliographic sources. Much of this kind of work is already being done in our cultural studies–based composition classes, where evaluation of film, advertisements, and audio files often form the basis for discussion and research projects. However, if students wish to bring these modes into compositions for courses that are not invested in such a pedagogy, they will have to teach both themselves and the instructors how validation of information through these various modes happens and assess the value of it for their particular arguments. This becomes a bit of a tricky proposition, though, because often the content of such sites—no matter what the mode of delivery—is constructed based on social memory practices. There is precedence for the use of communally built memory as part of argumentation strategies in classical and medieval rhetorical theory, as Mary Carruthers (1990, 24) has noted. This was often how political and moral decisions were made in cultures where individuals were educated in the communal memory that shaped civic values and shared meaning (ibid., 24). But the use of such communally built information, without the vetting process of the academic refereeing process in a modern society, where fewer assumptions can be made about shared values and meaning, might be a bit disconcerting to academics who value traditional notions of scholarship.

The sense that the canon of memory is a social construct is not new. It is true that modern scholarship lacked explicit use of the term "collective memory" until the work of sociologist Maurice Halbwachs and historian Marc Bloch in 1925 (Olick 2006).[2] However, classical and medieval notions of rhetorical memory were demonstrably communal, as Carruthers's (1990) scholarship shows, and accessible through education, which was to complete the uninformed individual experience. Shared meaning was important in the ability to engage in civic discourse (ibid., 24). One broad understanding of social memory contends that it is a "matter of how minds work together in society, how their operations are not simply mediated but are structured by social arrangements" (Olick and Robbins 1998, 109). Implicit in this statement is that social structures, structures of power and authority, help determine what does and does not get included in the social memory being built at every social level from family through nation-state. Social memory is an integral part of subjectivity formation (ibid.; Olick 2006). Mythology and cultural traditions are ancient, orally constructed social memories that are carried down through generations. Social memory is always externalized through shared narratives, cultural traditions, writing, monuments, and so on that are posited within a discourse community. Halbwachs (1992, 38) has argued that social memories are recalled externally; "the groups of which I am a part at any time give me the means to reconstruct" these memories.[3] Many studies of the external sites of social memory look at museums, monuments, political discourse, histories, and so forth.

The digital communicative practices with their malleability, archivability, and accessibility are an additional site of social memory construction. These can be the source of evidence and available designs for students doing multimodal work. From the aptly named Community Memory, the country's first electronic bulletin board developed in the early 1970s, to Wikipedia, Del.icio.us, Slashdot, and Digg, rhetors are constructing their storehouse for invention online. The construction of social memory, collective memory, communal memory, cultural memory—the terminology is highly contested between and within the disciplines that study it—is evolving its rhetorical means of development within each of these spaces as the communities figure out how and when to monitor themselves.

An example can help clarify this point. Digg.com (2007) is a site that allows users to either dig (approve of) or bury news items. These news items are then ranked by the number of times they are dug, and then the top items are feed through an RSS reader to the desktop of anyone who chooses to subscribe. Subscribers may or may not choose to be part of the community who develops the rankings. This ranking also determines which news items are archived and which are not. It isn't a perfect system, but the users are determining what is and is not noteworthy within the news categories offered. This has potential to be more egalitarian, but there is also potential for stories to be buried because the first user who posted it is widely disliked or because of other, sometimes arbitrary, choices in ratings. It isn't always clear what the community values are on Digg.com. The values are shifting as new categories and users are added and new difficulties with the community and its citizens crop up.

Lack of transparency about how content is vetted can be problematic in the academy. Authority and credibility are also problematic constructs in digital spaces. For instance, a community such as Slashdot, which is a group weblog about the latest developments in technology and the social and political happenings that might influence technology users, presumably is comprised mostly of peers within the world of information technology and technophiles, but, as comments made on the site often show, there is considerable bias based upon perceived expertise. This bias may or may not be built on legitimate evidence. It is hard to determine actual expertise when any information about a user is voluntary, anonymous posts are possible (although potentially subject to community ridicule as the FAQ point out), and posts are not subject to extensive review (Slashdot 2007). Students utilizing information, valued for its currency, from such a site may find themselves in an awkward position if they attempt to use the traditional criteria for determining whether or not the source is credible by academic standards.

Social memory in the case of Digg and Wikipedia is being developed in new loci with new participants forming groups outside of the standard of family, region, nation, institution, and so on. The social arrangements lead to those who have the most access, inclination, and time to devote to the activity as being the arbiters of what counts as social memory and what does not. This raises issues of suppression of memory that either diverges from the community's agreed norm or results from lack of access for those who might wish to participate in these communities. Andrea Smith (2004) has noted the heteroglossia of competing voices when she was developing an ethnographic study of oral memories of assimilation into the dominant French culture in Algeria. This is no less true in the spaces where memory is constructed online. Students need to learn to negotiate through the multiplicity of voices. Instances of flaming in these spaces are all too common when there is dissention. Learning the discourse conventions through FAQs or about pages, observation, and trial-and-error participation are often the only ways to discover how the hierarchies play out and how authority is established. For example, the viral video YouTube that shows former Senator George Allen making his infamous "macaca" comment had the power to influence an election (Zkman 2006). The comments in the responses range from outrage to mockery to debate over whether or not Allen knew what he was saying. It was still being commented on late into 2010. How does a YouTube video become evidence for a national debate and provide fodder for discussion about the values of the Republican Party? Understanding how this information becomes a valued commodity is still in the early stages of scholarly inquiry. Until this becomes more transparent, it is understandable that many academics might feel less than sanguine about allowing them into student work.

If students are both participant in and users of social memory that is built in digital spaces, then as instructors of rhetoric, we have an obligation to help them think through some of the issues that this new art of memory raise. Different social loci have different memory values, and students need to negotiate between the various discourse communities in which they have constructed (or wish to construct) participant identities. There is a potential for these sites of social memory to be memory of the masses. Students must also be taught to assess what each community values in the building of memory and in the use of memory for invention, especially when they are bringing in the social memory practices of one community—say that of Wikipedia—to that of the academic classroom for the creation of a digital composition. In part, some instruction can be done through modeling rhetorical practices in the classroom through using similar methods of delivery as well as analyzing spaces in which students already participate.

INCORPORATION: BRINGING THE CONTENT OF DIGITAL MEMORY INTO MULTIMODAL ARGUMENT

Recently I got an e-mail with a link to a video with comments in YouTube, where a good friend of mine complained about the storylines in a favorite science fiction show of ours. The writers had lost their way, he claimed. He played with this word—"lost"—referencing in the text the popular TV show *Lost*, which I have not watched but know of. More interestingly, the comments arrived next to a link to a series of campy false cliffhangers from the show *Lost in Space*, which we both have vague memories of watching in syndication as children. The campy nature and suggested plot content of the false cliffhangers underscored his opinion that the narrative of the show had gone from hard-hitting political commentary and social drama into the more clichéd realms of traditional science fiction narrative—some of which were referenced in the cliffhangers.

What struck me about this e-mail was how very ordinary it was, this use of the social memory of the video clip stored on the Web as device for invention, play, and evidence in an argument. I knew how to read this e-mail based upon the context of our previous discussions, knowledge of the rhetor and his sense of humor, and more critically through signposting developed by anchoring as Roland Barthes (2004) has defined it. The play on the word "lost" and its repetition allowed me to read this particular argument and the evidence it presented as interconnected. This anchoring acted as a metadiscourse, allowing the retrieved texts from various modes to create support for his thesis.

Metadiscourse and Signposting

In prose, metadiscourse creates cohesion and coherence of arrangement, allowing the reader to easily follow the points being made because overt connections through conjunctions, conjunctive adverbs, and punctuation. This is important in creating an argument because it allows the audience to make logical connections between the information being presented to arrive at conclusions that will, presumably, support the primary assertions of the rhetor. Questions of metadiscourse in multimodal compositions also need to be addressed because of the important rhetorical function it serves. There are already discussions in the field about metadiscourse at the visual level. For example, Eric Kumpf (2000) has argued that visual elements such as first impression, consistency, convention, chunking, style, and the external skeleton, among others, operate as metadiscursive functions as well. These elements serve memory functions by allowing the audience to be able to develop connections between each element. James Porter and Patricia Sullivan (2004) have made similar arguments regarding repetition in design. As a field, we have excellent research from visual rhetoric and technical communication to draw upon to discuss the principles for the inclusion of images (see, for example, Kostelnick and Roberts 1998; Kumpf 2000). We have fewer heuristics for determining what will operate as metadiscourse for multimodal texts.

Each of the forms of media that the modes are represented by—film, audio, interface, text, image—all have an internal metadiscourse. And within each media various genres have their own set of metadiscursive practices, with academic textual metadiscourse being some of the most studied (for instance, see Swales 1990). Even within traditional textual forms, metadiscourse conventions shift to suit audience, genre conventions, and rhetorical situations. For example, strategies like paragraph and topic transitions and formal, summative conclusions as metadiscourse are far less appropriate in certain genres of Western business settings where a premium is placed upon an economy of words. Memos, for instance, tend to use headings to guide readers, and reports often use a combination of headings, table of contents, and repurposed text to fill similar functions.

It becomes an even more difficult proposition for a composition instructor to consider metadiscourse practices and provide strategies to guide an audience when students are integrating modes. Film follows patterns of continuity, editing, lighting, and soundtrack conventions that all give specific information to the audience to understand how the narrative structure is progressing. However, the lighting conventions for a horror film—close and dark with light that tends to be intermittent or faulty to increase suspense—are quite different than those of your conventional Western, where big sky and outdoor scenes with natural lighting figure prominently. We are familiar with the genre conventions through frequent repetition, a conglomerate of memory based upon our long association with the medium. If a student wants to integrate a cinematic mode and a textual mode, there is some difficulty in mapping these types of cinematic metadiscursive practices onto textual practices like those mentioned earlier, especially as they fluctuate between genres. As Gunther Kress (2003, 107) notes, we can't transport our theories of how the modes work from one mode to the other without distortion. Kress himself, in *Literacy in the New Media Age*, talks about framing as one way into a discussion about reading, but our discussions about metadiscourse and its important function in meaning making and retention need to go further.

To help develop a way of speaking about how such a space works for the rhetor and the audience, rhetoric and composition instructors might turn again to the architectural mnemonic of the Greeks and Romans. Ellen Cushman (2004) has already suggested that in dealing with the space/time in new media, the use of spatial mnemonics of the ancients might become useful if they set markers within new media composing software to orient themselves. After all, the artificial mnemonic was a space (normally conceptualized as a house) in which visual keys or metaphors to evidence for creating an argument were arranged in order throughout an open, well-lighted architectural space. Conceptually, a rhetor using this type of mnemonic would be able to picture himself moving from space to space with the visual cues within providing the next piece of evidence for his oratory (see Quintilian 1998, XI.2, or Carruthers 1990 for a more thorough discussion).

The metaphoric representations of ideas were to be well connected through text and image and easily accessible. It is important to the architectural memory scheme that the space in which the memory images are located is constructed with care and precision, as it is a wax tablet upon which the memory images are to be impressed in a certain order for better recollection (Carruthers 1990, 72). Backgrounds should not be crowded, easily distinguished one from the other, to better facilitate the ability to start and end anywhere when remembering (ibid., 72). Memory images should be created by association with concepts, as they are more easily recalled than exact words (ibid., 73). Similar schemes might be devised for a multimodal text; design elements can be created to allow for the audience to track various shifts in modes while following the anchoring of meanings or disruption of common threads.

Although the architectural mnemonic has many possibilities, I believe that for multimodal work (indeed for many discussions of how the canon of memory can be found at work in digital spaces) the trope of the theater as a specific type of architectural space as opposed to the commonly used house might be far more useful. There is precedence for using the theater as a trope for artificial memory. Guilio Camillo in the Renaissance built an actual model theater designed as an interactive memory that allowed the rhetor to place within drawers and doors marked with images passages (mostly related to Cicero) (Yates 1966, 144). However, interestingly, audience seating was the place where memory was stored. The solitary spectator stands on the place where the stage would be (making him active) and looks out at the auditorium (ibid., 137). Robert Fludd in the English Renaissance also constructed what might be called an occult-based memory system upon a theater system. He emphasized the use of real buildings, in his work in the Elizabethan or Jacobean theater, and does not include the building proper in his system. Instead, he focuses on the stage. It is a place to story concepts and words (ibid., 328–29). Because so much is lost to time, it is unclear in Frances Yates's account how the rhetor was supposed to interact in these spaces.

In considering the theater as a present-day trope for memory, there are a number of attributes that are important to discuss. First, the stage is infinitely repeatable or infinitely changeable depending upon the drama, the director, and the actor's needs. But, outside of some of the more radical modern designs, the framework of the stage is always the same. There is the proscenium arch, the backdrops, stage-left, stage-right, and backstage for all the behind-the-scenes workings. It is a familiar space in this, much like the house or other piece of architecture recommended by the ancients or Camillo, Fludd, or the Englishman John Willis. The theater trope has precedence in scholarship about computer design. Brenda Laurel (1991, 17), in her classic work *Computers as Theatre*, advocates the use of the theater trope to think about interface design because it allows us to think of the computer as a virtual world: "All action within this space is confined to the world of [virtual] representation" (ibid., 18). The theater is a contained world for interaction between those who would communicate and be communicated with inside a specific scene that is designed by those who would exert some control over the means of communication.

On most stages there are props, scenery, and other actors with whom one can interact. They are manipulable (even the other actors to some degree). This is not unlike a computer, which has the same set of stages, similar choices of props, the same general space of the screen—each an ever-expanding set as the technology advances—within which the user can act and react. And yet there is certainly room for surprises, disruptions, asides, and audience participation—essentially breaking the fourth wall. While the actions might be somewhat different each time, the user determines the actions by the presence of things like icons, standard linking, common controls, and sometimes just scrubbing the screen to find hot spots. The navigational properties of such digital texts operate as a memory space both while the user is learning to read the text and by creating a series of indexible objects and interactions. After a period of repetition, the geography becomes familiar. All of these navigational properties can be developed into heuristics and strategies for composing in multimodal venues. To create appropriate connections in a multimodal text, information from the various modes should be indexed properly to create signposts for the audience that guide them through the connections.

Barthes (2004, 156) in "Rhetoric of the Image" discusses how each image is a "floating chain of signifieds"; each image requires the use of one of the scores of social techniques that use text for "anchoring" and "relaying" the chain so that there are fewer "uncertain signs" and the audience knows how to focus their gaze and understanding. This work can be done with the moving image of video, with audio, and with interaction as well.[4] It would be rhetorically beneficial to include strategies such as Barthes discusses as part of something much like the storyboarding techniques discussed by Nathaniel Córdova in chapter 6 of this collection as part of the invention process. This would not only help students conceptualize how they will make the multimodal composition memorable for their audience, but it would help them develop metadiscursive anchors that can guide their audience through connections in the work's argument. This work also foregrounds invention, memory, and delivery in ways that traditional textual work does not, which again complicates in productive ways for students and scholars the rhetorical situation.

ARCHITECTURAL MEMORY AND SIGNPOSTING IN PEDAGOGICAL PRACTICE

I teach an introduction to digital writing course at the sophomore/junior level. One of the projects I used the last time I taught this class was a digital discourse community analysis that is designed to encourage students to examine such questions as what counts as evidence in an online discourse community and what are the community's goals, preferred genres, and mechanisms for feedback. I carefully walk them through John Swales's (1990) six aspects of a discourse community as the foundation for this project. I also include examples of online discourse communities for class discussion so that they can see how these traits apply. I have a mock-up of a project that analyzes the site icanhascheezburger.com as a place where a discourse community convenes (fig. 9.1).

It starts with statements on a main page designed to mimic certain aspects of a threaded discussion board. (I keep everything within the mock-up at a technological level that they can replicate based upon what the class teaches.) Our discussion about the usage of digital genres for online discourse communities is referenced as I explain how I used this genre to create an interface for my mock-up by exploiting the nested nature of comments to make statements that can be explored as claims backed by evidence on the pages that are linked to. I use the names of the posters as the links, which is something often done on discussion boards when people want to share something about themselves or make a point regarding the post they've made. Essentially the mock-up is using some of the navigational strategies of threaded discussion boards as heuristics for moving through this page, despite the fact that it is clearly just a relatively standard web page.

For the genres page I created a short video of an unseen person watching a video posted on the site icanhascheezburger.com with a voice-over

Figure 9.1. "I Can Has Discourse Community"—mock-up of an interface.

explaining how it is a common genre and the way it is used. This is part of the evidence on the second page of the mock-up, the genre page. When I show them this video, I talk about it as part of the common genre of home video (moderately poor lighting and camera work). I then encourage discussion about how videos get incorporated into websites like icanhascheezburger.com. We talk about conventions for this insertion, how the video is arranged on the page and how that is related to the purpose of the video. I also refer them back to the early discussions we have on basic design principles. I apply the concept of the theater mnemonic in the analysis questions I provide regarding narrative interaction on the stage, props, memorability, and breaking the fourth wall:

1. What points are along the timeline(s) or narrative(s) of the digital project? Where do the reader and writer enter and act within the digital project?
2. What elements of previous design and experience might the audience have seen elsewhere? Do these elements act as devices to help the audience experience this timeline or narrative?
3. How is this particular digital project and the information in it made memorable for the audience so that they can recall and reuse the information within?
4. What, if anything, calls attention to the digital nature of the project? What is the value of this for the argument being made?

I then ask the class to use these analysis questions as an invention tool, along with others, in their planning of their own web-based reports.

A further purpose of the mock-up that I have included is to provide an example of what might be done with the types of evidence and genres they find online and to encourage a sense of play and the potential of various modes for producing valid academic discourse. It also is meant to demonstrate how you can use the navigational expectations of one genre as a heuristic for building interaction in another genre, even at a relatively unsophisticated level. I have discovered, though, that my attempts to encourage students to use a variety of evidence for their projects in a multimodal fashion often falls flat, even when the assignment's nature encourages the usage of a variety of modalities for presenting their evidence. I observe two forces at work in the anecdotal evidence provided by their post-project reflective writes. The first, and probably most critical, is that because this is an introductory class, many of the students don't feel comfortable adding into their web-based reports more than a few links and a picture. Perhaps my assignment description—which focuses on minimums that are designed to make students feel comfortable and calm openly expressed jitters about using the technology to create a web-based project—does not encourage enough of the sort of work I discuss with them in class.

The pages they produce very closely replicate the type of report they would produce in another class. They are also highly conditioned to rely upon textual evidence to demonstrate their claims; they feel that relying upon what they know is most likely to get them a good grade. It is difficult to get beyond discussions about how online sites are socially constructed, the first part of this chapter, to talk about presentation of the evidence, the second part of this chapter, when student are so wary about breaking away from traditional research papers in an English class, even one specifically about digital media. I do not yet have an answer to the first problem, because technology anxiety will always be an issue with the student population that takes this class. Perhaps as various technologies become easier to use this will change. It is already far easier to insert a video into web page through the use of a YouTube link than it was in the early days of teaching students to compose with digital media. The second issue I hope will also change over time as more students are taught throughout the academy and in their K–12 educations to take advantage of the full capacity of programs such as Microsoft PowerPoint, which allows for a wide variety of modalities. I recognize within my own pedagogy that I need to continue to experiment and refine my approaches so that students can deliberately apply aspects of class discussion and readings in their projects and not assume that such work is out of their technological reach.

IMPLICATIONS FOR MEMORY IN MULTIMODAL COMPOSITION

The canon of memory has potential to become more complexified as multimodal composition forces us to rethink the rhetorical canons. Memory as a canon can help instructors and students think through issues of evaluation and integration, even while its use with digital media makes the ties to the other canons more explicit. Memory as a canon in the past was often dropped from mention in textbooks because memorization of speeches is no longer a practice that most students need to do outside a speech communications course (Reynolds 1989). A more robust understanding of the history of the canon would assist instructors and students as they grapple with articulating the means of creating multimodal work. As we rethink issues of the canon of memory for multimodality, instructors can work with students on developing heuristics for assessing the value of multimodal texts that are constructed on social memory. Teaching students how to examine the practices of such sites through looking up FAQs, rules for posting, and political, social, and scholarly associations, as well as spending some time evaluating how conversations evolve and who is and is not legitimated as a participant, can be helpful in several ways. It can assist students in understanding why sites such as Wikipedia should be used with caution.

Students can also learn to understand knowledge formation at a deeper level and expand their ability to do quality research both in school and eventually workplace situations. Finally, such heuristics can help students make arguments to instructors and other authority figures in disciplines outside rhetoric for the value of such evidence in well-informed arguments.

In addition, conceptualizing multimodal compositions as spaces for interaction, much like a theater, can help emphasize the need for placing the texts students compose within a framework that takes into account both the need for memory strategies like anchoring to create cognitive cohesion between the different nodes/modes and for making the composition memorable so that it is better able to participate in the civic discourse practices it is inserting itself into.

NOTES

1. Certainly, the way that we theorize argument is going to be impacted by the use of multimodal composition as a means of communicating; however, this chapter looks more at the needs of the transitional phase as we work toward understanding how to create arguments that are valued by the academy while still moving toward an as-yet shifting set of argument strategies.

2. I use research in sociology and anthropology primarily because they are closer to rhetoric, history, and philosophy, and, unlike cognitive psychology, these disciplines focus less on individual memory (Olick and Robbins 1998).

3. Halbwachs was arguing against the Freudian tendency to locate all memory and identity strictly within the mind of one human being.

4. With interaction this might be a bit harder to see, but most interaction is meant to mimic certain material realities. For example, the mouse click in any Graphic User Interface application is meant to mimic selecting by hand. Scrolling on a screen in a word-processing program is meant to mimic the actions of a typewriter. Hitting a key in a first-person shooter video game is meant to mimic firing a gun. Each of these interactions is embedded within a larger context that gives you textual and image cues, letting you know what interactions you might anticipate.

REFERENCES

Barthes, Roland. 2004. "Rhetoric of the Image." In *Visual Rhetoric in a Digital World: A Critical Sourcebook*, edited by Carolyn Handa, 152–63. New York: Bedford/St. Martin's.

Carruthers, Mary. 1990. *The Book of Memory: A Study of Memory in Medieval Culture.* Cambridge: Cambridge University Press.

Crowley, Sharon, and Debra Hawhee. 2004. *Ancient Rhetorics for Contemporary Students*, third ed. New York: Longman.

Cushman, Ellen. 2004. "Composing New Media: Cultivating Landscapes of the Mind." *Kairos* 9 (1). Online at http://english.ttu.edu/KAIROS/9.1/binder.html?http://www.msu.edu/%7Ecushmane/one/landscape.html.

Digg, Inc. 2007. "What Is Digg?" Online at http://digg.com/about/.

Farkas, David, and Jean Farkas. 2001. *Principles of Web Design*, edited by Sam Dragga. New York: Longman.

Halbwachs, Maurice. 1992. *On Collective Memory*. Edited, translated, and with an introduction by Lewis A. Coser. Chicago: University of Chicago Press.

Horner, Winifred. 1998. *Rhetoric in the Classical Tradition*. New York: St. Martin's Press.

Kirk, Elizabeth. 2010. "Evaluating Information Found on the Internet." Johns Hopkins University. The Sheridan Libraries. Online at http://guides.library.jhu.edu/evaluatinginformation.

Kostlenick, Charles, and David Roberts. 1998. *Designing Visual Language: Strategies for Professional Communicators*, edited by Sam Dragg. Boston: Allyn and Bacon.

Kress, Gunther. 2003. *Literacy in the New Media Age*. New York: Routledge.

Kumpf, Eric. 2000. "Visual Metadiscourse: Designing the Considerate Text." *Technical Communication Quarterly* 9 (4): 401–24.

Laurel, Brenda. 1991. *Computers as Theatre*. Reading, MA: Addison-Wesley Press.

New London Group. 2000. "A Pedagogy of Multiliteracies: Designing Social Futures." In *Multiliteracies: Literacy Learning and the Design of Social Futures*, edited by Bill Cope and Mary Kalantzis, 9–37. New York: Routledge.

Olick, Jeffrey. 2006. "Products, Processes, and Practices: A Non-reificatory Approach to Collective Memory." *Biblical Theology Bulletin* 36 (1): 5–14.

———, and Joyce Robbins. 1998. "Social Memory Studies: From 'Collective Memory' to the Historical Sociology of Mnemonic Practices." *Annual Review of Sociology* 24: 105–40.

Pennsylvania State University Libraries. 2010. *How to Evaluate Information*. Online at http://www.libraries.psu.edu/psul/lls/students/research_resources/evaluate_info.html.

Porter, James, and Patricia Sullivan. 2004. "Repetition and the Rhetoric of Visual Design." In *Visual Rhetoric in a Digital World: A Critical Sourcebook*, edited by Carolyn Handa, 290–302. New York: Bedford/St. Martin's.

Purdue Online Writing Lab (OWL). 2010. "The Rhetorical Situation: Audience and Text." Online at http://owl.english.purdue.edu/owl/resource/625/2/.

Quintilian. 1998. *The Institutio Oratoria of Quintilian*. Cambridge: Harvard University Press.

Reynolds, John Fredrick. 1989. "Concepts of Memory in Contemporary Composition." *Rhetoric Society Quarterly* 19: 245–52.

Slashdot. 2007. "FAQ." Online at http://www.slashdot.org/faq/.

Smith, Andrea, L. 2004. "Heteroglossia, 'Common Sense,' and Social Memory." *American Ethnologist* 31 (2): 251–69.

Swales, John. 1990. *Genre Analysis: English in Academic and Research Settings.* Cambridge: Cambridge University Press.

University Library of the University of Illinois at Urbana-Champaign. 2009. "Evaluating Internet Sources." Online at http://www.library.uiuc.edu/ugl/howdoi/webeval.html.

Yates, Frances. 1966. *The Art of Memory.* Chicago: University of Chicago Press.

Zkman. 2006. "George Allen Introduces 'Macaca.'" Online at http://www.youtube.com/watch?v=r90z0PMnKwI.

PART III

The Changing Structure of Composition Programs

CHAPTER 10

Student Mastery in Metamodal Learning Environments

Moving beyond Multimodal Literacy

Mary Leigh Morbey and Carolyn Steele

ALTHOUGH THE ABILITIES TO INTERACT with and within virtually mediated spaces are rapidly becoming basic life skills, our awareness and understanding of how this interaction differs from traditional media is still in its infancy. The most advanced research in multimodal literacies is focused on schoolchildren, implying that the earlier technologically appropriate interventions are introduced, the greater their benefits. However, the most advanced usage of virtualized media is by teenagers and young adults, so note Henry Jenkins and coauthors (2006) and James Gee (2007) in their investigations into participatory culture and video game affinity groups. This has spawned an entire subfield of research hoping to translate the seemingly insatiable demand for gaming in virtual worlds into more compelling educational resources. Undergirding this demand is a divide between computer-savvy youth for whom the computer is a metamedium (an interface through which they negotiate their identity and interact on a global level), and the adults around them who see computers largely as a pragmatic technology of convenience and efficiency.

This divide is particularly foregrounded in universities where the range of computer use can stretch from nonexistent to deeply immersive virtual reality. This chapter concentrates specifically on North American university contexts where, for the most part, the bulk of computer use is still focused on text-based data processing within traditional disciplinary boundaries, most notably in the social sciences and humanities. Far from pushing the boundaries of computer-mediated research, in most cases, the level of computer literacy among university professors has been slow to change since the introduction of the graphical user interface (GUI), which opened up new modes of communication and typical administrative functions to the general population. The hiring of junior faculty, having been raised within a digital culture, is rapidly shifting these norms.

Many of the traditions and cultural practices that have solidified the university's position as the bedrock of Western intellectual culture for the past millennium have also impeded its ability to remain relevant in a digital and global economy.[1] For example, within the social sciences and humanities (which attract the majority of students in many universities) print-based scholarship continues to be privileged above all other forms, although increases in the cost of paper and printing are radically reducing the number of hard copy journals. The impact of this trend is still a matter of some debate. Likewise, academe has a well-earned reputation of being skeptical of innovation, although some of this can also be attributed to reductions in funding. Nonetheless, a university education is still considered a necessary prerequisite to a career in the knowledge economy. Universities are under increasing pressure from governments, industries, and parents to provide their graduates with mastery of current and emergent technological literacies. While millions of dollars are being spent on university-based research studying the impact of new technologies on society, few of these findings are being employed to transform how university students and instructors can use advanced, computer-based technologies in higher-level knowledge production for the organization of student experiences and composing practices. This contemporary context, containing traditional university educative philosophies and subsequent practices, creates the problematic faced in arguing toward a delitteralizing of approaches for student composition.

According to the Stanford Metaverse Roadmap Project, in 2016 students aged thirteen to thirty will be spending over forty hours a week using interactive, Internet-based, 3-D visual environments for a wide range of purposes including education (Smart et al. 2007).[2] For the vanguard of these young people, most of the technical knowledge and skills they will be using in these activities will not be learned in an educational environment but rather through means like social networking, entertainment technologies, and individual experimentation. Given the economic power of the telecommunications, entertainment, and computer industries, this raises serious concerns about the degree of agency and awareness the next generation will have in negotiating their identities and activities in a virtually mediated world.

More recently, we have seen the emergence of metamedia platforms within the realm of 3-D educative virtual environments (Young 2010). These are virtual environments that not only provide users with a dynamic, immersive experience but also enable them to create, construct, embed, unify, and archive multimedia content, social media, text, video, and 3-D artifacts, along with grid- and cloud-based on-demand computing services (Lombardi and Lombardi 2010). Metamedia are therefore not just another media type: they are virtual portals for delivering a range of media and media applications to both producers and consumers of media. They are distinct from "multimedia"; the emphasis in metamedia is not merely on the existence of more than one media type (as it is with multimedia) but on the creative environment in which multiple-types composition becomes a complex and diverse activity across media and can be manipulated for various semiotic and aesthetic purposes.

The focus of this chapter is the impact and potential of metamedia platforms to transform higher education into a learning "metaverse"—an emerging 3-D web of social spaces, technologies, and economies (Smart et al. 2007). Such a metaverse fosters many of the ideals of advanced knowledge production that are becoming increasingly relevant to university-level writing instruction: transdisciplinary research (conceptual space among disciplinary practices), creative synthesis of ideas and perspectives, and individual agency in the construction and mediation of multiple and complex lifeworlds (Welshons 2006) as well as more traditional writing skills. Using two contemporary virtual environments—*Second Life* (http://secondlife.com/) and Croquet-Open Cobalt (http://www.opencobalt.org/)—we examine the potential and promise for writing curricula in tertiary education to foster the development of metamodal mastery (MM) in metamedia environments. We are suggesting metamodal mastery as an alternative approach to traditional notions of literacy in the context of metamedia learning environments.

MM acknowledges the ability to work strategically and with a degree of personal agency across different media and disciplines (diSessa 2000;

Kahn and Kellner 2005; Kress 2003). Unlike discussions that prioritize individual ability (common with the term "literacy"), MM is a level of expertise that is only fully realized when students and researchers with such expertise in multiple fields come together to create a multimodal argument synthesizing their diverse perspectives in a way that crosses their disciplinary boundaries and emerges in a subsequent hybridity. In this sense, MM has a strong affinity with researchers who have focused on Web 2.0 usage, participatory culture, and remix culture (Gee 2007; Jenkins et al. 2006; Lankshear and Knobel 2003; Lessig 2008). Besides its affinity with popular culture, however, MM is also more generalized in its transdisciplinary or border-crossing realizations. This inquiry raises questions regarding the status of student participation in a virtual world and offers potential directions for further queries.

SHIFTING BOUNDARIES BETWEEN ACADEMIC DISCIPLINES

Gunther Kress, Carey Jewitt, and Charalambos Tsatsarelis (2000) have described the shift from modernism to postmodernism as one of destabilization in which the firm boundaries that structured modern, industrialized systems, and hierarchies became fluid and negotiable. This description frames the primary, secondary, and tertiary levels of education that these scholars examine as well as the disciplinary categories by which the North American university traditionally has been structured and through which expertise within that institution has been recognized. Universities have responded to these changes with varying degrees of enthusiasm. On the external public level, the epistemological blurring of academic boundaries has been articulated in university marketing and recruitment literature, presenting universities as interdisciplinary environments that offer an opportunity to see the world through different lenses.

Privately, however, in the internal professional realms of the academy—dissertations, academic journals, tenure reviews, and library holdings—traditional disciplinary divisions and practices are still strongly maintained. Bodies of knowledge articulated as disciplines are more than discursively realized: they are concretely situated within sites of education (Kress, Jewitt, and Tsatsarelis 2000), such as academic departments, faculty offices, and classrooms. Even in the archiving of knowledge within library holdings, the separation between disciplines is spatially reinforced in academic journals situated on different bookshelves, often on different floors of the library. To engage in transdisciplinary research, scholars must cross both conceptual and geographical boundaries into spaces where they are literally *strangers in a strange land*.[3]

To clarify what we mean by the notion of "transdisciplinary," a differentiation between the terms "interdisciplinary," "multidisciplinary," and "transdisciplinary" is needed. Here we draw on explorations of these differences occurring in two very different fields—science and visual design. The work of Michael Gibbons, Camille Limoges, Helga Nowotny, Simon Schwartzmann, Peter Scott, and Martin Trow (1994) on the Mode 2 theory of knowledge production (multidisciplinary teams working on specific problems for short time periods) focuses on applied context-driven research directed by problem solving outside traditional disciplinary distinctions. Within this dynamic, interdisciplinary teams collaborate on the development of approaches and concepts to problems that are a hybridization of their individual disciplinary affiliations. Gibbons et al. (1994) distinguish transdisciplinarity as different from multi- or interdisciplinarity because the resulting solutions of transdisciplinarity do not necessarily derive from traditional disciplinary frames at all, nor do they necessarily form new disciplines (Nowotny, Scott, and Gibbons 2003). A further expansion of transdisciplinarity is situated in a common theoretical understanding now accompanied by mutual interpenetrations of differing disciplinary epistemologies, leading to a cluster of disciplinary-based problem solving creating a transdisciplinary homogenized theory or model (Gibbons et al. 1994).

In light of their studies in industrial design, architecture collaborations, and fine art practice, John Marshall and Jon Pengelly (2006, 2007) posit that various computer technologies have been used to navigate and transverse disciplinary boundaries.[4] Furthermore, they argue that an increasing number of practitioners are able and willing to work across designated discipline domains, and they hypothesize that this has birthed a model of practice that engages cross-disciplinary discourse and yields convergence among distinct domains. Marshall and Pengelly (2006) employ transdisciplinarity in a way that ignores hierarchical distinctions, particularly of architecture, art, and design discourse and practice, and look to references from an expanded cultural field that can lead to new opportunities and practices, often in the *terrain vague* or conceptual space between disciplinary practices.

This transdisciplinary position effectively acknowledges creative approaches to knowledge production that synthesizes epistemologies and methodologies from inside disciplinary frames to spaces outside these frames, where innovative and unique ideas and solutions can emerge. We believe this conceptualization also holds promise for describing new compositional practices within and between genres for students to explore: fluid to-and-fro crossings of boundaries in a Heideggerian sense (Heidegger 1971). In essence, transdisciplinary practices explored from the realms of design and science are not just postmodernist manifestations of destabilization. They instead represent the transformation of actual disciplinary practices and artifacts to the virtual realm proposed by Pierre Lévy (1998) in *Becoming Virtual*. Lévy describes virtualization as a process wherein objects and events become deterritorialized from physical space to a nonmaterial realm: detached from their original contexts, easily shared among communities of interest, and transforming individual users through a process of heterogenesis—shifts in both media and media users as each is increasingly shaped by digital media use. We see Lévy's (1998) process of virtualization as particularly relevant to the digital dissemination of composition, text, illustrations, data, and artifacts through which disciplinary boundaries are fluidly crossed. This kind of process was recently acknowledged in *Our Cultural Commonwealth* (Welshons 2006), endorsing the potential of digital media to support the relatively seamless study of textual and nontextual objects and data in many fields.

FROM MULTIMODAL LITERACY TO METAMODAL MASTERY

There is an inherent affinity between metamedia platforms and transdisciplinary education. Both are characterized by permeable boundaries that require a broad palate of technical, analytical, and critical knowledge and skills on the part of both novice and expert, variously conceptualized as technoliteracy, multiliteracy, critical media, and visual, informational, and multimodal literacies (Kahn and Kellner 2005; Kress and Jewitt 2003; Kress and van Leeuwen 1996). Given that the virtual world is a visually mediated space in which print objects are embedded rather than a print-dominated environment where the visual takes a complementary, but rarely dominant role, it is not surprising that so many of these new literacies are focused on nonlinguistic semiotic modes. For this reason, in our articulation of metamodal mastery we reject the term "literacy" and its privileging of language in favor of the term "mastery."

As Andrea diSessa (2000, 227) claims, literacy "is about ideas that have their best expression in words" and, as such, is ill-suited to dynamic ideas like symmetry or momentum. Mastery thus effectively defers the question of the representational mode in favor of level of competency, generating new ideas, products, or perspectives, but is more appropriate to metamedia, which privileges the semiotic potential of visual over the linguistic (Anderson et al. 2001). Unlike paradigms of literacy that focus on skills needed within a single media type, or in the case of multimedia literacy acquiring literacies in more than one mode, MM focuses on the combinatory possibilities of multiple forms of media—using many of the same abilities identified by Henry Jenkins as typical within participatory culture—for example, play, simulation, appropriation, and distributed cognition (Jenkins et al. 2006).

The notion of metamodality emphasizes the ability to see patterns and strategically select and combine the typically unconnected fields of knowledge and practice rather than selecting and combining specific norms within a particular field.[5] Metamodality emphasizes semiotic effects and potentials of a myriad of ideas, genres, objects, and data, juxtaposed with those from different fields. Rather than positioning MM as a *new* concept, we see it in its very formulation as emulating what it describes—an epistemological hybrid.

Our preliminary definition of metamodal mastery, then, is the ability to discover, create, produce, analyze, synthesize, integrate, and share data, content, artifacts, vocabularies, and epistemologies from a variety of fields in many collaborative modes and media, within and across metamodal platforms to enhance student learning. We do not consider it to be a literacy around which curricula will be formed because it is inherently contingent and therefore evades the level of prescription and replication demanded by the term "literacy" (diSessa 2000). Instead, MM emerges in the *terrain vague* between institutional and disciplinary norms, where intuitive knowledge, innovation, and committed learning flourish (ibid.). MM emphasizes an aspect of transdisciplinarity that is underdeveloped in current literature and is necessary to understand and pursue if the potential of the metaverse is to be realized.

VIRTUALIZATION IN THE UNIVERSITY: TWO VIRTUAL LEARNING ENVIRONMENTS

We have chosen to focus the use of two metamedia platforms as sites of education because we see this evolution of computer technology as one of the first unique manifestations of digital media's potential since the introduction of hypertext. Much of the focus on new media in education generally, and within the university specifically, has been on the degree of difference between face-to-face and full or partial technically mediated learning environments: sites of inquiry in such studies included student satisfaction, grades, and quality of social interaction in peer-to-peer and student-to-teacher relationships.[6] The bulk of these studies focuses on technologies such as learning management systems (e.g., Blackboard, which now includes WebCT, Moodle, and Sakai), multifunctional conferencing software supporting video streaming, synchronized PowerPoint slides, chat and polling functions, and podcasts (e.g., MediaSite Live and Breeze), many of which were initially developed to support business practices rather than for educational purposes.

These environments are typically used to develop what Peter Horsfield (2003) has called "pseudo-reality" in that they mirror or imitate the traditional classroom dynamics, usually in the context of increasing access or flexibility in the time or site of learning rather than qualitatively transforming the educational experience. In so doing, these virtual learning environments extend the reach of traditional practices much in the same way that personal computers have been used largely to facilitate and extend traditional representational and communication activities (e.g., e-mailing, storing and displaying photographs, and editing video). Only recently has computer technology begun to realize new frontiers that are unique outside of an analogue world. The rise of immersive 3-D environments is the first visually based evolution of the qualities Horsfield identifies. Such environments move beyond merely imitating reality to also being creative, having "not just an 'as if' but 'not quite' character, but also a 'what if' quality as well" (ibid., 5), which is to say not only replicating the familiar but allowing for the construction of hypothetical or otherwise impossible sites of learning. This ability is very difficult, if not impossible, to render tangibly in other media.

Immersive 3-D worlds are the mainstay of the multibillion-dollar gaming industry, where the public demand for multiplayer, narrative-based games has financed the development of extremely realistic graphics. As well, such games include complex, unpredictable scenarios where players have a significant role in shaping the subsequent storylines that unfold. Public interest in these media has led to the recent introduction of professional leagues of video gamers, a development that promises to rival, if not surpass, traditional sports venues for entertainment dollars. The purpose of this chapter, however, is not to elaborate about immersive 3-D video gaming potential for education.

Even teaching practices within the university have not remained unaffected by the interest in 3-D worlds as the two virtual environments—*Second Life* and Croquet-Open Cobalt—illustrate. We examine their pedagogical use in tertiary-level education at early stages in their implementation. Are they being used merely to replicate and extend traditional classrooms, or are virtual worlds beginning to morph into Horsfield's what-if scenarios? Is there any evidence of metamodal learning and mastery being supported in these environments? What potential do metamodal environments have for the construction of knowledge across generic and disciplinary boundaries? We focus our examination of virtual environments on those that are accessible without the use of headgear or other technology beyond a computer screen and the Internet because they are increasingly available to the public and thus more familiar to both students and faculty.

SECOND LIFE

Second Life (*SL*)—the virtual, open-source, 3-D world inhabited and created by its users—drew international attention in late 2006 and early 2007 (Harkin 2006; Sege 2006). A downloadable client program enables its users, who are referred to as "residents," to interact with each other through avatars (personae of their own creation). These interactions form an advanced level of social networking: meetings, exploration, socialization, participation in group and individual activities, and the creation and trading of virtual property and services with each other. The purpose of Linden Lab is to create a world that is user-defined and in which people can interact, play, communicate, and transact business. By September 2008, *SL* had more than fifteen million residents registered, although this includes both active and inactive accounts, according to the *SL* economics site.[7] In an April 2, 2009, article in the *Guardian*, Glyn Moody (2009) noted *SL* is averaging 86,000 concurrent users with 640,000 active users who are expected to cash out—trading Linden dollars for real currency—the equivalent of $450 million. Although *Second Life* has facilitated many higher education developments over the past few years, recent disenchantment with its clunkiness and commercialization is leading educators to move away from it toward alternatives that are more open and flexible (Young 2010).

SL, however, goes beyond historic brick-and-mortar buildings to offer a 3-D virtual learning environment and community comprising the physical campuses of higher education and other learning spaces, opening up a world where an endless array of multimodal technologies can form new possibilities beyond the normal print text emphasis in higher education. *SL* as a virtual classroom is embraced by major colleges and universities, including Harvard University, Massachusetts Institute of

Figure 10.1. The York University virtual disaster and emergency lab in *Second Life*.

Technology, and Stanford University, to name but a few. This type of virtual environment for contemporary higher education students who have grown up in a wired world illustrates the kind of learning space attuned to those Web 2.0 students who keep updated and informed about current cyber developments through social networking sites such as Facebook, Twitter, YouTube, and grassroots information networks disseminated through wikis and blogs.

At York University in Toronto, Canada, a 2008 summer online course in disaster management used *Second Life* to recreate disaster simulations (figs. 10.1 and 10.2). The instructor, Professor Ali Asgary, had been teaching this course using learning management systems such as WebCT and Moodle. Because of the dynamic nature of the subject matter, moving from a print-based to a 3-D virtual environment offers a more realistic visual sense of the temporal spatial dimensions of a disaster scene, which distinguishes his course from the usual discussion-based simulations that occur in class. It would be prohibitively expensive and logistically too complex and dangerous to arrange real-life disaster simulations each time the course is offered, so the *SL* environment provides an opportunity for students normally outside the scope of what can be taught in a structured learning environment, exemplifying Horsfield's as-if scenario.

By utilizing the real-time audio function, students—who are assigned roles for the exercise such as mayor, fire chief, paramedic, and so on—are

FIGURE 10.2. A scene from a *Second Life* virtual disaster management exercise.

able to create and to coordinate their activities to manage the different aspects of a given disaster from their multiple perspectives by talking to each other in real time. The instructor is able to clearly see where everyone is and what they are doing throughout the exercise because his own point of view is not restricted by location. He can easily, and noninvasively, move throughout the simulation to assess the choices and activities of his students.

The disaster simulation is set in the York University Virtual Disaster and Emergency (DEM) Lab in *Second Life* on a private island. The lab includes a Virtual Emergency Operations Centre (VEOC), a Media and Training Room, and a Virtual Disaster and Emergency Management Exhibition Hall in which emergency management-related technology products are showcased and tested. It is this virtual scenario that is used for the live table-top exercises.[8]

Within *SL* environments participants can share slides, audio and video, engaging in discussions, presentations, and both textual and oral group projects. In this way, *SL* can be understood as a metamodal environment that not only delivers multiple media but also provides contexts in which students can develop MM regardless of their corporeal location or technical expertise. Although there were some technical glitches experienced during the simulation because of a lack of familiarity with the interface, the instructor finds *SL* no more difficult to use than other web-based teaching systems.

In terms of fostering *MM*, *SL* provides some ability to embed applications such as PowerPoint and video, but these features tend to be provided by the instructor for consumption by the students, similar to traditional learning environments. Therefore, although there is theoretically an interesting potential for instructors to leverage the virtual characteristics of this environment to facilitate MM through the construction of multimodal compositions, presentations, and new forms of data visualization, in York University's disaster management course the ability to navigate through this virtual space seems to be the primary consideration. Furthermore, this virtual space provided in *Second Life* is itself either preconstructed or constructed within narrowly predefined possibilities by the *SL* development team working alongside technicians from the host institution, not by the users themselves. Its effectiveness, then, in fostering MM is limited, depending on the degree of administrative control *SL* instructors are able or willing to grant their students.

CROQUET-OPEN COBALT

Croquet is based on the philosophy of Alan Kay and his mentor Seymour Papert, emphasizing constructionism and a repositioning of the learner as an active agent in the learning process (Papert and Harel 1991). The Croquet Consortium is an international collaboration of volunteers from university and industry developing a freely downloadable, open-source, 3-D environment that operates peer-to-peer, so no servers (thus no regulatory control) are required beyond those needed to get on the Internet. The Croquet architecture focuses on context-based collaboration inside a 3-D shared space, where users can see each other and what they are currently working on, as well as interact textually or verbally in real time (Smith et al. 2003). Artifacts of all modes (including 2-D web applications and multimedia) can be imported into the Croquet space to be shared and manipulated among users in real time. Portals provide visual, spatial links between Croquet spaces through which users fluidly move rather than hyperlink.

Unlike *SL*, the Croquet architecture is entirely built by users employing a developers' language called Squeak; there is no visual separation between development space and the user interface. This means that all maintenance and fixes happen in full view of users. It is a cross-platform application that works equally well on Mac, PC, and Linux-based computers and requires a bandwidth in only the tens of kilobytes range (Smith et al. 2003). Differing from most university offerings in *SL*, the Croquet projects developed during this preliminary iteration abandon the traditional classroom space in favor of more exploratory environments, exemplifying Horsfield's what-if possibilities of the virtual environment.

In 2006 the Croquet Consortium announced the development of a component-based architecture that extends the accessibility of Croquet to lay people. Labeled Brie, it was intended to scaffold users into authors who can easily construct their own 3-D environments, drawing directly on their expertise within their specializations or interests. Currently, attempts in higher education to develop sophisticated interfaces are impeded by exorbitant development costs and lack of access to appropriate expertise. By designing creative development functionality specifically for technically naïve users, Brie effectively avoided both these barriers while empowering "end users to actively participate in the creation, assembly, and architecture of the applications they use" (Stearns et al. 2006, 86–87).

In spring 2009 Brie evolved into Open Cobalt. Julian Lombardi and Mark Cahill, with support from the Andrew W. Mellon Foundation and more recently the U.S. National Science Foundation, began a Duke University–led effort to use the Croquet Software Developer's Kit (SDK) to build Open Cobalt, an open, free application to share and access richly provisioned and hyperlinked virtual work spaces to support research and education. Although to date there has been some success with Open Cobalt in the Edusim Project for the middle-school level (http://edusim3d.com/), Open Cobalt is still in the developmental stage for higher education working toward a more "user friendly" interface. Perhaps the evolution of Croquet is itself an excellent example of MM in situ as experts from a variety of fields and knowledge bases work together, usually virtually, to define, develop, and distribute metamodal products that require transdisciplinary collaboration to even be conceived of in the first place.

A particularly interesting example is the Arts Metaverse Project developed at the University of British Columbia (http://artsmetaverse.arts.ubc.ca/). Leveraging the ability of Croquet to build unique environments, Arts Metaverse constructs educational sites in places normally inaccessible because of time and space limitations, such as Machu Picchu in Peru. When combined with OGRE 3D, an open-source graphics engine, the resulting Ancient Spaces environments are even more visually detailed (http://ancient.arts.ubc.ca/index.html) and include ancient Athens and Egypt as well as an ancient Nisga'a village (a First Nations settlement on the northwestern coast of Canada) with a focus on the relationship between the architecture and the social structure of the village.

The project is the brainchild of three undergraduate students at the University of British Columbia (UBC) who in 2003 wanted to develop a massive multiplayer world in which to explore antiquity. A multidisciplinary team, including students from fields as diverse as classical studies and computer science along with staff from the Faculty of Arts Instructional Support and Information Technology (Arts ISIT) unit at the university, launched the project in 2004. With initial funding of eighty thousand dollars, the project exemplifies the principles laid out in *Our Cultural Commonwealth* to enable students, scholars, and the general public "to explore connections within a cultural record that is now scattered across libraries, archives, museums, galleries and private collections around the world" by creating "an integrated, digital representation of the cultural record, connecting its disparate parts and making the resulting whole more available" (Welshons 2006, 14).

The first course taught in this environment was UBC's Landscapes and Architecture of Pacific Northwest First Peoples offering, usually taught through lectures, quizzes, essays, and examinations. When the course was translated into a 3-D environment, Nancy Mackin, the course instructor, shifted the grading scheme from essay to construction of a 3-D presentation in which students were encouraged to cross disciplinary boundaries and to work in groups with students in other fields (fig. 10.3). The software became a lingua franca—a mode of communication across different discourse communities—among the students who were from archeology, architecture, landscape architecture, and First Nations studies. In Susan Star and James Griesemer's (1989) articulation, the virtual world is a "boundary object" operating as a functional scaffold between people or frames from different communities of practice. By enabling students to construct buildings or to manage landscapes in this virtual world, Mackin observes how the space has helped students "to understand that spaces are something with which people and other species interact, not aesthetic, abstract creations . . . history is something influenced by individuals creating and responding to change rather than as a series of events. . . . This in turn has implications for science, as the process of interweaving Traditional Knowledge (First Nations Knowledge) with Western Science has been verified by world agencies including the United Nations as vital to ecological and cultural diversity" (N. Mackin, personal communication with Carolyn Steele, July 5, 2007).

In effect, the Ancient Spaces environment *deliteralized* the students' understanding of the Nisga'a village—recontextualizing it from its linguistic representation in the regular face-to-face course where visuals

FIGURE 10.3. 3-D reconstruction of a Nisga'a village using both OGRE 3-D and Croquet.

supported the text description and discussion to a visual and spatially realized realm where the students' acts of construction were epistemologically integral to understanding historically what had impacted actual settlement. Here, the visual does not merely illustrate an authoritative narrative retelling of the truth; it replaces the traditional form of academic composition and in the process becomes a more semiotically complex process of deconstructing and reconstructing the village with full realization of the effects and implications inherent in the modes and processes used. In other words, this course began to develop the students' metamodal mastery, which opened up opportunities for a more complex and engaging site of learning. In the terminology of the New London Group (1996), the Arts Metaverse Ancient Spaces Project essentially redesigns the ancient world by recombining fragments of the cultural records separated in time and space in ways that not only make more accessible that which was lost but reconfigures the lifeworlds of users relative to their cultural pasts in the process.

The outcomes and foci of the Croquet-based Ancient Spaces course differ from that of the disaster management course based in *SL*. The Croquet-based course more strongly uses the unique potential of virtual

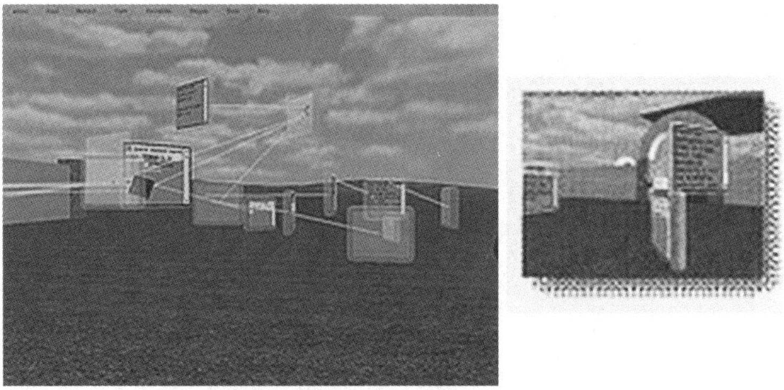

FIGURE 10.4. Screenshots of the Mindmap students created to brainstorm ideas about how Croquet could be used in an educational environment.

worlds to cross disciplinary boundaries and cultivate higher-level thinking. In this way, Croquet represents a significant movement toward being a true metamodal platform and, as such, a more effective environment for fostering MM than *SL*, although the complexity of the software still requires most students—and instructors—to negotiate their creativity with advanced groups of technologists. While this negotiation is in keeping with the collaborative nature of MM, the inability of most students to independently construct satisfying artifacts, or to embed multiple applications within a reasonable learning curve (like the length of a university course), mitigates that ability of *mastery* to be truly realized.

Another interesting application of Croquet was launched by the University of Minnesota, where the online Writing Center experimented with using a 3-D environment to explore collaborative writing strategies by embedding writing prompts in a 3-D environment, literally walking students through the elements of their written essays—introduction, body, and conclusion. In figure 10.4 the dark brown object in the center is a book the instructor first placed in the landscape to initiate the assignment. Students then added annotations to it; the text in the foreground describes how such embedded objects might be used in a writing classroom. By recontextualizing text into a dynamic 3-D environment, the essay form was redesigned in ways similar to the Ancient Spaces Project, imbued with new relevancy and meaning, transforming the lifeworlds of the students and the instructors in the process.

Lee-Ann Breuch, director of the Writing Center and the project instructor, has commented about her experience: "It's making me think

FIGURE 10.5. An environment constructed in a metamodal application.

that writing is more than text. Mind blowing! Writing is more than text. This is coming from a conservative person who is very tied to text. But communication is taking place not just through oral, written, and visual media, but also through animations, and movies" (Digital Media Centre 2005). The revelation Breuch describes can be reframed in terms of the same process of deliteralization realized in the Ancient Spaces course, where the text is loosened from its page-bound context, and virtualized, in Lévy's (1998) sense, or made a boundary object that reveals new potentials for understanding and meaning making in nonlinear terms.

Bernadette Longo, Breuch's co-instructor, points to the case of scientific writing, where traditionally much of what happens in an experiment is lost because all the details cannot be included within a scientific report, but if you redesign a scientific report by embedding it within a simulation of the experiment, then you radically expand and transform what a scientific report can communicate and represent, and what it means to compose such a report (Digital Media Centre 2005). Again, by developing learning environments that cross disciplinary boundaries and develop metamodal mastery, the potential for transformative learning is promising (fig. 10.5).

Croquet, Brie, and more recent Open Cobalt eclipse the pedagogical potential of *Second Life* and provide highly suggestive examples of the inherent compatibility of virtual environments and transdisciplinary metamedia modes of inquiry and representation. To function with agency in the twenty-first century, tertiary-level educators and students need to develop metamodal mastery of the creative possibilities available in an extraordinary range of modes, both available and emergent. We agree with many of the writers referenced in this chapter who believe that virtual environments hold considerable potential as heir apparent to a world historically dominated by print as the medium most conducive to the challenges and possibilities facing it. We are arguing for a more nuanced understanding of the differences between multiple literacies and mastery; the ability to discover, create, compose, and construct knowledge in a variety of modes that potentially hybridize our current knowledge structures. In relation to composition in the teaching of writing, this moves toward a deliteralizing of the written composition.

However, before virtual environments can take their place as dominant media of representation, they must overcome several obstacles. First, in many cases the benchmark of visual quality in the virtual world has been set by the entertainment industry at a level unmatched outside the economic power of the industry. In the disaster management course, the instructor found the interface style of *SL* too reminiscent of a video game, which interfered with some students being able to take the simulation seriously. However, the production of more realistic graphics requires software and hardware investments far beyond the budgets and expertise of educational institutions. Research funding in universities is not adequate to meet the ongoing demands of this technology, and until this changes, virtual worlds in the educational sector will continue to be rendered in animation-style graphics that appear both simplistic and often childish. This is not just an aesthetic issue: in many cases animation-style graphics also prevent the finesse required to render details finely enough to support close examination. The funding issue in higher education needs to be addressed so that universities possess the research, development, and financial support to build convincing 3-D immersive environments to metamodally develop appropriate learning-mastery and knowledge-shaping venues for students and educators. It remains to be seen if the current Open Cobalt initiatives will be able to address these issues on a large-scale basis. An open, free platform could greatly diminish the cost of 3-D virtual environments and educate students about the advantages of open-source software.

Second, along with the needed expansion of university research funding and development for which we are arguing, progress can be made from the ground level upward along with a well-financed top-down approach. The conceptualization and implementation of university 3-D immersive learning environments, such as those noted in this chapter, model possibilities to follow. Professors, instructors, and students need to be willing to experiment to create deeply collaborative research and learning spaces. Accompanying and illuminating these developments can be research conference presentations, symposia, proceedings, and subsequent publications to add to the expanding knowledge about immersive learning environments, which also can propel further research and funding.

Third, and most pressing for educators, is the need to better understand how to create pedagogically appropriate materials and learning environments for the 3-D virtual world. While York University disaster management courses, the Arts Metaverse Project, and the University of Minnesota online Writing Center provide strong models and directions for further development, we need more innovative approaches, grounded in critical and data-driven research across diverse fields and domains in order to understand the learning potential of metamedia. We do not yet have a clear understanding of the competencies that lead to metamodal mastery using metamedia platforms, nor do we have mechanisms and structures for recognizing and acknowledging this type of ability. Almost every North American system of recognition in our society is based on mastery within a single sphere of expertise.

In response to this dearth of understanding about how to use 3-D virtual platforms to reach pedagogical goals, the Immersive Education Initiative announced at the January 2008 Boston Digital Media Summit is a new collaboration of educational institutions and software developers, including *SL*, the community-supported, open-source Open Wonderland (http://openwonderland.org/; formerly Sun Microsystems Laboratory's Project Wonderland), and Open Cobalt, working to develop best practices, platforms, and support communities for virtual reality and game-based learning systems (see http://immersiveeducation.org/). Open Cobalt Alpha was featured at the 2010 Boston Immersive Education Initiative Summit; however, it remains to be seen how the Education Grid and Platform Ecosystem collaborations of the Immersive Education Initiative will address the emerging trends in higher education for more transdisciplinary research and experimentation in technologically immersive environments.

Finally, there will need to be a cultural shift in universities. Currently, computer technicians tend to be viewed as service providers rather than integral members of the teaching team. Until we have genuine collaboration among these contributors to research and pedagogy, two significant obstacles remain: the degree to which immersive environments will be adopted as viable and the suitability of the environments that are constructed for advanced-level knowledge construction.

This generation of often tech-savvy students coming through the current educational systems and moving toward a future we can hardly imagine today needs the knowledge bases so strongly argued for in the research of diSessa, Jenkins, Kress, Marshall, and Pengelly, the New London Group, and others. The rise of complex metamedia platforms that seem so advanced now will become antiquated before today's toddlers reach university. Universities will be increasingly forced to respond and, hopefully in time, will lead the rapidly paced transformations of the hypermodern world. While our conception of metamodal mastery is still in early unrefined stages, it addresses a level of human-computer interface that is as yet underdeveloped but of potential importance in the coming years. To this end, we urge sustained, theoretically based systematic research to more clearly develop and scrutinize its contribution to the strategic and innovative possibilities of 3-D immersive metamedia platforms in higher education.

The authors in this collection are taking important steps toward understanding and articulating how digital technologies are already impacting the traditional boundaries of disciplines and genres in the academy. We hope our proposal of metamodal mastery in media environments presses research possibilities for students and faculty to create new ways of knowing and constructing knowledge.

NOTES

1. Exceptions here include Stanford University's 2007 Metaverse Roadmap Project (http://metaverseroadmap.org/), the Humanities, Arts, Science, and Technology Advanced Collaboratory (http://www.hastac.org/), and *The 2010 Horizon Report* (Johnson et al. 2010).

2. The overview of the Stanford Metaverse Roadmap Project can be found at http://metaverseroadmap.org/MetaverseRoadmapOverview.pdf.

3. The reference here is made to science fiction writer Robert Heinlein's (1961) cult favorite *Stranger in a Strange Land*, which explores themes of cultural change.

4. Marshall and Pengelly (2006) derive much of their thinking about the semantic distinctions between transdisciplinary and interdisciplinary approaches from Michael Century (1999).

5. This is borrowed from Lev Manovich's (2001) discussion of the cultural database in which elements are selected and compiled in unique and creative ways to construct new representations.

6. Visit the *No Significant Difference* website at http://www.nosignificantdifference.org/ for a thorough reference list of research going back to 1928.

7. See *Second Life*'s economy stats at http://community.secondlife.com/t5/forums/searchpage/tab/message?q=Second+Life+Economy.

8. A running of the course in *Second Life* and focusing on a school shooting exercise videoed on March 27, 2011, can be viewed on YouTube at http://youtu.be/nVmxYKdQhZU.

REFERENCES

Anderson, Lorin W., David R. Krathwohl, Peter W. Airasian, Kathleen A. Cruikshank, Richard E. Mayer, Paul R. Pintrich, James Raths, and Merlin C. Wittrock, eds. 2001. *Taxonomy for Learning, Teaching, and Assessing: A Revision of Bloom's Taxonomy of Educational Objectives.* New York: Longman.

Century, Michael. 1999. *Pathways to Innovation in Digital Culture.* Montreal: McGill University Press.

Digital Media Center. 2005. *Using Croquet to Teach Writing: Interview.* Online at http://dmc.umn.edu/projects/breuch/

diSessa, Andrea. 2000. *Changing Minds: Computers, Learning, and Literacy.* Cambridge: MIT Press.

Gee, James Paul. 2007. *What Video Games Have to Teach Us about Learning and Literacy.* New York: Palgrave Macmillan.

Gibbons, Michael, Camille Limoges, Helga Nowotny, Simon Schwartzmann, Peter Scott, and Martin Trow. 1994. *The New Production of Knowledge: The Dynamics of Science and Research in Contemporary Societies.* London: Sage.

Harkin, James. 2006. "Get a (Second) Life." *Financial Times.* Online at http://www.ft.com/cms/s/0/cf9b81c2-753a-11db-aea1-0000779e2340.html#axzz24r36XSgC.

Heidegger, Martin. 1971. *Poetry, Language, Thought.* New York: Harper Colophon.

Heinlein, Robert. 1961. *Stranger in a Strange Land.* New York: Ace.

Horsfield, Peter. 2003. "Continuities and Discontinuities in Ethical Reflections on Digital Virtual Reality." *Journal of Mass Media Ethics* 18 (3–4): 155–72.

Jenkins, Henry, Katie Clinton, Ravi Purushotma, Alice J. Robison, and Margaret Weigel. 2006. *Confronting the Challenges of Participatory Culture: Media Education for the Twenty-first Century.* Online at http://digitallearning.macfound.org/atf/cf/%7B7E45C7E0-A3E0-4B89-AC9C-E807E1B0AE4E%7D/JENKINS_WHITE_PAPER.PDF.

Johnson, H., Alan Levine, Rachel Smith, and S. Stone. 2010. *The 2010 Horizon Report.* Austin: New Media Consortium. Online at http://wp.nmc.org/horizon2010/.

Kahn, Richard, and Douglas Kellner. 2005. "Reconstructing Technoliteracy: A Multiple Literacies Approach." *E-Learning and Digital Media* 2 (3): 238–51.

Kress, Gunther. 2003. *Literacy in the New Media Age*. London: Routledge.

———, and Carey Jewitt, eds. 2003. *Multimodal Literacy*. New York: Peter Lang.

Kress, Gunther, and Theo van Leeuwen. 1996. *Reading Images: The Grammar of Visual Design*. London: Routledge.

Kress, Gunther, Carey Jewitt, and Charalambos Tsatsarelis. 2000. "Knowledge, Identity, Pedagogy: Pedagogic Discourse and the Representational Environment of Education in Late Modernity." *Linguistics and Education* 11 (1): 7–30.

Lankshear, Colin, and Michele Knobel. 2003. *New Literacies*. Buckingham: Open University Press.

Lessig, Lawrence. 2008. *Remix: Making Art and Commerce Thrive in the Hybrid Economy*. London: Bloomsbury Academic.

Lévy, Pierre. 1998. *Becoming Virtual: Reality in the Digital Age*. New York: Plenum Trade.

Lombardi, Julian, and Marilyn Lombardi. 2010. "Opening the Metaverse." In *Online Worlds: Convergence of the Real and the Virtual*, edited by W. S. Bainbridge, 111–22. New York: Springer.

Manovich, Lev. 2001. *The Language of New Media*. Cambridge: MIT Press.

Marshall, John, and Jon Pengelly. 2006. "Computer Technologies and Transdisciplinary Discourse: Critical Drivers for Hybrid Design Practice?" *Co Design* 2 (2): 109–22.

———. 2007. "Computer Technologies and Transdisciplinary Discourse." *designedobjects*. Online at http://designedobjects.pbworks.com/w/page/17555005/Computer%20Technologies%20and%20Transdisciplinary%20Discourse.

Moody, Glyn. 2009. "Second Chance at Life." *Guardian*. Online at http://www.guardian.co.uk/technology/2009/apr/02/second-life-mark-kingdon.

New London Group. 1996. "A Pedagogy of New Literacies: Designing Social Futures." *Harvard Educational Review* 66 (1): 60–92.

Nowotny, Helga, Peter Scott, and Michael Gibbons. 2003. "'Mode 2' Revisited: The New Production of Knowledge." *Minerva* 41: 179–94.

Papert, Seymour, and Idit Harel, eds. 1991. *Constructionism*. Norwood, NJ: Albex.

Sege, Irene. 2006. "Leading a Double Life." *Boston Globe*. Online at http://msl1.mit.edu/furdlog/docs/b_globe/2006-10-25_bglobe_second_life.pdf.

Smart, John, Jamais Cascio, Jerry Paffendorf, Corey Bridges, Jochen Hummel, James Hursthouse, and Randal Moss. 2007. *Metaverse Roadmap Pathways to the 3-D Web: A Cross-industry Public Foresight Project*. Mountain View, CA:

Acceleration Studies Foundation. Online at http://metaverseroadmap.org/MetaverseRoadmapOverview.pdf.

Smith, David A., Alan Kay, Andreas Raab, and David P. Reed. 2003. *Croquet: A Collaboration System Architecture*. Online at http://doi.ieeecomputersociety.org/10.1109/C5.2003.1222325.

Star, Susan Leigh, and James Griesemer. 1989. "Institutional Ecology, 'Translations,' and Boundary Objects: Amateurs and Professionals in Berkeley's Museum of Vertebrate Zoology, 1907–39." *Social Studies of Science* 19 (3): 387–420.

Stearns, Howard, Joshua Gargus, Martin Schuetze, and Julian Lombardi. 2006. "Simplified Distributed Authoring via Component-based Object Construction and Deconstruction in Collaborative Croquet Spaces." In *Proceedings of the Fourth International Conference on Computing: Creating, Connecting, and Collaborating through Computing*, 79–87. Berkeley, CA: IEEE.

Welshons, Marlo. 2006. *Our Cultural Commonwealth: The Report of the American Council of Learned Societies Commission on Cyberinfrastructure for the Humanities and Social Sciences*. Online at http://www.acls.org/cyberinfrastructure/OurCulturalCommonwealth.pdf.

Young, Jeffrey. 2010. "After Frustrations in Second Life, Colleges Look to New Virtual Worlds." *Chronicle of Higher Education*. Online at http://chronicle.com/article/After-Frustrations-In-Second/64137/?sid=wc.

CHAPTER 11

Multivalent Composition and the Reinvention of Expertise

Tarez Samra Graban, Colin Charlton, and Jonikka Charlton

For the three of us writing this chapter, being multimodal is part of being human—part of living through a variety of overlapping and interactive discursive modes as teachers, writers, and thinkers. That does not mean we think all writers and writing teachers have the same conception of "multimodal," as this collection aptly demonstrates, or that all of us would use "multimodal" to describe our work with multiple texts, forms, ideas, genres, or delivery strategies. It does mean that we are attuned to the tensions that anyone putting two unlike or unfamiliar things together should think about, and that thinking about (teaching) multimodality heightens the tensions of praxis for us. These tensions are what led us to write this chapter—not only as we see them in the projects of our students, who take risks by working with several types of materials and/or modes of communicating, but also as we feel them when teaching other teachers how to handle a writing class that makes room for new connections, hybrid media, and uncertain technological applications. There is epistemic potential in articulating the unfamiliarities of form, meaning, and cohesion that can result from multimodal practices, but to tap it, we need to face head-on the pedagogical conventions and beliefs we strain against.

We have come to value multivalence in composition as a kind of definitional stasis on which other aspects of teaching rhetoric and writing rest. Simply making the case that "multivalent" composition is composition with "multiple meanings or values" is insignificant compared with the need to articulate multivalence with others. This activity holds the promise of getting teaching assistants and other instructors to deliver a curriculum that embraces multimodality and leads to a more complex definition of what counts as "writing." It has everything to do with what we think the purpose of the composition class is, how we see the roles and identities of "teachers," and what counts as appropriate "end products." More specifically, we understand that multivalent composition refers to multiple meanings of *composition* as the field to which we belong.

Yet getting students to embrace multivalence as a legitimate way of turning abstract goals into realized ones is not easy. Nor is using such a long-term process to sustain a first-year composition curriculum within institutional contexts that demand measurable "achievement." Although we cannot always revise those contexts or elide the material conditions that shape our jobs, we can inspire a new way of thinking and talking about achievement that doesn't preclude hybridity but more systematically draws on its critical potential. Thus the three of us have also come to value multivalence in composition as a kind of critical invention that puts us into conversation with our own and others' ideas, and this same kind of invention underscored the work we did while mentoring incoming teachers to teach first-year composition from two different approaches that grew out of the first-year curriculum reform at our institution, Purdue University.

Our goal with these teachers was the same as with our students—not to enculturate them to a particular style of teaching (or writing), nor to promote one kind of textbook/genre over others, nor even to make them believe in one approach and discount others, but rather to form the kinds of intellectual habits of mind that would lead them to their own grounded and cohesive practice. To encourage them to move through and beyond the discomfort of new tasks and accept that their principal task is to figure out the principal task. Our hope was that they could view what they were doing with unfamiliar genres as a kind of Atwillian productive knowledge making (Atwill 1998), specifically because it represents strategies that are guided by flexible and changing principles (ibid.,

48), and it potentially repositions teaching as helping students reach an "alternative destination" rather than a fixed path (ibid., 69), in turn helping all of us to arrive at a richer understanding of the occasion and possibilities for writing.

This position, we realize, is difficult for some educators to accept, and over the years we have advocated for it, each of us has become versed in some or another argument against it that emerged in local contexts—most notably that campuses are not uniformly equipped, teachers are not technically expert, and curricula dedicated to critical writing cannot also accommodate multivalent aims as they are delivered through unfamiliar technological contexts. Our goal with this chapter is not actually to laud a way of teaching on which we have come to rely, but neither is it to take up each of these arguments. Rather, our goal is to articulate how we have arrived at a way of rethinking "expertise" in the context of multivalent composition that we think ultimately serves our students, teachers, programs, and discipline. We do not need more material and technical support to break through the inertia of changing perceptions of writing. While changing the perception and culture of technology on campus is useful, what we really need is a philosophical change in how we see our relationship to technology so that a new teacher doesn't walk into a smart classroom and do the obvious—trade the old overhead for the new LCD, repeat, and rinse. If teachers begin to theorize writing and teaching in terms of the multiple charges we face instead of in terms of an expertise we hope to achieve—in short, if we make it our and our students' goal to think multivalently—maybe we can better temper our technological contexts with rhetorical invention.

OPENING PARENTHESES

Here's an epigraphic invitation: travel back in time, circa 2001, to David Byrne's digs in NYC; arrange to observe him as he begins to play with PowerPoint as a joke for an upcoming book tour; keep on the lookout for his gradual realization of PowerPoint as a medium for "artistic expression"; ask *what's happening?* and wait for it.

There is something inherently interactive and playful about the models of direction by artists like Marcel Duchamp and George Brecht, which the above epigraphic invitation plays on. It represents how the three of us—as friends, teachers, learners, and collaborators—thrive on the tensions that emerge in our professional lives, whether we're talking about writers creating hybrid genres, teachers learning how to become better teachers, or a discipline being informed by its progressive talk and somewhat less progressive practice. We hope this chapter will help us more honestly reflect on what we mean by "emergent," to, in turn, more accurately define "multivalence" and rethink what it means to be "expert"—to consider the potentiality of expertness as an art and of multivalence as a pedagogy. By considering why it can be difficult to bring teachers on board to a multimodal, multivalent type of pedagogy, we hope to argue more explicitly for its value.

To be clear early on, we advocate composing multimodally, not for what it helps us and our students to avoid in writing for academic and extra-academic contexts but for what it enables them to take on in those contexts. We advocate a rhetorical dexterity that comes from students having to grapple with the hard questions of how to enact those academic and extra-academic expectations in a new way. We are not aiming for a mere swapping out of genres or assignments—that is, pixels for paper because we think paper is limited. We see our roles in the classroom as helping teachers and students cultivate the critical capacities they need for writing, thinking, and participating in spheres where they are. Like David Fleming's (1998, 183) idea of rhetorical education in "Rhetoric as a Course of Study," we understand these critical capacities to be "productive and critical powers"—competencies resting somewhere between theory and craft. It requires frequent observation, reflection, and sustained inquiry. It is a kind of information literacy that often results in public or civic outcomes. And in our case, it involves emergent processes and unfamiliar genres.

In talking about definitions of writing, the field(s) of composition, and hybrid discourses, we realize that we're not breaking completely new ground here. Since Stephen North's *The Making of Knowledge in Composition* (1987), if not earlier, writers and thinkers have been trying to map networks of values in the field of composition, but very little is decided in our study of writing. The portrait is in flux, and so are we as audiences and contributors. But there are situations that we face, especially when we have the responsibility for training or working with new writing teachers that make such a fluctuating portrait untenable and counterproductive—for us as assumed authorities and for those mentored who often assume that authority is the endgame they and their students deserve. The trick is to enact an idea from Bill Readings (1996, 171) without imposing it as a mentor or sounding too mystical: "Change comes neither from within nor from without, but from the difficult space—neither inside nor outside—where one is."

But unimposing directions are hard to pull off. There is a spark of potentiality in such realistic direction sets as giving directions for how to invent music on a piano (Duchamp's "Erratum Musical"), how to begin a journey (Brecht's *Water Yam*), or how to reproduce a piece of art. Yet we've taken an unrealistic approach to a set of directions that will never escape the uncertainty of *what if*? Through the Internet and a bit of Googling, we do have access to an archive of action and response, and we can piece together how the relationships among particular mediums and messages emerge, by reading up on the history of Byrne's art (http://www.davidbyrne.com), PowerPoint's debated effects on thinking, and journalistic and popular responses to both. But we can't travel back in time, or voyeuristically observe a celebrity like David Byrne without risking restraining orders, or catch a glimpse of a turning point when one thing becomes another.

Thus the idea of the epigraphic invitation we've placed at the opening of this chapter is that the process (or processes) by which a composing approach emerges is not necessarily a path toward expertise as it has been traditionally defined. To parody the functions of presentation software, for example, is not to *know* PowerPoint but to *come* to know it, and come to use it, in an ingenious way. So much of what we do as writing teachers and mentors depends on helping students develop the courage and strategies for putting it out there, even when we are simultaneously exposing them to the realities of deadlines and format expectations that will affect their work beyond our classes. Of course, courage is only part of this approach. To assign paradigmatic status to this kind of *coming to know* means being able to argue, first for its effectiveness in helping new teachers theorize hybrid genre formation, and second for its kairotic appropriateness. We have to remind ourselves, in other words, to keep it (our penchant for innovation) rhetorical.

Jody Shipka (2005) has offered us one articulation of its effectiveness in "A Multimodal Task-Based Framework for Composing" by demonstrating how converting her writing assignments into multimodal communicative tasks has helped her students to understand, relearn, or rethink genre altogether. Beyond simply recasting the same assignment in a different mode or context, Shipka (ibid., 278) asks us to teach head-on the "wide variety of sign systems and technologies [that] students routinely engage" but that often become excluded in the writing class, perhaps because of what Gunther Kress (1999, 85) has historicized as the "single, exclusive and intensive focus on written language" dominating composition at the visual turn. In response, or by example, Shipka (2005, 284, emphasis in the original) characterizes multimodal composition as a "*three-dimensional layering* of words and visuals—as well as textures, sounds, scents, and even tastes" that does not preclude attention to written language or rhetorical sophistication.[1]

For Shipka (ibid., 290), this layering—or this "purposeful uptake, transformation, incorporation, combination, juxtaposition, . . . of words and visuals"—is not only complex enough to require its own framework for goal formation and attainment, but is inventive as well. This framework, in turn, leads to the uptake of new (or hybrid) genres in its defiance of "any easy attempt to categorize [assignments] by quality or kind" (ibid., 293). In other words, composing within a multimodal task-based framework heightens students' critical engagement and rhetorical flexibility, leading to what Shipka calls a more sophisticated way of attending to what, why, and how students compose for the audiences and contexts they do (ibid., 293).[2] Our understanding of multimodal composition, then, pushes us to help students develop productive, rhetorical, generic ways of responding to others' reactions—in turn helping us avoid a focus on what these assignments lack.

While we are doing all that, we also have to work through how technology is evolving in our classrooms, in our students' lives, and in mass-produced texts that inform our teaching and mentoring and the claims made about them (even when we do not adopt these texts). This is the moment to intervene in these claims. We look at textbook publishing trends over the past ten years, and we notice a pattern. Following an explosion of visual literacy books at the turn of the century, a new breed of writing textbook has emerged, arguing for the "naturalness" of visual literacy for today's college students who have grown up in the age of the image (McQuade and McQuade 2000; Atwan and Hacker 2003; Faigley et al. 2003). Ironically, this "naturalness" is what we fight against. These visually stunning and complexly designed books claim to appeal to and build out of the languages our students already speak and live in a multimodal and highly visual world. But in adopting them for our own classrooms, we have realized that the dirty little secret of the visual and electronic turn is that our students' abilities to multitask, their familiarity with navigating rich textual worlds, and their comfort with using multiple communication devices do not always ensure (and sometimes impede) the reflective acts that characterize the sophisticated rhetorical work we want them to do.

One need not be hooked on a "visual turn" in composition studies to see that Shipka (2005, 278) is noting—in Kress's moment, and in "the occasions for, as well as the reception and delivery of, the work they produce"—an opportunity to intervene in a different sign system and technological climate with student writers. We also note an opportunity for proactively theorizing the best way to draw on emerging technologies for recasting expertise in how to teach critical, rhetorical, and even linguistic skill. And, like Shipka, we agree that our interventions need to do more than "simply expand the media and communicative contexts in which students work," creating a greater awareness of the ways "systems of delivery, reception, and circulation shape (and take shape from) the means and modes of production" (ibid., 278). Too often we assume our students have thought through and theorized their own literacy practices. On the one hand, anyone can create a website or brochure with minimal knowledge of a what-you-see-is-what-you-get (WYSIWYG) application or template; on the other hand, we cannot say they are "creating" it until they have figured out and deliberately applied a methodology that guides the why and the how of their choices. This presents an interesting dilemma for bridging the "educational digital divide" that Mary Leigh Morbey and Carolyn Steele describe in chapter 10 of this edited volume: once it becomes apparent that our students' lived experiences are inadequate for what we recognize as truly rhetorical and critical work, we are more tempted to retreat or resist rather than take on the hard work of developing an appropriately multivalent pedagogy.

It is a concern for materials and modes of delivery that further helps us to deconstruct expertise for the processes of learning through composing that we value and want to more carefully teach, such as questioning, building a conceptual language, experimenting, building theory, and posing more questions. Our students are no closer to expertise in these often visually and electronically based media than they are outside of them until they have an exigency for adaptation. And, we would argue, neither are we. As teachers, mentors, and administrators with multimodal interests, we add another level of complexity to the scene of teaching when we add new teachers in unfamiliar environments, carrying out technologically rich course objectives or program goals. We often run up against new teachers' desires to avoid the technology because they do not feel "expert" in it (and thus cannot solve the problem of teaching writing once and for all). But for us, as experienced academics who are assumed to be on the side of expertise, it is not a matter of becoming expert. It is a matter of *kairotic doing* and a drive to leave the question of expertise open. We are now theorizing and practicing our teaching with technology with an idea of multivalent compositions, which openly function through multiple desires, values, and appeals.

This idea, coupled with the student projects that emerge from it, allows us to talk with new teachers about how to develop composition forms that don't depend on an expert use of a specific technology, the latest software update, or the most cutting-edge gadget. Sometimes ink on cardboard is more appropriate than digital video to get your message across. In fact, multivalent composition as we see it may live and thrive somewhere in the interstitial tension between the Dumpster and the iPhone as living archives, between accident and intention, between novice and expert.

Because the idea of the expert underlies so much of what gets written and disseminated in composition, we see an opportunity here for breaking new ground, or repurposing the grounds we have come across. We've inherited an acculturation and apprentice-based understanding of how knowledge is made in a university education (Nussbaum 1998, 15–16), whether we characterize such knowledge as created or inherited. There are signs that an uncomfortable awareness of this reality is getting attention in various institutional contexts. For instance, in November 2004, Cynthia Martin, the chair of developmental English and an assistant professor at the Community College of Denver, designed and mediated an online discussion entitled "Partners in Teaching Excellence: A Model for Transformative Mentoring." From the module's introduction, here is her analysis of what we would call an apprentice-based conception of mentoring:

> Typically these [GTA] mentor programs involve a hierarchical relationship between a senior faculty and a graduate student or new hire, in which the senior faculty acts as sponsor or "wise one" who socializes the new faculty . . . , provides career development . . . , or simply helps the new teacher "cope." . . . At the Community College of Denver, we believe that all teachers—from those with experience to those in training—benefit from on-going critical reflection on classroom practice and student learning. Going beyond these traditional models of mentoring, we seek to improve teaching practice for both the new teacher and the mentor. Our experienced faculty mentors co-participate with new teachers in the process of learning and growth based on the assumption that the experienced teacher has as much to discover as the new teacher does.

The problem is that, although it is becoming more and more of a necessity for teachers to create stories of success and progress within quantitatively driven university hierarchies, relying on a purely linear or developmental conception of writing privileges a loss of ineptitude over the acquisition of relational strategies. It's easy to assume that the local is implied by or incorporated in the global, but that does not explain the extreme reactions across generations of writing teachers toward the local-global type of source created by a student on a personal website or weblog. While seeing students as novices certainly maintains systems of credibility and demarcates discursive patterns or information channels for new- and old-comers alike, it functions to reproduce genres of academic discourse, genres of thinking, without necessarily incorporating habits of inquiry and strategies for production.

We would rather see these patterns and channels in the same way that Janet Atwill (1998) rediscovers *techne*: as an exchange from writer to audience using context-dependent strategies that potentially change or make something new out of that context. Like Atwill, we acknowledge that there is an inventive aspect to multivalence; we further state that our aim with multivalent composition isn't to formalize a singular method or to put forward a singular path but rather to "reach an end by way of a path that can [and must] be retraced, modified, adapted, and shared" (ibid., 69). In other words, rather than arriving at an assumed identity or a tidy pedagogical solution, students and teachers arrive at an understanding of their discursive struggles as a form of knowledge making.

We would also rather rely on Barbara Duffelmeyer's distinction between "training" and "practice" to resee the role of multimodal composition as an event in instructors' ongoing development as readers, writers, and thinkers. And we would embrace her commitment to "performance before competence" (Duffelmeyer 2003, 298) because we feel it puts the strangeness or ineffectiveness—not to mention the "almost arbitrary layer of stress and uncertainty" caused by having to function with unfamiliar tools and in unfamiliar genres—on more equitable grounds between instructor and student (ibid., 296). The more our assignments guide instructors and students to express their concerns reflexively so that they do not assume weakness on the part of the pedagogy, inappropriateness on the part of the curriculum, or unpreparedness on the part of themselves (ibid., 297), the more convincingly we can argue for their positive impact on students' rhetorical development.

For example, if we look at the classroom context of a composition project and suspend the question of how to best deliver a message to an intended audience, who better to work with a student in PowerPoint than a teacher with little PowerPoint experience? Through our mentoring experiences with a new multimodal curriculum, we noticed an interesting and very practical phenomenon: when we invited our students with experience (at the university or in any context) in a particular medium or piece of software to teach part of a class, other students saw their peer's knowledge being valued as equivalent to the teacher's instructions. To some extent, the class got decentered and more occasions arose for other students to demonstrate areas of expertise. The teacher got a chance to see how a familiar user worked with a medium. And, best of all, the experienced student got to demonstrate a set of examples that she or he put out there for a larger audience to see and use. It was an attractive strategy for getting students involved, dispersing authority, and avoiding unfamiliar territory in a curriculum that foregrounds rhetorical sophistication in multiple media. However, if we simply default to fetishizing the expert teacher and/or expert student, we run the risk of reinscribing a technique, a template, or a genre without considering its situated appropriateness because of our difficulties relinquishing disciplinary power. This, to us, perpetuates a cycle of expertise that depends on learning by example more than learning by doing. It positions the teacher and the role she or he assumes as the goal for authority in the class and for authority in a particular subject matter. It privileges how-to presentations over interactive demonstrations, which in turn privileges passive modeling over improvisation and experimentation.

MULTIVALENT PEDAGOGIES

What we are advocating, then, is a pedagogy that shifts the point of academic departure from analysis to invention from the beginning of a first-year composition class. This will involve working with what we don't know as rhetoric and composition teachers—that is, creating class projects that ask teachers and students to theorize composing for unfamiliar media (such as webliographies, photo essays, or movie trailers), spending large chunks of time at the beginning of a class finding and associating initially disparate texts, and challenging the hold that "academic clarity" has over writing pedagogy so that teachers and students can reinvest in first-year composition classes as sites for producing the unfamiliar through students' personal aesthetics, and as sites for regularly interrogating the pedagogical terms we let drive us.[3] "Mastery" may come later or not at all for all those invested in such pedagogical scenes.

Whatever the case, first-year writing can be explicitly about the study of language by people who might be reimagined as refugees (Haynes 2003, 687) from identities that are built either on foundational reasoning or on accidental happenings—identities that are not dependent on moves toward complete mastery of certain genres (as students) or certain teaching strategies (as teachers). To think in such a way defines the middle ground (of students and teachers working where they are) as its own epistemic space, rather than as a mere transitional space necessary to confront and overcome on the way to somewhere else. This is writing and teaching not for authority's sake but for invention's sake.

What we want for our writing students is not new or controversial at all. We want them to be rhetorical, to think carefully about what they want and need to say, who needs to hear it, and (here comes the potentially controversial part) how those two things affect the composition that gets produced. We want our students to take noticeable risks with multimodality, to compose something other than a traditional analytical essay if that's what makes sense. The devil we know allows us to compose blindly and in a vacuum. Too often, our students have chosen their forms for the wrong reasons—either refusing to do anything other than an essay because of fear, or choosing the "alternative" assignment because, for them, it's familiar and a way to avoid too much work and thought. PowerPoint was easy in high school, so they'll do it again—never mind that their audience would never have an occasion to be in a room somewhere watching it. What our curriculum aims for is that students come to understand multimodal composition as a normal kind of intellectual engagement, where they have to choose more selectively and reflectively—that, for every situation, they would come to see several options, not just one, and that they would choose not based on a memory of "what is familiar" but based on an understanding of what is successful or exigent. Understood this way, essays and ethnographic portraits and webliographies require us to think and rethink how we might use them.

Yet while the "shifting" pedagogies themselves are not new, we know that multivalent approaches to pedagogy have not yet caught on.[4] What we still lack is sufficient explanation, justification, and demonstration of their epistemic gains. How do they call up and call upon, over and over again, the knowledge-making processes we most value? And why is it so hard for new (and returning) teachers to believe it when they do? We likely cannot dispose of the "expert" because the business of education demands progress in measurable student outcomes, wanting to define the changes that occur for students as additive. Also, attempts to learn outside of this box may be looked upon suspiciously as naïve attempts to ignore the situatedness of learning and our dependence on the ostensible roles of teacher and student. Even when we look at a composition text that is trying to do something new, the idea of the expert pops up.

For example, when Colin was trying to design a graduate curriculum for a class titled Composition Techniques, he drew several ideas from Anne Wysocki, Johndan Johnson-Eilola, Cynthia Selfe, and Geoffrey Sirc's 2004 collection, *Writing New Media*. One way Wysocki (2004, 20) frames the book is in the terms of Stuart Hall who describes the taking of a position and how we retrospectively come to know who we are through the acts of composing. Wysocki (ibid., 20) connects this position taking to the materials of composition: "I argue that—because in acknowledging the broad material conditions of writing instruction we also acknowledge the contingent and necessarily limited structures of writing and writing instruction—people in our classes ought to be producing texts using a wide and alertly chosen range of materials—if they are to see their selves as positioned, as building positions in what they produce." Wysocki is talking about how writers can embody more meaningful positions and how we can materially realize messages in ways that don't pretend to distill abstraction and thought into a sensible and familiar form like a first-year composition "essay."

Wysocki (ibid., 20–21) then draws on Andrew Feenberg's ideas about alternatives to "system-congruent design" (designing around the familiar) and "expressive design." The resulting craft still "requires one to gain expertise," but Wysocki (ibid., 21) highlights how an expressive conception of design can redefine the designer's relationship to the objects she or he uses and the resulting self. Wysocki does not simply reinscribe the expert here. She's doing what we're doing—extracting the idea of multivalence (in terms of forming positions through work with objects) from an idea of craft that is still defined by the careful becoming of an expert craftsperson. Alternatives need standards to set them off; invention emerges from the uniform. But if a demonstration of expertise is what we're after, because it is an imposed or an assumed measure of self-worth, then we risk a loss of enjoyment and surprise in learning—especially in a first-year college writing class—that teachers and students need.

When you think about the readers and writers of any given text, there is always the potential for multiple readings, contradictory values, and multiple modes of delivery (whether intended or unexpected). Writers have their audiences and intentions as do readers, and even texts, we might think, harbor desires about what they can be. In one sense, when we suggest the phrase "multivalent composition," we are not announcing the dawn of a new age in the teaching of writing. We are not announcing the end of the analytical essay. We are calling for a perceptual change on the part of ourselves (as teachers) and our students as people trying to become better at writing and meaning making in any genre. So another way to think about multivalent composition is to talk about what it *is not* and why the perspective it values is worth consideration.

- *It isn't always an expert use of materials and technology.* An experimental hybrid of materials and technologies might look odd and unfamiliar because what it represents is in part a dimension of a new combination of materials, modes, and messages.
- *It isn't always slick.* An advertisement indebted to MasterCard's "priceless" model may not be a perfect replica ready for magazine publication or TV airing. And it probably won't be a simplistic inversion and criticism of corporate culture, mass-production either.
- *It isn't always finished.* This is not because the student has been a slacker, or the teacher is simply in love with the concept of a work in progress. The project isn't finished because it has not played to all its potential audiences outside of the context of the classroom in which it was created.
- *It isn't always "linear" or traditional in its modal development.* An essay doesn't have to become a screenplay for a short documentary film. A short video documentary can become a mixed-media essay, a researched argument paper can become a children's book, and so on.
- *It isn't always bound by the assignment.* It's one thing to have a student begin a project by trying to avoid certain requirements, like doing a personal interview. It is quite another to have a student experience multiple ways of collecting information about the profession of nursing and then make a proposal for why including personal interviews isn't appropriate to the project as it has developed for her.

Again, to be clear, we do not advocate composing multimodally as a devaluation of traditional academic genres, but rather as a validation and encouragement of the kinds of rhetorical experimentation that result in a first-year composition experience where students are full participants in the work. Multivalent composition is an idea of composition (as the work or works we do) that enacts several meanings or values in the classroom, in public discussions, in the larger university, and in the world.

ENACTMENTS

We were heading in this direction while working in the single-semester first-year composition curriculum at Purdue—helping students blend the idea of a newspaper profile with an architectural space to design a box that analyzed the "ins" and "outs" of a gated community; transforming an argument for a liberal arts education into a letter from the trees that students hung around campus to get student attention; touring areas of local graffiti art to get classes thinking about the variety and functions of student writing that take place on a college campus. The list of examples goes on and on, but the real impetus for us and our students came when we had the opportunity to showcase student work, which required that teachers and students work to convert class projects to a public, daylong presentation modeled after conference poster sessions.

As we worked with individual and group projects, we saw questions emerge that reflected the kind of agility we value: How do you frame and re-present a video mockumentary for a daylong presentation? How do you make an essay interactive when the student is interning out of state and unable to be present at the event? How do you represent a multivocally authored research project in a two-dimensional display? Do you display a set of rhetorical t-shirts virtually through a website or physically with hangers and fishing line? How do you make your critical exigency *pop* in a room full of sophisticated projects, movement, and noise? To address these questions with our students is only possible when we have built a pedagogical space that involves learning through adaptation and creative juxtaposition while suspending the notion and reward of being "expert."

This suspension with new teachers is productive for us because it causes us both to expand our range as writing teachers by enacting questions of critical pedagogy and epistemology. That is, it enacts our very notions of expertness, yet more than once we find new teachers rejecting or resisting this act unless it leads to a consensual notion of what it means to "teach writing." How do we then mentor new teachers into an understanding of the acts of invention, reflection, and reinvention that are at the heart of our teaching of multimodal composition? How do we get them to accept expertise not as an arrival but an *arriving*? Based on two approaches to teaching composition—a rhetorical humanities approach and visual ethnography—we discuss the principles that have helped us frame this reinvention of expertise in our composition classrooms and in our mentoring practica.

Enacting Multivalence in a Rhetorical Humanities Approach

What we're calling a "rhetorical humanities" approach to teaching composition is one which invites students to ask questions about our purposes and relationships to other people and institutions. We do this by reading difficult texts, which take on these types of questions, and we spend time thinking and writing about what we think. These questions matter if we see the classroom as a place for thinking. By foregrounding the rhetorical nature of asking them, we rearticulate what it means to do humanities work in composition—that is, using language to figure out what we think, what others think, and what we want to do with all that information. In this way we can productively and actively engage life. And though it may not seem like it to some, all this thinking actually does have everything to do with writing, if we can think of writing as "composing our thoughts." We constantly think-write-act through multimodal, always multivalent, compositions. Unfortunately, we only have most of our students for a semester or two, so we can only focus on asking a few questions—about the purposes and functions of higher education and work in our lives. What we hope they internalize is a habit of mind, a sense that they can act on exigency, and they can participate meaningfully in processes of inquiry. We want them to see the value of the humanities and rhetorical conceptions of being and acting in the world. Big goals indeed, and it is fair to ask, where is the *writing* in all this?

Colin and Jonikka had been using this approach for more than twelve years, but when the Introductory Composition program at Purdue revised the goals, means, and outcomes of first-year composition, they got a chance to think about how first-year composition curricula and students' rhetorical goals can benefit from thinking about writing in broader terms, as more than words on a page. It didn't hurt that around this time Colin took up painting. So, rather than assigning several essays throughout the term, they began to think in terms of "projects"—students would compose four major projects and a reflective cover letter to accompany the end-of-semester portfolio.[5]

The first major project of the sequence is designed to shake students out of their comfort zones and get them thinking about what it means to have their own message, a real audience that cares (or should), and a form that will help them deliver their message. This assignment—a "portrait" of themselves—is completely unexpected. It attempts to do what the literacy autobiographies or technology inventories that they have used do at the beginning of a class—build out of what students know or can

FIGURE 11.1. Final project poster created by Felipe Camacho, a student in Jonikka Charlton's English 106 class.

remember. The difference is that the portrait asks students to deliver the familiar in an unfamiliar form from the beginning. There is no leading up to mixed media or multimodality throughout the semester. It's the first project through which a student has to "compose a self-portrait that will make use of several technologies" readily available in the class "in order to discover and present aspects of who you are by considering yourself in relation to your surrounding culture." Once students have begun to orient themselves to the class and its goals, projects begin posing questions about the purposes and function of higher education in general and universities in particular: What are their social functions? What makes a university different from a two-year college or a technical school? Students read chapters from Stanley Aronowitz's (2000) *The Knowledge Factory* and Bill Readings's (1996) *The University in Ruins* alongside articles written about the value and changing role of liberal education. They begin to think about how they might shape their own education according to their own goals and vision of the experience, which is something most of them had not given a second thought to. At this point, they write a standard essay—their own theory about the purpose of higher education and the university (fig. 11.1). Felipe Camacho's poster enacts key elements of the rhetorical humanities approach, including extensive e-mail conferences with his instructor and a reflection piece in which he describes the theoretical springboard that led to his third and fourth projects. Because this poster was created for the showcase of student work, it also contains an instructor's reflection.

This is their theoretical springboard to the third project, which asks them to take a look around their own university and locate a problem they see related to their ideas about higher education—for example, too few engineering students do study-abroad (a group of people don't value something this student thinks should be valued), nursing students don't realize there are different types of nursing programs (liberal arts versus technical programs) that might better meet their needs, and so on. They then work to effect change on campus (or off campus at area high schools, if that's where the audiences are), to argue for the value of their own visions and priorities. To do this, students have to talk to real people on campus, to students, and to community members. They have to find relevant, credible information through any number of sources, both conventional and unconventional. And they have to figure out who their audience is, who has the power to make change, who needs information, and why current methods for reaching that audience might not have worked. (A typical university brochure doesn't really capture anyone's attention when you get fifteen in the mail every week for three months.) Then comes the fun part—students put their theories to work.

This third project offers another opportunity for multimodality. Colin and Jonikka have both had students create T-shirts as their "end product" out of an understanding that their peers—their audience—were much more likely to pay attention to a shirt than to another brochure (fig. 11.2). Others have created radio spots, videos, proposals to college administrators, Myspace sites, student organizations, board games for new college students, and more. The point is that the medium makes sense for the message and the audience. The difficulty is in learning these new genres at least in part on their own, without a lot of traditionally directive help from the instructor. In the end, students write a reflective cover letter for this project explaining the exigency for the project, its roots in the earlier theoretical project, and the rationale for the rhetorical choices made in its creation. This metadimension allows us, as teachers, to see what the students have learned, even if the actual thing—the T-shirt design or the cardboard viewbox or the interactive website—doesn't yet do everything the student hoped it would. Such a project foregrounds how messages change from medium to medium, from one context to another.

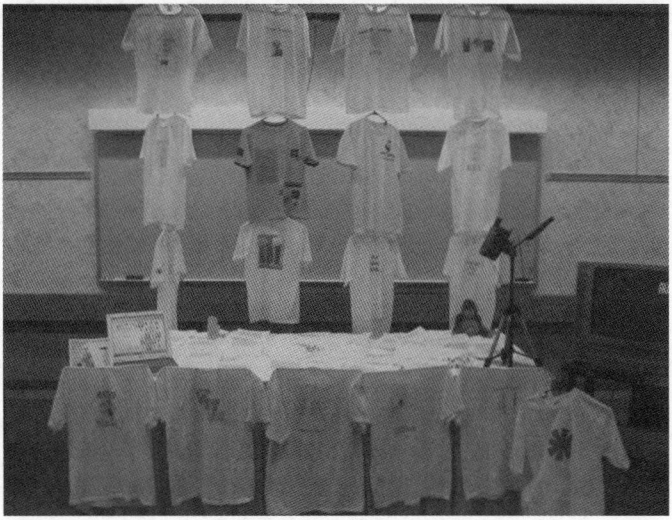

FIGURE 11.2. Interactive ICaP showcase exhibit featuring rhetorical T-shirt designs from Colin Charlton's English 106 class.

Most important, it asks students to produce knowledge *through medium* instead of defaulting to an "essay" format that reflects more than invents.

The students then move into a theoretical discussion of the nature and purpose of work in our world, from the micro—themselves and their families—to the macro. They have to design their own research question based on an issue of interest to them; the only caveat is that it must have something to do with the (huge) topic of work. Students can produce a more traditional researched argument essay for this fourth project if they wish, or they can choose to create their own purposes, audiences, and forms to meet the rhetorical goals of their research project and discoveries. And, finally, students reflect on their work for the semester and create a cover letter—with us as their audience—where they can write about what they've learned (or not). This, too, can be a multimodal project if the student chooses, with examples including soundtracks to a written portfolio, video documentaries of writing processes, architectural/metaphorical plans for the mind of a writer, and a series of paint-by-numbers head silhouettes with instructions on how, and how not, to color.

Enacting Multivalence in Visual Ethnography

Research and Writing through Ethnography, an approach Tarez uses, relies on the empirical observation of texts, people, and the world as a way of realizing that real inquiry can emerge from the "data" a writer collects alone and with others. Originally based on Bonnie Sunstein and Elizabeth Chiseri-Strater's *Fieldworking* (2001), this approach operates on the principle that observation, like other forms of invention-based inquiry, is a useful method for students to write themselves into current issues because it allows them to recognize and reflect on information in many forms—textual, visual, and interpersonal. The same *habit of mind* that we would want students to enact in a rhetorical humanities approach also gets enacted here. While similar approaches can result in only traditional genres and/or a strictly social-scientific orientation to writing, Tarez has framed her curriculum as a journey in information literacy, where assignments and genres are subservient to (and grow out of) broader goals or phases of rhetorical involvement.[6]

Tarez's approach asks students to pursue a semester-long inquiry project in a local field site or subculture they select. Students conduct between ten and twenty hours of observation over the semester, take field notes, conduct interviews, collect relevant images and artifacts, do archival and bibliographic research into their subculture, and ultimately develop a final project centered around a question they think is intrinsic to their field site. Along the way students compose several shorter projects and consider how to incorporate information from diverse sources in order to write in greater depth about an issue or a problem. Over the semester they keep a weblog on which they provide periodic updates in multiple modes (analytic and reflective) for an audience outside of the classroom, sometimes negotiating sensitive content with a reader's need for information and their own evolving biases about the work. At the end of the semester they compose a digital portfolio to showcase their work along with a one- or two-page rhetorical analysis in which they evaluate their own success as ethnographers, writers, and visual rhetoricians over the semester.

In revising and modifying the approach over eight years, Tarez has found that the ethnographic research process, as a whole, is an appropriate metaphor for students' rhetorical development, in much the same way that Colin and Jonikka use the rhetorical humanities approach to challenge students' notion of "relevant, credible information." Tarez's course is organized by five units of inquiry that represent ethnographers' reflexive relationships with their subjects—understanding contexts, defining the inquiry, envisioning the project, invoking other voices, and making (it) meaning(ful)—with each unit in turn centered around a major composing assignment and a series of minor assignments. The major assignments encourage conscious navigation of the various phases of ethnographic inquiry, while the minor assignments build students' understanding of abstract concepts (for example, developing research ethics, locating dissonance in physical spaces and artifacts, understanding "argument" as dialectical communication) and move them toward building a working knowledge of information literacies (that is, identifying information ends, accessing information, evaluating and using information effectively, and contributing to a body of information through their own projects).

The field-working portfolio acts as a thread for the course, allowing writers to make sense of each unit's rhetorical purpose and providing them with a space for reflection. At the end of the course their "big" ethnography provides a focused look into their subculture by drawing on the different forms of observation, reflection, and inquiry they have conducted all semester to argue—visually and alphanumerically—for that subculture's relevance. It is at this point in the course when students typically realize the cumulative purpose to navigating all five units. By the time they write the final project, they have learned to position themselves ethnographically, argue visually, synthesize multiple viewpoints, and "updraft" their observations in an ethical and accessible way. Their final rhetorical analysis invites them to use field notes and artifacts to tell two stories of their work: the story of their subculture, its plots, its movements and players that emerged from what they learned; and the story of their own role as a participant-observer in an unfamiliar place, including how they did or didn't fit into the subculture, where their archival research aligned or maligned with what they observed, and how—as rhetoricians—they chose to construct their final project for sometimes disparate audiences. For example, Erin Schefske's portfolio in fig. 11.3 presents a visual synthesis of the different components in her ethnographic study of the Purdue Child Development Lab School that ultimately led her to become interested in how curriculum can be designed to build self-esteem, despite her initial beliefs to the contrary.

In the year that Tarez used this approach with a group of new and incoming instructors, two projects seemed to reflect the rhetoricity of visual ethnography and its mutuality as a learning tool for students and teachers alike: the verbal/visual portrait, which was a major assignment in the second unit of the course ("envisioning the project") that ended up serving as a synthesis project in the middle stages of students' research,

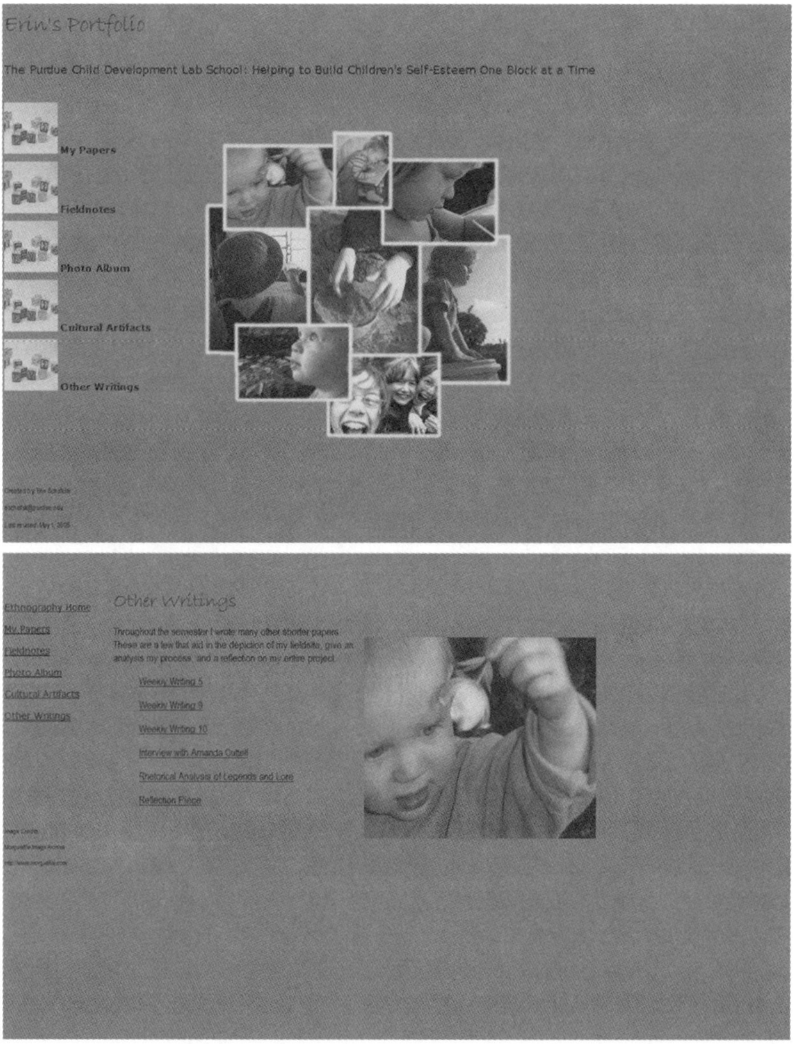

FIGURE 11.3. Final ethnographic portfolio created by Erin Schefske, a student in Tarez Graban's English 108 class.

and a Rhetoric of PowerPoint, which is a workshop Tarez originally devised for students that ended up serving as the basis for how she introduced new technology to the teachers she was mentoring.

The verbal/visual portrait has a written component and a visual component that students create in the medium of their choice. It asks students to interview, shadow, observe, and do some background research on a particular "insider" whom they think would represent their chosen subculture in a unique way—in fact, whose perspective their research project needs. Like project one of the rhetorical humanities approach, it is designed to foster students' growing realization of what makes the unfamiliar familiar about their subculture (or vice versa), and it pushes them to synthesize potentially dissonant and unconventional information as they triangulate facts from multiple sources for the first time. In preparation for guiding students through this act of triangulation, Tarez and the teachers she was mentoring studied different systems of invention heuristics before designing their own heuristics to use with students in class. These heuristics needed to help students arrive at a new point of dissonance that would then inspire the next point of their research, while also helping them identify a visual medium that best fitted the subject of their portrait.

This exercise led to several productive outcomes beyond the portrait assignment. For example, one student manipulated a digital photograph taken from her subculture in six different ways to arrive at a compelling sense of place, which then motivated her to repurpose her final paper as an advocacy project. Another student tried to construct a pathos-laden brochure on behalf of his field site but found that he was better equipped to refocus his research question more empathetically on the role of a single individual in that subculture rather than on depicting the whole place itself. One group of students completed direct and project-based service-learning at a local food pantry, for which they constructed a volunteer handbook that was inspired by their study of physical spaces. To demonstrate the pantry's holistic approach to subsistence and community education, students organized all of their information around this spatial map, which highlights the many functions of a single organization. Just as in writing this chapter we had to bring certain sections to closure to see new developments occur, composing what they think one audience might consider a convenient "end point" helps our students to get at the essence of another beginning point. This is critical to our understanding multivalent projects as having inventive potential even when they result in fairly unfamiliar products. This may also be critical to our understanding multimodal assignments as encouraging—rather than masking—a simultaneous realization of higher-learning, rhetorical, and compositional goals that guide our writing courses each semester (fig. 11.4).

Similarly, the Rhetoric of PowerPoint workshop grew out of a need for relevant, dynamic models of the kinds of applications that this approach to learning would require students to use, and also the kinds of thinking we want our students to do as users of these applications,

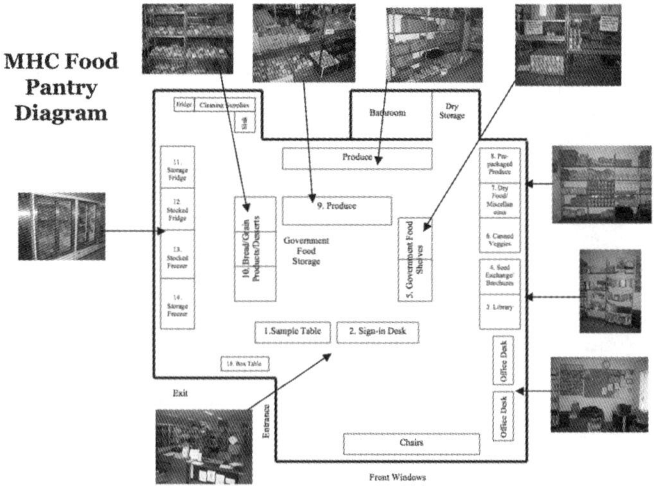

Figure 11.4. Part of a sixteen-page public document created by students in Tarez Graban's English W240 community-service writing class.

especially since we as teachers are still learning how to use them in compelling and situationally informed ways. Each semester she uses the approach, Tarez alternates between reading a full-length ethnography with her class or watching an ethnographic film and asking students to compose visual presentations of what they learn. This project gives her students an opportunity to witness different representations of research and question how certain audiences explicitly and implicitly influence those representations. Practically speaking, it allows students to collaborate on articulating visually how they do or do not understand what the ethnographer is trying to achieve. But if it is done consciously and reflectively, the PowerPoint project enables students to do more than just report: it can put them in the driver's seat should they want to use that medium to enact, re-present, or talk back to what they think *did* or *did not* work in the auteur's visual depiction of the subject. It is the juxtaposition of written or filmed arguments with the genre of student presentation that moves this assignment beyond merely a response or a summary. To express their learning, students have to learn a way to present their findings to peers in yet another format, one that hopefully draws on how the "readings" have asked to be read.

So that students and instructors don't shy away from letting the application help them determine that delivery (that is, to discourage them from merely transcribing a traditional essay onto a series of slides, or ourselves from expecting the same kind of linearity in a PowerPoint as we would a physical poster), Tarez encourages them to theorize the best way to use PowerPoint for visual depiction. Students read, unpack, and discuss several online articles by Peter Norvig, Edward Tufte, David Byrne (2003), and Julie Keller about the controversiality of PowerPoint before evaluating a series of amateur and professionally rendered PowerPoint presentations. Students then develop their "rhetoric"—a system determining everything from purpose and arrangement to layout and appearance—by critically examining the message, method, and medium of those presentations. Invariably, the students end up generating a list of criteria they feel should guide productive use not only of that program but also of web browsers, image editors, and word-processing software. Tarez uses the same activity when mentoring new instructors, urging them to generate a list of pedagogical uses for different technologies that supplement their instructional goals, rather than the other way around. She asks the instructors, in other words, to experiment with thinking from material to idea instead of letting an instructional goal—students will incorporate technology into their writing—define the use of technology as a "given" before its kairotic potential is explored.

INVENTING MULTIVALENCE

Other contributors in this collection point to the widespread possibility for us in rhetoric and composition to explain our multivalent teaching from a transdisciplinary perspective—that is, to embrace this as a viable project for the evolving rhetoric and composition tradition without sacrificing key disciplinary or historical goals. For example, in citing Heidegger and Lévy, Mary Leigh Morbey and Carolyn Steele mention in chapter 10 that we have available to us a language that helps position what we do as "theorizing from interspaces" between science and design, between literature and technology, and even between philosophy and art. In other words, where multimedia integration is concerned, we now have other options besides the "computers versus thesis statements" debate. *Either/or* becomes *both/and* as we consider how technological environments and technological contexts retain (and in many cases enhance) our students' exigency for developing rhetorical literacy. But if transdisciplinarity allows us to effectively acknowledge creative, synthesized approaches to knowledge production, what holds it back? Why hasn't this pedagogy taken off?

Perhaps teachers need a stronger understanding of what makes this "knowing" a hybrid art. When it comes to assessing our students' writing, we sometimes still fight against the tendency to separate out competence from performance as measures of student success, or to measure them using the same assessment tool. When it comes to mentoring our teachers, we have to work hard to invite productive discussion of failure or to invite dissonance and discomfort into the practicum. When it comes to developing assignments, we (in the discipline) may still be straining against purely literary conceptions of genre and not seeing that even our social-epistemic and/or transformative understandings of genre are bound by historically limited beliefs about what counts as a trustworthy text, an idea that Susan Miller (2008, 107) takes up in her critique of feature-driven views of print texts. In short, we haven't done enough to complicate rhetorical identity, rhetorical pedagogy, and rhetorical moments—haven't done enough to imagine (or accept) kairos as indicative of what's missing rather than indicative of what conditions are there (ibid.).

As composition teachers who value multimodality as rhetoricity, we have found that before dealing with the opportunities that these approaches afforded them, our students weren't always "focusing" or "inventing." More often they were calling up a familiar memory of some similar or conventional task and choosing what Melanie Kill (2006, 213) might call a "safe complicity" by reworking it, in the process robbing themselves of the opportunity to locate and solve a real problem in their writing. Our desires in teaching first-year composition go beyond the desire for repeated enacting (ibid., 214); it isn't enough for us to assign projects that ask students to *use* unconventional genres to do conventional things. Knowing a genre means more than just conforming to rules—it means knowing "how and when to deploy not only its conventions but also, and perhaps more importantly, the variations it enables" (ibid., 218). Inventing with a genre means playing with "the relationships between that genre and related genres, the paths they follow and the moves they make" (ibid.). Teaching a genre, then, means letting go of an assurance of how others see us in familiar roles. In the same way that our students may spend an open-ended literacy narrative assignment by writing about the awkwardness of writing it, we find our ways to not let go of the subject position we think our students (or others in the university) have asked us to assume (ibid., 223). Kill's idea of employing "uptake" (drawing on Anne Freadman's elaboration of J. L. Austin's use of the term) is inventive because it provides mentors, their students, and their teachers with a way to become less secure in the subject positions they occupy.

If we can suspend traditional notions of expertise in first-year writing situations, we take productive risks that we will:

- learn from our students as much as they learn from us,
- be surprised by the forms of writing that are produced and that we must learn to evaluate,
- strengthen and promote the idea that first-year writing is just a first year in college, suspended between a composing past and future, and
- foster students to develop their adaptive, rhetorical skills early in their post-secondary education so that they may be public intellectuals during and after their lives at colleges and universities.

We find that the "rhetorical humanities" and "visual ethnography" approaches to teaching composition overlap in their emphasis on using visual means to help the writer position herself and others, to position acts of inquiring and writing, and to consider the tensions between medium and message. At each stage of their research projects, students are faced with the questions of "What am I seeing here?" or "What's the difference between the 'real' and the 'perceived'?" or "What makes my subject unique?" or "How can I best arrange my information so that my reader sees it, too?" Our projects involve observing and participating in the intellectual work of a community, and they contain some aspect of argument as public discourse, research as service learning, or writing as social action. For example, students might compose a research study on affective behavior aimed at special educators or compile a lexicon of "insider" terms and urban legends to share with "outsiders."

But while we do ask students to articulate how they see a composition hanging together, this does not have to require traditional expertise in design principles or terminology. Those can emerge from class discussions and analyses of each other's work as much as from "handbooks" and "how-to" guides. This does not require a teacher to design individual workshops for each type of media or mode that students are using. Nor does it mean we have to put PowerPoint students with one another or group the nursing majors together when it comes time to generate feedback. That assumes that familiarity and similarity are more helpful than dissonance or fresh perspectives, which we don't think is the case.

The idea of multivalent composition requires us to reinvent that notion of "knowing" or "conforming" that we as teachers may desire, that our students may fixate on as an educational goal, and that new or future teachers may desire as a necessary step toward being a teacher (as opposed to thinking of oneself as always *becoming* a better teacher). The same goals we express for our students resonate with our hopes for new teachers: moving beyond binaries in figuring out difficult problems; recognizing that dissonance begins with what they see (and hear or feel in response to something); letting an issue guide but not drive their inquiry; devising rubrics and other evaluative tools with which to define their own learning goals; understanding sources as "voices" that need to be brought into mediated conversation with each other and their own (beyond just locating facts to support a preconception or premise); and breaking out of familiar generic molds long enough to flounder and reach out for a new foothold. Ultimately, we hope these kinds of experiences would equip teachers to think more independently as evaluators of unfamiliar genres—and beyond that, to realize that the intellectual work of teaching can be an inexpert becoming. This inexpert becoming—or reinvented expertise—looks the same for new teachers as it does for our students:

> *It challenges pedagogical devaluation by avoiding the theory-practice binary* (Salvatori 1994) in favor of creating sites for intensive rhetorical experimentation. Furthermore, it realizes theory not as an abstruse separation from practice but as the triangular intersection between the questions of "what," "why," and "how" we teach and write the way we do (Berthoff 1981, 41).
>
> *It leads to creative, transparent forms of resistance* because it is centered on writing projects that are contextualized in broader questions of definition and exigency (that is, How many ways are there to "write"? What are the familiar modal and material associations with my specific question?).
>
> *It deals inventively with resistance* by encouraging students, teachers, and mentors to be less secure in the subject position they think others want them to occupy, in order to reveal a subject position that participates more genuinely and—we hope—proffers a lasting rhetorical agility (Kill 2006, 223). For example, rather than capitulate to a teacher's and student's desire to simply be "trained" in the most efficient way to incorporate technology (a familiar outcome that doesn't recognize the pencil as technology), we would rather they spend a good deal of time considering the questions of technology emerging in a composition class: What counts as technology? What can technology affect? How are we affected by technology?
>
> *It relies on the idea of language as an impermanent space for identity* where we need only temporarily dwell instead of permanently reside. Especially for its invitation to reflect (that is, our multimodal assignments almost always

generate and emerge from reflexive writing), it presents opportunities to rethink the assumption that descriptions of experiences and events are universally shared, to take more ownership of a composition by working harder to clarify its purposes and bring readers along in cooperative understanding, and to understand that genres are not always fixed, determined, and stable.

It complicates the notion that certain kinds of tasks should only occur in certain kinds of spaces. For example, rather than focusing on the computer as the "locus of [students'] discomfort" (Duffelmeyer 2003, 299), we might rethink how we can adapt a familiarized computer lab space and repurpose the objects within it to better meet our needs for a particular class.

In writing, at least, it pushes students and teachers to consider how the acts of holding, storing, and indexing information and ideas affect the projects that emerge from them. When we think about how information is stored and how that storage affects meaning, the archive becomes an "arc-hive" of activity. Students and teachers can then more easily see how collecting is not about establishing expertise but building a network of potential.

CLOSING PARENTHESES

There is a strange ghost in our attempts here to reinvent expertise for ourselves, our students, and the teachers we mentor. In a field that pursues "self-efficacy" (Pajares, Johnson, and Usher 2007) as a good sign for progressive cognitive development, in a field where some scholar-teachers are suggesting that we do more theorizing with students about first-year composition (Downs and Wardle 2007), and in a performance culture that more and more values assessment to the detriment of engagement, we realize that an argument *against* notions of expertise in first-year composition may come across as counterproductive or, worse, as a naïve offshoot of a student-centered expressivism. That is not what we intend. Context, still, is everything.

However, at this juncture, the learning contexts in which we promise "expertise" in writing have lost the cohesion required for hybridized innovation. We see a need to regain that cohesion, not to fulfill the promise but to disrupt it, and one way to do this—beyond what we already suggest in terms of relinquishing our fixations on singularity in what counts as writing or technology—is to realize the evaluative possibilities in it. We suggest using reciprocal reflection to disrupt and to raise—rather than to avoid—contentious and productive conversations about how to determine when something has been done well.[7] Practically speaking, we see nine components of evaluation writ large that can be more deeply theorized or understood by teachers and students who grapple with the question of "expertise" in multivalent composing:

1. *Challenges of representation*—such as when writers realize their descriptions of experiences or events are not so universally shared.

2. *Situatedness and contextual nature of writing*—such as when writers have to work harder to articulate the significance (the "so what?") to someone less invested in their project.

3. *Ownership*—such as when the reciprocal reflective process demands that writers clarify their purposes and supporting points or rethink them altogether.

4. *Active/unstable genres*—such as when writers' and readers' understanding of genre is challenged beyond narrowly defined "types" of writing but as socially constructed forms.

5. *Style and delivery*—such as when writers experiment with different forms of delivery to achieve the desired interaction between what they write and how it is written.

6. *Organization and coherence*—such as when writers rely on the organization (for example, logical structure and coherence) of their piece to give the reader clues about its main point or significance.

7. *Dissonance (points of stasis)*—such as when writers see conflicts or problems emerge in what they might at first assume to be a stable or mundane situation.

8. *Process awareness*—such as when writers get into the habit of remembering how they act and think when putting their compositions together, and whether that process was effective.

9. *Active reading*—such as when writers and their peers realize that reading involves different forms of seeing—that is, noting and solving conflicts in one another's writing.

What this demonstrates, we think, is that enacting multivalence through rhetorical humanities and visual ethnography means focusing less on the generic differences between textual and visual and more on theorizing about a writing process even as students and teachers are experiencing it for the first time, and toward—not away from—being able to determine the efficacy of that process.

In other words, teaching ourselves to question what we do when we use the visual to "enhance" the alphanumeric is critical to our understanding multivalent composition as knowledge making, in lieu of arriving at a very fixed understanding of what "textual" should or shouldn't encompass. It means equipping students and teachers to critically understand problems through research and to understand what they want to achieve—and how it can be achieved—with others. It also means opening the lines of communication and work we've suggested here as productive and satisfying by framing our acts of learning and how we approach any act of composition. But we're thinking that each teacher has to find or call on a memory and story that allows him or her to show other people how he or she sees learning taking place in the world.

Like the memories of those we learn with. For Colin it is the memory of being in a graduate class taught by Dick Fulkerson, someone he knew had a name on important articles but was mostly a teacher on the way to becoming a friend. Although it was not easy for him to share, Dick had put five versions of a review article he was writing on the class bulletin board during the course of the semester, referring to the drafts sometimes, mostly criticizing what he saw as their shortcomings, in order to have a working example of writing for his students. Colin read the drafts closely and commented on them the way a coworker pitches in to solve a problem, or the way someone comes to the aid of a family member without thinking through the reasons. Working on personal projects with your students is not a necessity, nor is it something that a teacher should take on regardless of specific class dynamics, the culture of pedagogy in a department, or the amount and range of his or her teaching experiences. But for Colin it has become a means for promoting feedback and making room for others to talk about and question his writing while he is questioning theirs.

And the stories of how we adapt and invent. Tarez was able to witness a group of new and incoming instructors embrace (on their own) the idea that teaching writing required creativity, initiative, and engagement. This realization stemmed from the instructors' need to creatively adapt assignments that they thought were too sophisticated for students to grapple with but that they ultimately worked through in tandem with their students. One instructor adapted the verbal/visual portrait to create her own self-portrait assignment that she felt gave students more time to think about self-image and renderings of *self*, and aligned with her own interests in writing poetic portraits. In preparation for the final project, when students had to synthesize all of the data they had gathered over the semester for a thesis to emerge, another instructor devised a complex heuristic using visual and alphanumeric prompts to help students consider different rhetorical arrangements for their "data" and to start generalizing from all the details. As a result, Tarez's visual ethnography mentoring group ended up compiling a set of resources to pass along to other teachers and curriculum builders who were new to the approach and new to technology.[8]

And the public moments when writing classes and the work we do take on the gravity of a happening. When Jonikka, Jennifer Courtney, and Shirley Rose organized the first annual Showcase of Student Writing at Purdue, Jonikka knew that people across campus were wary of the change to a four-credit composition course and did not know what to expect from the new first-year composition course. At the time, Jonikka was in the middle of writing her dissertation, arguing that writing program administrators need to become more actively involved in articulating the goals, work, and value of their writing programs to people outside those programs. On the day of the event, faculty and administrators from all over campus came, and they were surprised at the different kinds of projects the students were working on—from traditional essays on the "market-driven university" to interactive websites to cardboard boxes representing students' portraits of themselves to their families. The dean of the college came twice that day, and what those who came witnessed was the (often invisible) intellectual work of a program—the way that first-year students engage in their own intellectual work as well.

And then there are your stories—which we look forward to hearing more about.[9]

NOTES

1. Contrary to the notion that composing in multimedia necessarily draws students' attention *away from* language, the kind of work we propose new teachers do may enhance students' understanding of what they do with language as "symbol-using" (Kenneth Burke, via Enoch 2004). By this we mean that traversing unfamiliar genres for making sophisticated arguments can potentially heighten students' sensitivity to all of the ways they must make their stances more critical, and all of the ways that language is used in conjunction with (or in lieu of) other media.

2. Here's how Shipka (2005, 284–85) might encourage us to convert our writing assignments into communicative tasks: (1) do not foreclose inquiry by signaling the specific ways students are to successfully accomplish the task; (2) do let the student come up with the scope and purpose of the work; (3) do not predetermine the methods, materials, and technologies they need to employ. Its most signature features are that students take responsibility for generating solution-procedure sequences, or steps, or complex action sequences (ibid., 286), and that students decide *how*, *why*, *where*, and even *when* an argument will be experienced by its recipients, especially when the argument is made based on outside or archival sources. For example, when Shipka's student Prakas received a fairly simple lexical assignment to look up in the *Oxford English Dictionary*, Prakas decided to create his own audiovisual rendering of the word "scare" because he felt that his rendering was a "prototype for a 'truer,' or more interactive, version of the *OED*" and of the lexical task (ibid.).

3. Geoffrey Sirc offers one such activity in "Box Logic" that offers an alternative to the "integrated coherence of college essayist prose" he sees as "increasingly untenable" (in Wysocki et al. 2004, 123). For his "Basic Box" activity, Sirc asks students to bring together a visual object and a text so that they comment on each other, making the student a multimodal "composer" who learns to invent connectivity in more than just words (ibid., 129–33). A pedagogy of juxtaposition, then, allows us to play with potentials instead of always *boxing* our message, style, and so on in an assumed ideal of the college essay or academic discourse.

4. See, for example, Dyehouse, Pennell, and Shamoon 2009 and Anderson et al. 2006.

5. What follows is a description of the curriculum Colin and Jonikka used at Purdue while teaching first-year composition as a one-semester course; they have since gone back to teaching the typical two-semester sequence at the University of Texas–Pan American, where the goals for the composition program are more traditional at the moment. The lessons of the curriculum they describe here are informing the revision of those goals, although a one-semester course for first-year writing is a long way off.

6. What follows is a description of the curriculum Tarez used at Purdue while teaching and mentoring first-year composition as a one-semester course. The unusual five-day-a-week format allowed for extensive work with technology and one-on-one conferencing. She has since adapted it for a community-service writing course at Indiana University that promoted various arts of research for community-based writing; lessons described here reflect the adaptation.

7. By "reciprocal reflection," we mean something like this, concretely described: a writer creates a text, then reflects on it by writing an analysis of what she thinks the text accomplishes; a reader then views the text and writes his own

analysis or interpretation of what he thinks the text accomplishes; finally, the writer reviews both analyses and reflects on the differences, in the process determining what could be changed and why those different interpretations might have occurred. And the cycle doesn't have to end there. In this way both reader and writer are reliant upon each other for making meaning out of a particular evaluation event.

8. See http://www.digitalparlor.org/icap/fieldir.

9. We welcome you to continue the conversation at our companion blog—http://multiv.blogspot.com—where you can find links to assignments and feedback activities, student projects, and our continuing discussion of what our idea of multivalence holds for composition and mentoring pedagogies.

REFERENCES

Anderson, Daniel, Anthony Atkins, Cheryl Ball, Krista Homicz Millar, Cynthia Selfe, and Richard Selfe. 2006. "Integrating Multimodality into Composition Curriculum: Survey Methodology and Results from a CCCC Research Grant." *Composition Studies* 34: 59–84.

Aronowitz, Stanley. 2000. *The Knowledge Factory: Dismantling the Corporate University and Creating True Higher Learning.* Boston: Beacon Press.

Atwan, Robert, and Diana Hacker. 2003. *Convergences: Message, Method, Medium.* New York: Bedford/St. Martin's.

Atwill, Janet M. 1998. *Rhetoric Reclaimed: Aristotle and the Liberal Arts Tradition.* Ithaca: Cornell University Press.

Berthoff, Ann. 1981. "A Curious Triangle and the Double-Entry Notebook: Or, How Theory Can Help Us Teach Reading and Writing." In *The Making of Meaning: Metaphors, Models, and Maxims for Writing Teachers*, 41–47. Montclair, NJ: Boynton/Cook.

Byrne, David. 2003. *E.E.E.I. (Envisioning Emotional Epistemological Information).* London: Steidl/Pace/MacGill Gallery.

Downs, Doug, and Elizabeth Wardle. 2007. "Teaching about Writing, Righting Misconceptions: (Re)Envisioning 'First-Year Composition' as 'Introduction to Writing Studies.'" *College Composition and Communication* 58 (4): 552–84.

Duffelmeyer, Barbara Blakely. 2003. "Learning to Learn: New TA Preparation in Computer Pedagogy." *Computers and Composition* 20: 295–311.

Dyehouse, Jeremiah, Michael Pennell, and Linda K. Shamoon. 2009. "'Writing in Electronic Environments': A Concept and Course for the Writing and Rhetoric Major." *College Composition and Communication* 61 (2): 330–50.

Enoch, Jessica. 2004. "Becoming Symbol-Wise: Kenneth Burke's Pedagogy of Critical Reflection." *College Composition and Communication* 56 (2): 272–96.

Faigley, Lester, Diana George, Anna Palchik, and Cynthia Selfe. 2003. *Picturing Texts*. New York: W. W. Norton.

Fleming, David. 1998. "Rhetoric as a Course of Study." *College English* 61 (2): 169–91.

Haynes, Cynthia. 2003. "Writing Offshore: The Disappearing Coastline of Composition Theory." *Journal of Rhetoric, Culture, and Politics* 23 (4): 667–724.

Kill, Melanie. 2006. "Acknowledging the Rough Edges of Resistance: Negotiation of Identities for First-Year Composition." *College Composition and Communication* 58 (2): 213–35.

Kress, Gunther. 1999. "English at the Crossroads: Rethinking Curricula of Communication in the Context of the Turn to the Visual." In *Passions, Pedagogies, and Twenty-first Century Technologies*, edited by Gail Hawisher and Cynthia Selfe, 66–88. Logan: Utah State University Press.

Martin, Cynthia. 2004. "Partners in Teaching Excellence: A Model for Transformative Mentoring." McGraw-Hill Higher Education. Online at http://www.mhhe.com/socscience/english/tc/martin/martinmodule.html.

McQuade, Donald, and Christine McQuade, eds. 2000. *Seeing and Writing*. New York: Bedford/St. Martin's.

Miller, Susan. 2008. *Trust in Texts: A Different History of Rhetoric*. Carbondale: Southern Illinois University Press.

North, Stephen M. 1987. *The Making of Knowledge in Composition: Portrait of an Emerging Field*. Portsmouth, NH: Boynton/Cook.

Nussbaum, Martha C. 1998. *Cultivating Humanity: A Classical Defense of Reform in Liberal Education*. Cambridge: Harvard University Press.

Pajares, F., M. J. Johnson, and E. L. Usher. 2007. "Sources of Writing Self-Efficacy Beliefs of Elementary, Middle, and High School Students." *Research in the Teaching of English* 42 (1): 104–20.

Readings, Bill. 1996. *The University in Ruins*. Cambridge: Harvard University Press.

Salvatori, Mariolina. 1994. "Pedagogy and the Academy: 'The Divine Skill of the Born Teacher's Instincts.'" In *Pedagogy in the Age of Politics: Writing and Reading (in) the Academy*, edited by Patricia Sullivan and Donna Qualley, 88–99. Urbana, IL: National Council of the Teachers of English.

Shipka, Jody. 2005. "A Multimodal Task-Based Framework for Composing." *College Composition and Communication* 57 (2): 277–306.

Sunstein, Bonnie, and Elizabeth Chiseri-Strater. 2006. *Fieldworking: Reading, Writing, and Research*, third ed. New York: Bedford/St. Martin's.

Wysocki, Anne F., Johndan Johnson-Eilola, Cynthia L. Selfe, and Geoffrey Sirc. 2004. *Writing New Media: Theory and Applications for Expanding the Teaching of Composition*. Logan: Utah State University Press.

CHAPTER 12

Going Multimodal

Programmatic, Curricular, and Classroom Change

Chanon Adsanatham, Phill Alexander, Kerrie Carsey, Abby Dubisar, Wioleta Fedeczko, Denise Landrum, Cynthia Lewiecki-Wilson, Heidi McKee, Kristen Moore, Gina Patterson, and Michele Polak

> In essence, multimodality lets the many-faceted world we live in be more accurately represented and analyzed. We experience life and learn through many different avenues and to try to confine our work to one, namely text, can constrict the possibilities immensely.
>
> —Zach Burns, Kenton Butcher, and Dirk Long, undergraduate students (Conference on College Composition and Communication presentation, March 2007)

As the students note in this epigraph, we do not live in a monomodal world. Rather, we experience the world and communicate through multiple modalities. "To confine" students to learning in only one mode, typically the textual mode in first-year writing courses, indeed limits students' understanding and creative potential—a point that has reemerged in considerations of education and the teaching of writing.[1] Instead, introducing students early in their college careers to the different ways of making meaning using a given mode and to a consideration of the contrastive affordances of other modes as they compose leads them to a deeper understanding of modality—that is, toward learning "the functional grammar" of modes, as the New London Group (2000) describes it.[2] Furthermore, to use the term of Mary Leigh Morbey and Carolyn Steele (see chapter 10 in this edited volume), such multimodal literacy can enable students eventually to develop "metamodal mastery," "the ability to work across different modes," to understand semiotic complexity, and to create hybrid genres that reach across disciplinary and academic and popular boundaries.

Given the increased complexity and importance of multimodality for learning and communication, the Composition Program at Miami University initiated programmatic, curricular, and classroom changes in 2005 to promote the teaching and learning of multimodal composition. In a dialectical and parallel process we also created the Digital Writing Collaborative (DWC), a network of teachers and students whose mission is to develop and sustain a culture and community of digital writing, learning, and teaching in all areas of English studies, especially in composition. In this chapter we discuss the process and elements of institutional change needed to initiate and sustain a digital composition program—from building alliances across campus to integrating the teaching and learning of multimodal digital composition into our first-year composition curriculum, classroom practices, and teacher training. We open by providing an overview of writing instruction and teacher preparation at Miami, followed by an account of how we worked from this base to develop a digital writing curriculum. We next present some examples of multimodal assignments and narratives of teaching specific modalities. We conclude with a brief summary of the ongoing developments of our program, now in its sixth year, and reflect on the challenges of assessing multimodal compositions and of sustaining digital writing programs.

THE PROGRAMMATIC LEVEL: THE FOUNDATIONS AND CONDITIONS FOR CHANGE

Miami's first-semester, rhetorically focused writing curriculum has included a space for multimodality for the better part of a decade, although we had no digital classrooms to explicitly support multimodal composing until our initiative to revise the program in 2005–2006. At that time the standard curriculum, laid out with detailed pedagogy and assignments in a four-hundred-page teacher's guide, included five recursive sequences organized around a common theme: autoethnography (critical analysis of one's experience, history, and beliefs in relation to the course theme); rhetorical analysis; argument and research; design your own project; and reflection. With an emphasis on the importance of considering audience, purpose, and appropriate form, the fourth sequence provided a capstone experience of rhetorical knowledge: Students selected, planned, and composed—either individually or collaboratively—an intensive project of their own choosing. Even before our digital initiative, some students pushed their writing outside the bounds of the traditional essay, creating multimodal projects, such as CDs of musical compositions, brochures with visual images, web pages, and documentary videos. In short, students were already leading us into multimodality—and digital multimodality—before we developed digital classrooms and consciously set out to revise our curriculum to be even more explicitly multimodal.[3] Our current curriculum includes five interrelated inquiries: self-inquiry/initial reflection, textual inquiry/rhetorical analysis, issue inquiry/public issue argument, media inquiry/remediation, and e-portfolio inquiry/final reflection.

Historically, our program at Miami has been alert to new technologies, incorporating these into the recommended pedagogy as they emerged—for example, in the early to mid-1990s Listservs started to be used for extending class discussions, and by 2000 course management systems like Blackboard, with its forums and other spaces for writing, were commonly used by most composition instructors. And in 2005 we set up a composition wiki (password-protected) for collaborative writing projects. Despite these examples of integrating technology, no sections of composition were taught in computerized classrooms (at least not since the late 1980s when the program's one computer classroom was released because of lack of adequate funding for computer maintenance and replacement). So, prior to 2005, while we did not focus our curriculum specifically on the integration of digital technologies, we did have many technologies already infused into the culture of composition teaching at Miami. Although computerized technologies are certainly not necessary for multimodal composing, the affordances they provide for integrating visual, aural, and textual elements enable multimodal composing to occur more seamlessly, apply to a wider range of rhetorical situations, and reach potentially more audiences.

As for teacher preparation, we extensively train graduate student instructors in a monthlong, four-credit summer graduate seminar in the teaching of composition before they step into a classroom and a two-semester practicum meeting once a week during their entire first year of teaching. By 2005 we had also incorporated Universal Design for

Learning (UDL) into teacher training. UDL, a philosophy and approach to teaching adapted from the field of architecture, is a movement to design spaces that are not only compliant with the guidelines of the Americans with Disabilities Act (ADA) but that meet the needs of all people throughout their lives. UDL emphasizes core principles for accessible and flexible goals, methods, materials, and assessment in teaching to meet the needs of diverse learners (see Bowe 2000; Bruch 2004; Dunn and DeMers 2002; "Fast Facts" 2007; "What Is" 2007). We thus had already been incorporating into teacher preparation discussion about the affordances of modes and technologies for teaching, learning, and composing, but we knew we needed some computerized classrooms where more direct teaching and learning with digital technologies could occur, especially as we sought to push our curriculum toward helping students analyze and compose more cutting-edge digital projects (for example, audio essays, video remixes, 3-D worlds).

Networking for Change

As we set out to develop digital laptop classrooms and a digital pedagogy, we needed to connect with stakeholders across campus. Although composition is a service course to the university, it has historically enjoyed a place of privilege and freedom at Miami: privilege in that it forms the foundation of the Miami Plan, the general education core curriculum, and freedom in that Miami emphasizes a strong liberal arts education. The Miami Plan and composition curriculum emphasize critical thinking, understanding contexts, engaging with other learners, and reflecting and acting. Unlike programs at some universities, the composition program was not pressured to emphasize a narrow range of skills. This meant, however, that in persuading stakeholders to help us develop digital classrooms and pedagogy, we had to reassure them that we were not diluting the intellectual focus of our writing classes.

To do this, we emphasized the ways in which digital technologies would help expand the possibilities for teaching and learning—presenting new rhetorical situations and potentially global audiences for communicating; allowing for the increased integration of images, audio, and video into print-based and web-based texts; developing in students more sophisticated research skills; and providing them direct instructional opportunities to become better critical writers, readers, and researchers in a variety of rhetorical contexts that they may face in their academic and professional careers. We made this argument in memos to and meetings with the president and provost and to other entities on campus—and in constructing it, we drew from the excellent article "Why Teach Digital Writing" (WIDE Research Center 2005). Key to our argument to those administrators who were less familiar with emerging trends in writing was that networked connectivity and multimodality have changed writing contexts, that students need opportunities in class to analyze and compose in these new contexts, and that doing so would improve their critical thinking, writing, and research—particularly their ability to evaluate online information and resources.

Because we were able to successfully argue for the need and the potential benefits of integrating digital technologies in the writing classroom and because Miami University was launching a laptop purchasing program where incoming students are strongly encouraged (although not required) to purchase laptop computers, we received internal funding from the provost and from the vice president of information technologies to develop several digital classrooms.[4] In 2006 we unveiled a new laptop classroom with a teacher station computer, projector, DVD player, document project, and wireless connectivity for use exclusively by the Composition Program and a desktop, high-end new media lab to be shared by English and Interactive Media Studies. In 2007 we opened another laptop classroom, enabling us to teach 30 percent of our more than 130 sections per semester with digital technologies. In 2008 we added another laptop classroom, enabling us to teach 42 percent of our sections with digital technologies. In 2009 we added one more laptop classroom, and in summer 2010 we added three more, enabling us by fall 2011 to teach more than 85 percent of our first-year writing classes in laptop or hard-wired classrooms. (Because of the Miami Notebook program, 98 percent of incoming students at Miami own laptop computers that they can bring to class. For those students who don't own laptops, they may enroll in sections offered in hard-wired labs.[5])

Materials Secured: On to Course Goals

Back in 2006, once we knew we'd secured the material spaces for teaching in digital classrooms, we administrators and graduate student instructors met to decide if we wanted special course goals for the digital sections. Our Composition Program's goals are adapted from the *WPA Outcomes Statement for First-Year Composition* (WPA 2000) and address both composing processes and rhetorical knowledge. We soon realized that we did not want to create new, special goals for the digital writing sections, but instead that we should revise the overall program goals, since all composition students—whether taught in rooms with digital technology access or not—benefit from explicit consideration of the multimodal elements of composing as they learn to make critical, rhetorical choices about modes and technologies for delivery.

Specifically, we added to some of our outcomes such elements as these (words in italic indicate changes): "A student should be able to choose appropriate conventions of form, structure, voice, tone, and diction *and appropriate technologies that assure accessibility to a range of audiences.* . . . By the end of the first year, students should understand how particular audiences, genres, *and technologies* shape reading and writing; *how multimodal elements of texts (images, sound, design) can have rhetorical effects; how to choose, critique, and experiment with multimodal elements, genre, or a mix of genres, for a rhetorical purpose*; the rhetorical, collaborative, social, and *technological aspects* of writing processes and products." Interestingly, as multimodal composing percolated through our program goals, it influenced rhetorical outcomes the most, not merely the composing skills, as might at first be imagined.

We might not have been prompted to make these changes to our outcomes if we hadn't been faced with the many teaching and learning opportunities made available by the digital classrooms. The biggest and most important changes, however, came in our instructor preparation programs. We wanted to ensure that we did not merely "add on" digital classrooms but fully integrated and supported a digital pedagogy. To that end, instructors and administrators redesigned the teacher-training classes, added a new practicum, and developed special multimodal workshops. We applied for and received several small internal grants to support these efforts, including funds to bring in nationally recognized leaders in multimodality for presentations and workshops.

INSTRUCTOR PREPARATION AND DEVELOPMENT

In the article "Beyond Imagination: The Internet and Global Digital Literacy," Lester Faigley (1999, 138) offered six characteristics for the "best possible learning environment with technology." Of these characteristics, we realized that the fifth, "training and support for integrating technology into the curriculum," would be one of the most important to the success of our digital initiative. In the late spring and early summer of 2006, interested writing instructors met with the aims of planning a digital curriculum and finding a name that could represent this diverse group. The Digital Writing Collaborative was chosen because it seemed appropriate to call ourselves a "collaborative" to emphasize the range of resources each person brought to the table. Our technological backgrounds and pedagogical interests ranged from those comfortable with high tech to those who call themselves "old school" when it comes to technology. We began with a commitment to validate this range of interests. With our various perspectives, we sketched out what it might look like to teach in multimodal ways with the affordances of technology. We were at once excited and intimidated to be part of this new movement in our composition program but also cautious about not getting too carried away with technology and losing sight of program goals.

One of the first actions of the new DWC was to meet with the director of Composition and the graduate student editors of *The Teacher's Guide*, a yearly internal publication that serves as a manual for teaching the major sequences of college composition courses. The bulk of the guide maps out composition goals, classroom activities, and major and minor writing assignments for the semester. The guide has always been a great resource for instructors, seasoned or new, and is updated yearly with new ideas and curriculum changes, and we felt it was important to include a new digital section—one that would adapt assignments to digital environments and provide some new ideas as well. Although the ideas published were helpful, each teacher needed to work them over to more fully develop, remix, or refine the assignments to suit their and their students' interests, technological abilities, and teaching and learning needs.[6]

The composition theory summer seminar required of first-year graduate instructors was an obvious place to infuse training and support for the digital initiative. The aim of the course is to help new graduate instructors think through how they will construct and teach the standard composition syllabus. The course had already been providing teachers with tools for incorporating technology and multimodal assignments into their first-year composition courses: for example, learning to use our course-management system (now Sakai-based), virtual chat rooms, digital journals, message boards, discussion forums, Listservs, and the composition wiki. The emphasis was not on using technology merely for technology's sake but on incorporating only what each instructor felt comfortable with and what furthered particular pedagogical and writing goals. In this first seminar for graduate instructors we did not introduce the specific technologies of the new multimodal curriculum (for example, building web pages or composing sound essays) but instead focused on developing a solid base of self-reflective, multimodal teaching habits. We did introduce the first-year graduate instructors to the new DWC and digital classrooms and invited them to consider teaching in them after they had completed this seminar and the two, semester-long teaching practica all new instructors must take during their first year of teaching. As of 2011 all new graduate teaching assistants are required to teach in laptop classrooms. There are no longer special digital practica because approaches for integrating digital and multimodal composing are woven throughout the curriculum of the standard instructor preparation programs.

Flying with (Limited) Radar

Back in 2006, the first semester of laptop classrooms and the new multimodal curriculum, volunteer seasoned instructors (tenure-line faculty, part-time faculty, and graduate students) formed the lead cohort of instructors in the digital classrooms. What proved most helpful were the opportunities to talk with each other about our experiences. Before the first semester began, we met for three half-day workshops that involved some "how-to" and room orientation as well as presentations from individuals across campus (the campus coordinator of our course management system, the lead IT classroom support contact, a library specialist in teaching students online research). To continue the support during that first semester teaching in the digital classrooms, the graduate students of the cohort met for a biweekly practicum to discuss issues that were surfacing in practice. We spent hours grappling with ways to effectively integrate digital technologies so as to meet students' learning needs and the goals of college composition. In essence, the first semester of teaching in the digital classrooms seemed like a collective experience of flying with only limited radar. Concerns that couldn't have possibly fit into the biweekly practicum spilled over into small networks of sponsorship, some of us meeting in coffee shops, chatting on the phone, via e-mail, and so on to swap ideas and tell our stories about how we were negotiating digital, multimodal pedagogy.

To encourage discussion and collaboration beyond the biweekly practicum, the DWC also offered sponsored workshops on specific techno-pedagogical issues. In all, the DWC offered twelve workshops during the 2006–7 school year: participants learned to blog, create audio essays, manipulate images, make movies, and build online gaming characters while considering how such technology changes the possibilities for multimodal composition. Workshops and lunchtime discussions are still a key component of our instructor outreach. Each semester, instructors in the DWC offer six to eight workshops and discussions. These opportunities to share our work and to learn from each other are crucial for the sustainability of the program.

Sustaining Flight

Faigley (1999) has argued that "training reduces anxiety and increases understanding in how to use technology." In the second year the DWC in its role in the Composition Program faced two challenges: continuing to develop digital, multimodal pedagogy and training instructors in its use, while sustaining the energy and commitment of the teaching community. To build on the knowledge and experience gained in the first year, a great deal of digital archiving of materials occurred, some available publicly on the Web and some available only to members of the Miami University community at the DWC Blackboard site.[7] In addition to the digital resources, face-to-face resources were and continue to be developed.[8] As well, the workshop series continues, led by DWC instructors, and there are weekly mentor meetings for all instructors who are (or who are interested in) integrating multimodal, digital composition in their classrooms (whether they are teaching in the digital classrooms or in more traditional classrooms).[9]

Many things did run more smoothly in our second and subsequent years of the digital initiative. For example, since we've all now actually taught in the digital classrooms, the assignments in the teacher's guide have been revised and refined. Our series of workshops and discussions (twelve per year) are known and expected events with topics changing each semester to meet changing needs. And the DWC will continue to bring in guest speakers and, with the generous help of Bedford/ St. Martin's, sponsor a prize for the best digital, multimodal composition for students enrolled in first-year writing courses.

INSTRUCTOR REFLECTIONS ON VARIOUS MODES AND MULTIMODAL ASSIGNMENTS

As with the integration of any pedagogy, the integration of multimodal composing occurs along various continua in our program. Most instructors develop assignments asking students to analyze the rhetorical effectiveness of various multimodal texts created by others (for example, commercials, YouTube videos, audio essays, digital storytelling projects).

But many instructors also develop assignments that engage students not just in analyzing but also in producing multimodal texts. This move to multimodal production wasn't, of course, entirely new. As Gina Patterson, one of the instructors from the lead cohort explained: "The biggest 'step' I experienced in the digital classroom was to slow down, not panic, and realize that I had previously been teaching multimodality and asking for multimodal assignments before I ever entered the wireless laptop classroom." The addition of access to digital technologies meant that instructors and students now had a wider array of options for multimodal analysis and composing, including opportunities to teach and to learn new genres and new technologies. In the sections that follow four instructors share narratives of their experiences engaging students with the analysis and production of multimodal texts. These narratives, from both experienced and new instructors, bring to the fore pedagogical benefits and issues to consider with multimodal composing.

Phill Alexander: Gaming as Multimodal Reading and Composing

An effective way to integrate multimodality and digital media in our composition classrooms is to meet students where many of them are already using digital media technology: video games (see Morbey and Steele's chapter 10 in this edited volume). At Miami University we ask our students to begin the second semester of first-year composition by creating an inventory of their reading and writing habits. Once, upon hearing the assignment, two students came to me with a concern, which I paraphrase here: "Um . . . we don't . . . um . . . read. And we only write what we have to." I asked, "So what do you do in your free time?" It turns out these two young men described themselves as "obsessed" with *Halo 2*, a first-person shooter game for the Xbox gaming system. They had a clan (a team of networked players), and their clan had a webpage with online discussion forums where they shared strategies, planned battles, and so on. One of the pair also spent hours playing a game called *The Elder Scrolls III: Morrowind*, a role-playing game that required the player to develop a complex character and interpret intricate visual, textual, and aural puzzles while exploring a digital world. The other played *Madden* football regularly and maintained "virtual" franchise webpages that tracked the progress of his team throughout the season(s) he played; the page included video clips, still images, box scores, and user-developed game summaries. Both spoke of hours of "playing," which included hours of reading forum posts, hours of posting messages and participating in game chats, hours of watching YouTube videos generated by other players to illustrate strategies and concepts, and the hours spent in all the other reading and writing activities that went into finding solutions to their gaming problems. In five minutes of banter, these two young men who claimed to "not read and write" described their roles as highly literate participants in a set of gamer discourse communities.

Gaming currently occupies an interesting position for scholars and teachers. As we seek to incorporate digital and multimodal elements in our classrooms, we must remember that we walk a fine line. Many students play with these technologies (whether it is in console games such as *The Sims* or *Halo* or in online worlds such as *World of Warcraft* or *Lineage* with thousands—or millions—of players). While that sense of play and desire to create can be harnessed for educational purposes, we also run the risk of alienating students by "invading" their discourse and making it "academic"—or in student's terms, we could potentially "suck the fun out of it."

At the same time, gaming is the ideal starting point for a discussion of multimodality that engages without feeling exactly like "work." During one course I had a group of students visit the online Adobe Flash game *The Crimson Room* (Takagi 2004). The goal of *The Crimson Room* is actually quite simple: The gamer is placed in a first-person gaming environment, told he or she had "too much to drink last night," and must find a way out of the room. Initially, it seems almost too easy, and anyone playing the game—seasoned gamer or gaming novice—begins clicking around the environment, reading visual, audio, and textual clues while using the mouse to explore the room. Most gamers click to "stand" and immediately try the doorknob. But the door is locked. This starts an exploration of the room that can take hours, as the gamer checks every remote corner of the small, simply rendered room/world, trying to locate the door key.

Something interesting happens when I show people *The Crimson Room*. It's meant to be a quick, easy example of a video game space. The interface and mechanics are simple. It can be played on any computer that can run Flash Player. And initially it looks boring. But players get sucked in. With both undergraduates and graduate students—and even a professor observing one of my presentations—there's a quick jump from "this is interesting" to "wait, wait, I think I've got it!" The game moves from being a simplistic example to presenting a challenge, the challenge becomes fun, and that fun generates energy. In some cases people have contacted me the next day to inform me that they continued playing late,

late into the night. A quick Google search for "Crimson Room" shows that those who e-mailed me are not alone; the game generates responses ranging from awe to anger each time a new gamer takes up the task of escaping the room.

What I have described here is *multimodal reading*, as the game requires visual, textual, and auditory observation for a gamer to have any real success in solving the puzzle. The input, however, might not seem like multimedia composing. The gamer, after all, is simply moving the mouse and clicking to explore. This is where one must consider the definition of gaming. Gamers who identify with the now expansive and multifaceted gaming community would define all actions involving the game to be a part of the gaming experience. The e-mails I received from people caught in the web of *The Crimson Room* would be game-related writing. The fan-generated websites, the image-based tutorials, and fascinating little pieces like a five-minute YouTube video entitled "Crimson Room Tutorial," which was created using a screen-capture program, a video editor, and music, would be considered game-related writing. The nature of gaming—the "jump in and play" concept that makes gaming fun and which snares even those who might skeptically think that *The Crimson Room* is a simple puzzle—serves as a multimodal digital echo for the "process" concept of composing.

Activities centered on gaming can—and, I would argue, *should*—be more complex than the one-session exploration of *The Crimson Room* described here, but the idea itself would work well for projects large or small in scope. Introducing students to a game, allowing them to explore, collaborate, and attempt to play/thrive/succeed, then asking them to create texts that analyze and reflect on their experiences is one way in to the reading and writing of multimodal compositions.

Michele Polak: Web Authoring and Digital Subjectivities

I didn't realize it when I first started teaching composition, but gradually I became aware of the fact that I would need to make the move toward incorporating multimodal forms of digital technologies into my pedagogy. Students in my classes were bringing their digital literacies to the classroom before I even thought to consider using the digital environment as part of their writing process.[10] They exchanged peer drafts through e-mail and responded to these drafts electronically, long before I finally gave in and followed suit. When the opportunity to teach in a digital classroom arose, I didn't just jump toward volunteering—I lunged.

At the start I had every intention of utilizing the digital environment to its fullest potential. The data were telling me that many teens with access were online; my dissertation research sent me into a whole netspace of active adolescent girls who were building and maintaining their own websites. I was hoping to see this in action, so I decided on a website assignment for the Design Your Own Project sequence, partnered with a paper based on an issue of public debate. Knowing that many professors would still require the standard "college paper," I didn't want students to be at a loss when they encountered traditional classrooms with no options for digital projects, so I used the argument sequence to assign a paper on a topic of public debate. I emphasized research during these weeks, teaching students how to navigate citation and plagiarism issues both traditionally and electronically; I still wanted them to familiarize themselves with the campus library and also to focus on how argument worked in both traditional paper-based as well as in web-based forms. When we discussed the upcoming website assignment, I encouraged students to choose topics they would be willing to research for the last half of the semester.

Once I responded and graded all the public debate papers, I introduced the new web-authoring sequence by placing students into groups based on similar topics. I designed the website assignment to include both a collaborative element and an individual effort. Each group was to create one homepage that introduced the shared issue of public debate with links to each student's own website. Each individual website required a minimum of four pages with a set number of graphics and other visual elements. Students used and revised text from their public debate research papers to build their pages and focused on making rhetorical choices as to how to compose and arrange text and image.

I was excited about this assignment. My research was telling me that this is a generation of students who grew up with technology; they have "never known life without the Internet" (Oblinger and Oblinger 2006, 8). I saw them surf the Web in the few minutes before class began, talk about chat discussions, and download music and videos. What I didn't expect was that out of my two course sections, not one student out of the forty-four had ever built a website. And what I didn't anticipate was how many students initially lacked the confidence to move forward with the assignment. As their drafting and website sketches proved, their ideas were strong. They utilized everything they had learned about rhetoric and argument to make creative choices about the visual and textual elements of their webpages. Yet despite how much they actually were using new technologies, they lacked the assurance that they could bring their writing to a digital platform. I slowly began to realize that it wasn't the software (Dreamweaver) that made them hesitant but some nervousness because their writing was going to be made public and available for anyone outside our class to view.

Many of their topics were highly political, and they realized that their websites could be viewed as representations of their identity. Joanne Addison and Michelle Comstock (1998, 374) have noted that "providing space for participants to articulate their positions is central" to many of the various websites created and posted on the Internet, and this was apparent for my students' sites. While the digital classroom obviously provides a space to compose in a variety of multimodal forms, I didn't fully appreciate how going multimodal also opens up a space for (re)considering and (re)presenting subjectivity. Ultimately, the website assignment surprised both my students and me. Despite their initial lack of confidence in moving forward, students produced websites based on strong rhetorical choices.

Tara acknowledged: "I was amazed that I was able to do something like making a website, so I'm pretty happy with the outcome. . . . The part I disliked about this assignment was first learning how to do everything. I didn't like being frustrated and not knowing what to do, but now that I finished it, I'm extremely happy with what I've done." By the completion of the assignment, reflections were generally positive. Meghan said: "Creating my own website has probably been the most rewarding project I have completed."[11] Although I probably won't change the website assignment structure much, I will add a day for discussing how moving our work to a public forum changes how we think about our writing and our identities. Placing myself alongside students in the learning curve, I will also need to revise my own pedagogy and assumptions that multimodality is just about verbal and visual texts; it also involves remaking subjectivity.

Abby Dubisar: Audio Projects and Public Audiences

With the ever-expanding network of mobile devices for accessing the Internet, the audio delivery of writing is omnipresent in our lives. As writing instructors preparing students for academic, professional, and personal writing in an age of YouTube and iTunes, we need to help students become better listeners to themselves and to one another, and to translate this better listening into improved understanding of writing and rhetoric. In an effort to show my students how they can improve their own writing by listening to themselves and their classmates, I incorporate audio components into my first-year writing courses. I wanted to make literal for them what I was hearing from their pages. For me, using audio in the classroom is a way to put into practice what I want my students to learn about audience, argument, organization, style, tone, and word choice (to name just a few). To these ends, I include in my courses published audio "texts" to be rhetorically analyzed and project assignments that ask students to write, record, edit, and revise their own audio essays.[12]

Another pedagogical goal associated with using audio is situating such projects within the curriculum to help students practice the analysis and production of arguments in different forms, for different purposes and audiences. Audio assignments create opportunities for class discussions about copyright (and copyleft), about Creative Commons, and about the importance of free software, since my favorite cross-platform audio program, Audacity, is free and open to everyone. Creating a course with an audio component therefore is an investment yielding a great return in the discussions, activities, and projects it produces. Instructors can incorporate audio components into classes in a variety of ways. One approach I've used is to have students create audio research-based essays. Students created NPR-style segments based on traditional research, which they included in their annotated bibliographies and written scripts. The goals of these essays were for students to collaboratively work together to extend knowledge of an issue, group, or event that had been discussed in class. To begin, students listened to examples of audio essays and then we discussed them together, noting what was more or less successful in the works we heard. In completing these projects, students had to make choices, such as deciding which information was most essential and informative, what their specific audience already knew about their topic, how to arrange information to catch listeners' attention, and how to layer music and other sound elements to transition sections of the narrative. Students first wrote their audio essays as scripts and created visual outlines to represent the layers of sound, revising, reordering, and editing as they worked. Because of the way these projects were scaffolded—starting with research questions, then investigating and (re)searching to narrow the focus of the project—and the amount of writing that went into all of these stages of planning and producing, it is evident that the work of such projects mirrors the same skills and practices of traditional writing assignments while allowing the students to experiment with the possibilities of a new technology.

Most recently I have asked students to collaborate in small groups when working on audio assignments, and instead of producing longer essay-style segments, I have assigned each group to compose three one-minute audio public service announcements (PSAs). These PSAs focus on a specific issue the group feels is important, and each of the three PSAs is directed at a different audience, reaching a different space or demographic (see Appendix A at the end of this chapter for the prompt for this assignment). I encourage students to choose local topics and audiences in an effort to make the work relevant and specific. For example, one group focused on resident hall safety, making three PSAs aimed at students, residential hall assistants, and university administrators.[13] Because the writing curriculum at Miami asks students to "enter public debate" in one of the writing sequences, I find the PSA to be a fitting assignment.

Beyond the curricular connections and practice in composing that audio assignments facilitate, I have also found peer response and revision to become more active when working with audio components in writing courses. I can conduct a whole class or partial group peer review during which classmates give written feedback about what is or is not working in a particular audio text. In doing so, the groups get a lot of feedback in a very short time, taking these feedback forms to their next group meeting to consider and potentially incorporate into their next revision. Furthermore, as a group's work is being critiqued, they watch their classmates' reactions to what they are hearing, noting what is confusing or enjoyable, if people laugh or grow silent. When the voice is broadcast and the listening is made literal, writing students can hear themselves and others in a productive and useful way. Including audio assignments can help students listen to themselves and their classmates, revise their compositions, and translate their ideas into a range of modes for different audiences and spaces.

Chanon Adsanatham: Video Projects and Collaboratively Building Multimodal Grading Criteria

In teaching composition, I aim to help students become informed and competent audience/authors of rhetorics. I work to raise their awareness that texts are ubiquitous by exposing them to and teaching them about different forms of discourse—alphabetic, visual, aural/oral. Students engage in critical reading, writing, listening, and viewing activities throughout the semester. Near the end of the term, they produce an argumentative multimodal clip that demonstrates their cumulative understanding of the rhetorical functions of sounds, images, and alphabetic texts.

While digital video is not a foreign media, students may not be cognizant of its rhetorical operations and effects. Teaching how to compose a multimodal clip helps learners become rhetorically aware and critically perceptive about a pervasive medium and enables them to see and use technology as rhetorical tools to enrich their communicative options and abilities. Students learn to acquire what Stuart Selber (2004, 25) has called functional, critical, and rhetorical literacies in which they become users, questioners, and producers of technology. To launch the multimodal project, I begin with a unit on research and argumentation.

Students in my class spend five weeks learning how to conduct research and write a five- to six-page scholarly argumentative essay about a public issue. They learn syllogism, enthymeme, fallacies, citations, and academic conventions. Once the essay is finished, I begin a sequence on multimodality in which students learn to recast their essay arguments into a three- to four-minute multimodal clip designed for a specific public audience. Their project must include still images, sounds, and alphabetic texts, and the finished product is exhibited on YouTube for public viewing. (Students know from the outset of the class that their video project will be posted to YouTube so they make rhetorical choices accordingly.) Altogether this unit requires four weeks to complete, and throughout this period I help students learn to use video-editing software such as iMovie (for Mac) and Movie Maker (for PC), introduce them to Creative Commons, and teach them about copyright ethics. Most important, I engage them in two crucial exercises that are designed to sharpen their multimodal senses and to prepare them to compose their own video project: biweekly critical viewing of sample clips and collaborating on the grading criteria for the final project.

For the critical viewing, twice a week during this unit I ask students as homework to watch three to five multimodal clips of disparate qualities on YouTube. Some works are made by amateurs, and some are created by professional organizations such as PETA and Barackobama.com. I want to expose students to a variety of examples so that they can learn to evaluate and judge the rhetorical effectiveness of various video media. Before assigning the homework, however, I introduce the concept of critical viewing. I explain to the class that critical viewing involves closely and rhetorically observing multimodal works by paying attention to how images, sounds, alphabetic texts, and digital effects are used to construct and cohere—and in some instances, detract from—a clip's message. To guide the viewing, I provide a set of critical questions that lead viewers to pay close attention to rhetorical elements in the clip (see Appendix B). The questions provide the scaffolding to help them build critical perception and awareness of how the text operates and how it is composed. After the viewing, they write responses to the critical questions and share them in an online discussion forum with classmates. This viewing assignment prepares learners for the next activity in the unit: building collaborative grading criteria for their multimodal project.

Rather than my simply handing students the criteria by which I'll grade their projects, I instead invite the class to develop the grading criteria in a collaborative, collective process. I first ask each person to design a grading criteria sheet that will be used to assess his or her work, providing the following instructions (see Appendix C for the full prompt): the criteria must clearly define the features of an effective clip; they must address the usage of images, sounds, transitions, text, clarity, persuasion, and arrangement; they must be thorough and thoughtful; and they must be specific. Once students have devised their criteria sheet, I have them post drafts on Blackboard for their classmates to review and comment upon. Students then revise what they have developed, depending on the feedback received. I then have them use their finished criteria to evaluate the biweekly videos assigned for homework viewing; they detail each clip's strengths and weaknesses by referencing the standards they have formulated.

Once all of the grading criteria are submitted, I consolidate them into a single comprehensive document. I have the option of revising, expanding, and building upon what the class produced, if necessary. What they delineate, however, is typically more complete and complex than what I might have designed on my own, so I have not had to add any additional criteria. I then distribute the finalized evaluation sheet to the class and use it to grade students' works (see Appendix C).

Building collaborative grading criteria is useful in many ways. First, it helps students synthesize their knowledge about what makes an effective multimedia clip, and this in turn provides an indirect way for me to assess their understanding of multimodality and rhetorical principles. Second, it enables me to intervene and correct any misunderstanding that a student might have about project requirements and expectations before she or he begins composing. A learner in my class, for instance, thought it was crucial that alphabetic texts accompanied every image and screen so that his arguments would be clear. He made that a required criterion. Having read what he submitted, I was able to talk to him about how having too much text can be problematic and to show him how to use sounds and images to assert and enhance his arguments. Third, collaborating on the evaluation criteria demystifies the grading procedure and allows students to see how they will be evaluated up front. Finally, the evaluation criteria can be used to guide peer response. All in all, building collaborative grading criteria for multimodal projects offers many pedagogical benefits for both students and instructor.

CLOSING IMPLICATIONS AND RECOMMENDATIONS

The teaching narratives offered by Phill, Michele, Abby, and Chanon are only a small sampling of the digital, multimodal assignments that instructors developed, but they demonstrate both the risks and rewards of teaching digital, multimodal writing. In addition to upping the fun factor, multimodal assignments can tap into students' creativity, hone their research skills, mobilize their rhetorical knowledge, and heighten their awareness of audience and writing's power to shape and represent identities. These are big rewards, but the risks in teaching multimodal composition are real as well and might be too daunting to some. Risks include the sharp learning curve needed to use software, glitches and unforeseen problems in carrying out assignments, students' discomfort with new technologies, the fear (or reality) that multimodal skills may not carry over to academic learning. This last risk can be a fear (of students, teachers, and program administrators) that undermines the reputation of a writing program, and so it needs to be addressed.

As any writing program administrator can attest, it's not enough to revise curriculum or even make it more appealing for students. Administrators also must be able to show that what they are doing is "working"—both to university stakeholders and grant sponsors who have supported curricular change. More important, we need such assessment information for students and teachers in our writing programs, as we seek to continue to revise and refine our curriculum and teacher training. In 2006, in our first year of the new digital and multimodal curriculum, we conducted a study that involved pre- and post-surveys of students, interviews with students, and a direct assessment of student writing in the digital sections. The findings from surveys and interviews showed that students enjoyed their learning more in the digital classrooms and felt that having access to computers and to multimodal composing expanded their opportunities for learning.[14]

Since our composition courses form the foundation level of the Miami Plan, we focused our direct assessment on how well student writing demonstrated critical thinking—one of the four learning goals of the Miami Plan. One of the important questions we and other university stakeholders had was whether students in digital classrooms, with an emphasis on multimodal pedagogy and composing, would develop their critical thinking at a level similar to students in traditional classrooms. There's always the worry that in computerized classrooms too much time might be spent on teaching basic-level "how-to" of technology issues and less class time might be given to serious intellectual inquiry. An important part of our assessment of the digital initiative, then, was to systematically collect and directly assess student writing from digital classes for evidence of critical thinking. For comparison, we chose to collect a sample from the same assignment (Sequence III: Argument and Research) that we had collected the year before from traditional classrooms, and to use the same rubric (one we adapted from the Washington State Rubric of Critical Thinking) to assess the digital writing sample.

Direct assessment scores showed that student writing done in digital classes compared favorably to writing produced in conventional classrooms. The scores of critical thinking traits in student writing done in digital classes were similar to the scores of writing produced in traditional classrooms. A two-sample t-test comparing the average of the 2005 nondigital classroom scores and the average of the 2006 digital classroom scores found that there was no significant difference between the two.[15] This data suggested that students' critical thinking abilities were being developed at a similar level in both regular and digital classrooms. We found these results encouraging, as did the higher administrators with whom we shared this information, because it showed that even as students write in more multimodal environments, producing blogs, websites, videos, audio essays, and gaming discourse, students are demonstrating as much critical thinking in their writing as they do in more text-centric composition courses. However, we are cautious about drawing too many conclusions from this direct assessment, because the assignment we collected was one that most students did as a traditional paper, not as a multimodal composition. We are currently in the midst of conducting direct assessment of students' multimodal projects for purposes of program assessment, piloting an assessment of students' e-portfolios that will include all of their major assignments, drafts, and reflective writer's letters for every assignment. We are especially interested in assessing how students' multimodal composing projects are meeting course and Miami Plan goals.

There are many essential components for sustaining a program-wide focus on multimodal pedagogy: preparing and supporting instructors, developing curriculum, securing and maintaining material and administrative resources, and conducting program-wide assessment. Balancing all of these is a challenge, but our institutional history—of commitment to the best practices of composition and to intensive training of our instructors—makes us hopeful that we can sustain the DWC. With a thirty-thousand-dollar internal grant from the provost for instructor training and curriculum development and with funding from IT for more digital classrooms, we have secured the needed resources to reach our goal of providing equitable learning opportunities for all first-year composition students at Miami's Oxford campus, being able to offer 100 percent of our English 111 sections in digital classrooms by fall 2011 and 75 percent of our English 112 sections.

One key ongoing concern is about access and fairness. In our digital classrooms we rely on students arriving with their own laptops. Although 98 percent of incoming students to Miami University's main campus bring laptops, 2 percent do not, and that 2 percent concerns us. In our discussions with administrators we have been active in urging the university to make laptops available to those who cannot afford to purchase one of their own. Each year Miami is able to provide approximately twenty-five laptops to incoming full-scholarship students who are enrolling under Miami's new access initiative for low-income students, but obviously that number is woefully inadequate for providing laptops to all students who need them. We will use our story of success with digital classrooms and our university network of supporters to continue to push for a program that will buy laptops for any student who cannot afford but wants one. We also continue to support and use a hard-wired lab for scheduling composition sections so that students who do not have access to laptops may be enrolled in sections with computers. As the first-year students who presented at the Conference on College Composition and Communication in 2007 noted, we live in a multimodal and increasingly digital world, and it's imperative that we ensure that all instructors and all students have opportunities to teach and learn in with digital multimodalities.

APPENDIX A. Entering Public Debate: Audio Public Service Announcement Assignment (Instructor Abby Dubisar)

Your assignment is to work with your group and compose three one-minute audio public service announcements on a topic of your choosing. You will also do a significant amount of writing as you prepare, plan, and compose this project.

Select a public issue topic that you care about and one that allows for discussion. I encourage you to rely on the work you've done for Sequences 1 and 2, thinking about public issues that are related to space. Choose something that is being discussed (that has been documented) and one that will allow you to continue the conversation, extending it in a new way. In this assignment you will be an inventor, constructing a new argument that doesn't just reinscribe arguments made by others but rather extends existing arguments and becomes your own.

This is a research project. Part of your task is to see how other authors have framed this issue. What arguments have been made? How can you use an understanding of existing arguments about an issue to construct your own argument about it?

This is a project where you will choose a *very specific audience* and address them through the use of a public service announcement. Think about your rhetorical situation and use it to your advantage. Consider the contexts in which your PSA will be broadcast and heard (for example, what television stations—played during what shows? what radio stations? if it is going to be broadcast, where will that happen?, and so on). How exactly will you reach your intended audience?

Once you have selected a topic, formulate a research question. A research question gives you a focus: your goal in this project will be to answer the question. The research you do is going to provide the evidence you need to answer this question; any conclusions you draw will come from the evidence. Your research question is a guiding feature that you can refer back to, revise, and use throughout the whole project. Ultimately you will have a project that intelligently discusses material that you have gathered and hopefully provides some new insight into the subject. This is a project where, through your research, you will become an expert on the topic you've chosen.

Research: The project requires that you have a minimum of five sources that appear in the final three PSAs. You should have considered and read at least ten sources by the end of this process in order to have chosen five good, appropriate sources. Include all these sources in your bibliography so it is evident that you have done a lot of work on the topic.

Incorporate sources: You will need to be able to appropriately place quotations, paraphrases, and summaries in your audio text. This includes introducing them properly and showing your audience why the quotations you use are important. Your project, in the end, will need to have the following: a main idea or thesis, focus, coherent points, and clarity. In constructing this announcement, you should use rhetorical strategies. One of the most important elements is audience selection. Who do you want to reach with your message and why? Because this is a group project, you will be spending time outside of class meeting with your group members and working on the project. I suggest you exchange phone numbers, e-mails, and so on to make sure you can find one another and schedule meetings.

APPENDIX B. Critical Viewing Assignment Prompt (Instructor Chanon Adsanatham)

Clip 1

As you watch the clip from the Humane Society of the United States, pay attention to the following:

1. How are the images arranged? In what order do they appear? Is there any logic to them?
2. What makes the clip memorable and why?
3. What sounds do you hear first, next, and afterward? Why do you think they are put in that order?
4. How are quotations used; why?
5. How is ethos utilized?
6. What do you like about this clip that you might try to emulate in your own?
7. Is there anything that you dislike?

Clip 2

As you watch the PETA clip, pay attention to the following:

1. How does the author create balance between logos and pathos? Be specific. Does she or he use interviews, factual descriptions, and so on?
2. Why do you think the clip doesn't contain music like other ones?

3. Listen to the voice of the narrator. Each voice has a distinctive style, and each one provokes different reactions. How would you describe the narrator's pitch and tone? What are their significance?
4. What colors are present in the clip? What rhetorical purposes do they accomplish?
5. Is there anything missing in the clip that you might add? What might you incorporate to make it more effective, if anything?

Clip 3

As you watch the clip about racial discrimination, pay attention to the following. Please watch it three times.

First round: Pay attention to how the arguments are conveyed—through images, quotations, sounds? Observe how colorations are used. What are their functions? Also, read the texts that are provided. How do they enhance or detract from the mood of the clip?

Second round: Pay attention to the Kilburn effects—that is, how images pan, focus, and zoom from one area to another (for example, begin in the middle and then zoom out). What effects do they create? Additionally, listen to the music provided. How does it correspond and sync (or not) with the images? What reactions are evoked?

Third round: Think about how images are organized. Do you see any coherent theme in their ordering? What do you see first, second, third, last? How does the sequence enhance or detract from the clip's effectiveness?

APPENDIX C. Final Evaluation Criteria for Multimodal Projects Compiled from Student-Generated Criteria (Instructor Chanon Adsanatham)

(Note: To validate students' work, the instructor quoted the criterion exactly as the students had submitted it, so there is a lack of parallelism in the entries.)

Images

1. Do the chosen images reflect creativity and efforts?
2. Are the images interesting, keeping the viewer's attention?
3. Be sure to leave the images up long enough for the viewer to see them but not so long as to bore them.
4. Do images visually explain the argument? That is, the images are a great

depiction of the argument and clearly and effectively persuade the audience.)

5. Images should be clear, and the viewer must be able to make out exactly what the picture is.
6. Do the images enhance and enrich your argument? That is, they are not irrelevant or "place holders." They convey rich meanings.
7. Does each image have high-quality resolution and no trace of graininess?

Sounds

1. Music or sounds are used appropriately and make sense with the rhetorical strategy being used. This is not a music video; the sound should enhance the message of the clip and not distract from the images or persuasiveness.
2. Do the sounds flow smoothly, eliminating choppiness or awkward transitions in the music?
3. Are the sounds matched up with the clips or message behind the clips and images?
4. Does the music match the theme of the argument? For example, no techno music for a video about dying children in Africa.
5. Is the audio at the same pace as the presentation and flows smoothly with the slides?
6. It is obvious that time was taken to search for unique sound effects that influence the argument.
7. Sounds are organized and helpful to the understanding of the argument. They are relevant to the argument and cut in a manner that makes sense with the pictures.
8. Is the sound high quality (everything can be understood and heard)?

Transitions

1. Are the transitions appropriate for the message of the clip? Are they professional looking and go along with the mood?
2. Do the transitions connect the slides together, making it a clip rather than a slideshow?
3. Transitions between images and sounds are used where appropriate to enhance rhetorical appeal without distracting the viewer from the images. Having a goofy transition between each image is not very persuasive and will most likely get annoying. Transitions should be used sparingly and only where they will have a specific purpose other than entertainment.

4. The transitions make sense to the emotions trying to be presented in the video.

Text

1. Is the text clear, legible, and provides only enough to get the point across?
2. Does the text correlate with the images and sounds, and adds another element without taking away from anything else from the clip?
3. Used when appropriate to support argument.
4. Enough time is provided to allow viewers to read and comprehend all text.
5. Is the amount of text controlled so the viewer isn't always reading?
6. Text is used effectively in its positioning, font, style, color, and content. It gives necessary information about the argument.
7. Is proper grammar used? There are no spelling mistakes, no capitalization errors, no punctuation errors.
8. Text is not mandatory to include within your multimedia clip if you don't want it. If used, it must be big enough and the color of text must stand out to be able to be read. Just like a PowerPoint presentation, too much text on one slide or image can be too overwhelming. Say what you need to say in as few words as possible.

Clarity

1. Do the pictures, sounds, text, and transitions create a flow as a whole that makes the clip enjoyable for the audience?
2. Is it easy to understand what the clip is trying to prove?
3. Is the information projected as easily digested and smooth?
4. Is the message of the clip focused and doesn't wander?

Persuasiveness

1. Would the audience walk away feeling affected by the video?
2. Does the clip provide enough information for the viewers to be convinced?
3. A variety of rhetorical appeals are used throughout the clip to persuade viewers to be for or against the topic.
4. All of the components above are used in a format that draws viewers into the clip and persuades them to keep watching. Make your clip memorable! Don't bore your viewer. Use exciting and bold images and music.
5. Does the clip make one want to help or further research the topic?

Arrangement

1. Are the pictures, clips, and sounds arranged in a way that allows for the audience to see the progression of the argument?
2. Is the arrangement in an order in which the audience can view the clip in a way that makes sense to them?
3. The arrangement creates a smooth flow that keeps the viewer interested.
4. Make sure your images and media are not scattered randomly throughout your clip; they should follow are particular sequence.
5. Does everything fit together as a whole?
6. Does the clip have any spots in which one part does not fit with the others?

NOTES

1. Howard Gardner (1993; 2000) has influentially argued for "multiple intelligences"; the New London Group (Kress 2003) charted modes and modalities and means to enact them in classroom settings. Gunther Kress and Theo van Leeuwen (2001) have theorized not only how modes work in isolation but also how the logic of each interacts and interanimates the other, arguing that rhetorical knowledge is even more important in designing the most effective interaction of verbal, visual, and kinesthetic modes. Bill Cope and Mary Kalantzis (2000) have moved outside the academy to consider how multimodalities and multiliteracies work in contemporary societal communications. In computers and writing studies, a number of special collections of journals—such as the sound issue of *Computers and Composition* (Ball and Hawke 2006), and a number of books, including Anne Wysocki et al.'s (2004) *Writing New Media* and Cynthia Selfe's (2007) *Multimodal Composition: Resources for Teachers*—have examined the intersections of multimodal composing and new digital writing technologies.

2. In using the terms "mode" and "multimodality," we draw most fully upon the New London Group (2000), who emphasize the importance of teaching multiliteracies and multiple modalities. Modes such as the linguistic, visual, aural, and kinesthetic have their own "functional grammars, the metalanguages that describe and explain patterns of meaning" (ibid., 25) through which to communicate. Multimodality then is the ultimate design of making meaning, "as it represents the patterns of interconnection among other modes" (ibid., 25).

3. See Mary Leigh Morbey and Carolyn Steele's chapter 10 in this edited volume for further discussion of the ways students, not educational institutions, lead the way into new digital technologies.

4. See http://www.muohio.edu/miaminotebook.

5. In 2006, 75 percent of Miami first-year students were already bringing laptops to college, so we were able to designate the digital sections "laptop required," indicating that students bring their own laptops to class. According to an IT survey, 70 percent of first-year students with laptops in 2006 were using PCs and 30 percent were using Macs. In 2010, 98 percent of first-year students brought laptops to college, and the ratio was 70 percent Mac and 35 percent PC. We plan all our curricula and prepare our instructor for cross-platform instruction.

6. In the fall 2009 teacher's guide, there is a special section on the Digital Writing Collaborative, but all sample syllabi for digital classes, assignment prompts, and class activities are integrated throughout the guide, a move that recognizes the increased integration of digital pedagogy in all aspects of the curriculum and for all instructors—those teaching in regular and laptop classrooms. In the 2011–12 academic year the teacher's guide migrated from being a PDF file available online to a folksonomic online collaboratory (hosted on the university Sakai course management system), where instructors and administrators can each upload and tag documents as well as add comments. Administrators are able to make suggestions to the table of contents through link structures that help new instructors plan their courses, and searching by such key words as "audio" or "peer response" also turn up documents. Thus there is flexibility and structure in the system.

7. See http://www.muohio.edu/dwc. Each year the Composition Program publishes exemplar, award-winning essays in a print-based text, *Composition at Miami*. Since 2006, with funding from Bedford-St. Martins, Miami also offers the Bedford-St. Martin Prize for Best Digital Composition, the winners of which are posted at http://www.muohio.edu/dwc.

8. Initially there was no official administrative recognition or support for the DWC. But in 2007 the English Department funded a part-time TA to serve as assistant coordinator of the DWC to help with administrative tasks and to be available as a resource to help instructors as they plan for and teach in the digital classrooms. Then, recognizing the need for a faculty administrator as well, in 2009 the department authorized a course release for the Digital Writing coordinator. Having administrative support is essential for the success and sustainability of our program.

9. In fall 2007 and in fall 2009, Miami hired two more specialists in digital writing and rhetoric (Jason Palmeri and James Porter).

10. According to a report sponsored by the Pew Internet and American Life Project, 93 percent of teens ages 12 to 17 and 95 percent of people ages 18 to 33

(so-called millennials) use the Internet (Purcell 2011; Zichuhr 2010). These are the students who enter our college composition classrooms—familiar with technology, bringing a digital literacy to their writing processes.

11. Student statements and texts are quoted with Institutional Review Board (IRB) approval and individual consent.

12. In all my classes I (Abby Dubisar) also address the sometimes limiting and noninclusive assumptions we have about who is an audience for our compositions. When writers imagine audiences with a range of sensory disabilities, they can use multimodality to reach a range of users. I have not yet taught the audio essay to a student who is deaf or hard of hearing, but I have thought about ways to universally design this assignment: all students would provide transcripts of their audio essays. A deaf student could make a video essay with signing and captioning, and if it is a group project, the other members could voice the audio components.

13. These PSAs may be heard at http://www.muohio.edu/dwc/student_projects/projects.htm.

14. See http://www.muohio.edu/dwc/perspectives.htm for video clips from the student interviews.

15. The t-test finding comparing the median rubric scores of 2005 and 2006 is T-value = -0.56, comparing 2005 mean of 5.104 to 2006 mean of 5.269. Because we kept a record of only the mean score for each trait, standard deviations could not be determined, and statistical significance of the changes in mean scores of individual traits could not be determined. We would like to thank Denise Krallman, Miami University director of institutional research, for calculating the statistical findings for us.

REFERENCES

Addison, Joanne, and Michelle Comstock. 1998. "Virtually Out: The Emergence of Lesbian, Bisexual, and Gay Youth Cyberculture." In *Generations of Youth: Youth Cultures and History in Twentieth-Century America*, edited by Joe Austin and Michael Willard, 367–78. New York: New York University Press.

Ball, Cheryl E., and Byron Hawke, eds. 2006. "Sound." Special issue, *Computers and Composition* 23 (3).

Bowe, Frank G. 2000. *Universal Design in Education: Teaching Non-traditional Students*. Westport, CT: Bergin and Garvey.

Bruch, Patrick L. 2004. "Universality in Basic Writing: Connecting Multicultural Justice, Universal Instructional Design, and Classroom Practices." *Basic Writing E-Journal* 5 (1). Online at http://orgs.tamu-commerce.edu/cbw/ASU/BWEspring2004.html.

Burns, Zachary, Kenton Butcher, and Dirk Long. 2007. "The Digital Generation Project: Multimodal Web Reports on College Students' Use of Digital Technologies." Conference on College Composition and Communication, New York City, March.

Cope, Bill, and Mary Kalantzis, eds. 2000. *Multiliteracies: Literacy Learning and the Design of Social Futures*. London: Routledge.

Dunn, Patricia A., and Kathleen Dunn DeMers. 2002. "Reversing Notions of Disability and Accommodation: Embracing Universal Design in Writing Pedagogy and Web Space." *Kairos* 7 (1). Online at http://english.ttu.edu/kairos/7.1.

Faigley, Lester. 1999. "Beyond Imagination: The Internet and Global Digital Literacy." In *Passions, Pedagogies, and Twenty-First Century Technologies*, edited by Gail E. Hawisher and Cynthia L. Selfe, 129–39. Logan: Utah State University Press.

"Fast Facts for Faculty: Universal Design for Learning, Elements of Good Teaching." 2007. *The Ohio State University Partnership Grant Improving the Quality of Education for Students with Disabilities*. Online at http://telr.osu.edu/dpg/fastfact/undesign.html.

Gardner, Howard. 1993. *Multiple Intelligences: The Theory in Practice*. New York: Basic.

———. 2000. *Intelligence Reframed: Multiple Intelligences for the Twenty-First Century*. New York: Basic.

Kress, Gunther. 2003. *Literacy in a New Age*. London: Routledge.

Kress, Gunther, and Theo van Leeuwen. 2001. *Multimodal Discourse: The Modes and Media of Contemporary Communication*. London: Oxford University Press.

New London Group. 2000. "A Pedagogy of Multiliteracies: Designing Social Futures." In *Multiliteracies: Literacy Learning and the Design of Social Futures*, edited by Bill Cope and Mary Kalantzis, 9–37. London: Routledge.

Oblinger, Diana, and James Oblinger. 2006. "Is It Age or IT?: First Steps toward Understanding the Net Generation." *CSLA Journal* 29 (2): 8–16.

Purcell, Amy. 2011. *Trends in Teen Communication and Social Media Use*. Pew Internet and American Life Project. Online at http://www.pewinternet.org/Presentations/2011/Feb/PIP-Girl-Scout-Webinar.aspx.

Selber, Stuart A. 2004. *Multiliteracies for a Digital Age*. Carbondale: Southern Illinois University Press.

Selfe, Cynthia L. 2007. *Multimodal Composition: Resources for Teachers*. Cresskill, NJ: Hampton.

Takagi, Toshimitsu. 2004. *The Crimson Room*. Online at http://www.albinoblacksheep.com/games/room.

van Leeuwen, Theo. 1999. *Speech, Music, Sound*. London: Macmillan.

"What Is Universal Design for Learning?" 2007. *CAST: Universal Design for Learning.* Online at http://www.cast.org/research/udl/index.html.

WIDE Research Center Collective. 2005. "Why Teach Digital Writing?" *Kairos* 10 (1). Online at http://english.ttu.edu/Kairos/10.1/binder2.html?coverweb/wide/index.html.

Writing Program Administration (WPA). 2000. *WPA Outcomes Statement for First-year Composition.* Online at http://wpacouncil.org/positions/outcomes.html.

Wysocki, Anne Francis, Johndan Johnson-Eilola, Cynthia L. Selfe, and Geoff Sirc, eds. 2004. *Writing New Media.* Logan: Utah State University Press.

Zichuhr, Kathryn. 2010. *Generations 2010.* Pew Internet and American Life Project. Online at http://www.pewinternet.org/Reports/2010/Generations-2010.aspx.

CHAPTER 13

Rhetoric across Modes, Rhetoric across Campus

Faculty and Students Building a Multimodal Curriculum

Traci Fordham and Hillory Oakes

> It's a current commonplace to acknowledge that writing is changing and that the look and functioning of texts are changing. Our conversations have been about how to respond responsibly—about how and what to teach—amidst the changes, about how people in our classes understand the changing textual landscapes, and about how they (and we) can be confident, effective, and ethical within that landscape.
>
> —Anne Wysocki, Johndan Johnson-Eilola, Cynthia Selfe, and Geoffrey Sirc (Wysocki et al. 2004, vii)

In her 2004 chair's address at the Conference on College Composition and Communication, Kathleen Blake Yancey (2004) articulated the concerns of composition colleagues curious—or anxious—about their pedagogical course of action in the "changing textual landscape." Yancey reminded listeners (and, important to note in a discussion of multimodality, also her *readers* in the substantially revised and published version of her talk) that in some ways compositionists were already engaged in teaching modes other than reading and writing, whether they had explicitly identified their strategies as multimodal or not: course management systems, for example, provided a digital framework for course material, while in-class peer-review sessions gave students a forum for communicating their ideas orally (ibid., 307). Yancey (ibid., 311) argues, however, that composition classes hadn't uniformly embraced some of the intellectual tasks necessary for negotiating the changing landscape, such as asking students to "consider what the best medium and the best delivery for such a communication might be," to "create and share those different communication pieces in those different media to different audiences," or to "think explicitly about what they might 'transfer' from one medium to the next." A successful approach to "new" composition teaching would depend on pedagogies dedicated to teaching these rhetorical skills.

A year after Yancey's address, the final report of the Twenty-First-Century Literacy Summit noted the growing need for attention to multiple modes of learning: "Fueled by media that increasingly are crafted for a global audience, pervasive access to goods and services from ever more distant locales, access to networks and communication services that span the planet, and generational ties between youth that transcend borders, a new concept of language—and what it means to be literate—is evolving" (New Media Consortium 2005, 1). These new media and the multimodal literacies required in their use present both challenges and promises to institutions of higher learning. If, in fact, our goal is to enhance student learning, we can no longer simply rely upon traditional pedagogies and singular, analogue-based modes of communication in the educational process.

As J. J. O'Donnell (1988,147–48) mused over a decade ago, opportunities for more substantive learning, and for richer, interdisciplinary dialogue, abound in these multimodal, discursive spaces: "What happens to higher education when every student has a link to a flood of words and images, metastasizing in every imaginable way from around the world, and when every teacher and every student can reach out to each other at all hours of the day and night? The short answer is that we don't know; we will soon, and are even now finding out; and in so doing we will reinvent pedagogy and the university as we know it now." In the years since O'Donnell wrote those words, we have witnessed this reinvention of pedagogy, or at least the first stages of it. Because new media and our understanding and employment of them, by definition, require an engagement with "old" media—a process called "circulation" by Yancey (2004) and "remediation" by J. David Bolter and Richard Grusin (2000)—we must reimagine communication in the twenty-first century as multimodal and intertextual. New media and multimodal literacies require a fluid exchange—interstices—between analogue-based and other forms of literacies. It is imperative, then, that we see our responsibilities as educators as creating teaching and learning contexts in which students can communicate effectively, and ethically, within and between these multiple modalities.

What do multimodal literacies "look" and "sound" like, in an educational context? What abilities and skills do students need in order to learn and to perform in a multimodal environment? Multimodal pedagogies are by nature dialogic and thus engender in students abilities that go beyond "traditional notions of language and literacy" (New Media Consortium 2005, 1). Multimodal communication environments, by definition, require broader, more integrated epistemologies: one must be able to entertain multiple perspectives and multiple strategies for communication. Multimodal literacy, then, is a dimension of cognitive complexity (Delia, Clark, and Switzer 1974, 299–308).

These multiliteracies are not only necessary for learning disciplinary knowledge in a classroom context but are also central to citizenship in a plural, global society. Citizenship in a multicultural democracy requires more complex and integrated ways of being in the world, in order to conceptually and communicatively move back and forth, within and between, multiple rhetorical situations: "[Citizens] must be able to invent valued knowledge, and so they must be able to use complex information technologies. . . . they must be able to produce the professional and technical performances expected in contemporary civic forums" (Simmons and Grabill 2007, 422). And multimodal literacy involves more than the cultivation of these integrated performativities; W. Michele Simmons and Jeffrey Grabill (ibid., 442) remind us that it also requires the ability to analyze and critique the rhetorical choices of others—whether choices about writing, speaking, visual imagery, or technological applications: "Rhetorical theory is useful as well, not just in terms of connecting students to a long and meaningful history of people communicating to change communities but also to help students develop habits of mind that will enable them to recognize problems and design inquiry strategies to work toward solutions." Educators, then, must renovate curricula into those that emphasize rhetorically integrated pedagogies.

We believe that the curricular and pedagogical foci of Writing across the Curriculum (WAC)—and Communication across the Curriculum (CAC)—efforts have been crucial to cultivating more critical teaching and learning cultures in the academy. We are convinced, however, that writing and speaking (and other modes) inevitably share the metalanguage of rhetoric. Students must become more proficient at communicating within and between various modes; this proficiency, though, requires not only skill at employing these modes but, more important, skill at making more sophisticated rhetorical choices. We believe that a focus on rhetoric (instead of on the use of any one or two modes per se) brings WAC, CAC, and other such cross-curricular/cross-disciplinary programs to another, more sophisticated level.

Designing multimodal and integrated learning environments and cultivating in students critical design abilities is a "dialogic, third-space" endeavor that requires attendance to issues of critical pedagogy, intertextuality, and rhetoric (Bhabha 1994). This chapter explores the ways in which a small liberal arts institution has worked with faculty and students to move beyond the "transmission" and "acquisition" of skills or literacies and toward the fostering of a critical and rhetorical approach to multimodal pedagogies, both inside and outside of the classroom context. We believe that our curricular initiatives are the beginning of an answer to a question posed by Yancey (2004, 308): "If we cannot go home again to the days when print was the sole medium, what will the new curricular home for composition look like?"

A LOCAL HISTORY OF RHETORIC

As higher education came fully into the digital age, many colleges and universities began to scrutinize their undergraduate, general education, or core requirements. Although "essential skills" such as writing and critical thinking remain important, several colleges and universities now also include references to media literacy, cross-cultural communication, democracy, and global citizenship. The discourses of general education themselves also seem to be shifting from a "breadth" and "depth" dialectic to one of integration and multiple literacies.

At St. Lawrence University (a small, private liberal arts institution in New York), the second "aim and objective" of the school's mission statement declares that students should graduate with "the ability to read, write, speak, and listen well" (St. Lawrence University 2000, 6). The first goal here, "reading well," is, many faculty assume, covered by the emphasis on "content" and "coverage" in a variety of courses, problematic as those pedagogical goals can be (whether reading copious amounts equates to "reading *well*" is a question for another study). The second of the four abilities, to write well, has been carefully fostered by the university's commitment to writing in a number of ways: a university writing program doing WAC work, a writing center supporting students, a writing requirement for graduates, and more. By contrast, the third and fourth critical abilities outlined in the St. Lawrence mission—to speak and listen well—have until recently been left to fend for themselves financially and programmatically. Moreover, any goal for students to acquire more than just written and oral communication proficiency—such as visual literacy or skillful use of technology—is not articulated at all in the mission statement, save for one vaguely worded objective of "an expansion of aesthetic sensibilities and capacities."

This official prioritizing of reading and writing over all other essential rhetorical capabilities is especially strange at an institution where the first-year program requires students to complete a number of oral presentations, where an annual "Festival of Scholarship" features posters and multimedia presentations of student work, and where an expensively equipped arts technology center opened to great fanfare. Over the past decade many faculty had been venturing into various types of multimodal pedagogies, incorporating more than just writing into their courses, but they had no visible campus support for these other modes, nor a metalanguage with which to discuss these multiliteracy pedagogies (New Media Consortium 2005, 13). Meanwhile, students were tackling the oral, visual, and multimodal assignments these faculty were creating without, for the most part, having the kind of formalized, integrated assistance with speaking, visual work, and technology that they could get with their writing assignments by visiting the writing center. Both faculty and students struggled separately to make sense of the interconnections between words, images, and sounds as interrelated modes for learning, and few instructors made explicit the way rhetoric bound all these endeavors together.

Motivated by the disconnect between actual multimodal pedagogical practices on campus and the university's lack of acknowledgment of and support for these pedagogies, a group of faculty and administrators—which became known as the Rhetoric and Communication Initiative (RCI)—began exploring the transformation of our University Writing Program into a Rhetoric and Communication across the Curriculum Program, with attendant requirements for students to work on writing, oral communication, visual literacy, and information literacy in integrated ways throughout their four years. Although curricular change is a long and still ongoing project, St. Lawrence has implemented parallel programs aimed at improving multimodal literacy in courses throughout campus: a series of intensive workshops to help faculty redesign an existing course, a rhetoric and communication class for student mentors being trained to assist both other students and faculty, and a transformation of the writing center into a rhetoric and communication center focusing on multimodal literacies. These initiatives have worked to move faculty and students beyond the usual pedagogical concerns with demonstrable "skills" or conventional literacies and instead toward conscious choices about how to teach and how to learn, design, and perform in a multimodal, rhetorically integrated environment.

We see *rhetoric* as the transmodal frame, the metalanguage, for our approach to multiliteracies. After much internal wrestling over the connotations of the term "rhetoric"—other possible labels for our work put forward by our group included "critical literacies," "discourse studies," and "twenty-first-century literacies"—we came to some agreement that no other term captures the ways in which positionality, agency, intentionality, design, and engagement with audience operate within a communication situation. While we understood the reservations of some that too many people now use "rhetoric" simply as a synonym for "rhetrickery," we decided to reclaim the word as a way to underscore the fact that communicators always encounter a multitude of choices and that each of these choices might bring different outcomes and consequences (Booth 2004). As Richard Lanham (1993, 110) wrote: "A fit between the rhetorical paideia and the social and technological conditions that are helping to revive it makes intrinsic sense. It is not simply an accident. This revival of our traditional paideia includes those parts of contemporary literary criticism and cultural studies which have rediscovered that all arguments are constructed with a purpose, to serve an interest." Our work within the Rhetoric and Communication Initiative places primacy on these choices, not simply on the skills or modalities employed in any given context.

As we engage students with issues of rhetoric (such as voice, audience, purpose, context, and medium) in specific courses and assignments, we also help them cultivate a more critical consciousness about communication in their everyday lives. If we insist on seeing student learning as an isolated text-based activity, we place undue limitations on their and our potential in the making of knowledge. Therefore we must explore learning contexts (be they classrooms, laboratories, stages, studios, or fields) in which meanings are created and maintained through use of multiple media and multiple genres. When we plan purposefully interrelated modes of communication in our course design, classroom pedagogies, and assignments, we can help students achieve more substantive learning. The promises, and the challenges, of this work come from the fact that there are myriad ways to create these learning opportunities.

Challenges of this rhetorical approach to multimodal pedagogies include fully integrating the modes toward a singular objective of learning and thinking carefully about the rhetorical choices motivating the integration. In RCI workshops we advise faculty who want more rhetorically rich courses to think as much about the *why* of syllabus and assignment design as about the *what* and to ask themselves why they do or don't bring modes and assignments into closer contact as interrelated, intertextual ways of making meaning. Why ask students to maintain a class blog if they'll never have a chance to bring that online conversation into a class discussion or debate? Why require students to use a visual aid with a seminar presentation but offer them no guidance as to what the visual might add to the overall arguments in their oral communication? And why not encourage students to move from Word document essays to the more media-rich, such as video-embedded PDFs?

The irony is that those of us who facilitate faculty development workshops on this topic of multimodality often find ourselves feeling as if we have to isolate the modes of communication for explanatory purposes. While the rhetorical integration of courses and assignments is the end goal of our faculty development efforts, successful integration of modes still necessitates successful engagement with each mode, individually: we must learn how to teach writing and speaking and visual literacy effectively before we can effectively integrate them in our teaching. Our rhetoric and communication workshop does not, in fact, "train" participants in these modes (follow-up sessions and other faculty development resources exist for that purpose); instead, it encourages them to think about the ways in which each mode might function, rhetorically and epistemologically, with other modes within the matrix of courses, assignments, and activities. Invariably, what one instructor might consider a non-negotiable literacy in relation to a course might be different from what another might deem as important, since our respective disciplines provide rhetorical and discursive parameters for the pedagogical process. An instructor's expectations for and definitions of what constitutes "literacy" may also vary from course to course; indeed, even within a single course, instructors might ask students to tackle a number of genres, genres that themselves are not "discrete sets of constraints but . . . representative of a point in a multidimensional genre space" (Allen, Bateman, and Delin 1999, 28). The point is not to standardize our expectations for any one mode but to cultivate a greater degree of pedagogical intentionality in relation to the communication that students do in and for our courses.

If we trace the genealogy of our work with rhetoric and communication at St. Lawrence, we can see how easy it can be to fall into an artificial separation of rhetorical modes. For ten straight years the University Writing Program sponsored a Summer Writing Institute for Faculty (SWI), a two- or three-day workshop series covering both broader philosophies of process, commenting, and grading as well as more hands-on practice with designing assignments, creating in-class writing exercises, and reviewing strategies for better instruction in grammar and mechanics. The SWI was strictly concerned with writing, however; discussion of other modes was completely absent, and when one year one of the authors gave a presentation on something as simple as using the Comment function in Word to give more thorough feedback on drafts, most of her audience shook their heads at this surely silly interference of technology with the "real" task of writing.

The Oral Communication Institute (OCI) was one response to both the success of the SWI and to its exclusion of other pedagogies. In 2001 the Hewlett Foundation awarded a grant to St. Lawrence to explore the ways in which the university might bring oral communication to the same level of importance on campus as writing. The OCI, a three-day January workshop with follow-up meetings during the spring semester, enabled faculty participants to create or redesign a course by incorporating more dialogue-centered activities and pedagogies, from class discussions to group presentations. The OCI focused less on specific pedagogical strategies or "best practices" than it did on working with faculty to imagine the teaching-learning context as a discursive space and the pedagogical process as a rhetorical enterprise (Mooney, Fordham, and Lehr 2004, 220–35).

Several foundational assumptions guided our work with oral communication and dialogue-centered pedagogies. Because learning is an active and dynamic process, students must be engaged, not passive. As social constructivists in all fields have long argued, meaning making is a collaborative process, created and maintained in conversation with others. Effective oral communication in a learning context involves more than simply designing and articulating an argument; it involves listening to and coming to understand the diverse arguments and perspectives of others. If a broader notion of literacy involves learning to negotiate "a multiplicity of discourses," pedagogies that involve students in conversing, discussing, and creating meaning together enable the development of this broader notion of literacy (New London Group 1996, 1). Communication across the curriculum is fine, but we should also think of how students communicate outside our curricular walls: by definition, literacy can and should transcend the classroom context. Because engaging others in meaningful dialogue is central to citizenship in a plural society, we see the design and enactment of dialogue-centered pedagogies as contributing to the creation and enhancement of global citizenship (McCoy and Scully 2002, 117–35).

Ultimately, our institutional conversations about the uses of dialogue-centered pedagogies led to discussions about the relationship between writing, speaking, visual, kinesthetic, and other modes of communication, with the overall consensus being that the university needed to be more integrative and multimodal in our approach to faculty development and curriculum design. For instance, while our focus on oral communication in the OCI was important, we may have overlooked the fact that meaningful dialogue between diverse others also occurs across and between multiple modes of communication; digital technologies and social networking sites, among other new media, have hybridized the contexts for human communication and meaning construction (Freidman 1997), yet at the time our campus had held virtually zero faculty conversations on these technologies. Although our writing and oral communication institutes were useful projects, their very existence artificially isolated modes of communication and reinforced pedagogical strategies that are clearly less effective than more intertextual and multimodal ones.

Our first steps toward integrating these curricular efforts occurred in 2004, when our dean of academic affairs convened a group of faculty and asked us to think more broadly about the ways in which oral communication and multimedia projects might be integrated into the work of the peer mentors in the writing center.[1] This first conversation about transforming writing tutoring quickly led us to agree that since the role of student academic support centers must grow out of the classroom pedagogies of our faculty, and because those pedagogies must extend from the curriculum as a whole, we needed to take a few steps backward and think about broader curricular issues. We agreed that we ought to begin by reaching out to faculty to see what kind of knowledge and experience they had and what kind of support they needed in order to design multimodal curricula and pedagogies. A precedent for a January institute format was already established by the OCI, which had run for three consecutive years. It made sense to simply transform the faculty development institute that focused on oral communication into one that focused on rhetoric and multimodal integration.

MULTILITERATE FACULTY: THE RHETORIC AND COMMUNICATION INSTITUTE

Each iteration of the January RCI institute has been slightly different in content, focus, and participants, but each has had basic logistical similarities.[2] In mid-November all faculty receive a letter of invitation to participate in the institute (which includes the three-day January symposium and several follow-up meetings during the spring semester). To apply, faculty are asked to identify a particular course (ideally one they will be teaching during the following fall semester) that they would like to revise to include more multimodal pedagogies. Participating faculty receive reading materials, a stipend, and the guarantee of a course-linked peer mentor to assist them when they begin to implement what they had learned. (The training and responsibility of those student mentors is covered in more detail in the second half of the chapter.) RCI participants have come from a variety of departments: biology, history, government, English, fine arts, chemistry, physics, global studies, performance and communication arts, and psychology.[3] The RCI institute has been facilitated by the authors, along with one year the director of the Center for Teaching and Learning and another year a member of the performance and communication arts department. Generous funding for readings, stipends, and costs of the institute was provided by the Center for Teaching and Learning.

During the RCI institute we seek to keep rhetoric, as a concept and as a process, at the center of our conversations; we use Wayne Booth's *The Rhetoric of Rhetoric* (2004) as our jumping-off text and have found it extremely provocative, since even those faculty who have volunteered for this workshop on rhetoric often express doubts about the definition of or the necessity for "rhetoric" in our students' educations. Our foundational assumption is that students learn material more substantively when they are given opportunities to express their learning sequentially and through integrated modalities. Thus we begin the institute by underscoring for participants the notion that helping students to develop rhetorical sensitivity and communicative competencies has less to do with students acquiring specific multimodal skill sets than it does with helping them to cultivate transmodal conceptual abilities.

The full syllabus for the institute is a lengthy document; here is a truncated schedule.

DAY ONE

- Definitions of *rhetoric* and *communication*
- History of WAC and CAC efforts
- Goals for rhetoric and communication at a liberal arts college
- Definitions of *multimodal pedagogy*
- Analysis of successful multimodal assignments created by St. Lawrence University colleagues
- Discussion of learning goals for individual courses
- Planning syllabi that include assignments that will support learning goals

DAY TWO

- Discussion of writing and speaking as rhetorical enterprises
- Discussion of writing to learn and speaking to learn
- Generating low-stakes writing and speaking assignments
- Generating assignments that integrate writing and speaking
- Discussion of visual literacy
- Discussion of research as a rhetorical enterprise
- Generating assignments that integrate research and a visual/multimedia element

DAY THREE

- Discussion of goals of multimodal, integrated assignments and courses
- Meeting past RCI faculty participants to discuss their experiences
- Working together to generate multimodal assignments for each other's courses
- Workshopping of created multimodal assignments
- Time for individual work on syllabus and assignment design
- Discussion of faculty-peer mentor relationship

Throughout the institute we attempt to balance theoretical discussions of multimodal literacies with opportunities for participants to try out applications of these theories by doing a number of interactive exercises that they could easily adapt for their own courses, such as making a visual representation of a key course concept (easy for the physicist, more challenging for the historian). We believe that by doing the work they might ask of students, participants see that these rhetorically integrated, multimodal pedagogies are not completely "new"—only our ways of thinking about them are.

Employing multimodal, rhetorically integrated pedagogies necessitates a critical conceptual shift regarding teaching and learning. As instructors, our focus must move from a primary concern with the *coverage* of material (a teacher-centered focus on content) toward a commitment to *learning* (a student-centered focus on process). When we do this and do it well, the foundational knowledge of a course doesn't change, but the methods and modalities through which students learn and synthesize this knowledge do. Herein lays the largest resistance we have faced with our RCI work, something that has surfaced in every iteration of the RCI institute: the assumption that course content and pedagogical process somehow exist in a binary, antagonistic relationship. In the latter part of the first day of the institute, we lead faculty participants in a number of different exercises and discussions designed to address this apparent tension. Dee Fink's (2003) work in course and assignment design informs our discussion of learning goals. We stress that the entire tenor of a course will change by simply moving the conceptual energy from a focus on content coverage to a focus on goals for student learning and by channeling course-planning energy into generating assignments and activities that are clearly supporting those goals (rather than, say, simply assigning two papers and a presentation because those are "measures" you need to gather). Despite our best efforts, not every participant leaves the institute fully convinced that adding multimodal pedagogies that will enrich their students' learning of content is worth the relatively small amount of "coverage" they may have to set aside.

If participants grant that changing their pedagogical strategies will actually enhance their teaching of this content, we then have to work with them to expand their notion of the pedagogical modes appropriate for their practice. Not surprisingly, the majority of faculty participants are the most comfortable with teaching writing, even if they'd like to explore new approaches to this mode. Formal and informal oral communication is the second most prominent in the faculty playbook, although faculty confidence in their oral communication pedagogy is often quite low. The use of visual and multimedia components in a course is by far the least common among participants. Cynthia Selfe (2004, 67) explained the phenomenon of lack of pedagogical curiosity about modes other than writing: "Faculty may limit their teaching in this way because they lack familiarity with a range of new media texts that they consider appropriate for study in composition classrooms. Given their educational backgrounds and expertise, after all, most faculty remain book readers, primarily. . . . In addition, faculty may feel that they lack the analytical skills they need to conduct serious study of these texts, an effective vocabulary and set of strategies for discussing the structure and composition of new media texts, or that they lack the expertise with the software packages typically used to create such texts."

Typically, the institute is one of the first contexts in which faculty have been able to spend a great deal of time thinking about how different media shape the learning process, and how integrating modalities might enhance it. Hearing from their colleagues, they learn that everyone is making some attempt at this pedagogy: a mathematician provides students with visual representations of fractals; a gender-studies scholar uses performance and corporeal pedagogies as a way to explore standpoint epistemologies; a global-studies professor requires students to create a news website and maintain its podcast. As faculty share their learning goals and choices of media, others learn new ways to incorporate these modes into their own courses.

Once participants' resistance to using multiple rhetorical modes has softened, the next potential hazard comes when someone inevitably asks, "But how am I supposed to grade them on this?" We have found quite useful for such a discussion Madeleine Sorapure's (2006) article "Between Modes: Assessing Students' New Media Compositions" in which she argues that educators must create new ways of conceptualizing and assessing student work, based on the emerging realities of intertextual communication modes and assignments:

> Complicating discussions of new media assessment is the fact that there are so many different types of projects being assigned: websites, images, image/text combinations, videos, audio projects, Flash projects, and others. With each type, somewhat different considerations come into play. A broadly rhetorical approach can accommodate these differences—that is, an approach that focuses assessment on how effectively the project addresses a specific audience to achieve a specific purpose . . . assessment is very much about context and needs to take into account the particular circumstances of the course, the students, and the teacher, as well as the possibilities afforded by the assignment, the modes, and the medium.

After noting Sorapure's reminder that even assessment is a rhetorical endeavor, we encourage participants to realize that they need not grade or formally assess every activity or assignment in order to know whether their pedagogy is working, whether students are learning; the ensuing discussions about various faculty's approach to the assessment question have been some of our most heated institute conversations but also some of the most informative. Just as a small number of participants leave feeling strongly that they will not give up control of content or coverage, some faculty can get frustrated that we are not, for instance, handing them a ready-to-go multimodal assignment rubric with checkboxes and points.

Thinking beyond the traditional epistemological boundaries of a given discipline can be both overwhelming and exhilarating. Multimodal, rhetorically integrated pedagogies are less concerned with technological wizardry than with thinking strategically about the modes through which meanings are created in the teaching and learning context. On the third day of the institute, participants are asked to imagine a possible integrated, multimodal assignment, or a sequence of assignments that could be integrated throughout the semester. When they protest that this is an impossible task to even attempt in the time allotted, we remind them that our goal is not for them to construct a single massive multimodal assignment, but for them to design integrated and sequenced learning opportunities for students in their courses.

Participants are the most valuable resources to one another; they offer insights, suggestions, and possible solutions. The questions and concerns to which faculty give voice at this point in the institute serve as the foundation for our follow-up meetings, which convene monthly during the spring semester and have addressed a range of topics such as *ethos*, *logos*, and *pathos*; the rhetoric of technology; responding to drafts of visual projects; and power dynamics among faculty, students, and peer mentors. Certainly we ask much of the faculty during these long but productive three days, but we don't expect them to redesign an entire course in seventy-two hours; the spring semester follow-up meetings are vital to helping them sustain their inquiry into these new pedagogical practices. (Because the RCI has shifted to a single-department format, these follow-up sessions have been even more interesting, as the members of, for example, the psychology department compare notes on how they've been teaching the required methods course differently during the follow-up semester.) Equally important is the promise of a peer mentor attached to participants' courses; these mentors assist students once the redesigned course is running, much like writing fellows programs elsewhere. However, a somewhat unusual aspect of this peer-mentor program is that the student peers are also asked to help the faculty before the course begins by designing sample assignments and supporting the use of multiple media.

MULTILITERATE STUDENTS: THE RHETORIC AND COMMUNICATION THEORY AND PRACTICE COURSE

Just as the Rhetoric and Communication Institute for faculty built on the successful model of the Oral Communication Institute, our plans for training and employing rhetoric and communication peer mentors were modeled on our well-established First-Year Program mentor positions—course-linked tutors who provide writing and oral communication support for all of our first-year seminar classes. First-Year Program mentors have always been considered employees of the Writing Center (and now of the reconfigured Rhetoric and Communication Center), and as such receive the same training as the center's tutors: three days of intensive work before the start of each academic year, along with weekly or biweekly follow-up meetings and individual conferences with the director of the center twice a semester. Before the RCI group began its work, no tutor-training course was on the books as a regularly offered full-credit course, although one had been taught occasionally as a special-topics class.

From the beginning of our shift toward Rhetoric and Communication across the Curriculum, we felt it vital to include student mentors who would work both with other students and with faculty. The peer-mentoring piece was practically a given on our campus, where constructivism and collaborative learning pedagogies underlie most faculty members' teaching and inform the support services offered our undergraduates. As part of their application process for the January RCI institute, faculty must identify one student they would like to work as mentor for the course they are revising; the selected mentors are then required to take a training course, Rhetoric and Communication Theory and Practice for Peer Mentors, during the spring semester, with successful completion guaranteeing them a paid position as a rhetoric and communication mentor for the faculty members the following fall.

We felt strongly that these mentors should not be responsible solely for working with students but that they should be involved in an important way with designing the course itself. To that end, we defined their role as sort of demi-pedagogues, asking faculty to consider the mentors not merely tutors but instead fellow rhetors exploring interrelated modes of communication. During the follow-up semester after the January RCI institute, faculty make several revisions to the syllabi and assignments they began drafting during the workshops; mentors in the training course have to consult with faculty about these syllabi and multimodal assignments to complete their own work for the rhetoric and communication class, for they are asked to reflect constantly on the way the rhetorical theories and tutoring praxis discussed in class relate to the learning goals of their faculty member's course.

Our approach to both the student course and the faculty institute has been to emphasize both theory/practice discourse and teaching/learning discourse. If faculty can let students see the theory underlying their pedagogical praxis—letting students learn about teaching (and opening up discussion about it)—the learning environment for students in their courses will inevitably take on new and productive dimensions. Some of the most powerful sessions in the course have arisen out of frank conversations about pedagogy; within the confidential confines of the classroom, students feel free to discuss the ineffective pedagogies they've been subject to while using their newly acquired vocabulary—*constructivism, multimodal, minimalism, rhetorical stance*—to think aloud and together about how rhetorical approaches enhance both teaching and learning.

Although each syllabus has varied slightly, the topics covered generally include a history of rhetoric; a history of communication studies; a history of rhetoric and composition studies, including the productive tension between writing across the curriculum and writing in the disciplines; theories of tutoring; pedagogies of writing, oral communication, research, and visual design; and theories and pedagogies of multimodal learning. The assignments the students complete have also varied slightly semester to semester but always include a mix of modes: writing a conference proposal, designing a PowerPoint with multimedia elements, maintaining a course blog, designing a research poster, and giving a panel presentation, among others.

The most important assignments mentors complete for the course, however, are the assignments they themselves design. Working from the syllabi faculty participants draft during the RCI institute, students in the course create a sequence of assignments that could potentially be used in the faculty's fall course: one combining written and oral components, one requiring a creative visual representation of research, and one multimodal assignment that combines written, oral, and visual elements. Students consult with faculty about each of the assignments they turn in, although in the end their grade is up to the course instructors alone. During the last RCI follow-up session in the spring, faculty meet with all mentors for presentations of the final mentor-designed multimodal assignments, allowing everyone a chance to share the campus-wide growth of rhetorical approaches to this pedagogy. Faculty are not ultimately obligated to use the assignments the mentors design, but many have either adapted them or used them almost verbatim.

Although we might sometimes feel slight resistance from instructors about taking on the challenge of multimodal pedagogy, student mentors clearly express a desire for increased multimodal approaches in the classroom and more support for students in those classrooms; it simply makes sense to them. These students already have a year or more experience with the St. Lawrence curriculum and know that faculty across campus are asking them to push themselves beyond mere writing-as-product, but until they take the course, they haven't had the language to explain their experiences or to articulate what would make their learning in these cases even more profound. (Indeed, if faculty members use the assignments their mentors have designed, the mentors have a direct impact on their peers' learning.)

After completing the course, the mentors take on their job responsibilities the next fall; these duties include attending the class for which they're mentoring and holding five to ten office hours each week to conference with students. Mentors also meet regularly with their faculty members to discuss the progress of the course and the outcome of the assignments. We intend for the work of both faculty and students to continue in other venues; faculty, for instance, can replicate and adapt their multimodal assignments for other courses they teach. Likewise, some mentors will go on to be tutors in the Rhetoric and Communication Center or mentors for the First-Year Program, thus ensuring that the multimodal work faculty do across campus will be supported by the availability of highly trained peer mentors. (Now, all student employees of the Rhetoric and Communication Center must complete the training course before beginning work.)

A staff of tutors trained in multimodal pedagogies offers two benefits to their peers: those students who are taking courses in which faculty are engaged in multimodal pedagogies work with tutors who already understand the demands of multimodal assignments, while those who are in more traditionally structured courses may still get exposure to other modes through conversation with tutors (for example, "Have you considered bringing images [or audio clips or video] into this section of your project?"). The likelihood of students doing multimodal work in their courses and needing the input of tutors trained in multimodal pedagogies will continue to increase as St. Lawrence takes further steps toward Rhetoric and Communication across the Curriculum.

LOOKING FORWARD TO A MULTILITERATE CURRICULUM

Beginning in fall 2007, St. Lawrence made campus-wide curricular moves in support of rhetoric and communication visible to both faculty and students, in part because of receiving a gift to endow a chair in rhetoric and communication. The faculty member who holds this chair (which will rotate every three years) is also the director of the Rhetoric and Communication across the Curriculum Program. This director is responsible for such things as facilitating the RCI, team-teaching the rhetoric and communication course for mentors, and working with colleagues on a department-by-department basis to make all course offerings more rhetorically and multimodally rich.

Simultaneously, the Writing Center has been renamed the Rhetoric and Communication Center (with the more student-friendly nickname of the WORD Studio—WORD being an acronym for writing, oral communication, research, and visual design); in fall 2007 we dedicated a new rehearsal space in which students can practice their multimedia presentations while filming their rehearsal for review with a tutor. Future plans for center expansion include more square footage and more equipment for video- and audio-editing, large-format printing, and more. We see the center not as a mere workspace for students but as a place where they will sit down to have a conference with a tutor trained in rhetoric and communication and multimodal pedagogy, with their conversations ranging over modes and media.

The largest challenge facing the school is the economic straits it finds itself in. The chair of rhetoric and communication is now endowed, but pressures mount to cut back, for example, on funding for peer tutoring. We believe that taking peer tutors—and the collaborative learning environments they support—away from the First-Year Seminars and other rhetorically and pedagogically rich courses throughout the curriculum will set the RCI's efforts back substantially, as would trimming support for RCI faculty workshops. We have been striving for everyone to make use of multiple modes and genres in thoughtful, intentional, and collaborative ways, but it would be difficult to get that message across to students if the classroom is once again reduced to simply one teacher and a captive audience of students fending for themselves.

As the university prepared for reaccreditation, some faculty and administrators began making noises about thoroughly revising the school's mission statement with its vaguely worded and not exactly ambitious aims and objectives. Certainly that sort of bureaucratic project won't happen soon or be easy to achieve. Still, we believe that the curricular work of the Rhetoric and Communication Program—helping both teachers and students to take charge of multiple modes of making knowledge and meaning—will leave a legacy in whatever revamped mission we finally accept: St. Lawrence won't ask its graduates simply to "read, write, speak, and listen well" but to speak about reading, write about seeing, create imagery about sound, and create sound about text—to *do* rhetoric.

Rhetoric is the ability to critically analyze a communication situation and to employ strategies and media that are appropriate to that situation. Rhetorical sensitivity inevitably *must* transcend specific skills in the use of discrete or even integrated modalities; rhetoric is the transmodal metalanguage for multiliteracies. When we reimagine our learning environments as spaces for "doing" rhetoric, the possibilities for engagement with multiple media and modes of communication are endless. In partial answer to her question about the future of composition studies in an era of "circulation" of modes, Yancey (2004, 313) mused: "Located in the rhetoric of purpose, audience, genre, this model of circulation is particularly oriented to medium and technology; it permits a student . . . to define composition as 'the thoughtful gathering, construction, or reconstruction of a literate act in any given media.'"

Rhetoric is the contact zone (Pratt 1992), the third space (Bhabha 1994), where message and medium—*any* given medium—intersect. Composition and communication instructors must not only think critically about the ways in which multiliteracies might address the contingencies of our global and digital world, but we must also think carefully about the ways in which teaching and learning through a rhetorical framework bring this world together.

APPENDIX A. Sample Rhetoric and Communication Institute Faculty Assignments

Associate Professor, Department of History

RCI Institute Participant, 2006

Multimedia Assignment for Elementary Chinese and Advanced Beginnings Chinese

This assignment was created spontaneously for Elementary Chinese and Advanced Beginning Chinese courses; thus no formal assignment sheet exists. The following is an excerpt from a report about the project. Three examples of student videos may be found at http://www.stlawu.edu/bestpractices/csete.

Students in all Chinese classes were invited to combine a digital image of their choice with an original composition in Chinese and to perform their original poem, in both Chinese and English, at a Poetry for Peace event. Five students accepted the challenge. Of the five students, four had been to China; of those, three used images they personally captured in China. Students used standard technology—PowerPoint and digital projection—as well as Chinese writing software (Microsoft Input Method Editor) to compose their original work of poetry. During the performance the visual image and text were displayed while each student read. As a final step, audio recordings of the performed poems were added to the images and text for media-rich PDF documents that could be shared with others.

Students who participated were interested in the idea from the start and worked on it with impressive focus; the professor was surprised by the ease with which lovely poems emerged. One of the most advanced students sat down quietly with a dictionary and wrote his poem in one sitting, checking periodically with the rest of the class on a few words. Another student quickly came up with a basic idea, chose two images from among her Tibet collection, and after some discussion with the class over word choice and order, wrote a striking, passionate poem. Some students used photos they had taken in China with special personal meaning and worked more closely with the professor and the dictionary to translate their thoughts into Chinese. The professor worked most closely with the single elementary Chinese student, who came to her office with a finished poem in English to be translated into Chinese. After all poems were complete, they were put into pinyin (the romanized form to aid in pronunciation) and practiced for the performance.

APPENDIX B. Final Sketch Assignment for Colonial Latin America

Associate Professor, Department of History
RCI Institute Participant, 2006

Within the context of colonial Latin American history (1492–1825), you will each choose an actual historical character (for example, Moctezuma, Tupac Amaru I, Columbus, Juan Garrido, La Malinche, Pedro de Gante) or create a fictional character from a specific historical time and place. You will research the historical context in which this person lived, the types of people with whom she or he might have interacted, and so on. You will prepare the following:

1. A short (two pages) written biography of this person.

2. Four documents or sources *that you create* that reveal something about your person and her or his interactions with others (around five pages, in total)—for example, imagined journals, maps, deeds, legal documents. At least one of these created sources should have a visual component beyond standard language text.
3. Oral presentation. Imagining yourself as your chosen person, you will give a ten-minute oral presentation as that person in a way that communicates answers to such questions as: Who are you in the context of the colonial society in which you live? How and why do you interact with other people? What do you think of them and why? What impact might your life have beyond your own lifetime?
4. A five-page paper (plus a bibliography) written *in the voice of a historian and biographer of your subject* that covers the following points: What materials did you use to understand the historical context and create the examples of sources? Where does this person fit into narratives and themes of colonial Latin American history that we studied this semester? How did you decide which elements to include in your presentation; what did you choose to leave out and why? What can we say we know about your person's life? What kinds of things remain unknowable and why? Did this affect how you presented your person in your presentation or in writing?
5. You will turn in a portfolio of all the final project materials on the day you do your oral presentation—the short bio, an outline of your oral sketch, the examples of your created sources, the paper, and a full bibliography.

NOTES

1. This group was first composed of the dean of academic affairs, the director of the Center for Teaching and Learning, the director of the University Writing Program, the director of the Writing Center, three members of the performance and communication arts department, the head reference librarian, the associate dean of the First Year, and a member of the gender studies department. Later, three others would become involved: the director of instructional technology, the director of the Arts Technology Center, and a member of the global studies department.

2. A note on names and abbreviations: The original advisory group was called the Rhetoric and Communication Initiative (RCI); the faculty development workshops are known as the Rhetoric and Communication Institute (also known as RCI). To avoid confusion, we will refer to the first as the RCI group

and the second as the RCI workshops or institute. The curricular program that has emerged from the work of the RCI group is known as the Rhetoric and Communication Program (RCP).

3. Recently, the RCI has tried a new model, working with members of an entire department to improve the multimodal work they do across their courses. The first two departments to work through the institute under this new model were psychology and modern languages. This new approach of course requires RCI facilitators to grapple with the differences between an "across the curriculum" approach and an "in the disciplines" one.

REFERENCES

Allen, Patrick, John Bateman, and Judy Delin. 1999. "Genre and Layout in Multimodal Documents: Towards an Empirical Account." In *Proceedings of the AAAI Fall Symposium on Using Layout for the Generation, Understanding, or Retrieval of Documents*, edited by Richard Power, 27–34. Cape Cod, MA: American Association for Artificial Intelligence.

Bhabha, Homi. 1994. *The Location of Culture.* New York: Routledge.

Bolter, J. David, and Richard Grusin. 2000. *Remediation: Understanding New Media*. Cambridge: MIT Press.

Booth, Wayne. 2004. *The Rhetoric of Rhetoric: The Quest for Effective Communication.* Malden, MA: Blackwell.

Delia, Jesse, Ruth Anne Clark, and David Switzer. 1974. "Cognitive Complexity and Impression Formation in Informal Social Interaction." *Speech Monographs* 41: 299–308.

Fink, Dee L. 2003. *Creating Significant Learning Experiences: An Integrated Approach to Designing College Courses.* San Francisco: Jossey-Bass.

Freidman, Matthew. 2007. *Fuzzy Logic: Dispatches from the Information Revolution.* Montreal: Véhicule Press.

Lanham, Richard. 1993. *The Electronic Word: Democracy, Technology and the Arts.* Chicago: University of Chicago Press.

McCoy, Martha, and Patrick Scully. 2002. "Deliberative Dialogue to Expand Civic Engagement: What Kind of Talk Does Democracy Need?" *National Civic Review* 91: 117–35.

Mooney, Kim M., Traci Fordham, and Valerie Lehr. 2004. "A Faculty Development Program to Promote Engaged Classroom Dialogue: The Oral Communication Institute." *To Improve the Academy* 23: 220–35.

New London Group. 1996. "A Pedagogy of Multiliteracies: Designing Social Futures." *Harvard Educational Review* 66: 1–22.

New Media Consortium. 2005. *A Global Imperative: The Report of the Twenty-First-Century Literacy Summit*. Austin: New Media Consortium.

O'Donnell, J. J. 1998. *Avatars of the Word: From Papyrus to Cyberspace*. Cambridge: Harvard University Press, 1998.

Pratt, Mary Louise. 1992. *Imperial Eyes: Travel Writing and Transculturation*. London: Routledge.

Selfe, Cynthia. 2004. "Toward New Media Texts: Taking up the Challenges of Visual Literacy." In *Writing New Media: Theory and Applications for Expanding the Teaching of Composition*, edited by Anne Wysocki, Johndan Johnson-Eilola, Cynthia Selfe, and Geoffrey Sirc, 67–110. Logan: Utah State University Press.

Simmons, W. Michele, and Jeffrey T. Grabill. 2007. "Toward a Civic Rhetoric for Technologically and Scientifically Complex Places: Invention, Performance, and Participation." *College Composition and Communication* 58 (2): 419–48.

Sorapure, Madeleine. 2006. "Between Modes: Assessing Student New Media Compositions." *Kairos* 10 (2). Online at http://english.ttu.edu/kairos/10.2/binder2.html?coverweb/sorapure/index.html.

St. Lawrence University. 2000. *University Catalog*. Canton, NY.

Wysocki, Anne, Johndan Johnson-Eilola, Cynthia Selfe, and Geoffrey Sirc. 2004. *Writing New Media: Theory and Applications for Expanding the Teaching of Composition*. Logan: Utah State University Press.

Yancey, Kathleen Blake. 2004. "Made Not Only in Words: Composition in a New Key." *College Composition and Communication* 56 (2): 297–328.

CONTRIBUTORS

Chanon Adsanatham, doctoral candidate at Miami University, researches comparative rhetoric, Thai rhetoric, multimodality, and digital multimodal pedagogy. His works examine theories and heuristics for teaching multimodal composing and rhetorics beyond the Euroamerican tradition. At Miami he has worked as a digital pedagogy consultant and as the assistant director of the portfolio assessment program.

Cheryl E. Ball is associate professor of New Media Studies at Illinois State University, previously of Utah State University, from 2004–7, where she met Tia Bowen and Tyrell Brent Fenn in a 2006 class. She is editor of *Kairos: Rhetoric, Technology, and Pedagogy*, and her interests include editorial pedagogies, multimodal composition, digital media scholarship, and digital publishing. Her portfolio can be found at http://www.ceball.com/.

Tia Scoffield Bowen graduated from Utah State University with a BS in exercise science and an English minor. She is an event videographer working independently toward incorporation and has filmed weddings and couples, documentary-style interviews, birth stories, and company projects. Her online portfolio can be found at http://www.tiasbowen.blogspot.com.

Tracey Bowen is a lecturer on mass communications and popular culture and coordinates an internship program for the Institute of Communications, Culture, and Information Technology at the University of Toronto–Mississauga. Her research focuses on visual literacy and the use of visual rhetoric within digital environments, particularly in terms of globalization and counternormative narratives. Her work has been published through *Inter-Disciplinary Press*, the *Journal of Popular Culture*, *Studies in Art Education*, and *Higher Education Research and Development*. She coedited *Cultural Production in Virtual and Imagined Worlds* with Mary Lou Nemanic (2010).

Jerome Bump (http://www.cwrl.utexas.edu/~bump/) is a professor of English at the University of Texas–Austin. His latest publication is "Racism and Appearance in *The Bluest Eye*: A Template for an Ethical Emotive Criticism," *College Literature* 37, no. 2 (Spring 2010): 147–70. He was the first director of the Digital Writing and Research Lab (http://www.dwrl.utexas.edu/) and the author of essays in *Computers and Education*, *Computers and the Humanities*, and *Currents in Electronic Literacy*. He has written papers on computers and English presented at NCTE, CCCC, CCTE, Computers and Writing conferences, and at the Universities of Paris, Pittsburgh, and Indiana.

Kerrie L. Carsey is an assistant professor of composition and rhetoric at York College of Pennsylvania. Her research interests include rhetorical theory, religious rhetorics, composition pedagogy, and the history of rhetoric. She received her PhD from Miami University in 2011.

Colin Charlton is an associate professor of rhetoric and composition at the University of Texas–Pan American. He coordinates the Transitional Reading/Writing Program, runs an immersive writing STUDIO for developmental students, and publishes the multimodal online magazine *inQuiry* (http://infiniteinq.blogspot.com). In all these projects he looks for ways to write, read, and learn with colleagues and students in innovative forms that compel engagement and dispel myths.

Jonikka Charlton is an associate professor of rhetoric and composition and an associate vice provost for Student Success Initiatives at the University of Texas–Pan American. In both of these positions she pursues opportunities to support programs that help students engage in meaningful intellectual work. One of her biggest hopes is that students will come to see themselves as belonging to a dynamic intellectual community, one whose borders extend well beyond the university.

Nathaniel I. Córdova was a professor of rhetoric and media studies at Willamette University in Oregon. He was killed in a motorcycle accident on July 16, 2011. His website (http://www.nachocordova.org/) reads: "The temple bell stops but the sound keeps coming out of the flowers." An e-memorial for Nacho is maintained at http://nacho-cordova.blogspot.com/2011/07/it-is-with-deep-regret-that-we-are.html?show.

Abby M. Dubisar, assistant professor of English and affiliate faculty member in women's and gender studies at Iowa State University, works in the areas of multimodal writing, activist and feminist rhetorics, disability studies, and writing in the disciplines.

Erik Ellis is a lecturer in the Program in Writing and Rhetoric at Stanford University. His multimedia piece "'Completely out of My Domain': An Institutional Narrative of Multimedia Collaboration," coauthored with Dave Underwood, appears in the special issue of *CCC Online* devoted to infrastructures of twenty-first-century writing instruction, edited by Christine Alfano.

Wioleta Fedeczko is an assistant professor of English and administrator of the Associate Writing Program at Utah Valley University. In addition to teaching courses in rhetoric and professional writing, she also works with faculty at the Higher School of Economics in Nizhny Novgorod, Russia, where she conducts research and teaches courses on cold war rhetorics.

Tyrell Brent Fenn is pursuing a master's of science degree in instructional technology and learning science at Utah State University. He is interested in how technology can improve and, in some cases, provide self-directed, collaborative, and social learning environments. He works as the technology services manager at New Dawn Technologies.

Traci Fordham is an associate professor of rhetoric and communication studies at St. Lawrence University. She has been creating and conducting faculty development programs around intercultural, interpersonal, and small group communication for two decades. Her areas of research include dialogue and civic engagement, multimodal literacies, and cross-cultural adaptation.

Tarez Samra Graban is an assistant professor of English at Florida State University, where she teaches for the undergraduate major in editing, writing, and media and for the graduate program in rhetoric and composition. The pedagogy described here largely represents her experiences while teaching and mentoring in introductory composition at Purdue University and while teaching and mentoring teachers for writing-intensive courses at Indiana University–Bloomington. In all these roles she is interested in helping students consider their own expert orientations to text.

Susan M. Katz is an associate professor in the Department of English at North Carolina State University. She coordinates the internship program and teaches courses such as Professional Internships and Writing in Nonacademic Settings. She is also a Community Engaged Faculty Fellow. Her research interests include the assessment of multimodal discourse, the use of narrative in professional discourse, and the value of internships for both students and the academy.

Penny Kinnear works as an instructor with the Engineering Communication Program at the University of Toronto, where the use of visualization as a mediating activity continues to play a part in her pedagogy and research. Her research projects include a longitudinal study of chemical engineering portfolios as sites of identity transformation and an activity theory–based study of the integration of communication and engineering expertise with engineering graduate students as communication instructors.

Denise Landrum-Geyer is an assistant professor and writing center coordinator in the Department of Language and Literature at Southwestern Oklahoma State University, where she teaches courses in basic writing, composition, peer tutoring, creative nonfiction, writing across the professions, and rhetorical theories. Her research interests include rhetorical genre theories, composition histories and theories, the history of the essay, writing center theory, and writing-across-the-curriculum work.

Cynthia Lewiecki-Wilson, a former director of the composition program and professor of English at Miami University, teaches courses in composition and rhetoric and in disability and women's studies. She is author or coeditor of five books, including *Embodied Rhetorics: Disability in Language and Culture* and *Disability and the Teaching of Writing.* She has published in *College Composition and Communication*, *Disability Studies Quarterly*, *JAC*, *Journal of Basic Writing*, *Rhetoric Review*, *TETYC*, as well as in edited collections.

Heidi A. McKee is an associate professor in the Department of English and an affiliate faculty member of the Armstrong Center for Interactive Media Studies at Miami University. She is coeditor of *Technological Ecologies and Sustainability* (2009) and *Digital Writing Research: Technologies, Methodologies, and Ethical Issues* (2007). She is currently coediting *Digital Writing Assessment*. With James Porter, she cowrote *The Ethics of Internet Research: A Rhetorical, Case-based Process* (2009).

Kristen Moore is an assistant professor in Texas Tech University's Technical Communication and Rhetoric Program. Her scholarship focuses on technical communication, specifically the rhetorics of public policy, planning, and participation.

Mary Leigh Morbey is an associate professor of culture and technology in the York University Faculty of Education, Toronto, and serves as the associate codirector of the York Institute for Research on Learning Technologies. She researches and publishes widely on the theory, history, practice, and education of web participatory and social media technologies and technological mediations in visual culture, with an emphasis on the Global South.

Hillory Oakes is the director of the Learning Commons and the director of writing at Bates College. She was for seven years the director of the Munn Center for Rhetoric and Communication at St. Lawrence University, where she was also a cofounder of the Rhetoric and Communication Institute. The connections between writing, speaking, and visual communication are the foundation for her work developing pedagogical support for faculty and academic resources for students.

Lee Odell is a professor of composition at Rensselaer Polytechnic Institute, where he teaches writing courses such as Writing for Classroom and Career and Writing about Science. His principal scholarly interest is in developing a conceptual framework that, for purposes of both teaching and assessment, integrates written and visual information. His books include *Writing Now* and *Writing in a Visual Age*, both with Susan Katz; *Evaluating Writing*, with Charles Cooper; and *Writing in Non-Academic Settings*, with Dixie Goswami.

Gina Patterson is a visiting assistant professor of English and Women's, Gender, and Sexuality Studies at Miami University–Hamilton. Her core research interests include rhetorics and ethics, queer rhetorics, working-class studies, and social justice pedagogies. Her dissertation work focuses on how English studies teachers navigate the intersections between LGBTQ issues and religious discourse in the classroom.

Donna Reiss (http://wordsworth2.net) retired in 2008 as director of LitOnline, a faculty development project for interactive learning in online education at Clemson University, where she taught in the English department. She is professor emerita of English at Tidewater Community College in Virginia, where she taught computer-enhanced and Web-based writing, literature, and humanities; directed the Writing Center, Writing Across the Curriculum, and Online Learning; and won the Cowan Award for teaching and service.

Julia Romberger is the program coordinator for Professional Writing at Old Dominion University. She has published in *Computers and Composition* and *International Journal of the Image* and contributed to the edited collections *Rhetoric, Sex, Technology: Ecofeminist Perspectives on Discourse* and *Digital Writing Research: Technologies, Methodologies, and Ethical Issues.* She researches at the intersection of digital media, memoria, and visual rhetoric.

Jody Shipka is an associate professor of English at the University of Maryland–Baltimore County, where she teaches courses in the communication and technology track. She is the author of *Toward a Composition Made Whole* and the editor of *Play! A Collection of Toy Camera Photographs.* Her work has appeared in *College Composition and Communication*, *Computers and Composition*, *Enculturation*, *Kairos*, *Text and Talk*, *Writing Selves/Writing Societies*, and other edited collections.

Carolyn Steele is adjunct faculty in the humanities department of York University, where she develops and teaches courses on digital culture and art in 3-D multiuser environments, including *Second Life*. She also collaborates with Gail Vanstone (of York University) on an interactive multimedia installation that reflects on feminist ideas documented over the past century in diaries, media, and video, fusing augmented reality with traditional quilt making. Her own research explores the historical emergence and transformation of interactive media at the National Film Board of Canada.

Carl Whithaus studies the impact of information technologies on literacy practices, writing in the disciplines and professions, and writing assessment. He has published two books that focus on writing instruction and information technologies: *Writing Across Distances and Disciplines: Research and Pedagogy in Distributed Learning* (2008) and *Teaching and Evaluating Writing in the Age of Computers and*

High-Stakes Testing (2005). He teaches courses ranging from first-year writing to graduate-level classes in traditional, hybrid, and distance-learning environments. His articles have appeared in *Technical Communication Quarterly*, *Kairos*, *Assessing Writing*, and the *Journal of Basic Writing*.

Art Young (http://www.clemson.edu/~apyoung) is Robert S. Campbell Chair and Professor of English Emeritus at Clemson University. He retired from Clemson in 2009 and was the founder and coordinator (1990–2009) of Clemson's Communication Across the Curriculum program. He received the Exemplar Award (2002) from the Conference on College Composition and Communication for outstanding achievement in teaching, research, and service, and he received Clemson's Class of 1939 Award for Faculty Excellence (2004). He co-edited *Teaching and Learning Creatively: Inspirations and Reflections* (2006), an anthology of creative works by Clemson students with accompanying reflections by their teachers.

INDEX

NOTE: Page numbers in italic type indicate illustrations